Chinese Dictionary of Individual Characters

個別字辭典

Chinese Dictionary of Individual Characters

Comparing
Simplified, Traditional, Small Seal, and Large Seal Scripts

個別字辭典

比較

现代 ， 传统 ， 小篆 ， 大篆

現代 ， 傳統 ， 小篆 ， 大篆

Copyright © 2022. Russel Tingley. All rights reserved.
Registered U.S. Copyright # TXu 2-303-990. February 3, 2022.

Brief portions of this publication may be reproduced or transmitted in any form or by any means electronic or mechanical for personal non-commercial use only, on the condition that acknowledgment of the source is given. Complete copies of the entire publication is prohibited without written authorization from the author.

ISBN: 978-0-9968404-2-2
Printed in the United States of America. First edition.
Compiled by Russel Tingley.

Fonts:
  Book Antiqua   (English)
  TW-Kai   (Simplified and Traditional Characters)
  TW-Kai Ext-B   (Simplified and Traditional Characters)
  Traditional Chinese Seal Script (HDZB_25)   (Large Seal)
  汉仪篆书繁 (HYZhuanShu)   (Small Seal)

This work was not compiled by a native Chinese scholar nor a professional staff. Though perfect accuracy was pursued, it is entirely my fault if errors remain.

Another book by the author is
"Historic Dinosaurs - Evidence that dragons are not mythological beasts"

Russel Tingley
P.O. Box 32118
San Jose, CA 95152

Notes

This work is intended to aid in comparing traditional characters with three other styles for calligraphy and transliteration.

Simplified   Traditional   Small Seal   Large Seal

亿 億 億 億	Mandarin (*Pinyin*) Cantonese (*Yale*) (*alternates*)
	English basic definitions

The method for locating 4 character styles by their radical or stroke count is problematic. Some characters are categorized under different radicals between simplified, traditional, small seal, and large seal scripts, and each style has a different stroke count. Therefore, due to my bias towards the traditional character set, **the traditional radical system is the method used. They are further arranged by stroke-count order** (see the top corners of each page for quick reference) and grouped loosely on their visual similarities.

Though simplified characters are more practical for writing, two main issues arise when comparing them with the traditional. First, the core meaning of a character is reduced and offers little help in understanding it. (i.e., the simplified character for "love" has the heart removed). Second, simplified characters do not visually convey certain objects or concepts as well as the traditional. (i.e., the character "vehicle" no longer looks like a top-down view of a chariot). Some traditional characters have yet to be simplified.

All four styles have characters that have various artistic and/or regional versions of how they are written. It would be too cumbersome to present all the various artistic forms here, particularly for small and large seal scripts. Simplicity is the goal. Thus, a single representative character for each script is given as a suggested standard. In some cases, alternate traditional forms are included for reference. Since this work is focused on just Chinese characters, various-toned words that utilize the same written character are not necessarily included. Some transliterated words into English (particularly Cantonese) may not be accurate or available, in other words. Nevertheless, three general indicative marks representing the various tones [(rising (á); falling (à); falling-rising (ǎ)] are used to help in pronunciation. If there is no mark, the tone is flat.

Furthermore, many Chinese words are formed by two or more characters and is beyond the scope of this work to indicate these combinations. The generic conceptual definitions for these individual characters often refer to more specific and complete multiple-character word combinations. Though some individual characters are words in themselves, many characters reflect generic associated terms that are only specified when combined with other characters. For example, the single representative character for "middle, center, China" is nebulous on its own since a specific definition is not obvious, but when combined with other characters it clearly conveys specific words:

Generic: 中   = middle; center; China
Specific: 中間 = intermediate; middle
            中心 = center; core
            中国 = China

An excellent source for character combinations is:
"Understanding Chinese" by Rita Mei-Wah Choy.

Preface

After searching through various Chinese dictionaries for large and small seal scripts, I could not find one that incorporated a side-by-side comparison of the four main character styles with only one Seal character chosen as a standard from alternate calligraphic forms of the same character. So I set out to compile my own. I hope you find this useful.

One motivating factor in compiling this dictionary, apart from my interest in Chinese traditional culture, comes from several books and online presentations that give evidence on how the ancient Chinese incorporated into their writing system some commonly-known historical events of the early ages of mankind and creation as described in the Bible. For example, the Bible describes the creator of the universe as God and further explains that God has three aspects of his character; commonly called the Trinity [Father, Son (Jesus), and the Holy Spirit]. While God was creating the earth, His Spirit was actively involved with the work and is identified in Genesis 1:2.

"Now the earth was formless and empty, darkness was over the surface
of the deep, and the Spirit of God was hovering over the waters."

Before various religions worked their way into ancient China, history reveals that the Chinese believed in a single creator God (上帝). Not only did they believe in a single God but it also appears that they understood the concept of the Trinity.

heaven + cover + water = rain   + 3 mouths/persons + worker of magic = Spirit

When we examine the character "spirit", the top horizontal stroke, because of its position, represents heaven or above. The second stroke means "cover". The remaining portion of the top part of the character is "water". Thus the top portion represents what the Bible describes the Holy Spirit doing in His initial decent upon the earth – "hovering over (covering) the face of the waters". The next lower section contains three "mouths" which could imply three persons that speak via the Spirit (consistent with the concept of the Trinity). The bottom section of this character means "a worker of magic". What better way could the ancient Chinese describe the creative and miraculous work of God other than great "magic"? Why use this combination of characters to make the word spirit? The similarity with the Bible description is notable.

This single example is not very impressive on its own, but when combined with many other characters, as well as ancient traditions, such as the border sacrifice, the evidence is compelling that the ancient Chinese specifically believed in the God of the Bible.

I highly recommend these two books for those who are interested in this unusual topic.

"Genesis and the Mystery Confucius Couldn't Solve" by Nelson/Broadberry
"The Beginning of Chinese Characters" by Nelson/Broadberry/Wang

Page	Radical		Page	Radical	
	1 stroke			**3 strokes**	
1-2	一	一	34-55	口	口
2	丨	丨	55-57	囗	囗
2	丶		57-66	土	土
2-3	丿乁乀	乁	66	士	
3	乙乚⺃		66-67	夂	
3-4	亅		67	夕	
			67-69	大	
	2 strokes		69-77	女	
4	二	二	77-79	子	
4-5	亠		79-83	宀	
5-17	人亻	人 亻	83	寸	
17-18	儿		83-84	小	
18-19	入		84	尢	
19-20	八丷		84-86	尸	
20	冂		86	屮	
20	冖		86-91	山	
21-22	冫		91	巛巜川	
22	几		91	工	
22	凵		91-92	己	
22-26	刀刂	刀	92-94	巾	
27-28	力		94	干	
28-29	勹		94-95	幺	
29	匕		95-98	广	广
29-30	匚		98	廴	
30	匸		98	廾	
30-31	十	十	99	弋	
31-32	卜		99-100	弓	
32	卩		100	彐彑	
32-33	厂	厂	100-101	彡	
33	厶		101-103	彳 (also 行)	
33-34	又				

Page	Radical		Page	Radical
	4 strokes			**5 strokes**
103-117	心忄		216	玄
117-118	戈		216-222	玉王
119	戶		222	瓜
119-139	手扌		222-223	瓦
139	支		223	甘
139-141	攴攵		223	生
141	文		223-224	用
141	斗		224-226	田
142	斤		226	疋
142-143	方		226-232	疒
143	无旡		232-233	癶
143-149	日		233	白
149-150	曰		234	皮
150-151	月 (also 肉)		234-235	皿
151-170	木朩		235-240	目
170-171	欠		240	矛
171-172	止		240-241	矢
172-173	歹歺		241-247	石
173	殳		247-249	示礻
174	毋		249	肉
174	比		249-252	禾
174-175	毛		253-255	穴
175	氏		255	立
175-176	气氣			
176-201	水氵			
201-208	火灬			
209	爪爫			
209	父			
209	爻			
209-210	爿			
210	片			
210	牙			
210-211	牛牜			
212-216	犬犭			

Page	Radical		Page	Radical	
6 strokes			**7 strokes**		
255-263	竹	竹	334	見 [见]	
263-265	米		335	角	
265-276	糸		335-346	言 [讠]	
276	缶		346	谷	
276-277	网 四		346	豆	
278-279	羊		346-347	豕	
279-280	羽		347-348	豸	
280-281	老		348-352	貝 [贝]	
281	而		352	赤	
281-282	耒		353-354	走	
282-283	耳		354-359	足	
283-284	聿		359-360	身	
284-292	肉 月 (also 月)		360-363	車 [车]	
292	臣		363-364	辛	
292	自		364	辰	
292-293	至		364-371	辵 辶	
293	臼		371-374	邑 阝(右)	
293-294	舌		375-378	酉	
294	舛		378	釆	
294-296	舟		378-379	里	
296	艮				
296	色				
296-316	艸 艹				
316-317	虍				
317-327	虫				
327-328	血				
328	行 (also 彳)				
328-333	衣 衤				
333	西				

[Bracketed characters are simplified forms]

Page	Radical		Page	Radical	
	8 strokes			**11 strokes**	
379-392	金	金 金	420-424	魚 [鱼]	魚 魚
392	長 [长]	長 長	424-428	鳥 [鸟]	鳥 鳥
392-395	門 [门]	門 門	428-429	鹵	鹵 鹵
395-399	阜 阝(左)	阜 阜	429	鹿	鹿 鹿
399	隶	隶 隶	429-430	麥 [麦]	麥 麥
399-400	隹	隹 隹	430	麻	麻
400-402	雨	雨 雨			
403	青	青 青		**12 strokes**	
403	非	非 非	430	黃	黃 黃
			430	黍	黍 黍
	9 strokes		430-431	黑	黑 黑
403	面	面 面	431	黹	黹
403-404	革	革 革			
404-405	韋 [韦]	韋 韋		**13 strokes**	
405	韭	韭 韭	432	黽 [黾]	黽 黽
405	音	音 音	432	鼎	鼎 鼎
405-408	頁 [页]	頁 頁	432	鼓	鼓 鼓
408-409	風 [风]	風 風	432	鼠	鼠
409	飛 [飞]	飛 飛			
409-412	食 飠[饣]	食 食		**14 strokes**	
412	首	首 首	432-433	鼻	鼻 鼻
412	香	香 香	433	齊 [齐齐]	齊 齊
	10 strokes			**15 strokes**	
412-416	馬 [马]	馬 馬	433-434	齒 [齿齿]	齒 齒
416-417	骨	骨 骨			
417	高	高 高		**16 strokes**	
417-418	髟	髟 髟	434	龍 [龙竜]	龍 龍
418-419	鬥	鬥 鬥	434	龜 [龟亀]	龜 龜
419	鬯	鬯			
419	鬲	鬲		**17 strokes**	
419-420	鬼	鬼 鬼	434	龠	龠

一	一		弍	yi one	yàt	弌 醫 壹 (financial)
丁	丁	个	帀	ding person; servant; 4th heavenly stem (4th day of a 10 day week - Shang Dynasty)	dìng	
七	七	卡	亡	qi seven	chàt	柒 (financial)
三	三	三	弎	san three	sàam	叁 弎 叄 (financial)
丈	丈	丈	岁	zhàng unit of measurement; survey; gentleman	jéung	
上	上	上	上	shàng up; above; ascend; high	séuhng	丄
下	下	下	下	xià down; below; decend; low	hah	丅
不	不	不	不	bù no; not	bàt	
丕	丕	不	丕	pi large; grand; to act on; to follow; distinguished	pei	㔻 秊 秊
丐	丐	匄	丐	gài beggar	koi	
丑	丑	丑	丑	chǒu clown; comedian	cháu	
且	且	且	且	qiě and; besides; moreover	ché	且 且
世	世	世	世	shì world; life; lifetime; generation	sai	
丘	丘	丠	丠	qiu small hill, mound, grave	yàu	
丙	丙	丙	丙	bǐng 3rd heavenly stem (3rd day of a 10 day week - Shang Dynasty)	bíng	

一 5　｜ 3-6　、2-4　丿 1-4

	丢	𠚍	𠚍	diu　　　diù throw; lose
并	並	竝	竝	bìng　　　bihng and; side by side; in a row; coexist; simultaneously; actually; in fact; (used before a negative for emphasis)
	｜	｜		gǔn　　　gwan rod, up and down
	中	中	中	zhong　　　jùng middle; center; China; Chinese
	串	貫	串	chùan　　　chyun string
	、	｜		zhǔ　　　jyu dot
	丸	仈	仈	wán　　　yún　　凡 pill; pellet; bolus
	丹	丹	丹	dan　　　dàan cinnabar; red
	主	主	主	zhǔ　　　jyú master; emporer; lord
	丿	丿		piě　　　piht　　〳〵 angled line
	乃	𠄎	𠄎	nǎi　　　náaih therefore; then; so; thus
	久	久	久	jiǔ　　　gáu long time
	之	㞢	㞢	zhí　　　jì of
	乏	乏	乏	fá　　　faht to lack; tired
	乎	乎	乎	hu　　　fùh in; at; on; (a suffix placed after adjectives and adverbs expressing amazement)

乓	乓	乒		ping ping	ping-pong; "ping!"
乒	乒	乒		pang pong	ping-pong; "bang!"
乍	怔	岜		zhà ja	first; suddenly; abrupt	乍
乖	𡗞	𡗞		guai gwàai	obedient; well behaved; good; clever
乘	乘	乘		chéng sìhng	ascend; mount; ride; make use of
乙	乁	乁		yǐ yuht	2nd heavenly stem (2nd day of a 10 day week - Shang Dynasty)
九	九	九		jiǔ gáu	nine	玖 (financial)
乞	乞	乞		qǐ hàt	beg; begging
也	也	也		yě yáh	also; too
乳	乳	乳		rǔ yúh	milk; breast; to suckle
乾	乾	乾		gan gòn	dry; waterless	乹
乱	亂	亂	亂	lùan lyuhn	chaos; disorder
	丨			júe kyut	hook
了	了	了		le; liǎo líuh; lak	know; finish; understand (ending word showing past tense)
	予	予		yǔ yúh	give; grant

事	事	事	shì sih thing; matter; affair; business; fact
二	二	弍	èr yih 貳 弍 (financial) two
亍	亍		chù juk to stop; stand still; take small steps
互	互	冱	hù wuh mutual; each other
五	㐅	㐅	wǔ ńgh 伍 (financial) five
井	井	丼	jǐng jéng a well
亘	囘	亘	xuan - 囘 revolve around
亚 亞	亞	亞	yà a second; inferior
些	些	些	xie sè some; few; several
亟	亟	亟	jí gik urgent
亠	亠		tóu tau cap, head
亡	亾	亾	wáng mòhng die; lose
亢	亢	亢	kàng kong arrogant; haughty; extreme; excessive; resolute; ridge of a roof
交	交	交	jiao gàau cross; pay; deal
亥	亥	亥	hai hoi boar (Chinese zodiac); 9-11 pm

亦	夾	亦	yì also; likewise	yihk	夾
京	京	京	jing capital; artificial tall mound; large barn	gìng	京
亨	喜	亯	heng smoothly progressing; prosperous	hang	
享	喜	亯	xiǎng enjoy	héung	亯
亭	亭	亭	tíng pavilion; kiosk	tìhng	亭
亮	亮	亮	liàng bright; brilliant; radiant; very clear	leuhng	
亳	亳	亳	bó capital of Yin	bok	
人	儿	人	rén man	yahn	亻
什	什	什	shén troop of 10 men; miscellaneous	sahm	亭 十
仁	仁	仁	rén benevolent	yàhn	
仂	仂		lè surplus; excess; remainder	lak	
仄	仄	仄	zè slant; oblique; narrow uneasy; worried	jak	庆厌厣广疨
仇	仇	仇	chóu hate; hatred; enemy	sàuh	
仃	仃	仃	ding (used only in 伶仃; meaning isolated; alone; scrawny)	ding	
介	介	介	jiè introduce; situated between	gaai	

人 2-4

今	仒	今		jīn　　　　gàm now; presently
令	令	令		lìng　　　　lihng cause; make; command; order
仍	仍	仍		réng　　　　yìhng still
仞	仞	仞		rèn　　　　jan to fathom; to measure depth or height
仟	仟	仟		qian　　　chin　　千 leader of a thousand men; (*the financial form of one thousand*)
仔	仔	仔		zǎi　　　　jái kid; son; young (*person or animal*); meticulous; fine
仕	仕	仕		shì　　　　sih official; gentleman; scholar
他	他	他		ta　　　　tà he; him; other
仗	仗	仗		zhàng　　　jeuhng battle; to rely on
付	付	付		fù　　　　fuh to pay; hand over
仙	仙	仙		xian　　　sìn　　僊 immortal; fairy
代	代	代		dài　　　　doih generation; to replace; substitute
以	以	以		yǐ　　　　yíh with; by; in order to; so as to
仰	仰	仰		yǎng　　　yéuhng look up; raise the head; to respect
仳	仳	仳		pǐ　　　　pei to part; to leave each other; to distinguish; to tell apart

仲	仲	𠉧		zhòng — juhng (*second in seniority*)
件	件	𠈄		jiàn — gihn item; clothes; (*classifier for piece*)
任	任	𢓊		rèn — yahm office; responsibility
企	𨲠	𨲠		qǐ — kéih hope; to stand; enterprise
份	份	𠁙		fèn — fahn share; part; portion
仿	仿	㑖		fǎng — fóng imitate; copy
伉	伉	㐉		kàng — kong to match; to be equal to; tall; upright; arrogant
伊	伊	𠈌		yi — yì he; she; this; that
伍	伍	伍		wǔ — ńgh five; a company (*military*)
伎	伎			jì — gei performer (*sing/dance; primarily female*)
伏	伏	伏		fú — fuhk to lie prostrate; conceal
伐	伐	伐		fá — faht cut; cutting; chop
休	休	休		xiu — yàu rest
伢	伢			yá — nga child
佇	佇	佇	𠋗	zhù — jyu stand or stay (*for a long time*); to wait; hope for; to store; accumulate 竚 佇 㣥

人 5

伯	伯	伯	bó　　　　baak	father or husband's older brother; uncle
估	估	估	gu　　　　gú	estimate; appraise
你	你	你	nǐ　　　　néih	you
伴	伴	伴	bàn　　　　buhn	partner; companion; company
伶	伶	伶	líng　　　　lìhng	clever; quick-witted
伸	伸	伸	shen　　　　sàn	stretch; extend
似	似	似	shì　　　　chíh	similar; like; seem; appear
但	但	但	dàn　　　　daahn	but; however; yet
伽	伽	伽	qié　　　　ke (*original form of* 茄)	
位	位	位	wèi　　　　wái	position; place; location
布	布	布	bù　　　　bou	announce; proclaim; to arrange
低	低	低	di　　　　dài	low
佑	佑	佑	yòu　　　　jau	bless; assist; help; protect
住	住	住	zhù　　　　jyuh	live; dwell; reside; stop
佐	佐	佐	zuǒ　　　　jó	assist; assistant; subordinate

人 5-6

	佑	司	祐	yòu　　　yau assist; help; protect
	何	何	何	hé　　　hòh what; how; why; which
	佝	何	何	gou　　　kau rickets disease
	伺	同	伺	sì　　　jih spy; watch; examine; wait
	佃	佃	佃	diàn　　　dihn tenant farmer
	佛	佛	佛	fó　　　faht Buddha; Buddhism
	作	作	作	zùo　　　jok make; do; compose
	佩	佩	佩	pèi　　　pui pendant; ornament; to wear; hold; carry; admire; respect
来	來	來	來	lái　　　lòih come; arrive
	佯	陽	佯	yáng　　　johng pretend; false
	佰	佰	佰	bǎi　　　baak　　百 troop of 100 soldiers; hundred (*financial*)
	佳	佳	佳	jia　　　gàai good; auspicious; beautiful; excellent; fine
	佻	佻	佻	tiao　　　tiù frivolous
	使	使	使	shǐ　　　sí　　　駛駛洗 order to do; need to; make cause; to employ; messenger; envoy
	侃	侃	侃	kǎn　　　khán　　侃砍 upright; outspoken; straightforward; harmonious; to chat

9

	侈	侈	侈	chǐ　　　chí	extravagant; luxurious; wasteful
	例	例	例	lì　　　laih	case; instance; illustration; example
	侍	侍	侍	shì　　　sih	serve; wait upon; attendant
	侏	侏	侏	zhu　　　jyu	small; little; dwarf
	侑	侑	侑	yòu　　　yau	to urge (*to eat or drink*); help; to assist; requite
仑	侖	侖	侖	lún　　　leuhn　　崙	flute
	侗	侗		tóng　　　tung	childish; unenlightened; ignorant; frivolous; flippant
	供	供	供	gong　　　gùng	for; confess; supply; provide; offer
	依	依	依	yi　　　yì	rely on; depend; yield; according to; judging by
	佬	佬	佬	lǎo　　　lou	middle-aged man; guy; fellow; chap (*Cantonese dialect - slightly derogatory*)
	侮	侮	侮	wǔ　　　móuh	insult; humiliate
	候	候	候	hóu　　　hàuh　　候 候	observe; to survey; scout; lookout; wait for; attend; predict (*by divination*); vanguard
	侵	侵	侵	qin　　　chàm　　侵 侵	invade; encroach
侣	侣	侣	侣	lǚ　　　léuih	companion
局	侷	侷	侷	jú　　　guhk	narrow; cramped; confined

	促	促	促	cù　　　chùk urgent; hurried
	俗	俗	俗	sú　　　juhk vulgar; common; vernacular; cheap; custom; practice; habit
	便	便	便	biàn　　bihn make convenient; handy; nimble; agile informal; ordinary; human waste
系	係	系	系	xì　　　haih to be; relation; yes
	俊	俊	俊	jùn　　jeun　　　僬 僬 talented; handsome; pretty
	俎	俎	俎	zǔ　　chó　　　俎 chopping board; chopping block
们	們	們	們	men　　mùhn (suffix indicating plural)
	俏	俏	俏	qiào　　chiu good looking; smart; charming; lovely fast-selling; high demand
	俑	俑	俑	yǒng　　juhng tomb figurine
	俘	俘	俘	fú　　　fù captive; prisoner of war
	俚	俚	俚	lǐ　　　lei rely on; rustic; vulgar; unpolished; folk; popular (general name for ethnic groups in southern China)
	保	保	保	bǎo　　bóu to raise; to rear; keep; maintain; protect; ensure; guarantee
	俟	俟	俟	sì　　　ji　　　　俟 俟 wait
侠	俠	俠	俠	xiá　　hahp heroic; chivalrous
	信	信	信	xìn　　seun true; accurate; verifiable; trustworthy; to believe; letter; courier; messenger

人 7-8

	俄	俄	俄(seal)	é　　　ngòh suddenly; soon
	修	修	修(seal)	xiu　　　sàu　　　修 decorate; embellish; repair; study (education); cultivate
	俞	俞	俞(seal)	yú　　　jyu　　　俞 to approve
仓	倉	倉	倉(seal)	cang　　　chòng　　　舱艙舱艙 warehouse; storehouse; barn; cabin
	俯	俯	俯(seal)	fǔ　　　fú bend down; bow; look down
	俱	俱	俱(seal)	jù　　　kèui all; together
俩	倆	倆	倆(seal)	liǎng　　　léuhng both (classifier for a pair; couple)
	俳	俳	俳(seal)	pái　　　paai actor; vaudeville show; funny
	俸	俸	俸(seal)	fèng　　　fung wages; salary
	俺	俺	俺(seal)	ǎn　　　aan (Mandarin dialect) I; me; my (Mandarin dialect only) we; us; our
	俾	俾	俾(seal)	bǐ　　　béi in order that; so that; so as to cause
伥	倀	倀	倀(seal)	chang　　　cheung bewildered; reckless; rash;
并	併	併	併(seal)	bìng　　　bing　　　併 combine
	倌	倌	倌(seal)	guan　　　gun servant who drives a carriage; groom; keeper of domestic animals; worker in a teahouse
	倍	倍	倍(seal)	bèi　　　pui to double; times; hundredfold; (classifier for the number of times a value is multiplied)

	倒	倒	倒	倒	dǎo　　dóu to fall; collapse; decline; damaged; discontinue (*Cantonese*) to pour out; to tip over; to dump
	倚	倚	倚	倚	yǐ　　yí rely on; depend
	借	借	借	借	jiè　　je lend; borrow; take advantage of an opportunity
	倡	倡	倡	倡	chàng　　chèung guide; leader
伦	倫	倫	倫	倫	lún　　lèuhn relationship; kinship
	值	值	值	值	zhí　　jihk price; worth; worthwhile
条	條	條	條	條	tiáo　　tiu article; item; strip; stripe; (*classifier for long thin objects*)
	倘	倘	倘	倘	tǎng　　tóng if; suppose
	倔	倔	倔	倔	jué　　gwaht stubborn; rude; obstinate
个	個	個	個	個	gè　　go (*classifier for people and objects*)
	偎	偎	偎	偎	wei　　wui be close to; draw near; comfort; sit down
	倦	倦	倦	倦	jùan　　guhn tired; weary
	假	假	假	假	jiǎ　　gá pretend; false; fake
	偏	偏	偏	偏	pián　　pìn inclined; slanting
伟	偉	偉	偉	偉	wěi　　wáih great; large

人 9-10

	做			zùo jouh to do; perform; make; produce
	偕			xié gàai accompany; in harmony with
伪	偽			wěi ngaih hypocritical; fake; spurious
	健			jiàn gihn strong; robust; healthy; adept
侧	側			cè jàk side; to lean to one side; to incline; to slant
	偷			tou tàu steal; stealthy; covert; thief; burglar
侦	偵			zhen jìng to spy; detective
	停			tíng tìhng stop; halt; to park (car)
	偶			ǒu ngáuh idol; couple; pair; accidentally; coincidentally
伧	傖			cang càhng vulgar person; country man
家	傢			jia gà stubborn; obstinate; intransigent; furniture
	傀			kui faai puppet; exotic; strange
杰	傑			jié giht hero; distinguished person
伞	傘			sǎn saan umbrella; parasol
备	備			bèi beih prepare; provide; put in order; get ready; completeness

人 10-12

	傅			fù　　　　　fuh tutor; teacher; to assist; teach; instruct; attach
传	傳			chúan　　　　chyùhn transfer; transmit; impart; spread; circulate; disseminate
	傲			ào　　　　　ngouh proud; haughty; distainful; to despise; stubborn
	催			cui　　　　　chèui urge; pushy; hasten; speed up
佣	傭			yong　　　　yùhng servant; maid; employ; hire
伛	傴			yǔ　　　　　jyu humpback; stoop; bend down
侨	僑			qiáo　　　　kiùh reside abroad; emigrate; sojourn; lodge
	像			xiàng　　　　jeuhng figure; image; portrait; resemble
债	債			zhài　　　　chaai debt; loan; liabilities
伤	傷			shang　　　　sèung injure; hurt; wound
倾	傾			qing　　　　kìng lean; tilt; incline; collapse; overpower; overwhelm; compete; entire; whole
仅	僅			gán　　　　　jín only; merely
	傻			shǎ　　　　　sòh foolish; silly; stupid; naïvely stubborn
仆	僕			pú　　　　　fuh fall forward
雇	僱			gù　　　　　gu hire; employ

15

人 12-14

	僚	僚	僚	liáo liùh officials; companion; colleague
侥	僥	僥	僥	jiǎo hiù lucky; by chance
	僧	僧	僧	seng jàng Buddhist monk
	僖	僖	僖	xi hei joy; gladness; delight
价	價	價	價	jià ga price; value
	僵	僵	僵	jiang gèuhng fall down; stiff; rigid; motionless; deadlock
亿	億	億	億	yì yìk hundred million
侬	儂	儂	儂	nóng nung 人仏農农 person associated with an identity or trait; other people; I; me; you; (*suffix for pronouns*)
侩	儈	儈	儈	kùai kui go-between; broker; proxy
俭	儉	儉	儉	jiǎn gihm thrifty; frugal; modest
仪	儀	儀	儀	yí yìh instrument; apparatus; ritual; manner
	載	載	載	zài choi ride; travel; carry; support; to set out; cause; undertaking; things loaded ("to download")
	僻	僻	僻	pì pìk 俟 覓 avoid; depraved; secluded; unorthodox; eccentric
	儒	儒	儒	rú yùh scholar; Confucianism
尽	儘	盡	盡	jǐn jeuhn utmost; extreme; furthest; to do one's best; give priority to

傧	儐	儐	儐	bīn　bān entertain guests; display; exhibit
俦	儔	儔	儔	chóu　kàu companion; mate; colleague; on par with
偿	償	償	償	cháng　sèuhng repay; recompense; restitution; compensation
优	優	優	優	yōu　yāu excellent; superior; exceptional; actor
储	儲	儲	儲	chǔ　chyúh store; reserve; save money; heir
俪	儷	儷	儷	lì　laih married couple; a pair
傩	儺	儺		nuó　nò walk gracefully; to move to measured steps (*Nuo ceremony*)
傥	儻	儻	儻	tǎng　tóng if; supposing; in case
俨	儼	儼	儼	yǎn　jím solemn; respectful; dignified; majestic
	儿	儿		rén　yàn legs, stand
	兀	兀	兀	wù　ngaht towering; lofty; bald; still; yet; cut off the feet; unpeaceful
	元	元	元	yúan　yùhn chief; first; dollar
	允	允	允	yǔn　wáhn promise; allow
	兄	兄	兄	xiōng　hìng older brother
	充	充	充	chōng　chùng fill; full; to serve as

儿 4-12　入

兆	州	𠈌	zhào　　siuh omen; million
光	炎	𤉨	guang　　gwòng bright; light; empty
先	兂	兂	xian　　sìn first; before; ancestor; former
凶	兇	凶 凶	xiong　　hùng fierce; cruel
克	亨	𠅏	kè　　hàk competent; win; encroach; restrain; gram
兑	兌	兌	dùi　　deui exchange; convert
儿	兒	兒 兒	ér　　yìh son; child
免	兔	兔	miǎn　　míhn take off; release; set free; exempt; discharge; waive; forgive; dismiss from office; forbidden; avoid
兔	兔	兔	tú　　tou rabbit
兕	兕	兕	sì　　chi　　舰兕咒兕兜兕 a bovine-like animal; rhinoceros (female)
兗	兗	兗	yǎn　　jin (used only in 兖州)
党	黨	黨	dǎng　　dong (used only in 党項); surname
兜	兜	兜	dóu　　dàu　　兜 helmet; to wrap; to encase; armor; bag; pouch; pocket; move in a circle; to peddle; to hawk; to save
兢	兢	兢	jing　　ging fearful; cautious
入	入	入	rù　　yahp enter

內	內	內	nèi　　　noih inside; within
全	全	全	qúan　　　chyùhn all; whole; entire; complete
兩	兩	兩	liǎng　　　léuhng two; both; ounce
俞	俞	俞	yú　　　jyu　　　俞 approve
八	八	八	ba　　　baat　　　ㄨ 捌 (financial) eight
公	公	公	gong　　　gùng public; common; fair; male; husband's father; father-in-law
六	六	六	liù　　　luhk　　　陸 陆 (financial) six
兮	兮	兮	xi　　　hai (sentence-final exclamatory particle, or possessive particle)
共	共	共	gòng　　　guhng total; altogether; common
兵	兵	兵	bing　　　bìng soldier; troops; army; military
其	其	其	qí　　　kèih (possessive pronoun) it; its; their; that; they; those; his; her; he; she
具	具	具	jù　　　geuih tool; equipment; device
典	典	典	diǎn　　　dín　　　棋 law; canon; documentation; scripture
兹	兹	兹	zi　　　ji　　　兹 black; muddy; dirty
兼	兼	兼	jian　　　gìm do two or more things or hold two or more positions simultaneously; double

八 14　　冂 2-9　　冖 2-14

冀	冀	冀		jì　　　　　kei look forward to; hope for; wish
冂	冂			jiong　　　gwing suburbs
内	內	內		nèi　　　　noih inside, within
册	冊	冊		cè　　　　chaak book, booklet, volume
冉	冉	冉		rǎn　　　　jim　　　　冄 tender; weak; proceed gradually
再	再	再		zài　　　　joi again; once more; another
冒	冒	冒		mào　　　　mouh　　　冃 冐 to cover; sack for corpses; fake; feign; to risk
冕	冕	冕		miǎn　　　míhn ceremonial cap or crown
冖	冖			mi　　　　　mik cover
冗	冗	冗		rǒng　　　yúng　　　冘 superfluous; unnecessary; surplus; excessive; redundant; complicated and tedious
冠	冠	冠		gúan　　　gùn　　　　冠 㡚 冠 帽 hat; cap
冢	冢	冢		zhǒng　　chung　　　塚 mausoleum; tomb; burial mound; mountain summit
冥	冥	冥		míng　　　ming dark; deep; profound; gloomy; night
冤	冤	冤		yuan　　　jyun　　　　寃 寃 冕 寃 怨 to wrong; to treat unjustly; grievance; unjust
幂	冪	幎	幎	mì　　　　mik to cover with cloth; (*mathematics*) power

				bing　　　bìng ice
	冬			dong　　　dùng winter
	冰			bing　　　bìng ice
	冱			hù　　　wu freezing; stopped up; closed off
	决			júe　　　kyut determine, decide, definitely
	况			kùang　　　fong condition; situation; furthermore
	冶			yě　　　yéh smelt; metallurgy
	冷			lěng　　　láahng cold; frosty; indifferent
冻	凍			dòng　　　dung freeze; very cold
	准			zhǔn　　　jéun allow; grant; permit
	凇			sòng　　　- icicle, dewdrop
	凋			diao　　　diù wither; fade
	凌			líng　　　ling rise high; place oneself above; to override; insult; invade
冯	馮			féng　　　fung gallop
凛	凜			lǐn　　　láhm shivering; solemn; freezing cold

冫 14   几 1-12   凵 3-6   刀

凝	癡	凝	níng　　　　yìhng coagulate; congeal; to freeze; concentrate	冰 冸 癡 癡
几	兀		jí　　　　gèi small table; stool; chair	
凡	尺	凡	fán　　　　fàahn common, every	
凩	凬		mù　　　　do wintery wind	
凰	皇	凰	húang　　　　wòng Chinese phoenix (female)	皇鵟
凱	愷	凱	kǎi　　　　hói victory; triumphant	
凳	櫈		dèng　　　　dang stool; bench	櫈
凵	ㄩ		qiǎn　　　　ham open mouth, receptacle	
凸	凸	凸	tú　　　　daht convex; protrude; raised	
凹	凹	凹	ao　　　　nàp concave; indent	
出	凷	出	chu　　　　chèut out; to go out; to come out	
凶 兇	凶	凶	xiong　　　　hùng evil; fierce; ferocious; terrible; ominous	
函	圅	圅	hán　　　　hàahm letter; note; correspondence; box; case	圅
刀	刀	刀	dao　　　　dòu knife; blade	刂
刁	刁	刁	diao　　　　diù tricky; sly	

22

刀 1-5

刃	刃	刃	rèn yahn edge of a blade
分	分	分	fēn fahn minute; cent, point; fraction; branch partition; separate; divide
切	切	切	qiè chai cut; slice
刈	刈	刈	yì ngáai to weed; weeding tool; uproot
刊	刊	刊	kān hón publication
刎	刎	刎	wěn mahn behead; to cut one's throat
刑	刑	刑	xíng yìhng punishment
刖	刖	刖	yuè jyut 䏍 punishment by cutting off one or both feet; (one of the 五刑, "Five Punishments")
列	列	列	liè liht column, row; series, file
初	初	初	chū chò early; first; beginning; start; initial; inceptive; primary
刪	刪	刪	shān sàan delete; eliminate
判	判	判	pàn pun sentence; judge; discern
刨	刨	刨	páo pàauh dig; plane (woodworking)
別	別	別	bié biht do not; another; other; separate
利	利	利	lì leih benefit; profit; interest; advantage; favorable

23

刀 5-7

	劫	劫	劫	jié　　　gip robbery; plunder; disaster	
	刮	刮	刮	gua　　　gwaat scratch; scrape; shave; wipe; sweep	
	到	到	到	dào　　　dou arrive; go to; attain	
	刳	刳		ku　　　fu cut open; dig; rip up; scoop out	
	制	制	制	zhì　　　jai regulate; ration; restrain; restrict; limit; control	
	刷	刷	刷	shua　　　chaat a brush; to brush; scrub	
	券	券	券	qùan　　　hyun ticket; certificate; coupon; deed of trust; bond	
	刺	刺	刺	qì　　　chik thorn; sting; stab; prick; puncture; assassinate; to criticise with pointed words	
	刻	刻	刻	kè　　　hàk engrave; cut; carve; moment; quarter hour	
	剂	剂	剂	jì　　　jai trim; prune; medication; to concoct; medicinal preparation	劑剤
	刹	刹	刹	chà　　　saat brake; buddhist monastery	
则	則	則	則	zé　　　jàk then, standard, rule	則則則則
	削	削	削	xue　　　seuk peel with a knife; cut; scrape off the surface; slice; divide; split; separate; reduce	
	剌	剌	剌	là　　　laat contradict; slash; cut in two	
	前	前	前	qián　　　chin front; forepart	偂歬

24

到	到	剄		jǐng　　　ging cut one's throat (*Chinese ritual suicide*)	
	剃	鬀	鬄	tì　　　tai shave	
	剔	剔	剔	ti　　　tihk to pick (*with a pointed instrument*); weed out (*Cantonese*) tick; checkmark	
	剖	剖	剖	pou　　　fau cut open; divide; analyze; dissect	
刚	剛	剛	剛	gáng　　　gòng just; only; barely; strong; firm	
	剜	剜	剜	wan　　　wun cut out; pick out; scoop out	
	剞	剞		ji　　　gei to rob	
	剡	剡		shàn　　　sim sharp; sharpen	
剥	剝	剝	剝	bao　　　mok cut apart; peel; to skin; to shell; fall off or erode	
	剪	剪	剪	jiǎn　　　jihn cut (*i.e.*, *paper*)	前劗
	副	副	副	fù　　　fu secondary, auxiliary; assistant (*classifier for pairs, sets of things, and facial expressions*)	
剐	剮	冎		guǎ　　　gwaa cut flesh off the bone	咼 呙 呙 另
	剩	賸	剩	shèng　　　sihng extra; left over; remainder	賸 剰 剩 剩
	割	割	割	ge　　　got cut; cut apart	
创	創	創	創	chùang　　　chong create; achieve; wound; invasive	

刀 10-14

剀	剴	剴	剴	kǎi　　hoi sharpen; carefully; thorough
	剽	剽	剽	piao　　piu rob; plunder; cut off; swift; nimble
	剿	剿	剿	jiǎo　　jiu　　勦 剿 剿 destroy; exterminate; annihilate; plagiarize
	劁	劁		qiáo　　chiu cut; geld
	劂	劂	劂	júe　　kyut a chisel; engraving
划	劃	劃	畫	hùa, húa　　waahk draw; stroke; row; divide
	劈	劈	劈	pi　　pek chop; split open
刘	劉	劉	劉	liú　　làuh kill; slaughter
刽	劊	劊	劊	gùi　　gur cut open; chop off
刿	劌	劌		gùi　　gwái injure; stab
剑	劍	劍	劍	jiàn　　gim sword
剧	劇	劇	劇	jù　　kehk opera; extremely
	劐	劐		huo　　fok destroy
	劓	劓	劓	yì　　ji punishment by cutting off the nose (*one of the* 五刑, *"Five Punishments"*)
	劑	劑	劑	jì　　jai trim, prune, medication, to concoct, medicinal preparation

26

	力			lì　　　lihk strength; force; power; energy
	功			gong　　　gùng merit; achievement; service
	加			jia　　　gà add; plus; increase
	劣			liè　　　lyut inferior
	助			zhù　　　joh help; aid; assist
	努			nǔ　　　nóuh strive; exert
	劫			jié　　　gip robbery; plunder; disaster
	劬			qú　　　keui diligent; toil; endeavor
	劭			shao　　　siu encourage; excel; excellent
	劾			hé　　　hat examine; impeach; charge
劲	勁			jìn　　　ging strength; vigor; energy; powerful
	勃			bó　　　buht push; to drive; exuberant; vigorous; suddenly (*changing countenance*)
	勇			yǒng　　　yúhng brave; courageous
	勉			miǎn　　　míhn encourage; endeavor; make an effort
动	動			dòng　　　duhng move; motion

力 7-17   勹 1

	勒	勒	勒	lei　　　lahk bridle (*with bit*); rein in; restrain; lead; bind tight; tighten; restrict; limit; compel
	勘	勘	勘	kan　　　hahm proofread; compare; investigate
务	務	務	務	wù　　　mouh business; duty; responsibility
	勖	勖		xù　　　juk　　　勗 encouragement to work hard
胜	勝	勝	勝	sheng　　　sing to bear; withstand; equal to; match; completely
劳	勞	勞	勞	láo　　　lòuh labor; work hard; fatigue
	募	募	募	mù　　　mouh levy; raise; summon; recruit
剿	勦	勦	勦	jiǎo　　　jíu　　　勦 剿 勦 suppress; destroy; exterminate; annihilate; plagiarize
势	勢	勢	勢	shì　　　sai potential; force; power; momentum; situation; tendency
	勤	勤	勤	qín　　　kàhn diligent; attentive; industrious
勋	勳	勳	勳	xun　　　fàn　　　勛 勲 merit; rank; meritorious deed
励	勵	勵	勵	lì　　　laih encourage
劝	勸	勸	勸	qùan　　　hyun advise; urge; encourage
	勹	勹		bao　　　baau wrap
	勺	勺	勺	sháo　　　cheuk　　　杓 spoon; ladle; unit of volume

勻	匀	匀	yún　　wàhn uniform; even; evenly
勾	勾	勾	gou　　ngàu hook, tick (*mark*)
勿	勿	勿	wù　　maht do not
包	包	包	bao　　bàau package; packet; bundle; wrap
匆	匆	匆	cong　　cung hasty; hurried
匈	匈	匈	xiong　　hùng tumultuous, Hungary
匍	匍	匍	pú　　pouh crawl; creep; prostrate
匏	匏	匏	páo　　pauh gourd; musical instrument
匐	匐	匐	fú　　fuhk crawl; creep; prostrate (*used only in* 匍匐)
匕	匕	匕	bǐ　　bei ladle; spoon; daggar
化	化	化	huà　　fa convert; transform (*suffix*): -ify, -ize, -ization
北	北	北	béi　　bàk North
匙	匙	匙	chí　　sìh spoon
匚	匚	匚	fang　　fong container
匝	匝	匝	za　　jahp (*classifier for circuits or circles*) surround; all over; throughout

匚 4-12   匸 2-9   十 1-2

	匠	匠	匠	jiàng　　jeuhng craftsman; carpenter
	匡	匡	匡	kuang　　hong upright; to correct; save; assist; expect; shell of crabs
	匣	匣	匣	xiá　　hahp box; case; cassette
匭	匭	匭		guǐ　　gwai small box; chest; casket
	匪	匪	匪	fěi　　féi robber; thief; bandit; gangster
匮	匱	匱	匱	kùi　　gwai to lack; deficient
		匸		xì　　hai cover; conceal
	匹	匹	匹	pǐ　　pàt match; equal; opponent; mate; spouse (*classifier for bolts of cloth*)
区	區	區	區	qu　　kèui area; region; zone; district
	匿	匿	匿	nì　　nìk flee; hide; conceal; anonymous
	匾	匾	匾	biǎn　　bin flat; horizontal inscribed board; plaque; silk banner embroidered with eulogy; a round shallow basket
	十	十	十	shí　　sahp　　　拾(*financial*) ten
	千	千	千	qian　　chìn thousand; many
	午	午	午	wǔ　　ńgh noon; midday
	升	升	升	sheng　　sìng liter; rise; ascend; promote

	卅	卅	卅	sà thirty	sà	
	卉	芔	芔	huì wai (generic term for plants); flower		芔 卉
	半	半	半	bàn bun half; halfway; semi-		
协	協	協	協	xié hihp assist; help; association; harmonize		
	卑	卑	卑	bei bei inferior; humble		
	卒	卒	卒	zú jyùt soldier, servant, pawn		卒 卒
	卓	卓	卓	zhuo cheuk outstanding; eminent; distinguished; lofty		
	南	南	南	nán nahm south; southern		
华	華	華	華	húa wàh Chinese; China; magnificent		
卖	賣	賣	賣	mài maaih sell; sale; betray		
	單	單	單	dan dàan single; solitary; simple; only; faint		
	博	博	博	bó bok abundant; plentiful; rich; wide; broad; win; gamble		
	卜	卜	卜	bǔ bùk foretell		
	卞	卞	卞	biàn bin law; impatient; irritable; impetuous		
	占	占	占	zhan jìm foretell, divine		

卜 3-6　卩 2-9　厂

卡	卡	卡	kǎ　　kàat wedge; get stuck; jammed; clip; fasten; choke (*computing*) freeze up; buffer; stop loading; lag
卣	卣		yǒu　　jau　　卣 卤 an ancient lidded bronze vessel used for storing wine offerings for rituals
卦	卦	卦	gùa　　gwa divine; change; (*divinatory trigram of the I Ching*)
卩	卩		jié　　jit　　㔾 seal (*stamp*)
卯	卯	卯	mǎo　　mauh 5-7 a.m.; early morning; mortise
卮	卮	卮	zhi　　ji　　巵 an ancient round Chinese goblet; (*classifier for the volume of liquid in one* 卮 / *goblet*)
危	危	危	wéi　　ngai dangerous; precarious; high
印	印	印	yìn　　jan print; seal; stamp
卵	卵	卵	lǔan　　léun egg; ovum
即	即	即	jí　　jìk　　卽 immediately; prompt; which is
却 卻	卻	卻	qùe　　keuk but; however; yet; while; refuse
卸	卸	卸	xìe　　se unload; discharge; remove
卷	卷	卷	jùan　　gyún scroll; roll; to curl
卿	卿	卿	qing　　hing noble; high officer
厂			hǎn　　hon cliff; habitable cave in a cliff

	厄	厃	厄	è / ak / 戹阨厄 harrowing; miserable; disaster; calamity; catastrophe; adversity; difficulty; distress; stranded
	厚	厚	厚	hǒu / háuh / 垕 thick; large; substantial; deep; rich; strong; generous; kind
	原	厵	原	yúan / yùhn / 原邍 plain; field; prairie; wilderness; source; origin; basic; fundamental; primary; forgive; pardon
	厝	厝	厝	cùo / cok / 厝錯错礛 whetstone
	厥	厥		júe / kyùt faint; lose consciousness
厉	厲	厲	厲	lì / laih severe; stern; strict; harsh
厌	厭	厭	厭	yàn / yim be disgusted with; loathe
厣	厴	厴		yǎn / jim operculum (*a covering flap*)
	厶	ㄕ		mǒu / mauh private; secret
	去	杏	去	qù / heui go; leave
	叄	三	弎	san / sàam / 三弎叄 three
参	參	參	參	shen / sam / 曑叁叅 three objects in a group; mix; join; attend; participate; disorder; uneven; ginseng
	又	ㄋ	ㄋ	yòu / yauh also; again
	叉	ㄋ	ㄋ	cha / chà fork; prong
	及	及	及	jí / kahp and; reach

	友	💠	💠	yǒu yáuh friend; friendly
	反	💠	💠	fǎn fáan turn over; rebel (*prefix*: anti-; counter-)
	叔	💠	💠	shu suhk paternal uncle (*father's younger brother*); brother-in-law (*husband's younger brother*)
	取	💠	💠	qǔ chéui take; fetch; get
	受	💠	💠	shòu sauh accept; receive; to bear
叙	敘	💠	💠	xù jeui talk; chat; narrate; recount; relate; assess; appraise
	叛	💠	💠	pàn buhn revolt; rebel
	叟	💠	💠	sǒu sau 叜 叟 傁 俊 old man; old gentleman; sir
丛	叢	💠	💠	cóng cung cluster; collection
	口	💠	💠	kǒu háu mouth; opening
	古	💠	💠	gǔ gú ancient; old
	右	💠	💠	yòu yauh right side
	另	💠	💠	lìng ling another; seperate; other
	召	💠	💠	zhào jiuh call; summon; convene
	叨	💠	💠	dao dou excessively talkative

口 2-3

叻	㔹	㓕	lè lek 喔 叻 叻	
			smart; clever; able; (used in place names)	
叩	㪣	㞢	kòu kau	
			knock; kowtow; to bow; enquire; to ask	
只	只	只	zhǐ jí	
			only; just; merely; exclusively	
叭	叭	㕷	ba bà	
			a sharp noise; a trumpet "ba" sound	
叫	呌	噭	jiào giu	
			call; shout; make	
吁	吁	吁	yù jyu	
			appeal; plead; call; implore; (to slow/stop animals) whoa!	
叮	叮	叮	ding dìng	
			sting; bite	
可	可	可	hó kě	
			can; may; able	
司	司	司	si sì	
			manage; division; department	
句	句	句	jù geui	
			sentence; clause; phrase; to hook	
叵	叵	叵	pǒ po	
			cannot; unable; impossible; (contraction of 不可); thereupon	
叱	叱	叱	chi chik	
			scold; shout at; bawl out	
史	史	史	shǐ sí	
			history; historical	
叼	叼	叼	diao diu	
			to hang from the mouth	
吃	吃	吃	chi hek	
			eat; eating; take	

口 3-4

吒	吒	吒	zhà　　jaak shout; roar; bellow; scold	咤
各	甙	㕸	gè　　gok each; every; apiece	
吆	吆	吆	yao　　jiù to yell; shout	
合	合	合	hé　　hahp close; shut; gather; combine; join; fit	
吉	吉	吉	jí　　gāt lucky	
吊	吊	吊	diào　　diu hang; suspend	弔
同	同	同	tóng　　tùhng with; same; alike; and	
名	名	名	míng　　mìhng name; title; reputation	
吏	吏	吏	lì　　leih minor government official	
后	后	后	hòu　　hauh after; later; rear; back	
吐	吐	吐	tǔ　　tou to spit; vomit; throw up	
向	向	向	xiàng　　heung to; towards; direction	
吖	吖		ya　　ah shout; cry out	
君	君	君	jun　　gwàn king; ruler; gentleman	
吝	吝	吝	lìn　　leuhn miserly; stingy; mean	

	吞	窑	呑	tún　　　tàn to swallow; gulp	
	否	渝	盃	fǒu　　　fáu not; deny; negate	
	吾	吾	吾	wú　　　ng I; my	
	告	告	峕	gào　　　gou tell; inform; accuse; announce	
呂	吕	呂	呂	lu　　　leui a spine; even number of music notes; an ancient Chinese state	
	呈	呈	呈	chéng　　　chìhng show; present; offer	
吴	吴	吴	吴	wú　　　ng speak loudly; shout	吳 吴 吴 荞 荠
	呆	呆	呆	dái　　　ngòih stay; dull	獃 騃 痴
	吠	吠	吠	fèi　　　faih a dog bark; barking	
	呲	批		bǐ　　　bei blame; slander; denounce; rebuke; compare	
	吧	呭	呭	ba　　　bà sound of a bang; (*final article indicating decisiveness*)	
	吭	亢	坑	keng　　　hang throat; to utter	
	吮	吮	吮	shun　　　shyun suck	
	吱	吱	吱	zhi　　　gei squeak	
	吲	吲		yǐn　　　jan smile; sneer	

口 4-5

吵	訬	吵(seal)	chǎo cháau	noisy; quarrel
吸	吸(seal)	吸(seal)	xi kàp	suck; inhale; absorb
吹	吹(seal)	吹(seal)	chúi chèui	blow; brag; boast
吻	吻(seal)	吻(seal)	wěn máhn	kiss; lip
吼	吼(seal)	吼(seal)	hǒu hàau	roar (*animal*); shout (*people*); squeal (*inanimate objects; i.e. a car*)
呀	呀(seal)	呀(seal)	ya ah	ah!; yeah; (*exclamation point*)
呃	呃(seal)	呃(seal)	è ak	belch; hiccup
吶 吶	吶(seal)	吶(seal)	nà naap	raise voice; yell; shout; stammer
呔	呔(seal)		tǎi toi 畚 噠	an exclamation to get attention; foreign accent
吩	吩(seal)	吩(seal)	fen fan	(*no direct English translation, used in compound words for order, instruct*)
吟	吟(seal)	吟(seal)	yín yàhm	chant; recite; moan
含	含(seal)	含(seal)	hán hàhm	contain; harbor
呤	呤(seal)		lìng ling	speak with a soft voice; whisper
呦	呦(seal)		you jau	an expression of surprise or sudden awareness
呱	呱(seal)	呱(seal)	gua gu, gwa 哌	wail; crying of a child; to swear at

呰	呰		zi ji chant	
味	味	味	wèi meih taste; flavor; smell; odor	
呵	訶	呵	he, o hò, òu shout; cry out; laughter; breathe slowly; (*exclamation of surprise*) "ah!"	
呶	呶	呶	náo nauh babble; to clamour; bulge; move; shift	
呸	呸	呸	pei pei (*an expression of reprimand*) "Bah!"	
呷	呷	呷	xia haap sip; suck; drink	
呻	呻	呻	shen sàn groan; chant; recite	吟 叺 哼 瘖
呼	呼	呼	hu fù call; shout; breath out; exhale; greet; (*onomatopoeia of wind howling*)	
命	命	命	mìng mihng 俞 life; existence; lifespan; destiny; fate; luck; command; order; instruction	
咀	咀	咀	jǔ jéui chew; masticate; mouth	
咂	咂		za jaap suck; smack the lips	咂 咂 咂
咄	咄	咄	duo deuht cry out in anger; berate	
咆	咆	咆	páo paau roar; thunder	
咋	咋	咋	zǎ jaa how; why	唝 咱 囉
和	咊	和	hé wòh peace; harmony; and; with; kind	

口 5-6

咎	㕤	㕤	jiù　　　　gau fault; defect; error; mistake; calamity; misfortune
咐	呮	㕻	fù　　　　fu direct; command
咒	詶	呪	zhòu　　　jau　　　呪 curse; incantation; swear
咔	吒		kǎ　　　　kaa (*onomatopoeia*) click
咕	咕	呫	gu　　　　gu (*onomatopoeia*) "goo", "coo"; fail to show up
咖	咖	㗊	ga, ka　　gaa coffee
咚	嘡	㗎	dong　　　dung (*onomatopoeia*) boom; thump; thud
咩	咩	羋	mie　　　　me　　　芈芈哔哔 "baa!" (*the bleating of sheep*)
咪	咪	咪	mi　　　　mai "meow"
咦	咦	姨	yí　　　　ji (*an interjection to express confusion*) huh?
咧	咧		lie　　　　le grimace; grin
咨	詙	㗖	zi　　　　ji consult; official document; sigh (*an interjection used to indicate appreciation*)
品	品	品	pǐn　　　　bán article; item; commodity; rank; grade; personality; character
虽	雖	雖	sui　　　　seui although; even if
咫	䟽	䟽	zhǐ　　　　chi few; little; short; (*a unit of measurement during the Zhou dynasty equal to 8 cun*)

咬	齩	𠰍	yǎo to bite	ngáauh	
哀	㤅	㤅	ai sorrow	òi	
咳	欬	欬	ké to cough	kàt	
咴	噅		hui fui (onomatopoeia of the sound a horse makes)		
咭	咭		ji card (borrowed from English)	kat	卡
咯	喀	𠹭	lùo expel from the throat	kat	
咱	喒	㛚	zán we; us; I; me	jà	
咸	咸	咸	xián also	hàahm	
哉	𢦏	𢦏	zai exclamation	jòi	
咻	咻		ziu shout	jau	
咽	咽	咽	yan throat	yìn	
哂	㗚	哂	shěn smile	can	
咿	㖈	㖈	yi moan in pain or grief	ji	咿
哆	哆		duo sound of hitting; tattoo; to purse lips	do	
哇	哇	哇	wa (interjection indicating surprise or amazement)	waah	

口 6-7

	哈	哈	哈	ha　　　hà laughing sound; exclamation of joy
	哎	哎	哎	ai　　　aai (interjection of surprise)
	哚	哚		duǒ　　　do to support someone powerful
	哞	哞		mou　　　mau (sound a cow makes)
呙	咼	咼		wai　　　waah slanting
	哥	哥	哥	ge　　　goh older brother
	哦	哦		ó　　　oh recite poetry; chant; nag
	哨	哨	哨	shào　　　saau guard; outpost; whistle
	哩	哩		lǐ　　　lei (archaic term for a mile)
	哪	哪	哪	nǎ　　　náh where; which; that; (final article)
	哮	哮	哮	xiáo　　　hàau roar; howl; asthma
	哲	哲	哲	zhé　　　jit wise; sagacious; sage　　　喆 嚞 悊
	哼	哼	哼	heng　　　hang hum; sing softly; moan
	哽	哽		geng　　　gang choked with grief
	唆	唆		suo　　　so tempt; seduce; instigate

	唉	唉	唉	ái àai oh!; alas; (exclamation)
	唏	唏	唏	xi hei weep; sob; grieve
	唧	唧		ji jik chirping of insects
	唁	唁	唁	yàn jin offer condolences
	哺	哺	哺	bǔ bou to feed; nurse
呗	唄	唄		bei bui (colloquial; particle indicating obviousness or grudging agreement)
唢	嗩	嗩		suǒ so a double reed wind instrument similar to an oboe
员	員	員	員	yúan yùhn staff member; personnel
	唔	唔		mh (Cantonese) a direct equivalent of 不 in most cases
	唇	唇		chún sèuhn lip
	唐	唐	唐	táng tòhng Tang Dynasty
	哿	哿		gě go excellent; commend
	哭	哭	哭	ku hùk cry
	唪	唪		fěng fung recite; chant
	唬	唬	唬	hǔ fú intimidate; scare

口 8

售	䔍	𦉫	shòu sauh	sell
唯	唯	唯	wéi wàih	sole; only; answer quickly
唰	唰		shua syut	swish; rustle
唱	唱	唱	chàng cheung	sing
唳	唳	唳	li leui	cry of a bird
唷	唷	唷	yo jo	(final particle)
啑	啑		shà jaap	peck; eat; suck
唾	唾	唾	tùo tou	spit; saliva
唿	唿		hu fat	sad; bit; part
啁	啁	啁	zhao jau	chirp; twitter
啃	啃		kěn hang	gnaw; chew; bite
啄	啄	啄	zhúo doek	peck; slander
商	商	商	shang sèung	trade; commerce; business; businessman; dealer; quotient
念 唸	念	念	niàn nim	recite; read; chant
	啉	啉	lán laam 替 飲 饮 啖	pour a round of alcoholic drink; finish drinking

	啊	嘚	婀	a	à
				ah!	
	啐	啐		cui	cheui
				drink; taste; expectorate; spit; start	
问	問	問	問	wèn	mahn
				ask; inquire	
启	啟	啟	啟	qǐ	kái
				to open; enlighten; educate; inspire; start; begin; explain; note	
	啕	啕	啕	táo	tou
				wail	
	啖	啖	啖	dàn	dahm
				eat; feed; chew; bite; entice	
	啜	啜	啜	chùo	chyut	嚽 歠 嗽 嗜 饡
				sip; suck up; sob; weep	
哑	啞	啞	啞	yǎ	ngá
				dumb; mute	
	啡	啡	啡	fei	fe
				coffee; morphine	
	啤	啤	啤	pí	be
				beer	
	啥	啥		shà	sá
				what	
	啦	啦	啦	la	là
				"la" (*final article; exclamation point*)	
	啪	啪		pa	paak
				pop; pow	
	啷	啷		lang	long
				clanging or rattling sound	
	啻	啻	啻	chì	chi
				only; merely; just like	

口 9

啼	嚧	嚧	tí　　　　tàih cry loudly; wail; (*birds and beasts*) crow; howl	嚧 啼 嗁 渧 諦 謕
啾	啾	啾	jiu　　　jau wailing of a child; chirp	
喀	喀		kà　　　haak (*onomatopoeia*) noise made by coughing	
喁	喁		yóng　　　jung the mouth of a fish at the surface of the water; gasping for breath	
喂	喂	喂	wèi　　　waih hello	
喃	喃	喃	nán　　　naam keep talking; chattering; mumble	
善	善	善	shàn　　　sihn good; kind; skillful; familiar; easily	譱
喇	喇	喇	lǎ　　　laa horn; bugle; lama; (*final particle*)	
喈	喈		jie　　　gaai music; melody	
喉	喉	喉	hóu　　　hàuh throat	
喊	喊	喊	hǎn　　　haam shout	
喋	喋		dié　　　dip talkative	
喏	喏		nùo　　　je (*interjection for drawing attention to*) here!, look! ; respectful reply of assent to superiors	
喑	喑		yin　　　ngam cry continuously	
喔	喔	喔	wò　　　ngak sound of a chicken cluck	

46

	喘	喘	喘	chuǎn　　chyún gasp; pant; breathe heavily	
	喙	喙	喙	huì　　fui beak; snout	嘴
唤	唤	喚	喚	huàn　　wuhn call; summon; invite	
	喜	喜	喜	xǐ　　héi joy; happiness; like	
	喝	喝	喝	he　　hot to drink; to cheer	欲
	喟	喟		kùi　　wai sigh	咽
乔	喬	喬	喬	qiáo　　kiu tall; lofty; area on the shaft of a spear (near the tip) for hanging a feather	高
单	單	單	單	dan　　daan single; individual; solitary; thin; narrow; faint; simple; uncomplicated	单
丧	喪	喪	喪	sang　　sòng mourning; funeral ceremony; corpse; dead body; misfortune; misadventure	喪
	喧	譁	喧	xuan　　hyùn noisy; uproarious; clamouring	叫
	喳	喳	喳	cha　　chaa chirp; twitter; whispering	
哟	哟	喲		yo　　jo (final particle; an interjection used when surprised)	
	喻	諭	喻	yù　　yuh tell; understand; inform	喻
哟	哟	喲		yo　　yò o! ; (final article, an exclamation point)	
唤	唤	喚	喚	huàn　　wun call; summon	

口 10

嗒	㗳		tà　　　　taap	absent-minded; careless
嗄	嚍		sha　　　　saah	hoarse
嗅	齅	嗅	xiù　　　　chau	smell; scent; sniff
嗉	嗉	嗉	sù　　　　sou	a bird's crop
嗦	嗦		suo　　　　sò	to suck; shiver
嗌	嗌		yì　　　　jik	throat; shout; yell, speak loudly
唢	唢		suo　　　　sok　　　軟喋	to suck
嗑	嗑	嗑	kè　　　　gaap	crack between the teeth; talk; gab
嗓	嗓	嗓	sǎng　　　sòng	throat; voice
嗔	嗔		chen　　　cahn	scold; rebuke; anger
嗖	嗖		sou　　　　sau	whizzing sound
嗜	嗜	嗜	shì　　　　si	fond of; hobby
嗝	嗝		gé　　　　gaak	hiccup; burp; call of a bird
嗟	嗟	嗟	jie　　　　jè	sigh; mourn
嗡	嗡	嗡	weng　　　jung	(sound of flying bees and airplanes) "buzz"

48

	嗣	嗣	嗣	sì　　ji connect; descendants; inherit; heirs
	嗤	嗤		chi　　chi laugh at; ridicule; sneer; snort
	嗥	嗥		háo　　hòu roar; call out; wail; howl; bark; yelp
	嗨	嗨		hai　　hoi hi! ; hey!
	嗬	嗬		he　　ho (Cantonese) interrogative particle
	嗯	嗯	嗯	en　　ng used as an interjection to express doubt, curiosity, surprise, agreement; a groaning sound
	嗲	嗲		diǎ　　de inviting; coquettish; intensifying particle; (Cantonese) saliva
吗	嗎	嗎	嗎	ma　　mà (question mark)
呜	嗚	嗚	嗚	wu　　wù (onomatopoeia) sound of sobbing or crying
呛	嗆	嗆	嗆	qiang　　chòng to choke from smoke; to irritate the nose
啬	嗇	嗇	嗇	sè　　sik　　嗇 嗇 cherish; save; conserve; miserly; thrifty; stingy; covet; lack; to be insufficient; poor harvest
	嗷	嗷	嗷	áo　　ngou (onomatopoeia) sound of wailing; clamor
	嗽	嗽	嗽	sòu　　sau cough; clear the throat
	嗾	嗾	嗾	sǒu　　sàu incite; instigate
唛	嘜	嘜		mà　　màk　　嘜 trademark; brand

口 11

	嘀	嘀	嘀	dí　　　　dik backbite; (*onomatopoeia*)	啾
	喊	喊		qi　　　　chi grieved; ashamed; (*onomatopoeia*)	
	嘈	嘈	嘈	cáo　　　chau noisy; tumultuous	
	嘉	嘉	嘉	jia　　　　gà fine; nice; good	
尝	嘗	嘗	嘗	cháng　　sèuhng taste; flavor	
慨	嘅	嘅	嘅	gá　　　　ge (*Cantonese possessive particle*)	噶
	嘌	嘌		piào　　　piu passing swiftly; speak	
	嘎	嘎		ga　　　　gaa (*onomatopoeia*); crack; creak; screech	
	嘏	嘏		gǔ　　　　gu felicity; prosperity; longevity; good fortune; grand	
	嘛	嘛		ma　　　　mah (*stresses the obvious*) of course! (*signals a pause in a sentence, similar to a comma*)	
	嘞	嘞		lei　　　　laak (*final particle used to emphasize the certainty of a changed condition or completed action; an exclamation*)	
	嘣	嘣		beng　　　bang (*onomatopoeia*) a throbbing or popping sound	
叹	嘆	嘆	嘆	tàn　　　　taan sigh	嘩
呕	嘔	嘔	嘔	ǒu　　　　ngáu vomit; throw up	歐 咯 欸 欣 蝫
	哔	嗶	嗶	bì　　　　bat (*onomatopoeia*) beep	

50

唛	嚜	嘜		mài　　　mak (*dialect*) mark; brand; trademark
啧	嘖	嚍	嘖	zé　　　tsak to argue; attempt; (*onomatopoeia*) sound of tongue clicking
喽	嘍	嘍	嘍	lóu　　　lau (*Cantonese*) invite someone to take part in something
	嘟	嘟		du　　　dou (*colloquial*) to pout; to pucker up
	嘬	嘬		chùai　　　chaai to lap; suck; suction
	嘭	嘭		peng　　　baang chase; drive away; (*onomatopoeia*) bang
	嘲	嘲	嘲	cháo　　　sau　　　謿 ridicule; deride; scorn; jeer; mock
	嘴	嘴	嘴	zǔi　　　jéui mouth; beak; (*Cantonese*) kiss
	嘶	嘶	嘶	si　　　sai hiss; neigh; husky throated
	嘹	嘹	嘹	liáo　　　liu clarity of voice; resonant
	嘻	嘻	嘻	xi　　　hei mirth; happy; laugh; giggle
	嘿	嘿	嘿	hàk　　　hei hey!
	噌	噌		cheng　　　chaang bass; scold
	噍	噍		jiào　　　jiu chew; eat; munch
	噎	噎	噎	ye　　　jit choke; burp

口 12-13

	噔	噔		deng / dang (*onomatopoeia*) thump; thud; (*Cantonese*) for a recipient of sympathy
	噗	噗	噗	pu / pok (*onomatopoeia*); sudden laughter; the release of liquid or gas
	嗷	嗷		jue / kyut pouting
	噙	噙		qin / kam hold in mouth; bite
叽	嘰	嘰	嘰	ji / gei sigh in disapproval; grumble
呒	嘸	嘸		fǔ / fu unclear; not; stunned; stupefied
咝	噝	噝		si / si hiss; call to come
哓	嘵	嘵		xiao / hiu fear; shout garrulously; argue; chatter
哗	嘩	嘩	嘩	hwa / waa rushing sound; noise; be noisy
唠	嘮	嘮	嘮	láu / lou nag; chatter
啸	嘯	嘯	嘯	xiào / siu roar; howl; scream; whistle
喷	噴	噴	噴	pen / pan to spray; strong; fragrant; (colloquial) angrily rebuke or scold
嘘	噓	噓	噓	xu / heoi slowly exhale; sigh; lament; praise; flatter; heat by steam or fire
	噢	噢	噢	yǔ / jyu interjection for pain or sadness; realization: "oh!"
	噤	噤	噤	jìn / gam refrain from speaking; close; silent

52

	器	櫐	器		qì　　　hei　　　器 嚻 嚣 器 vessel; device; tool; utensil; organ; capacity; tolerance; ability
	噩	噩	噩		è　　　ngok frightening; startling; shocking; bad omen; unlucky; disaster
	噪	譟	噪		zào　　　chou noisy; chirp loudly
	噫	噫	噫		yi　　　ji belch; burp; alas! (*expressing regret or surprise*)
	噬	噬			shì　　　saih to bite
	噱	噱	噱		júe　　　cheuk hearty laughter
	噶	噶	噶		gá　　　gaa (*used in transliteration*)
	嚏	嚏			sai　　　sak (*used in transcription*)
	噼	噼			pi　　　pek (*Cantonese*) buttocks
吨	噸	噸	噸		dun　　　dèun a ton
哒	噠	噠			da　　　daat clamor; sound made to get a horse to move forward
哕	噦	噦			yue　　　jyut hiccup; retch
哙	噲	噲			kùai　　　faai swallow; gulp; greedy
哝	噥	噥	噥		nóng　　　nung whisper
嗳	嗳	噯	噯		ǎi　　　ói (*interjection of disagreement*) "ai!", "oh!"; (*exclamation*)

口 13-16

当	噹	嘗	嘗	dang　　　dong sound of a bell
	嚅	嚅	嚅	rú　　　yùh indistinct and faltering speach
	噶	嚆		hao　　　hou make noise; sound
	嚎	嚎	嚎	háo　　　hòu cry loudly; bawl; yell; scream
	嚏	嚏	嚏	tì　　　tai sneeze
	嚓	嚓		ca　　　chaat cracking or snapping sound
吓	嚇	嚇	嚇	xià　　　haak threaten; frighten; scare
咛	嚀	嚀	嚀	níng　　　ning enjoin; instruct; charge
哜	嚌	嚌		jì　　　chai sip
啮	嚙	嚙		niè　　　ngat　　　齧 bite; gnaw
噜	嚕	嚕	嚕	lu　　　lou verbose; talkative; chatter; grumble
嚯	嚯	嚯		hùo　　　ho (*interjection expressing surprise or admiration*) oh! wow!; sound of laughter
呖	嚦	嚦		lì　　　lik (*onomatopoeia*)
咙	嚨	嚨	嚨	lóng　　　lùhng throat
向	嚮	向	向	xiàng　　　heung direction; orientation; turn towards

咽	嚥			yàn / yin	to swallow; gulp
	嚷			rǎng / yeuhng	shout; clamor; cry out; uproar
嚳	嚳			kù / guk	urgent; inform quickly; (historical) Emperor Ku
嚶	嚶			ying / jing	call of a bird
严	嚴			yán / yìhm	strict; severe
	嚼			jiáo / jeuk	chew
嚣	囂			xiao / hiù	clamor
啭	囀			zhùan / jyun	sing; chirp; warble; twitter
嗫	囁			niè / jip	move lips as when speaking; hesitation
呓	囈			yì / ngai	talk in your sleep
嘱	囑			zhǔ / jùk	to direct; urge; entrust
	囊			náng / nòhng	bag; sack
	口			wéi / wai	fence; enclosure
	囚			qiú / chàuh	prisoner
	四			sì / sei	four — 肆 (financial)

□ 3-8

回	⊙	回	huí wùih return, go back	田 同
孑	孑	孚	jiǎn chai son; child; infant	仔
囟	囟		xìn seun skull; top of the head	
因	因	因	yin yàn because; cause; reason	
囡	囡		nan naam daughter; child	
勿	勿	勿	é fat entire; whole	
囪	囱	囱	cong tung chimney; funnel	
屯	屯	屯	dùn deuhn storage bin; to hoard	
困	困	困	kùn kwan difficult; exhausted; fatigued; sleepy; stranded	
固	固	固	gù gu solid; strength; firm; stubborn	
囹	囹		líng ling prison; enclosure	
囿	囿	囿	yòu yau pen up; limit; constrain	
圃	圃	圃	pǔ pou garden; orchard; gardener; lush	
圄	圄	圄	yǔ jyu prison; jail; horse keeper	
圈	圈	圈	quǎn hyùn ring; circle; loop; enclose	

	圊	圊		qing　　ching pigsty; pigpen; latrine
仑	侖	侖		lún　　leuhn all; complete; entire
国	國	國	國	gúo　　gwok country; empire
围	圍	圍	圍	wéi　　wàih surround; enclosure
圆	圓	圓	圓	yúan　　yùhn round; circular
园	園	園	園	yúan　　yùhn garden; park; yard
图	圖	圖	圖	tú　　tòuh picture; illustration; pattern
团	團	團	團	túan　　tyùhn group; lump; mass
	圜	圜		húan　　waan heaven; celestial realm
土	土	土		tǔ　　tóu earth; soil; ground
	在	在	在	zài　　joih in; at; to be; exist
	圩	圩	圩	wéi　　heui dike; embankment
	圬	圬	圬	wu　　wu whitewash; plaster
	圭	圭	圭	gui　　gwai jade tablet (*used by officials when addressing the emperor in court*)
	圮	圮		pǐ　　pei destroyed; ruined; collapse; to subvert; to injure

土 4-5

圯	圯		yí / ji bridge; bank
地	坔		dì / deih place; land; ground; earth
圳	𠫓		zhèn / chùn furrow, small drainage in a field
址	坁		zhǐ / ji site; location; land for house; foundation
圻	圻		qi / kei border; boundary
坎	坎		kǎn / ham 埳 pit; hole; snare; trap; threshold; crisis
均	均		jun / gwàn all; uniform; even; equalize
坊	坊		fang / fòng 阪岅 lane; street; square; city subdivision
坌	坐		bèn / ban earth; dust; assemble; to gather; gush (of dust) to fly up or settle on something else
坍	坍		tan / taan collapse; landslide
坐	坐		zuò / joh sit; ride
坑	坑		keng / hàang pit; hole
圾	圾		ji / saap garbage; rubbish
垃	垃		la / laahp garbage; rubbish
坦	坦		tǎn / táan flat; level; smooth; frank; calm; honest

土 5-6

坩	坩	𤰈	gan　　ham earthenware; crucible; earthenware vessel
坨	坨		túo　　to lump; spherical object
坤	坤	𤮼	kún　　kwàn earth; feminine; female
坪	坪	𡊡	píng　　pìhng level ground; plain
坭	坭		nǐ　　nai mud; mire; paste; plaster
坯	坯		pei　　pui　　坏 unburnt pottery and bricks; base; abode; hill (*figurative*) unfinished or semifinished product
坳	坳		ào　　aau flat land between mountains; a hollow in the ground; a cavity; depression
坷	坷	𡍄	kě　　ho a placename in ancient China
坡	坡	𡊜	po　　bo slope, bank, hillside
坻	坻		chí　　chih islet; small island; shore; embankment
坼	坼	𡍺	chè　　chaak crack; split; tear open
垂	坙	𡉴	chúi　　sèuih　　垂巫才物 hang; droop; dangle; suspend; bend down
垌	垌		dòng　　dung field; farmland
垓	垓	𡍙	gai　　goi border; boundary; frontier
垛	垛		dùo　　do pile; heap; buttress

土 6-8

垠	垠	垠	yín　　　ngan	bank, boundary
垢	垢	垢	gòu　　　gau	filth; dirt; dust; shame
垣	垣	垣	yúan　　　wùhn	wall; town
垮	垮	垮	kǔa　　　kwà	collapse; defeated; fail
城	城	城	chéng　　　sihng	city; town; fortified settlement
型	型	型	xíng　　　yìhng	mold; model; type; pattern
垤	垤		dié　　　dit	mound; small hill; anthill
垸	垸		yúan　　　jyun	dike; embankment
埃	埃	埃	ai　　　oi	fine dust; dirt; angstrom; one ten-billionth
埋	埋	埋	mái　　　màaih	bury; hide; conceal
埂	埂	埂	gěng　　　gang	earth dyke; irrigation channel
埔	埔	埔	pǔ　　　bou	plain; flatland
埕	埕		chéng　　　chìhng	a large pear-shaped earthenware jar for alcohol
埝	埝		niàn　　　nim	earth embankment used to retain water; dike around a paddy field
域	域		yù　　　wihk	region; district; fief; cemetery

	埠	埠	埠	bù　　　fauh	port; wharf; pier; dock
垭	埡	埡		yà　　　a	character used in place names; (*dialect*) strip of land between hills; narrow mountain pass
	埤	埤	埤	pí　　　pei	increase; parapet; low; inferior; reservoir used in irrigation
	野	野	野	yě　　　je　　　埜壄埜壄壄	countryside; field; outskirts; plain; wild; feral; untamed; unrestrained; coarse; informal; illegal
	埭	埭		dài　　　dai	dam; inclined plane on a canal (*where boats can be launched*)
	埯	埯		ǎn　　　ám	cover with earth; hole (*for seeds*)
	埴	埴		zhí　　　jik	soil with high clay content
执	執	執	執	zhí　　　jàp　　　执秇㚔執埶	hold; grasp; keep; (*Cantonese*) to pick up rubbish; clean up
	埸	埸		yì　　　jik	border; edge
	培	培	培	péi　　　pùih	cultivate; nourish; to create a hill or embankment for agriculture
	基	基	基	jī　　　gèi	foundation; basic
	埽	埽		sào　　　sou	broom; sweep; clear away
	堀	堀		ku　　　fat	cavity; cave; to bore a hole
	堂	堂	堂	táng　　　tòhng	hall; court; large room
坚	堅	堅	堅	jián　　　gìn	strong; firm; durable; hard; solid; resolute

土 8-9

	堆	堆	堆	dui / dèui — heap; stack; pile; accumulate
	堇	堇		jǐn / gan — clay; violet (flower)
垩	堊	堊	堊	è / ok — chalk; whitewash
	堋	堋		péng / bing — bury; archery target
	堍	堍		tù / tou — flat ground on either end of a bridge
	堙	堙		yin / jan — mound; dam; bury; to block up
埚	堝	堝	堝	gwo / wo — crucible
	堞	堞		dié / dip — plate
	堠	堠	堠	hòu / hau — mound for a beacon; battlements; battlement wall
	堡	堡	堡	bǎo / bóu — fort; castle; stronghold
	堤	堤	堤	di / tàih — embankment; barrier
尧	堯	堯	堯	yáo / yiu — lofty; high; Emperor Yao (legendary ruler of ancient China) 垚 尧 尧 尧 杭
	堪	堪	堪	kan / hàm — may; capable; to bear; to stand; resist; worthy
	堰	堰	堰	yàn / yím — weir; dam; dike
报	報	報	報	bào / bou — reciprocate; avenge; inform; newspaper; telegram

土 9-10

场	場	場	場	cháng　　　chèuhng yard; field; open space	坊 場
	堵	墻	墻	dǔ　　　dóu obstruct; block	
	塄	塄		léng　　　ling elevated bank in a field	
坚	堅	堅	堅	jian　　　gin firm; strong; hard; solid; resolute	
茔	塋	塋	塋	yíng　　　jing grave; tomb; cemetary	
	塌	塌	塌	ta　　　taap collapse; fall down; sink; droop	
坞	塢	塢	塢	wù　　　ou dock; castle; village; hamlet	
	塍	塍		chéng　　　sing raised path between fields; dyke	
垲	塏	塏		kǎi　　　hoi high and dry place; dry terrain	
	塑	塑	塑	sù　　　sou mould; to model; plastic	
	塒	塒		shí　　　si roost for hens	
	塔	塔	塔	tǎ　　　taap pagoda; tower; spire; tall building	墖
涂	塗	塗		tú　　　tòuh mud; shoal; daub; smear; apply; paint; cross out; scrawl over	
	塘	塘	塘	táng　　　tòhng pond; pool; embankment	
	塞	塞	塞	sai　　　sak block; stop up; cork; stuff; jammed; prohibit	

63

土 10-11

埙	塤	塤		xun　　　hyun　　　壎 an ancient egg-shaped flute made of clay or ceramic
	塥	塥		gé　　　gaak dry clay lump
	填	填	填	tián　　　tìhn fill out a form; fill a gap or shortcoming
	塬	塬		yúan　　　jyun plateau; highland
块	塊	塊	塊	kùai　　　faai piece; lump; mass
	墀	墀	墀	chí　　　chi step; porch
	墁	墁		màn　　　maan plaster; pave
	境	境	境	jìng　　　gíng region; boundary; territory; border; condition; situation
	墉	墉		yong　　　yung fortified wall
	墒	墒		sháng　　　sèung moisture in the soil
	墓	墓	墓	mù　　　mouh grave; tomb; mausoleum
	墚	墚		liáng　　　loeng mountain range
尘	塵	塵	塵	chén　　　chàhn　　　麈 塵 dust; dirt; ashes; cinders
堑	塹	塹	塹	qiàn　　　chim chasm; moat; deep trench
垫	墊	墊		diàn　　　dihn pad; mat; cushion; place under

	塾	塾	塾	shú　　　suhk	old style family or village school
坠	墜	墜	墜	zhuì　　　jeuih	fall; drop; sink
堕	墮	墮	墮	duò　　　doh	fall; degenerate; sink
	墅	墅	墅	shù　　　seuih	villa; cottage; country house
	墟	墟	墟	xu　　　hèui	market; fair; wasteland; ruins
	墩	墩	墩	dun　　　dan　　墪	mound; block of stone or wood; (classifier for dense foliage; a cluster; rounds in a card game)
坟	墳	墳	墳	fén　　　fàhn	grave; mound; bulge
	增	增	增	zeng　　　jàng	increase; add to; expand; gain
	墨	墨	墨	mò　　　mahk	ink; black; dark; embezzle; learning; knowledge; (poetry, handwriting, painting)
坛	壇	壇	壇	tán　　　tàahn	altar
	壁	壁	壁	bì　　　bìk	wall; partition; rampart; cliff
	壅	壅	壅	yong　　　jung	obstruct; block; barricade
垦	墾	墾	墾	kěn　　　hán	plow land; cultivate
	壕	壕	壕	háo　　　hòu	moat; channel; trench
	壑	壑	壑	hè　　　kok	ravine; gully

土 11-14

土 15-21 士 1-11 夂

垒	壘	壘	壘	lěi　　　　léuih rampart; military wall	
圹	壙	壙	壙	kuàng　　　kwong grave; prairie	
垆	壚	壚		lú　　　　lou clay; shop	
坜	壢	壢	壢	lì　　　　lik hole; pit	
坏	壞	壞	壞	huài　　　waaih ruin; bad; rotten; spoiled	
垄	壟	壠	壟	lǒng　　　lung mound; grave	壟 垅
	壤	壤	壤	ràng　　　yeuhng soil; earth	
坝	壩	壩	壩	bà　　　　ba dam; embankment	
	士	士	士	shì　　　　sih scholar, officer, soldier	
	壬	壬	壬	rén　　　　jam 9th heavenly stem (9th day of a 10 day week - Shang Dynasty)	
壮	壯	壯	壯	zhuàng　　jong strong; healthy; robust	
	壹	壹	壹	yi　　　　yàt one	一
壶	壺	壺		hú　　　　wùh kettle; jug; canteen; bottle; flask	
寿	壽	壽	壽	shòu　　　sauh longevity; age; lifespan	壽 寿
	夂	夂		zhǐ　　　　chi approach from behind	

66

	复	復			fù　　　　　fuk complex; compound; duplicate
	夏				xià　　　　　haa summer; great; grand; magnificent; Xia dynasty
夔	夒				kúi　　　　　kwai walrus
	夕				xí　　　　　jihk evening; sunset
	外				wai　　　　　ngoi outside, foreign, external
	多				duo　　　　　dò　　　　 夛 many, much, numerous, multi- (prefix)
	夙				sù　　　　　suk　　　　 侊 㐁 dawn; early morning; past
	夜				yè　　　　　yeh　　　　 亱 㐉 night, evening
	夠				gòu　　　　　gau enough; sufficient
	夤				yín　　　　　jan distant; remote; deep
梦	夢				mèng　　　　　muhng dream; aspiration
伙	夥				hǔo　　　　　fó many; group; companion
	大				dà　　　　　daaih big; large; great; older
	太				tài　　　　　taai too; very; extreme; elder; Mrs.
	天				tian　　　　　tìn sky; heaven; day; overhead; weather

大 1-6

夭			yao / yiù	delicate; tender; die prematurely
夫			fu / fù	husband; man
失			shi / sàt	lost; missed; mistake
央			yang / yeung	central; center; to beg
夷			yí / yìh	barbarian; safe; even; level
夾			jia / gaap	squeeze between; pinch; clamp; carry under one's arm; wedged between; clip; folder; layer
奇			qí / kèih	remarkable; strange; curious; odd
奈			nái / noih	how; why (*rhetorical*); bear; endure
奏			zòu / jau	play (*musical instrument*); achieve; report; memorial
奄			yǎn / jim	hasty; quickly; suddenly; cover; castrate
奉			fèng / fuhng	offer; receive; serve; respect
奔			ben / bàn	run; hasten
奕			yì / jik	grand; beautiful; skilled; adept; bright 弈 預 预 意 咿
契			qì / kai	contract; deed; conform; carve; engrave
奎			kúi / fui	stride; legs

奘	奘	奘	zàng stout; fat	jong	
套	套	套	tào case; cover; wrapper; envelope	tou	夳套
奚	奚	奚	xi what; why; where; how	hai	
奢	奢	奢	shé extravagant; wasteful; exaggerate	chè	
奠	奠	奠	diàn make offerings to the dead; libation	din	
奧	奧	奧	ào difficult to understand	ou	
奪	奪		dúo take by force; seize	deuht	
獎	獎	獎	jiǎng praise; reward; prize; award	jéung	獎弊
奮	奮	奮	fèn strive; struggle; exertion; shake; vibrate; wave; (*bird*) to spread and flutter the wings	fáhn	
女	女	女	nǔ female; woman; girl; daughter	néuih	
奴	奴	奴	nú slave	nòuh	
奶	奶	奶	nǎi milk; breast; suckle	náaih	
妁	妁	妁	shùo matchmaker; act as go-between	jeuk	
如	如	如	rú as; if	yùh	
妃	妃	妃	fei couple; spouse; imperial concubine	fei	

女 3-4

	她	(seal)	(seal)	tá / tà she; her
	妄	(seal)	(seal)	wàng / móhng absurd; preposterous
	好	(seal)	(seal)	hǎo / hóu good; well; fine; OK; very
	妤	(seal)	(seal)	yú / jyu beautiful; fair; handsome
	妓	(seal)	(seal)	jì / geih prostitute
	妖	(seal)	(seal)	yao / yiú phantom; demon; succubus; bewitching
	妙	(seal)	(seal)	miào / miuh wonderful; splendid; clever; subtle; fine; excellent
	妨	(seal)	(seal)	fáng / fòhng harm; hinder
	妍	(seal)	(seal)	yán / jin beautiful; handsome; seductive
	妊	(seal)	(seal)	rèn / jam conceive; pregnant
	妞	(seal)	(seal)	niu / nau girl
	妣	(seal)	(seal)	bǐ / bei a posthumous name for a mother
妆	妝	(seal)	(seal)	zhuang / chong apply makeup; adorn oneself
	妥	(seal)	(seal)	tuǒ / to proper; appropriate; ready
	妒	(seal)	(seal)	dù / douh jealous; envy

	妮	柅	柅	ni / nei	servant girl
	妯	妯	妯	zhóu / juk	a brother's wife
	妹	妹	妹	mèi / múi	younger sister
	姆	姆	姆	mǔ / móuh	woman who looks after children; baby sitter; female tutor; governess
姗	姍	姍	姍	shan / saan	deprecate; slander; ridicule
	姊	姊	姊	zǐ / jeh	older sister
	姐	姐	姐	jiě / jé	older sister; miss
	始	始	始	shǐ / chí (乿 乱 乿 乿)	beginning; start; origin; initial; first
	姑	姑	姑	gu / gù	aunt; father's sister; husband's sister; husband's mother
	姒	姒	姒	sì / chíh	elder brother's wife
	姓	姓	姓	xìng / sing	family name; clan name
	妻	妻	妻	qi / chài	wife
	妾	妾	妾	qiè / chip	slave woman; concubine
	委	委	委	wěi / wái	appoint; delegate; entrust; commit
	姘	姘	姘	pin / ping	mistress; paramour; extramarital sex

女 6-7

	姚	㛮	㚪	yáo jiu handsome; elegant
	姝	姝		shu jyu beautiful woman; charming
	姣	姣	姣	jiao gaau graceful; beautiful; cunning
	姥	姥	姥	lǎo lou maternal grandmother; midwife
	姨	姨	姨	yí yìh aunt; mother's sister
	姻	姻	姻	yin yàn marriage
	娃	娃	娃	wá wah girl; infant; doll
	姜	姜	姜	jiang geung ginger
	姿	姿	姿	zi ji posture; position; appearance; gesture; manner; bearing
	威	威	威	wei wai prestige; power; might
奸	姦	姦	姦	jian gaan evil; wicked; treacherous; traitor; betrayer; adultery; rape
	姬	姬	姬	ji gei imperial concubine; beauty
	娉	娉	娉	ping ping beautiful; attractive; charming; graceful
	娌	娌	娌	lǐ lei brother's wife
	娓	娓	娓	wěi mei comply; agreeable

	娠			shen　　　san pregnant
	娘			niáng　　　niang young woman; mother; wife
	娜			núo　　　no beautiful; graceful
	娣			di　　　dai younger brother's wife
	娥			é　　　ngo beautiful; good
	娩			miǎn　　　min give birth; agreeable
	娟			juan　　　gyun beautiful; graceful
娛	娱			yú　　　jyu amuse; entertain; enjoyment; pleasure
嫻	嫻			xián　　　haan　　嫺 嫻 elegant; refined; skillful
	娑			suo　　　so dance; frolic
	婆			pó　　　pòh old lady; mother-in-law; husband's mother; grandmother
	娶			qú　　　chéui marry; to take a wife
	婪			lán　　　laam greed; covetous; avaricious
	娼			chang　　　cheung prostitute
	婀			e　　　o be beautiful; be graceful

女 8-10

	婉	㛅	㛅	wǎn　　jyun amiable; congenial; restrained
	婊	㿧	㿧	biǎo　　biu (*slang, derogatory*) prostitute; whore; wrongly accused
	婕	倢		jié　　jit handsome
	婚	婚	婚	hun　　fan marriage; wedding
	婧	婧		jìng　　jing modest; supple; slender; delicate
婵	嬋	嬋	嬋	chán　　sim beautiful; lovely; pretty; graceful
	婢	婢	婢	bì　　pei female slave; servant girl
妇	婦	婦	婦	fù　　fu married woman
	婷	婷	婷	tíng　　ting pretty; attractive; graceful
	婺	婺		wù　　mou disobey
	媚	媚		mèi　　mei charming; attractive; flatter
	婿	婿	婿	xù　　sai son-in-law; husband
	媒	媒	媒	méi　　mui go-between; matchmaker; medium; introduce; yeast
	媛	媛	媛	yúan　　jyun beauty
	媪	媪	媪	ǎo　　ou old woman

女 10-11

妈	媽			ma / mà mother, mom
	媲			pì / bei pair; match; marry off
	媳			xí / sik daughter-in-law
	媾			gòu / gau to marry; dote on; make peace; agreement; negotiate peace; copulate
	嫁			jià / gaa marry; become married to; give a daughter in marriage; transfer; shift blame
	嫉			jí / jat jealousy
	嫌			xián / jim hate; detest; suspect; criticize
	嫂			sǎo / sou sister-in-law (older brother's wife); friend's wife
嫒	嬡			ai / oi (*your*) daughter
嫔	嬪			pín / ban court lady; palace maid
	媵			yìng / jing to accompany; bridesmaid
	嫣			yan / jin beauty; charming; fascinating
	嫖			piáo / piu to patronise prostitutes; nimble; agile
	嫘			léi / leui (*sirname*)
	嫠			lí / lei widow 釐 嫠 娌

女 11-14

	嫡	嫡	嫡	dí　　　　dik legitimate wife; closely related; orthodox; authentic
	嫦	嫦	嫦	cháng　　　chèung (ngo)　　常娥 Cháng'é (*mythical moon goddess*)
	嫩	嫩	嫩	nèn　　　　nyun tender; delicate; inexperienced; unskilled
	嫫	嫫		mó　　　　mou ugly woman; calm
嫱	嫱	嫱		qiáng　　　chèuhng lady; female court official
娇	嬌	嬌	嬌	jiao　　　　giu seductive; loveable; tender; delicate
妪	嫗	嫗	嫗	yǔ　　　　yu old woman; brood over
	嬉	嬉	嬉	xi　　　　hei enjoy; play; amusement
娆	嬈	嬈	嬈	ráo　　　　jiu graceful; charming; fascinating
娴	嫻	嫻	嫻	xián　　　　- refined; elegant; gracious
妩	嫵	嫵	嫵	wu　　　　mou charming; enchanting; flatter
	嬗	嬗		shàn　　　sin succession to the throne
	嬴	嬴	嬴	yíng　　　jing win; gain; surplus
	嬖	嬖		bì　　　　pei favorite
婴	嬰	嬰	嬰	ying　　　jing infant; baby

	嬤	嬤		ma / ma	mother; mamma
	嬲	嬲		niǎo / niu	flirt; tease
婶	嬸	嬸	嬸	shěn / sam	aunt (*wife of father's younger brother*)
	孀	孀		shuang / song	widow (霜 姌)
	孌	孌		lúan / lyun	lovely; beautiful; docile; obedient
	子	子	子	zǐ / jí	son, boy
	孑	孑	孑	jié / kit	alone; single
	孓	孓	孓	júe / kyut	missing a right arm; short (孑亥)
	孔	孔	孔	kǒng / húng	hole; aperture; opening
	孕	孕	孕	yùn / yahn	conceive; pregnant; give birth
	字	字	字	zì / jih	word; character
	存	存	存	cún / chyùhn	exist; save; keep
	孚	孚	孚	fu / fu	confidence; trust
	孛	孛	孛	bèi / bui	luxuriant; lush; flourishing; comet
	孝	孝	孝	ziào / haau	pay respect to parents; filial piety

子 4-14

	孜	攷	辪	zi / zi diligent; hard working; industrious
	孟	盈	盈	mèng / maahng senior; oldest
	孢	坤		bao / baau spore
	季	𩰀	𩰀	jì / gwai season; period; youngest brother
	孤	𤖅	𤖅	gu / gù orphan; lonely
	孥	孥		nú / nou offspring; one's children
	孩	𡥷	𡥷	hái / hàai child; baby
孙	孫	𡥥	𡥥	sun / syùn grandson
	孬	孬		nao / naau not good; cowardly; contemptible
	孰	孰	孰	shú / suhk who? whoever? which? which one? what? what else?
	孱	孱		càn / saan weak; small; frail; feeble; meager; mean; shallow; cautious
	孳	孳	孳	zi / zi 孳 breed; propogate; procreation
	孵	孵	孵	fú / fù hatch; brood
学	學	學	學	xúe / hohk learn; knowledge; study
	孺	孺	孺	rú / yùh child

78

子 17-19　宀 2-5

	孽	孼	孼	niè / jip son of a concubine; ghost; monster; disaster; calamity; evil; sin; treacherous
孪	孿	孿	孿	lúan / lyùhn twins
	宀	宀		mián / min roof
	它	它	它	tá / tà it (*third-person singular pronoun for inanimate objects*)
	宄	宄		gǔi / gwai traitor; villain
	宅	宅	宅	zhái / jaahk residence; abode
	宇	宇	宇	yǔ / yuh house; universe
	守	守	守	shǒu / sáu guard; keep
	安	安	安	an / òn peaceful; safe; secure
	宋	宋	宋	sòng / sung Sung Dynasty
	完	完	完	wán / yùhn finish(ed); complete(d)
	宏	宏	宏	hóng / wàhng vast; great
	牢	牢	牢	láo / lou prison; stable; firm
	宓	宓		fú / fuk quiet; silent; good health
	宕	宕		dàng / dong stone quarry; cave dwelling; put off

宀 5-7

	宗	宗	宗	zong / jùng — ancestor; clan
	宙	宙	宙	zhòu / jauh — universe; eon
	定	定	定	dìng / dihng — certain; decided; finalized; definite
	宛	宛	宛	wǎn / yun — as if; seem; crooked; winding
	宜	宜	宜	yí / yìh — suitable; proper
	官	官	官	guan / gún — officer; official; organ (body)
	宦	宦	宦	huàn / waan — government official; eunuch
	客	客	客	kè / haak — guest; visitor; customer; passenger; objective
	宣	宣	宣	xuan / syùn — announce; declare; proclaim
	室	室	室	shì / sàt — room; office
	宥	宥	宥	yòu / jau — forgive; pardon
宮	宮	宮	宮	gong / gùng — palace; temple; castration (one of the 五刑, "Five Punishments": aka 淫刑, 腐刑, or 蠶室刑)
	宰	宰	宰	zǎi / choi — slaughter; butcher; govern
	害	害	害	hài / hoih — harm; hurt; misfortune
	宴	宴	宴	yàn / yin — feast; entertain; banquet

宵	宵	宵	xiao　　siu	night; evening
家	家	家	jia　　ga	family; home; household
宸	宸	宸	chén　　san	eaves; roof; great mansion; imperial palace
容	容	容	róng　　yùhng	hold; contain; tolerate; allow; permit; facial appearance; bearing; posture
宿	宿	宿	sù　　sùk	dormitory; lodging
寂	寂	寂	jì　　jihk	silent; lonely; still; quiet
寄	寄	寄	jì　　gei	send; mail; post
寅	寅	寅	yín　　jan	polite; respectful; revere
密	密	密	mì　　mat	dense; thick; close; intimate; secret; confidential
寇	寇	寇	kòu　　kau	plunderer; robber
寒	寒	寒	hán　　hòhn	cold; chilly
富	富	富	fù　　fu	rich; wealthy
寐	寐	寐	mèi　　mei	sleep soundly
冤 寃	寃	寃	yuan　　yùn	injustice; false accusation
	寓	寓	yù　　yu	residence; lodge; dwell

宀 7-9

宀 11-16

实	實	實	實	shí　　　　saht solid; true; real; sincere
宁	寧	寧	寧	níng　　　　nìhng rather; peaceful
寝	寢	寢	寢	qín　　　　chám sleep; lie down; bedroom
	寞	寞	寞	mò　　　　mohk lonely; deserted
	察	察	察	chá　　　　chaat observe; inspect
	寡	寡	寡	guǎ　　　　gwa widowed; alone; friendless; few
	寤	寤	寤	wù　　　　ng wake up
	寥	寥	寥	liáo　　　　liùh very few; scarce; empty
	寨	寨	寨	zhài　　　　chai stockade; stronghold; fort; bandit den
宽	寬	寬	寬	kúan　　　　fùn wide; width; broad; breadth
审	審	審	審	shěn　　　　sám examine; judge
写	寫	寫	寫	xié　　　　sé write; compose
	寮	寮	寮	liáo　　　　liu small house; shack; hut
	寰	寰	寰	húan　　　　waan large domain; country; world
宠	寵	寵	寵	chǒng　　　　chúng pamper; spoil; favor

宝	寶	寳	寶	bǎo	bóu
				treasure; precious; jewel	
寸	寸	ㄢ	㝷	cùn	chyun
				inch	
	寺	寺	㞢	sì	jí
				temple; Buddhist monastery	
	封	封	封	féng	fùng
				seal; close; (*classifier for correspondence*)	
	射	躲	躲	shè	seh
				shoot; squirt	
将	將	將	將	jiang	jèung
				will; would; shall; commander; general	
专	專	專	專	zhuan	jyùn
				specialized; expert	
	尉	尉	尉	wèi	wai
				military officer	
	尊	尊	尊	zun	jyùn
				respect; honor	
寻	尋	尋	尋	xún	chàhm
				search; seek	
对	對	對	對	dùi	deui
				correct; right; to	
导	導	導	導	dáo	douh
				lead; direct; guide; conduct	
	小	小	小	xiǎo	siú
				small; little; tiny; young	
	少	少	少	xiǎo	siú
				few; less; little	
	尕	尕		gǎ	gaa
				small	

小 3-6　尤 4-14　尸 1-4

尖	尖	尖	jian　　jìm	sharp; pointed; acute; shrewd
尚	尚	尚	shàng　　seuhng	still; yet; revere; hold in high esteem; admire; virtuous
尜	尜		gá　　gaat　　嘎	a spinning top that is spun with a string
尤	尤	尤	yóu　　yàuh　　尣	especially; particularly
尬	尬	尬	gà　　gaai	embarrass
就	就	就	jiù　　jauh	on; then; that; approach; arrive at; undertake; succeed; suffer; subjected to; concerning; right away
尷	尷	尷	gan　　gaam	embarrassed
尸	尸	尸	shi　　si　　屍	corpse; carcass; impersonate the dead
尺	尺	尺	chǐ　　chek	foot (*measure*); ruler
尻	尻		kao　　haau	tailbone (*coccyx*); sacrum
尼	尼	尼	ní　　nèih	Buddhist nun
尾	尾	尾	wěi　　méih	tail; end; last
尿	尿	尿	niào　　niu　　溺 屎 屄 尾	urine; urinate
局	局	局	jú　　guhk	bent; crooked; restrict; coerce; close; tolerance; circumstances; office; bureau; gathering; chessboard
屁	屁	屁	pì　　pei　　糞 尾 屎 屁 屄	fart

尸 5-12

		居	居	居	ju　　　　gèui occupy; house; residence; dwelling
届	居	居	居		jiè　　　　gaai session; arrive at
		屈	屈	屈	qú　　　　wàt bend; stoop; flex; crouch
		屋	屋	屋	wú　　　　ùk house; building; room
		屎	屎		shǐ　　　　sí excrement; feces; dung
		屏	屏	屏	píng　　　　bing a screen wall; folding screen; shield; wall scroll; shelter
		屐	屐		ji　　　　kehk wooden shoes; clogs
		屑	屑		xiè　　　　sit fragment; scrap; crumb
		展	展	展	zhán　　　　tsin open; unfold; stretch; extend; postpone; exhibit; display; show
		屙	屙		e　　　　o　　　痾疴阿屙屙 defecate; excrete
		屉	屉	屉	tì　　　　tai drawer; tray
		屠	屠	屠	tú　　　　tòuh slaughter; butcher
		屣	屣		xi　　　　saai straw sandal/slipper
屡	屡	屡	屡		lǚ　　　　léuih frequent; often; repeatedly
层	层	层	层		céng　　　　chàhng story; floor; layer; level

85

尸 12-18　屮 2　山 3-5

履	履	履	履	lǚ　　　　lei　　　　履 屦 履 復 踶 shoe; footwear; foot; territory; walk on; put on shoes; assume a role; experience; undergo; carry out
屦	屨	屨	屨	jù　　　　geoi straw sandals; trample
属	屬	屬	屬	shǔ　　　　suhk belong to; subject to
	屮	屮		chè　　　　chit sprout; initial bud; left hand
屯	屯	屯		tún　　　　tyùhn village; hamlet; station
山	山	山		shan　　　　sàan mountain; hill
屹	屹	屹		yì　　　　ngat towering; firm; unyielding; high
屺	屺			qǐ　　　　hei hill without trees or vegetation
岈	岈			yá　　　　nga towering; cragginess
岌	岌	岌		jí　　　　kap perilous; hazardous; steep
岐	岐	岐		qí　　　　kei high; majestic; divergent
岑	岑	岑		cén　　　　sam steep; precipitous; peak
岔	岔	岔		chà　　　　chà intersection; fork; contradictory
岜	岜			ba　　　　baa (used in placenames in Guangxi province)
冈	岡	岡	岡	gang　　　　gong　　　　崗 岗 ridge or crest of a mountain; mound

岩	巖	岩	yán　　　　ngàahm rock; cliff	巖巌岊嵓
岫	岫	岫	xiù　　　　jau cave; cavern; mountain peak	
岬	岬		jiá　　　　gaap cape; promontory; headland	
岱	岱	岱	dài　　　　doi (*a nickname for mount Tai (Dàishan), one of the five sacred mountains in China*)	
岳	嶽	岳	yuè　　　　ngohk tall mountain; parent-in-law; wife's parents	
岵	岵		hù　　　　wu a woodland hill	
岷	崏	岷	mín　　　　man the Min River and mountains in Sichuan	
岸	岸	岸	àn　　　　ngohn shore; bank; coast	
峁	峁		mǎo　　　　maau yellow dirt mound (*Loess hills*)	
峋	峋		xún　　　　seun a range of hills	
峒	峒	峒	dòng　　　　dung a mountain in Gansu province (*Tong mountain*)	
峙	峙	峙	zhì　　　　si stand erect; stand up; tower; pile up	
峨	峨		é　　　　ngo lofty	
峪	峪		yù　　　　yuk valley; ravine	
峭	峭	峭	qiào　　　　chiu steep; precipitous	

	峰	峯	峯	feng / fùng — peak; summit
岘	岘	峴	峴	xiàn / jin — steep hill; mount Xian (*south of Xiangyang, Hubei*)
岛	島	島	島	dǎo / dóu — island
	峻	峻	峻	jùn / jeun — steep; lofty; severe; high
峡	峽	陝	峽	xiá / hahp — gorge; mountain pass
	崆	崆	崆	kong / hung — Kongdòng mountains (崆峒山); (*used in place names*)
	崇	崇	崇	chóng / sùhng — worship; honor; esteem; dignified; lofty
	崎	崎	崎	qí / kèi — rugged; rough; craggy
	崔	崔	崔	cui / cheui — high; lofty; towering
	崖	崖	崖	yá / ngàaih — cliff; precipice; limit; boundary; margin
岗	崗	岡	岡	gǎng / gòng — ridge of a hill; mound; hillock; guard; post
仑	崙	侖	侖	lún / leon — Kunlún mountains (崑崙山) 崘
	崛	崛		júe / gwat — towering; eminent; rise abruptly; peak
	崞	崞		guo / gwok — (*a mountain in Shanxi province*)
峥	崢	崢	崢	zheng / jang — high; lofty; noble; steep; perilous

崤	崤	崤	xiáo　　ngaau mount Xiáo in Henan
崦	崦		yan　　yim a mountain in Kansu province (*that has a cave into which the sun is said to sink at night*)
崩	崩		beng　　bàng to collapse
崴	崴	崴	wǎi　　wai sprain one's ankle; high; lofty
崽	崽		zǎi　　jai cub, young animal
嵇	嵇	嵇	ji　　kai a mountain in Henan province
嵋	嵋		méi　　mei a mountain in Sichuan province
嵌	嵌	嵌	qiàn　　hahm inlay; embed; grotto; sink into
岚 嵐	嵐	嵐	lán　　laam mountain mist; haze
	嵎	嵎	yú　　jyu a county in Shandong province
	嵩	嵩	song　　sung lofty; sublime; grand; one of the 5 peaks in Hunan
	嵬	嵬	wéi　　ngai high; rugged; rocky
	嵯	嵯	cúo　　cho irregular; rugged
	嵴	嵴	jí　　jek crest; mountain ridge
嵝	嶁	嶁	lou　　lau Gǒulou (岣嶁), a mountain peak in Hunan province

	嶂	嶂		zhàng　　jeung cliff; mountain barrier
崭	嶄	嶄	嶄	zhǎn　　chaam high; steep; precipitous
岖	嶇	嶇	嶇	qu　　kèui rugged; rough
崂	嶗	嶗		láo　　lou a mountain in Shandong province
	嶙	嶙		lín　　leon precipitous
	嶝	嶝	嶝	dèng　　dang a path leading up a mountain
峤	嶠	嶠		jiào　　giu highest peak
峄	嶧	嶧		yì　　jik　　峄 a range of peaks in Shandong and Jiangsu provinces
岙	嶴	嶴		ào　　ou flat land between mountains; (*used in place names in coastal regions such as Zhejiang and Fujian*)
	嶷	嶷		yí　　jik a mountain in Hunan province
嵘	嶸	嶸	嶸	róng　　wang high; steep; towering
岭	嶺	嶺	嶺	lǐng　　líhng ridge; mountain range
屿	嶼	嶼	嶼	yǔ　　jeuih small island; islet; (*one of the Hong Kong islands*)
岿	巋	巋		kui　　kwai grand; stately; secure; lasting
峦	巒	巒	巒	lúan　　lyun pointed mountain

巔	巓	巓	巓	dian　　　dìn peak; mountain top
	巛	巛		chuan　　chyùn　　巛 川 stream; river; brook; flow
川	川	巛		chuan　　chyùn stream; river; brook; flow
州	州	州		zhou　　jau　　州 prefecture; state; province
巢	巢	巢		cháo　　caau nest
工	工	工		góng　　gùng　　刑王巨珍 labor; work; industry; profession; workman
左	左	左		zuǒ　　jó　　ナ差左 left side; inferior position; unorthodox; wrong; erroneously
巧	巧	巧		qiǎo　　háau skillful; dextrous; ingenious; clever
巨	巨	巨		jù　　geuih　　王飞五王 huge; enormous; gigantic
巫	巫	巫		wu　　mòuh wizard; shaman; witch; witch doctor
差	差	差		cha　　chà　　差莕壓叁戶 different; incongruous; incorrect; erroneous; discrepancy; inferior; substandard; nearly; almost
巯	巯	巯		qiú　　kau sulfhydryl (*chemistry*)
己	己	己		jǐ　　géi oneself; 6th heavenly stem (*6th day of a 10 day week - Shang Dynasty*)
已	已	已		yǐ　　yíh already; stopped
巳	巳	巳		sì　　jih (*sixth earthly branch*); snake (*Chinese zodiac*)

己 1-9　巾 2-5

巴			ba　　　bà slap; wish; *(suffix)*: objects below or behind; clumped due to dryness/stickiness
巷			xiàng　　hohng　　騹 鄉 巷 alley; lane; tunnel
巽			xùn　　　seon obedient; modest
巾			jin　　　　gàn towel; kerchief; napkin
市			shì　　　síh city; town; market
布			bù　　　　bou cloth; fabric
帆			fán　　　fàahn sail; canvas
希			xi　　　　hèi hope; rare; infrequent
帑			tăng　　　tong treasury; storehouse of money
帚			zhǒu　　　jáau　　　箒 蒂 蒂 broom; broomstick
帛			bó　　　　baahk silk; fabric; wealth
帕			pà　　　　paak wrap; handkerchief
帖			tie　　　　típ invitation card; note
帙			zhì　　　　dit book cover; satchel; bag
帔			pèi　　　　pei skirt; a long robe for women *(no sleeves and fastens down the front)*

	帝	帝	帝	dì　　　dai emperor; God
帅	帥	帥	帥	shùai　　　seui leader; general; command; designate; guide; example; rapid; sudden
师	師	師	師	shi　　　sì　　　棄皁帯帶阵 teacher; expert; division of 2500 soldiers; armed force; general public; capital city
	席	席	席	xí　　　jihk seat; mat; table; banquet
	常	常	常	cháng　　　sèuhng regular; frequent; often
带	帶	帶	帶	dài　　　daai belt; band; ribbon
	帷	帷	帷	wéi　　　wàih curtain; screen; tent
帐	帳	帳	帳	zhàng　　　jeung account; debt; mosquito net
	帽	帽	帽	mào　　　mouh cap; hat
帧	幀	幀	幀	zhèng　　　jìng (classifier for pictures); frame; scroll
帏	幃	幃	幃	wéi　　　wai curtain that forms a wall
	幅	幅	幅	fú　　　fùk piece; strip; breadth; hem; (classifier for textiles)
	幌	幌	幌	huǎng　　　fong advertising sign; curtain
	幔	幔	幔	màn　　　maam curtain; mantle
	幕	幕	幕	mù　　　mohk curtain; veil

巾 10-14　干 2-10　幺 1

幗	幗	幗	幗	gúo　　gwok hat worn by women; mourning cap
	幛	幛	幛	zhàng　　cheung silk scroll
帜	幟	幟	幟	zhì　　chi banner; flag; standard
	幡	幡	幡	fan　　faan pennant; banner; streamer; flag
	幢	幢	幢	chúang　　chòhng wooden pole; umbrella; tent
币	幣	幣	幣	bì　　baih money; currency
帮	幫	幫	幫	bang　　bòng help; assist
帱	幬	幬		chóu　　chàuh bed curtain; mosquito net; carriage curtain
	干	干	干	gan　　gòn concern; implication; shield; request; offend; encroach; interfere; intervene
	平	平	平	píng　　pìhng　　丂 丂 丂 even; level; flat; draw, tie; calm; peaceful; pacify
	年	秊	秊	nián　　nìhn　　季 秊 year; harvest; annual
	幸	幸	幸	xìng　　hahng fortunate; luck
干	幹	干	干	gàn　　gon main part of something; body; trunk; to do; work (*vulgar*): "f--k" / kill / steal / blame / condemn
	幺	幺		yao　　jiu　　幺 tiny; minute; youngest; ace one (*alternative way of saying the numeral*)
	幻	幻	幻	hùan　　waahn mystical; mysterious; illusion; fantasy; mirage; unreal; imaginary

	幼	翝	舒	yòu　　　yau young; early age; child
	幽	幽	幽	you　　　yàu quiet; secluded; hidden; dim; dark
几	幾	纍	絲	jǐ　　　géi　　幾 how many?; few; several; some; almost
	广	广		an　　　yim shelter; cliff; wide; broad; extensive; vast; large
	庀	庀		pǐ　　　pei prepare; regulate
	庇	庥	庥	bì　　　bei shelter; protect; cover; shield
	床	牀	牀	chúang　　　chohng bed; couch
	庋	庪		jǐ　　　gei cupboard; pantry
	序	序	序	xù　　　jeuih sequence; order; preface
	庖	庖	庖	páo　　　paau kitchen; chef; cook
	店	坫	店	diàn　　　dim store; shop; inn
	府	府	府	fǔ　　　fu government warehouse; storehouse; residence; prefectural capital
	庚	庚	庚	geng　　　gang age; 7th heavenly stem (7th day of a 10 day week - Shang Dynasty)
	底	底	底	dǐ　　　dái bottom; base; ground; foundation; end
	度	度	度	dù　　　douh measure; size; consideration; thought; standard; rule; convention; limit; quota; tolerance; degree; level

广 6-9

	庠	庠	庠	xiáng　　chèuhng village school; teach
	庥	庥		xiu　　yau shade; shelter; protection
	庭	庭	庭	tíng　　tìhng courtyard
	座	座	座	zùo　　joh seat; base; pedestal; stand
库	庫	庫	庫	kù　　fu warehouse; storehouse; file library
	庳	庳		bì　　pei low-lying; short
	庵	庵	庵	an　　am dome-shaped grass house; hut; (*Buddhism*) monastery; nunnery
	庶	庶	庶	shù　　syu many; various; ordinary; common people
	康	康	康	kang　　hòng healthy; peaceful
	庸	庸	庸	yong　　yùhng common; ordinary; mediocre
	庹	庹		tǔo　　tok span; the length of both outstretched arms
	庾	庾	庾	yǔ　　jyu grainery; storehouse
厕	廁	廁	廁	cè　　chi toilet
厢	廂	廂	廂	xiáng　　sèung side room; wing; compartment; train carriage
	廊	廊	廊	láng　　lòhng porch; veranda; corridor

厦	廈	廈	廈	shà　　　hah large house; building; mansion
	廉	廉	廉	lián　　　lìhm　　　廉 厫 槏 厭 薕 honest; clean; incorruptible; honorable; inexpensive
	廑	廑		jǐn　　　gan careful; a hut
	廒	廒		áo　　　ngou granery
	廓	廓	廓	kuò　　　kwok broad; wide; open; empty; expand; outline
荫	蔭	蔭	蔭	yin　　　yam shade; shelter; protect
	廖	廖	廖	liào　　　liu deserted; silent; Zhou dynasty state of Liao
厨	廚	廚	廚	chú　　　chèuih kitchen; cook
厮	廝	廝		si　　　si servant
庙	廟	廟	廟	miào　　　miú temple; shrine; monastery
厂	廠	廠	廠	chǎng　　　chóng factory; mill; plant
废	廢	廢	廢	fèi　　　fai abandon; waste; ruined; depose
庑	廡	廡		wǔ　　　mou　　　庄 veranda
	廛	廛		chán　　　chìhn marketplace; store; shop
广	廣	廣	廣	guǎng　　　gwong　　　広 broad; wide; extensive; vast

广 13-22　　 廴 4-6　　 廾 1-12

	廨	廨		xiè　　　　gaai government office; workplace; headquarters
廪	廩	廩		lǐn　　　　lam granary; stockpile; store
庐	廬	廬	廬	lú　　　　lou hut; cottage
庞	龐	龐	龐	páng　　　　pòhng huge; colossal; enormous
厅	廳	廳	廳	tīng　　　　tìng　　　　廰廳厅所 hall; large room
	廴	廴		yǐn　　　　jan stride
廷	廷	廷		tíng　　　　tìhng palace; imperial court
延	延	延		yán　　　　yìhn lengthen; postpone; delay
建	建	建		jiàn　　　　gin establish; build; suggest; construct
廾	廾	廾		gǒng　　　　gung two hands; twenty
廿	廿	廿		niàn　　　　jaa　　　　卄廿念 twenty
弁	弁	弁		biàn　　　　bin conical cap worn during the Zhou dynasty
弄	弄	弄		nòng　　　　nuhng make; play; cause; get; do
弈	弈	弈		yì　　　　jik Chinese chess
弊	弊			bì　　　　baih defect; corruption; disadvantage; fraud; harm

弋				yì　　　jik catch; arrest; shoot with a bow
式				shì　　　sìk form; formula; style
弑	弑			shì　　　si to kill a parent or superior
弓				góng　　　gùng bow (archery); curved; arched
引				yǐn　　　yáhn pull; lead; guide; introduce; cause
弔				diào　　　diu hang; suspend
弗				fú　　　fat not (obsolete)
弘				hóng　　　wang　　弘 弘 弘 㢬 spread; enlarge; expand; great
弛				chí　　　chìh loosen; relax; slacken; loosen a bow
弟				dì　　　daih younger brother
弦				xián　　　yìhn string of a bow or musical instrument
弧				hú　　　wùh wooden bow; arc; crescent
弩				nǔ　　　nou crossbow
弭				mǐ　　　mai stop; desist; end; quell
弱				ruò　　　yeuhk weak; inferior; young

弓 7-19   ヨ 7-9   彡

弳	弳		jìng　　　ging radius
張	張	張	zháng　　　jèung stretch; spread; open up
強	強	強	qiáng　　　daahn strong; power; force
弼	弼	弼	bì　　　baht aid; assist; assistant; help; correct
彀	彀		gòu　　　gau enough; adequate
彈	彈	彈	tán　　　daan bomb; bullet; shell; catapult; eject; flick; strike; spring; leap; play (*stringed instrument*)
彌	彌	彌	mí　　　nèih full
彎	彎	彎	wan　　　wàan bend; bent; curve; curved; turn; crooked
ヨ	ヰ		jì　　　gai　　　　　屮 pig nose; snout
彖	彖		tùan　　　teun hog; hedgehog; porcupine
彗	彗	彗	hùi　　　seuih　　　　彗 broomstick; comet
彘	彘		zhì　　　zi pig; swine; boar; sow
汇	匯	匯	匯	hùi　　　wui exchange; remit; converge; assemble; gather
彝	彝	彝	yí　　　ji　　　　彜 彝 彝 rule; tripod; wine vessel; Yi people (*an ethnic Chinese group*)
	彡	彡	shan　　　saam hair

	形	形	形	xíng　　yìhng	shape; form; figure; appearance
	彤	彤	彤	tóng　　tung	red; vermillion
彥	彥	彥	彥	yàn　　yihn	educated; accomplished; handsome; elegant
	彪	彪	彪	biáo　　biù	little tiger; tiger stripes; Asian golden cat (*catopuma temminckii*)
	彩	彩	彩	cǎi　　chói	beautiful variegated colors; brilliance; gracefulness
	彬	彬	彬	bin　　bàn　　斌	elegant; refined
	彭	彭	彭	péng　　pang	name of an ancient country
	彰	彰	彰	zhang　　jèung	apparent; show; evident; manifest
	影	影	影	yǐng　　yìng	shadow; image; presence; occurrence; picture
	彳	彳		chì　　chik	walk slowly; step with the left foot first
	役	役	役	yì　　yihk	event; service; servant; work; labor; event; incident; soldier; war
	彷	彷	彷	fǎng　　fóng	like; resembling; resemble
	往	往	往	wǎng　　wóhng	go to; head for; towards; past; previous; former
	徂	徂		cú　　chou	go; reach
	彼	彼	彼	bǐ　　béi	he; she; it; they; that; those

彳 6-8

	後	后	后	hòu　　　hauh back; behind; later; after
	很	很		hěn　　　hán very; quite
	待	待	待	dài　　　doih wait; need; about to; intend to; treat; entertain; receive
	徉	佯	徉	yáng　　　jeung wonder; stray; hesitating; rove; walk back and forth
	律	律	律	lù　　　leuht laws; rules; discipline; control
	徇	徇	徇	xùn　　　seon comply; follow
	徊	回		húai　　　wùih linger; walk to and fro; hesitate; tarry; irresolute
	徐	徐	徐	xú　　　chèuih slow; at ease
径	徑	徑	徑	jìng　　　ging　　　逕 path; track
	徒	赴	徒	tú　　　tòuh　　　往徑 disciple; follower; foot soldier; prison sentence
	徙	沁	徙	xǐ　　　sáai move; shift; migrate
	徘	裴	徘	pái　　　pùih walk aimlessly
从	從	從	從	cóng　　　chùhng from; follow; obey; join
	徠	徠	徠	lái　　　loi induce; encourage to come
	徜	徜	徜	cháng　　　seuhng walking to and fro; lingering

	得	得	得	dé　　　dak get; obtain; acquire; must; need; contract (disease); result in; to produce; be ready; fit; proper; satisfied
复	復	復	復	fù　　　fuhk recover; return; repeat; duplicate
	徨	徨	徨	huáng　　　wòhng hesitation; confusion; doubt; irresolute
	循	循	循	xún　　　chèuhn to follow; accord; obey; comply
彷	徬	彷	彷	páng　　　pòhng uncertain; wander
	徭	徭		yáo　　　jiu compulsory labor
	微	微	微	wéi　　　mèih small; tiny; micro-
彻	徹	徹	徹	chè　　　chit penetrate; pierce; pervade
征	徵	征	征	zheng　　　jìng collect; levy
	德	德	德	dé　　　dàk　　　德惪悳惪悳 morality; virtue; faith; character
	徼	徼		jiào　　　giu frontier; border; inspect; patrol
	徽	徽	徽	húi　　　fài symbol; badge; insignia
	心	心	心	xin　　　sàm　　　忄 heart; mind; center; core
	必	必	必	bì　　　bìt surely; certainly; must; necessarily
	忉	忉		dao　　　dou grieved

心 3-4

忌	忌	忌		jì　　　　gei avoid; abstain; fear; dread; jealous
忍	忍	忍		rěn　　　　yán endure; bear; patience; tolerate
忐	忐			tǎn　　　　taan nervous (*used only in* 忐忑)
忑	忑			tè　　　　tik nervous; jumpy; fearful (*used only in* 忐忑)
忒	忒			tè　　　　tik excessive; too; to err; mistake; changeable
志	志	志		zhì　　　　ji　　　　誌 識 痣 will; determination; aspiration; ambition; annals; records
忘	忘	忘		wàng　　　　mòhng forget; neglect
忙	忙	忙		máng　　　　mòhng busy; occupied; hurried
忖	忖	忖		cǔn　　　　chyún guess; suppose; conjecture; consider; ponder
忡	忡			chong　　　　chung sad; distressed; uneasy
忤	忤			wǔ　　　　ng insubordinate; stubborn; disobedient; wrong
忭	忭			biàn　　　　bin delighted; glad; happy; joyful; pleased
忪	忪	忪		song　　　　sung quiet; calm; tranquil; peaceful
快	快	快		kuài　　　　faai pleased; happy; forthright; rapid; quick; speedy; fast; clever; sharp (*knife blade*)
伎	伎			zhì　　　　gei stubborn; perverse; aggressive; invasive; belligerent

忱			chén / sam sincerity; honesty
忸			niǔ / nuk blush; bashful; ashamed
忻			xin / jan delight in; joy; be glad; pleasant
忝			tiǎn / tim shame; self-deprecating; ashamedly; with disgrace
芯			xin / sam core; pith; wick; pencil lead
忠			zhong / jùng loyal; faithful; sincere; devoted; fidelity
忽			hu / fàt suddenly; neglect; ignore
忿			fèn / fan be angry; be indignant; to hate
念			niàn / nihm think about; thought
怠			dài / tóih lazy; idle; slack
急			jí / gàp hasty; urgent; anxious
怨			yùan / yun hatred; grumble; complain
思			si / sì think; miss; thought
怎			zěn / jám how; why
怍			zùo / jok ahsamed; abashed

心 5

怔	怔	怔	zheng　jing terrified; startled; panic stricken
性	性	性	xìng　sing nature; character; gender; sex; intercourse
怊	怊		chao　chiu sad; sorrowful; disconsolate; disappointed
怙	怙		hù　wu rely on; presume; persist
怡	怡	怡	yí　ji harmony; pleasure; joy; cheerful; happy; content; pleased
怏	怏	怏	yàng　yeung discontented; dispirited; sad
怒	怒	怒	nù　nouh angry; anger
怕	怕	怕	pà　pa fear; dread; afraid
怛	怛	怛	dá　daat grieved; worried; distressed; shocked
怖	怖	怖	bù　bou terror; fear
怦	怦		peng　paang eager; ardent; impulsive; anxious; thumping; palpitating
怩	怩	怩	ní　nei shy; timid; bashful
怪	怪	怪	gùai　gwaai　恠 怪 strange; odd; unusual; peculiar; weird; queer; to blame; quite; rather
怫	怫	怫	fú　fat sorry; anxious; depressed
怯	怯	怯	qiè　hip timid; cowardly

106

怵	怵	怵		chù	cheut
				fear; be afraid; sad; sorrowful	
恐	恐	恐		kǒng	húng
				afraid; fearful; apprehensive	
恕	恕	恕		shù	syu
				pardon; excuse; forgive	
恙	恙	恙		yàng	yeuhng
				sickness; illness; worry	
恚	恚			huì	wai
				anger; rage; resentment	
恝	恝			jiá	aat
				carefree; indifferent	
恣	恣	恣		zì	chi
				indulge; unrestrained; profligate; wanton; to change	
恧	恧			nù	nuk
				ashamed	
恩	恩	恩		en	yàn
				favor; benevolence; grace	
息	息	息		xi	sìk
				interest; rest; breath; news	
恂	恂			xún	seon
				careful; sincere; honest; trust; genuine	
恫	恫	恫		dòng	dung
				sorrowful; pain	
恃	恃	恃		shì	chíh
				rely; presume; trust	
恍	恍	恍		huǎng	fong
				seemingly; indistinct; as if; absent-minded	
恒	恆	恒	恆	héng	hàhng
				permanent; constant	

心 6-7

	恢			húi　　　　fùi　　　　忄 great; vast; recover; restore
	恨			hèn　　　　hahn hate; resentment
	恪			kè　　　　kok respectful; reverent; solemn; serious
	恬			tián　　　　tim quiet; calm; tranquil; peaceful; simple and content; indifferent to fame or fortune
	恰			qià　　　　hàp just; exact; appropriate
	恤			xù　　　　syùt　　　　卹 pity; sympathize; compensate
	恭			gōng　　　　gùng respectful; reverent; polite
耻	恥			chǐ　　　　chí humiliate; shame; disgrace
	恿			yǒng　　　　júng urge; instigate; incite; alarm
	悉			xī　　　　sīk know; learn; be informed; comprehend; to exhaust; all; fully; entirely
	您			nín　　　　néih respectful form of "you"
	悠			yōu　　　　yàuh remote; distant; leisurely; drawn out; sad; to swing
	患			huàn　　　　waahn to contract (*illness*); suffer; afflicted; worry; danger; misfortune; trouble; peril
	悃			kǔn　　　　kwán sincere; genuine; loyal; honest
	悔			huǐ　　　　fui　　　　毎 regret; repent; show remorse

108

	悄	悄	悄	qiǎo　　chiu quiet; silent; sad; sorrowful; whisper
	悌	悌	悌	tì　　dai to love and respect one's elder brothers
	悍	悍	悍	hàn　　hon brave; bold; fierce; ferocious; vigorous; valiant
	悒	悒		yì　　jap miserable; depressed; heartbreaking; worried; distressing; discouraging; apprehensive; anxiety
	悖	悖	悖	bèi　　bui paradox; contrary; perverse; erroneous; confused; puzzled; rebel; revolt; cover
	悚	悚	悚	sǒng　　sung afraid; scared; frightened; horrified; terrified
	悛	悛		quan　　syun repent; regret; reform; amend
	悝	悝		kui　　fui tease; mock; ridicule; afflicted; sad
	悟	悟	悟	wù　　ngh apprehend; comprehend; realize; become aware
悦	悦	說	悦	yùe　　yuht delight; happy; pleasant
闷	悶	悶	悶	mèn　　muhn bored; melancholy; sultry; suffocating
	惠	惠	惠	huì　　waih favor; benefit; kindness; advantage; benevolent; kindhearted
恶	惡	惡	惡	è　　ok bad; wicked; disgusting; evil; detest
	悲	悲	悲	bei　　bèi sad; sorrowful; pessimistic; grief; pity
	悱	悱		fěi　　fei (to have the desire to speak but are unable)

心 8

悴			cùi　séuih haggard; distressed
悸			jì　gwai fearful; apprehensive; perturbed
悻			xìng　hang angry; resentful; vexed
悼			dào　douh lament; greive; mourn
情			qíng　chìhng feeling; sentiment; emotion; love; affection; friendship; reputation; situation; circumstances; obviously
惋			wǎn　yún sympathize; regret; be sorry
惕			tì　tìk cautious; watchful; alert; careful
惘			wǎng　mong disconcerted; dejected; discouraged; desolate; frustrated
惆			chóu　chàuh disappointed; vexed; grieved; forlorn
惚			hu　fat absent-minded; confused; indistinct
惜			xi　sìk　錫 锡 嚗 pity; regret; grieve; rue; cherish; begrudge; value greatly; love dearly
惝			chǎng　chóng disappointed; dejected; fearful; terrified; undeceived; frustrated
惟			wéi　wàih but; however; nevertheless; only; to think; to contemplate
惦			diàn　dim to think of someone; to miss
怅	悵		chàng　cheung despair; upset; disappointed; dissatisfied

110

惑			hùo gám	doubt; suspicion; confused; puzzled
感			gǎn gám	feel; emotion; influence
想			xiǎng séung	think; miss; want; consider
惹			rě yéh	incite; cause; tease; provoke; offend
愁			chóu sàuh	worry; sad; gloomy
愆			qian hin	fault; mistake; error; transgression
慈			cí chìh	loving; merciful; compassionate; gentle; kind; charitable; benevolent
愈			yù yuht	more; further
愍			mǐn man 憫 悯	pity; sympathize; sorrow
意			yì yi	thought; opinion; idea; Italy; Italian
愚			yú yùh	foolish; to fool; stupid; to dupe
惰			dùo do	indolent; careless; lazy; idle
惴			zhùi chyún	afraid; apprehensive; nervous; anxious; worried
惶			húang wòhng	fearful; afraid; anxious; nervous; confused
惺			xing sing	intelligent; clever; astute; realize; tranquil; quiet; serene

	愀	愀	愀	qiǎo　　chiú change one's countenance; anxious; blush
	愉	愉	愉	yú　　yùh happy; pleased
	愎	愎	愎	bì　　bīk stubborn; obstinate; headstrong
	愕	愕	愕	è　　ngohk startled; frightened
恻	惻	惻	惻	cè　　chāk grieve for; pity
恼	惱	惱		nǎo　　nóuh irritated; distressed; upset
恽	惲	惲		yùn　　wan devise; plan; deliberate; consult
惬	愜	愜	愜	qiè　　hip satisfied; comfortable; cheerful
	愣	愣		lèng　　ling be in a daze; dumbfounded
	慨	慨	慨	kái　　koi indignant; resentful; impassioned; vehement; to rue; be sad; generous
爱	愛	愛	愛	ài　　oi　　悉愛 love; fondness; to treasure; to value
态	態	態	態	tài　　taai condition; state; form; shape; manner; bearing; attitude; situation; posture; voice (*grammar*)
悫	愨	愨		què　　kok sincerity; honesty; cautious
	愧	愧	愧	kùi　　kwáih ashamed; abashed; feeling guilty
	愫	愫		sù　　sou guileless; sincere; honest; truthful; candid; frank; upright

心 10-11

忾	愾	𢙁	𢙁	kài　　　hei anger; wrath; hatred; enmity
怆	愴	𢠵	𢠵	chuàng　　chong sad; mournful; grieved; disconsolate; broken-hearted
恺	愷	𢝆	𢝆	kǎi　　　hoi peaceful; harmonious; contented; joyful
愠	慍	𢥠	𢥠	yùn　　　wan indignant; resentful; angry
	慊	慊		qiàn　　　hip resent; content; satisfied
慌	慌	𢡖	𢡖	huāng　　fòng fear; alarmed; nervous; panic; confused; flustered; frantic; flee
慎	慎	𢛓		shèn　　　sahn cautious; careful
	慝	慝		tè　　　tik evil thought; evil; vice
	慧	慧	慧	huì　　　wai bright; intelligent
	慰	慰	慰	wèi　　　wai pleased; comfortable; console; relieved
怂	慫	𢝫	𢝫	sǒng　　sung alarm; instigate; arouse; incite; fear
	慢	慢	慢	màn　　　maahn slow; negligent; sluggish; leisurely
沤	慪	慪		òu　　　au　　　悥嘔呕 displeased; irritated; annoyed; (Sichuan) broken-hearted
惯	慣	慣	慣	guàn　　gwaan habitual; habit; accustomed, be used to
	慵	慵	慵	yōng　　jung careless; indolent; easygoing; lazy; happy-go-lucky

113

心 11-12

	慷	忼	慷	káng　　hóng generous; bountiful; magnanimous
忧	憂	憂	憂	you　　yàu　　惪 worry; distress; sorrow; grieved; melancholy
悭	慳	慳		qian　　haan miserly; stingy; parsimonious
	慕	慕	慕	mù　　mou admire; adore; long for; desire; yearn
惨	慘	慘	慘	cǎn　　cháam trajic; cruel; severe; miserable
惭	慚	慚	慚	cán　　chàahm ashamed; embarrassed
恸	慟	慟	慟	tòng　　duhng grief; sorrow; sadness; mourn
怂	慫	慫	慫	sǒng　　súng instigate; urge; alarm; arouse; incite
宪	憲	憲	憲	xiàn　　hin law; constitution
虑	慮	慮	慮	lù　　leuih think through; worry; concerned; consider
	憋	憋		bie　　bit hold; suppress inner feelings; suffocate
	憝	憝		dùi　　deui resentment; grudge; wicked; evil
	憨	憨		han　　ham silly; simple-minded; naive; innocent
	憩	憩	憩	qì　　hei to rest
凭	憑	憑	憑	píng　　pàhng　　凴 lean/depend/rely on; proof; on the basis of

惫	憊	憊	憊	bèi baaih; exhausted; tired; weary; fatigued
	憎	憎	憎	zeng jàng; hate; detest; abhor; dislike
	憔	憔	憔	qiáo chiùh 顦; haggard; worn out
怃	憮	憮	憮	wǔ móuh; disappointed; regretful
	憧	憧	憧	chong chung; irresolute; unsettled; indecisive
	憬	憬	憬	jǐng ging; rouse; awaken; become conscious
怜	憐	憐	憐	lián lìhn; pity; sympathize; love tenderly
悯	憫	閔		mǐn máhn 愍; sad; pity; sympathize; grieve for
惮	憚	憚	憚	dàn daan; dread; shrink from; shirk; fear
愤	憤	憤	憤	fèn fan; resent; hate; indignant
愦	憒	憒		kùi kui; confused; befuddled; troubled
应	應	應	應	yíng yìng; should; ought to; reply; respond
懑	懣	懣		mèn mun; sick at heart; sorrowful; sad; melancholy
	懋	懋	懋	mào mau; splendid; grand; majestic
恳	懇	懇	懇	kěn hán; sincere; earnest; request

忆	憶	意篆	憶篆	yì / yìk — recall; remember
	憷	憷篆		chǔ / chó — painful; suffering; privation
	憾	感篆	憾篆	hàn / hahm — regret; resentment; unpleasant
	懂	懂篆	懂篆	dǒng / dúng — understand; comprehend
	懈	懈篆	懈篆	xiè / haaih — lazy; idle; negligent; lax 解
	懊	懊篆	懊篆	ào / ou — regret; irritated; vexed 怏
懒	懶	懶篆	懶篆	lǎn / láahn — lazy; idle; slothful
懔	懍	懍篆	懍篆	lǐn / lam — afraid of; in awe; fear
怿	懌	懌篆		yì / jik — pleased; delighted; happy; rejoice; exult
怼	懟	懟篆		duì / deui — hate; abhor; resentment 譈
	懦	懦篆	懦篆	nuò / noh — weak; cowardly; timid
恹	懨	懨篆		yan / jim — feeble; sickly; tranquil; calm; contented; relaxed; serene; peaceful
惩	懲	懲篆	懲篆	chéng / chìhng — punish; penalize
悬	懸	懸篆		xúan / jyun — hang; suspend; hoist; announce; raise; unsettled; unresolved
	懵	懵篆		měng / mung — absent-minded; stupid

怀	懷	懷	懷	húai wàaih	bosom; breast; heart; mind; affection; think of; cherish; pregnant
忏	懺	懺	懺	chàn chaam	regret; repent 懺 讖 讖
	懿	懿	懿	yì ji	virtuous; admirable; esteemed; righteous; worthy
慑	懾	懾	懾	shè sip	afraid; scared; fearful; frighten; intimidate
惧	懼	懼	懼	jù geuih	fear; afraid; scare; frighten
恋	戀	戀	戀	liàn lyún	long for; love
戆	戆	戆		zhùang jong	stupid; blunt; tactless
	戈	戈	戈	ge gwo	dagger-axe; halberd
	戊	戊	戊	wù mou	5th heavenly stem (5th day of a 10 day week - Shang Dynasty)
	戍	戍	戍	shù syu	guard the frontier; defend the border
	戌	戌	戌	xu sèut	military affairs
	戎	戎	戎	róng yùhng	weapon; armament
	成	成	成	chéng sìhng	make; accomplish; finish; succeed; become
	我	我	我	wǒ ngóh	I; me 吾
	戒	戒	戒	jiè gaai	warn; caution; admonish; forbid; guard against

戈 4-14

	戕	㸦	牂	qiang　　chèuhng kill; harm; destroy
	或	或	或	hùo　　waahk or; either; perhaps; probably
	戚	槭	槭	qi　　chìk　　感 戚 慽 鏚 relative; sorrow; sad
	戛	戛	戛	jiá　　aat lance; tap; strike lightly
	戟	戟	戟	jǐ　　gik　　𢧄 戟 ancient Chinese halberd with crescent blade
	戢	戢	戢	jí　　chap store up (*weapons*); draw back; fold back; stop; put an end to
	戡	戡	戡	kan　　ham subjugate; subdue; quell
	戤	戤		gài　　koi infringe a trademark; pledge an article
	戥	戥		děng　　dang small stilyard for weighing money and small items
	截	截	截	jié　　jiht intercept; cut off; sever
	戮	戮	戮	lù　　luk kill; humiliate; join forces
战	戰	戰	戰	zhàn　　jin　　戦 fight; battle; war; fear; tremble
	戴	戴	戴	dài　　daai put on; to wear (*hat, jewelry, glasses, or other "attachments"*); support; respect; esteem
戏	戲	戲	戲	xì　　hei　　戱 戲 play; drama; show; game; amuse; tease
戳	戳	戳	戳	chuo　　cheuk prick; stab; stamp; seal; chop

戶	戶	戶	hù　　　wuh door; household; family	
所	所	所	suǒ　　　só place; location; institute	䀹 所 所
戽	戽		hu　　　fu bale out water; water bucket for irrigation	
戾	戾	戾	lì　　　lai perverse; recalcitrant; rebellious; brutal; go against	
房	房	房	fáng　　　fòhng room; house; apartment; building	
扃	扃		jiong　　　gwing shut; a door bar	
扁	扁		biǎn　　　bín flat and thin; to inscribe on a door; curl one's lips; underestimate	
扇	扇	扇	shàn　　　sin fan; flap; leaf of a door	搧 煽
扈	扈	扈	hù　　　wu escort; retinue; restrain; prevent	
扉	扉	扉	fei　　　fèi door panel or door leaf; back cover of a book	
手	手	手	shǒu　　　sáu hand; arm; handy	扌
才	才	才	cái　　　chòih ability; talent; only; just	
扎	扎	扎	zha　　　jaat prick; pierce; puncture; tie up	
扒	扒	扒	pá　　　pàh gather; rake up; scratch; pickpocket; crouch	爬
扔	扔	扔	reng　　　yìng throw; throw away	

手 2-4

打	打	打		dǎ / dá — strike; hit; slap
扦	扦			qian / chin — skewer; impale; stick in; graft
托	托	托		tuo / tok — support with the hand; palm; entrust
扛	扛	扛	椌枆掆摃摃	káng / gòng — lift with both hands; lift with two or more people; carry on shoulders; contradict
扣	扣	扣		kòu / kau — fasten a button; buckle; knot; clasp; subtract; deduct
叉 扠	叉	叉		cha / cha — fork; pick up with a fork or pincers; cross-out
扳	扳	扳		ban / baan — pull; turn; win back; debate; dispute
扼	扼	扼		è / ak — grasp; clutch; guard; control; choke; strangle
折	折	折		zhé / sit — break off; snap; bend
扭	扭	扭		niǔ / nau — twist; wring; contort
扮	扮	扮		bàn / baan — dress up; disguise oneself; act, play; put on an expression
扯	扯	扯		chě / ché — pull; tear; leave; rip up
批	批	批	剕剠剕剖	pi / pài — comment; criticize; wholesale
技	技	技		jì / geih — skill; technique; ability; talent; creativity
投	投	投		tóu / tàuh — throw; cast; hurl

120

抉			júe / kyut determine; choice; select; gouge; pluck out; pierce; puncture; reveal
抄			chao / chàau copy; confiscate; transcribe; plagiarize; seize; take a shortcut
把			bǎ / bá hold; grasp; control; handle; knob; grip; be near; (*classifier for objects that can be held by a handle or knob*)
抑			yì / yìk restrain; repress; restrict; suppress; hinder; furthermore
抒			shu / syù express; convey
抖			dǒu / dáu shake; tremble; shiver
抗			kàng / kong resist; object; oppose; anti-
找			zhǎo / jáau seek; look for; find
抓			zhua / jáau scratch (*with nails/claws*); seize; grab; supervise; take control of; ensure
承			chéng / sìhng 丞 receive; acknowledge; inherit; support; undertake; carry on
扶			fú / fùh hold onto something as support; support; help someone up; aid; assist
抹			mǒ / mut wipe; smear; apply; remove; erase; play; cut
拔			bá / baht pluck; pull up/off/out; select; promote
拖			tuo / tò drag; tow; haul; dangle; sag; hold hands; delay; procrastinate; prolong; pin down
抨			peng / ping shoot with a catapult; censure; attack; impeach; pat; beat; slap with the palm of the hand

手 5

抵	㧪	𢪐	dǐ　　　　dái prop up; support; resist; oppose; offend; equivalent; balance; compensate
披	𢁣	𢁤	pi　　　　pèi put on; unroll; spread out
拓	𢪙	𢪚	tùo　　　tok　　　搨 open up; push open; develop; expand; stretch
抬	𢬘	𢭃	tái　　　tòih lift; raise; carry between two people
招	𢭄	𢭅	zhao　　jiù beckon; recruit; enlist; enroll; incite; cause; provoke; tease; confess
拈	𢪏	𢫦	nian　　nim nip; to grasp with the fingers
拒	𢪕	𢪖	jù　　　kéuih resist; refuse; reject
抱	𢬶	𢭨	bào　　　póuh embrace; hold; hug; carry in the arms
拘	𢭩	𢭪	ju　　　　kèui arrest; restrict; restrain; seize; detain
拐	𢭫	𢭬	gǔai　　gwáai kidnap; abduction; swindle; misappropriate; crutches
拍	𢫕	𢫖	pai　　　paak pat; slap; clap; swat; hit; shoot (*picture, video*); send (*telegram*); to suck up; (*classifier for rhythm*)
抽	𢪱	𢪲	chou　　chàu pull; pump water; draw out; draw lots; put forth; to smoke; take in; (*slang*) to become abnormal
抻	𢪳		chen　　chán stretch; pull
押	𢪴	𢪵	ya　　　ngaat sign; signature; mortgage; pledge; arrest; detain; accompany; bet; rhyme
拇	𢬋	𢬌	mǔ　　　móuh　　　跨 thumb; big toe

拂	拂	拂	fú　　　fàt stroke; touch lightly; to flick; brush off; sweep
抿	抿	抿	mǐn　　　man sip; pucker the lips
拄	拄	拄	zhǔ　　　jyu prop; support; lean on; ridicule; talk back; to prod; poke; block; to plug
拆	拆	拆	chai　　　chaak dismantle; take apart; demolish; destroy
拉	拉	拉	la　　　làai pull; drag
拊	拊		fǔ　　　fu pat; slap; clap
抛	抛	抛	pao　　　pàau throw; cast; raject; abandon
拎	拎	拎	lin　　　ling lift; take; hold; carry in one's hand
拗	拗	拗	ào　　　aau defy; disobey; bend; stubborn
拙	拙	拙	zhuo　　　chyut clumsy; awkward
拌	拌	拌	bàn　　　buhn mix; stir
拜	拜	拜	bài　　　baai worship; obeisance; to bow
括	括	括	kùo　　　kut include; encompass; embrace; enclose
拮	拮	拮	jié　　　gat laboring hard; occuped; pursued; antagonistic
拾	拾	拾	shí　　　sahp pick up; collect; ten

手 6

拭	拭		shì　　　　sìk rub; wipe	
拽	拽		yè　　　　jai drag; tow	曳 擗
拯	拯	拯	zhěng　　　chíng rescue; save; aid; lift; raise	丞 抍
拶	拶		za　　　　jaat force; compel; press	
拱	拱		gǒng　　　gung fold hands on breast; bow; salute; surround	廾
拷	拷	拷	kǎo　　　háau beat; flog; torture	
拼	拼	拼	pin　　　　ping order; command; accompany; follow; join together; put together; pronounce; spell (*writing*)	拚
持	持	持	chí　　　　chìh hold; support; maintain	
指	指	指	zhǐ　　　　jí finger; digit; point out; indicate; direct	
挈	挈		qiè　　　　kit lift; carry; raise; take along	
按	按	按	àn　　　　on according to; press; push; put aside; restrain; stop	
挎	挎		kùa　　　　kwaa to carry (*slung over the arm, shoulder, or side*)	
拳	拳	拳	quán　　　kyùhn fist; Chinese boxing	
挑	挑	挑	tiáo　　　tiù provoke; incite; bring into the open; make public; select; choose; carry something on a shoulder pole	
挖	挖		wa　　　　waat dig; excavate; gouge out; scoop	

手 6

拴	拴	拴	shuan　　sàan fasten; tie; bind
拿	拏	拿	ná　　nàh　　挐挈舒 take; hold; grasp; seize; capture; apprehend; bring
摀	摀		wǔ　　wu　　搗 to cover
捃	捃		jùn　　kwan　　擄攄攎 gather; pick; pluck; pick up; collect; tidy up; sort
挹	挹		yì　　jap pour; ladle out; bale out; decant liquids; drizzle
捐	捐	捐	juan　　gyun　　甌蜎 contribute; give up; renounce; remove; donate; spend; tax; dissipate; burrow; writhe through
捎	捎		shao　　sàau carry; send; select; take
捉	捉		zhuo　　jùk catch; arrest; capture; grasp; clutch
挫	挫	挫	cùo　　cho obstruction; defeat; frustrate
挨	挨	挨	ái　　àai near; next to; to lean; suffer; endure; hit from behind; depend on; to crowd; push and squeeze; sequence
振	振	振	zhèn　　jan shake; vibrate; stimulate; excite; arouse action
挺	挺	挺	tǐng　　tíhng stick out; to straighten up; stiff; proud; endure; stand; persist and overcome; quite; rather
挪	挪	挪	núo　　nòh shift; move
挽	挽	挽	wǎn　　wáahn pull; draw back; pluck
挟 挟	挟		xié　　hip　　挾 clasp under the arm; carry; coerce; to harbor (*resentment*)

125

手 7-8

	捋	捋		lǚ　　　lyut stroke; hit; strike; slap with slender bamboo stick
	捌	捌	捌	ba　　　baat (*the financial form of eight*)
	捍	捍	捍	hàn　　　hohn　　扞 guard; defend; protect; resist; firm; solid
	捏	捏		nie　　　nia pick with fingers; pinch; clench; knead; mold; bring together; concoct
	捆	捆		kǔn　　　kwan tie up; bind; to truss; bundle; bunch; sheaf
	捅	捅		tǒng　　　tung stab; poke through; disclose
	捕	捕	捕	bǔ　　　bouh arrest; catch; seize
	挲	挲		suo　　　so　　抄 stroke; caress; fondle
舍	捨	捨	捨	shě　　　se discard; abandon; give up; bestow
	捊	捊		póu　　　pau break up; hit; attack; split
	捧	捧	捧	pěng　　　búng hold in both hands; flatter; exalt
	捭	捭		bǎi　　　baai weed; spread out; open; strike with hands
	掉	掉		diào　　　diu　　擲 drop; fall; lose; to part; to shed; shake; wag; reduce; turn
	挼	挼	挼	liè　　　lai twist with hands; snap; tear
扪	捫	捫		mén　　　mun stroke; pat; grope

	捲	𦥯	𢪎	juǎn　　gyún roll up; curl
	捶	𢱧	𢳂	chúi　　chèuih beat with a stick; strike
	推	𢱦	𢲖	tui　　tèui push; refuse; delay; postpone
	捷	𢫦	𢳫	jié　　jiht prompt; quick; win; victorious; succeed
	捺	𢳅		nà　　naat press down firmly with the hand
	捻	𢴈	𢴇	niǎn　　nim twist with the fingers
	掀	𢴵	𢴶	xian　　hìn raise; stir up; lift; expose
扫	掃	埽		sǎo　　sou sweep; clean with a broom; clear away
抡	掄	𢯶	𢯷	lún　　leun whip; swing; brandish; select
	掇	𢪎	叕	duo　　jyut collect; gather; pluck (*a flower*); select; obtain
	授	𢱧	𢱨	shòu　　sauh give; confer; impart; teach; transmit
	掎	𢮦		jǐ　　gei drag aside; pull
	掏	𢭢	𢰶	táo　　tòuh draw/take/pull/clean out
	掐	𢭣		qia　　haap hold; pinch; strangle; choke
	排	𢯱	𢯲	pái　　pàaih line; rank; row; platoon; discharge

手 8

	掖			ye — jik — 腋 support with the arms; stick in; tuck in; fold up
	掘			júe — gwat dig; excavate
	掮			qián — kin carry on the shoulders
挣	掙			zheng — jàng struggle; strive; endeavor; earn
挂	掛			gùa — gwa hang up; suspend; register
	掠			lùe — leuk rob; ransack; plunder; pillage
	掂			dian — dim — 战 weigh in the hand; break; snap off; haggle over; take
采	採			cǎi — chói select; choose; pick
	探			tàn — taam find; locate; search; visit; test; try
	控			kòng — hung control; take charge of; accuse; turn upside down to empty; draw the bowstring; bend
	接			jié — jip recieve; connect; accept; come close to; pick up (*person*)
	掩			yǎn — jim cover; conceal; hide; close; shut
	措			cùo — chou place; arrange; manage
	掬			ju — guk — 掏 匊 grasp; hold with both hands
	捵			tiàn — tim manipulate

手 8-9

	掣	㸷	𢯱	chè　　　jai obstruct; pull; drag
	掌	赏	赏	zhǎng　　jéung palm of hand; sole of foot; shoe sole or heel; horseshoe; slap; hold; control
	掰	掰		bai　　　baai break apart with both hands; bend; argue; end a relationship
	搿	搿		gé　　　gaap hug tightly; clutch
	捶	捶	捶	chúi　　chèuih　　搥 beat with a stick; strike; lash
	掾	掾		yùan　　jyun auxiliary; general designation for officials
拣	揀	柬	揀	jiǎn　　gáan choose; select; pick; get; obtain
	揄	揄		yú　　　jyu pull; lift
抢	搶	搶	搶	qiǎng　　chéung fight over; scramble for; compete; steal; snatch away
	揆	揆	揆	kúi　　　kwai prime minister; guess; estimate
	揉	揉	揉	rou　　　jau knead; rub; massage; crush by hand
	揍	揍		zòu　　　jau hit; beat; smash; break
	揎	揎		xuan　　syun pull up the sleeves and stretch out the arms; strike with bare fists
	描	描		miáo　　miu copy; trace; sketch; depict; describe
扬	揚	揚	揚	yáng　　yèuhng lift; raise; hoist; scatter (*in the wind*); spread; praise

	提	提	提	tí　　　tàih　　　拿拂 carry; lift; raise; increase; mention; nominate; point out; put forward
揑	捏	捏		nie　　　nip fabricate
	插	插	插	cha　　　chaap　　　挿 insert; interpolate; stick into; to plant; (*Cantonese*) to scold; to criticize
	揖	揖	揖	yí　　　yāp bow; salute; greet; defer; yield
換	換	換		hùan　　　wun change; exchange; swap; switch; substitute
	揞	揞		ǎn　　　ám cover with hands; apply medicine to a wound
	揠	揠		yà　　　aat pull up; promote; eradicate
	握	握	握	wò　　　ngàak grasp; hold; grip
	揣	揣		chǔai　　　chéui　　　敪 speculate; guess; surmise; measure; estimate; assess; try; attempt; grab
	揩	揩	揩	kai　　　hàai wipe; clean; brush; come into slight contact with
	揪	揪	揪	jiú　　　chàu　　　揫 grasp; pinch; hold tight
	揭	揭	揭	jié　　　kit raise; lift up; uncover; expose
揮	揮	揮	揮	hui　　　fài shake; wave; wield; brandish; direct; command
	揲	揲		dié　　　dip (*sorting out the stalks used in divination*)
	援	援	援	yúan　　　wùhn rescue; help; aid; assist

手 9-10

	揶	揶		yé　　　yeh make fun of; ridicule	撒揶
	揸	揸		zha　　　jaa hold in the hand; grasp; drive a vehicle	
背	揹	揹		bei　　　bui (to carry things on your back) [simplified form is identical to bèi/bui in 肉 section]	
	搋	搋		chuai　　chaai knead with hands; rub	
捶	搥	搥	搥	chúi　　　chèuih beat; strike; pound; hammer	
	搞	搞	搞	gǎo　　　gáau make; do; produce; disturb; engaged in	
损	损	損	損	sǔn　　　syún hurt; injure; damage; diminish; impair	
	搏	搏	搏	bó　　　bok wrestle; fight; strive; sudden attack	
	搐	搐		chù　　　chuk cramp; spasm; convulsion; twitch	
	搓	搓		cuo　　　chaai rub between the hands	
	搔	搔	搔	sau　　　sòu to scratch	
	搖	搖		yáo　　　jiu wag; wave; swing	摇
捣	搗	搗	搗	dǎo　　　dóu pound with a pestle; beat with a stick; make trouble; disturb; attack (an enemy); mount an offensive	擣
	搜	搜	搜	sou　　　sau seek; search; collect	搜
	搠	搠		shùo　　　sok daub; thrust; pinch	

131

手 10-11

	搡	㩙		sǎng　　sóng push over; push back
	搦	㩗		nùo　　nik repress; restrain; grasp; capture; seize; hold in the hand; provoke
	搧	扇	扇	shan　　sin　　扇 to fan; slap
	搌	㩏		zhǎn　　jin　　展 wipe; bind
	搪	㯖	㯖	táng　　tong ward off; evade; parry; block
	搬	㩘		ban　　bun move; shift the position of; transport (*a large item*); (*slang*) to rake in money
	搭	㩁	㩁	da　　daap build; join; pile up; add to; cover; ride
	搽	㩛	㩛	chá　　chàh to rub on; apply; anoint
	搴	㩜		qian　　gin extract; seize; pluck up
	榨	㭰		zhà　　jaa　　榨 press or extract juices; squeeze; (*figurative*) exploit; oppress
	摁	㩰		èn　　on to press with the hand
摑	摑	㩴	㩴	gúo　　gwok box one's ears; slap
抠	摳	㩽		kou　　kau lift up; raise; dig out; carve; cut; stingy; delve into; study meticulously
折	摺	㧈	㧈	zhé　　jip fold; foldable; booklet; side; destroy
	摘	㩷	㩷	zhái　　jaahk pick; pluck; select; to take (*something*) off of

132

手 11-12

	摔	摔(seal)	摔(seal)	shuai　　syùt fall down; stumble; trip; throw down
掼	掼	掼(seal)		gùan　　gwaan throw to the ground; know; be familiar with
搂	摟	摟(seal)	摟(seal)	lǒu　　láuh embrace; hug; cuddle; drag
	摞	摞(seal)		lùo　　lo stack; to pile up; (classifier for objects in a pile or stack)
	摧	摧(seal)	摧(seal)	cui　　chèui destroy; break
	摭	摭(seal)		zhí　　jek pick up; gather; assemblage
搀	摻	摻(seal)	摻(seal)	shǎn　　sáam hold; pull; support by the arm; mix in
	撂	撂(seal)		liào　　liu put down; put aside; drop
	摒	摒(seal)		bìng　　bing　　屏 expel; cast off
抟	摶	摶(seal)		túan　　tyun roll around with a hand
	摸	摸(seal)	摸(seal)	mo　　mó　　摹 touch; feel; caress; grope; fumble
	摩	摩(seal)	摩(seal)	mó　　mò rub; massage; stroke
	摹	摹(seal)	摹(seal)	mó　　mouh imitate; copy; follow a pattern
	摯	摯(seal)	摯(seal)	zhì　　ji sincere; warm; cordial; sincere; close; bosom
	撅	撅(seal)		jue　　kyut lift; raise; stick up; snap off

手 12

	捞	撈	撈	lao　làauh dredge; scoop up; fish for; make money
撑	撐	撐	撐	cheng　chaang prop up; support; pole; brace; stay
挠	撓	撓	撓	náo　nàauh scratch lightly; disturb; bother; upset; flinch
捻	撚	撚	撚	niǎn　nín　捻 pinch; pick up; take; hold; fiddle; fidget; tease; twist; trample; tread
抚	撫	撫	撫	fǔ　fú stroke; caress; pat; console; to comfort; nurture; foster
	撕	撕	撕	si　sì tear; break in pieces; shred; rend
	撙	撙	撙	zǔn　jyún economize; regulate; comply; abide with
	撞	撞	撞	zhùang　johng　搪衝 collide; offend; bump against; strike; come across
挢	撟	撟		jiǎo　giu to correct; rectify; bend; twist; raise the hand
掸	撣	撣		dǎn　daan　撣 to dust; make contact with
	撇	撇		pie　pit　擎 discard; abandon; throw away; to skim (*a stroke in Chinese calligraphy:* ノ)
	撒	撒	撒	sá　saat to cast; distribute; spread; scatter; let go; urinate
	撖	撖		hàn　haam (*sirname*)
	撤	撤	撤	chè　chit　抑 delete; dismiss; withdraw; retreat; remove
拨	撥	撥	撥	bó　buht dispel; distribute; allocate; set aside (money); push aside (using something); poke (a fire); turn around

	撩	撩	撩	liáo liùh arrange; wind up; pick up; tease; incite; provoke; banter; flirt
	撬	撬	撬	qiào giuh force open; pry open; lift; raise
	播	播	播	bó bo 抪 sow; to seed; broadcast; spread; migrate; to go into exile; scatter; disseminate
	撮	撮		cuo chyut 熶 pick up powder using the fingers; scoop up with a dustpan; gather; assemble; extract; eat as a group
	撰	撰	撰	zhùan jaan 撰 compose; write; compile
扑	撲	撲	撲	pu pok pound; beat; attack; strike
揿	撳	撳	撳	qìn gam 搇 㩒 push; press down firmly
挞	撻	撻	撻	tà taat to whip; flog; chastise
挝	撾	撾	撾	zhua jaa beat; strike; (*name of an ancient Chinese weapon*)
	撼	撼	撼	hàn hahm move; shake; vibrate; fight
拥	擁	擁	擁	yóng yúng [illegible] embrace; hug; wrap around; squeeze; to crowd; provide support
据	據	據	據	jù geui 搋 [illegible] occupy; take possession of; depend on; evidence; according to
掳	擄	擄	擄	lǔ lóuh 虏 seize; capture; plunder; rob
捡	撿	撿	撿	jiǎn gim 拣 pick up; collect; put in order
	擀	擀		gǎn gon to roll flat

手 13-14

	擅	擅	擅	shàn　　　sihn monopolize; claim; arbitrarily; dare; be good at; act without authority
择	擇	擇	擇	zé　　　jaahk choose; prefer; select; pick out
	擐	擐		huàn　　　gwaan to put on
	擂	擂	擂	léi　　　lèuih grind; beat; drum; boxing ring
挡	擋	擋	擋	dǎng　　　dóng block; resist; obstruct
	操	操	操	cao　　　chòu conduct; to run; control; manage; drill (*military*); calisthenics; exercise; self-discipline
	擒	擒	擒	qín　　　kam　　擥 catch; capture; seize; arrest; hold; grasp
担	擔	擔	擔	dán　　　dàam carry on a shoulder pole; undertake; to bear
	擗	擗		pǐ　　　pik to beat the breast
	擘	擘		bò　　　maak　　擘 thumb; outstanding person; split; break; tear; open; spread
击	擊	擊	擊	jí　　　gìk strike; attack; hit
	擎	擎		qíng　　　ging prop up; hold up; lift up
挤	擠	擠	擠	jǐ　　　jài squeeze; crowd; push; press
	擤	擤		xǐng　　　sang　　醒揎 blow the nose
摈	擯	擯		bìn　　　ban discard; abandon; get rid of; reject; exclude; expel; (*Cantonese*) to braid hair

手 14-16

	擢	擢	擢	zhúo johk pull up; draw up; select
搁	擱	擱	擱	ge gok put aside; to place down; add; hold; contain; delay; to bear; stand; endure
		擦	擦	ca chaat rub; wipe; scour; scrub; be close to; be near; apply; shred
拧	擰	擰	擰	nǐng nihng twist; spin; screw; wring; stubborn; obstinate; wrong
拟	擬	擬	擬	nǐ yíh draft; plan; intend; compare; imitate; copy
扰	擾	擾	擾	rǎo yiú disturb; annoy; trouble; confused; disordered
掷	擲	擲	擲	zhì jaahk throw; fling; hurl
扩	擴	擴	擴	kùo kong stretch; enlarge; expand
撷	擷	擷	擷	xié kit capture; collect; pick; pluck
摆	擺	擺	擺	bǎi báai place; display; show; swing; pendulum
擞	擻	擻		sǒu sau shake; trembling; quake; flutter
摅	攄	攄		shu syu spread; disperse; scatter; to vent; express; set forth; jump up
撵	撵	撵	撵	niǎn lin 撵 趁 expel; oust; chase after; push with the hands
	攀	攀	攀	pan paan climb; ascend; clamber; pull; hang on to
		攉	攉	huo fok shovel coal, ore, etc. from one place to another; flip one's hands over; beat someone up

手 16-21

拢	攏	攏	攏	lǒng　　lúhng collect; gather; approach
拦	攔	攔	攔	lán　　làahn obstruct; block; hinder
撄	攖	攖		ying　　jing oppose; offend; assault; harass; opposition to; contest; resist
	攘	攘	攘	ráng　　jeung repel; expel; steal; snatch; invade; seize by force; pull up the sleeves
搀	攙	攙		chan　　chaam stab; insert; sharp; mix; support by the arm; take by force; seize
撺	攛	攛		cuan　　chyun hurry; urge; throw
携	攜	攜	攜	xié　　kwàih carry; bring; lead by the hand
摄	攝	攝	攝	shè　　sip absorb; take in; manage; administer; photograph
攒	攢	攢		zǎn　　jaan bend; save; assemble
孪	孿	孿	孿	lúan　　lyùhn bent; crooked; tangled; entwined
摊	攤	攤	攤	tan　　tàan spread; share; display; booth; stall; vendor
	攥	攥		zùan　　jaan hold tight
搅	攪	攪		jiǎo　　gáau disturb; annoy; mix; stir
	攫	攫		júe　　fok to grab; snatch; seize; (*animals*) to grab using claws
揽	攬	攬	攬	lǎn　　láam grasp; take hold of; monopolize

	攮	攮		nǎng　　　nong fend off; stab
	支	支	支	zhi　　　jì support; sustain; disburse; pay; defray; prop up; send away; branch; offshoot; subdivision
	攴	攴		pu　　　bok　　　夂符 tap; hit lightly
	收	收	收	shou　　　sàu arrest; keep; detain; accept; receive; to admit into; gather; harvest; reap; close; stop; withdraw
	攸	攸	攸	you　　　jau distant; far; (prefix)
	改	改	改	gǎi　　　gói change; correct; alter; improve
	攻	攻	攻	gong　　　gùng assault; attack; criticize
放	放	放	放	fàng　　　fong set free; release; liberate; let go; banish; exile; put something down
	政	政	政	zhèng　　　jing government; govern; political power; regulation; rule; decree; politics; correct; comment
	故	故	故	gù　　　gu cause; reason; therefore; purposely; old; dead; deliberately
	效	效	效	xiào　　　haauh result; devote; effectiveness; imitate
	救	救	救	jiù　　　gau save; rescue; pacify; stabilize
启	啟	啟	啟	qǐ　　　kai　　　启啟 open; enlighten; educate; inspire; start; commence; inform; state; explain; note; short letter
	敏	敏	敏	mǐn　　　máhn　　　勄 swift; quick; clever
	救	救	救	jiù　　　gau save; rescue; salvage

攴 7-11

	敕	敕	敕	chì / chik imperial order; decree
	敖	敖	敖	áo / ngou ramble; haughty; loud; leisurely
	教	教	教	jiào / gaau 敎 敎 direct; teach; instruct; religion
败	敗	敗		bài / baaih defeat; ruin; lose; fail
	敘	敘	敘	xù / jeuih converse; talk; chat; narrate; recount
	敝	敝	敝	bì / baih my; our; this; worn-out; shabby; tattered; decayed; corrupted; tired; fatigued; defeated; destroy; poor
	敞	敞		chǎng / tóng spacious; open; roomy; disclose
	敢	敢	敢	gǎn / gám to dare; venture; bold; brave
	散	散	散	sàn / saan scatter; dispurse; mixed; free; at ease
	敦	敦	敦	dun / dèun honest; sincere
	敬	敬	敬	jìng / ging respect; honor
	敫	敫		jiǎo / giu an ancient musical instrument
	敲	敲	敲	qiao / hàau knock; hit; strike; extort; blackmail
数	數	數	數	shù / sou number; several; count; enumerate; criticize
敌	敵	敵	敵	dí / dihk enemy; opponent; rival; fight against

	敷	敷	敷	fu　　　　fù administer medicine; spread; apply; diffuse
	整	整	整	zhěng　　　jíng complete; whole; entire; uniform; neat; orderly
敛	斂	斂	斂	liǎn　　　lim draw back; fold back; restrain; gather; collect; arrange
毙	斃	斃	斃	bì　　　　baih die violently; kill; execution; fall down; collapse
	文	文	文	wén　　　màhn written language; literature; culture; essay; refined
	斐	斐	斐	fěi　　　　féi graceful; elegant; beautiful
	斌	斌		bin　　　　bàn graceful; genteel; refined; ornamental
	斑	斑	斑	bán　　　bàan spot; stripe
斓	斕	斕	斕	lán　　　　laan variegated; multi-colored
	斗	斗	斗	dǒu　　　dáu fight; struggle; ancient Chinese wine vessel; unit of dry measure (~1 *decaliter*)
	料	料	料	liào　　　liuh anticipate; predict; material; estimate; manage; ingredient; component
	斛	斛		hú　　　　huk unit of measure equal to about five or ten dou (斗)
	斜	斜		xié　　　chèh tilted; slope; inclined; oblique; slanted
	斟	斟	斟	zhen　　　jàm to pour a drink; consider; deliberate
	斡	斡		wò　　　　waat revolve; rotate; spin

斤 1-14　方 4-6

	斤	斤	斤	jīn　　　gàn　　　釿 劤 catty (0.5 *kilogram*); an axe; keen; shrewd
	斥	庠	庠	chì　　　chìk scold; accuse; reproach; expel; dismiss; expand; enlarge; to allocate funds
	斧	斧	斧	fǔ　　　fú axe; hatchet
	斫	斫	斫	zhuó　　　cheuk　　　斲 斮 chop; cut
斬	斬	斬	斬	zhǎn　　　jáam chop; cut; behead
	断	斷	斷	duàn　　　dyun sever; cut off; interrupt
	斯	斯	斯	sī　　　sì this; thus; such; lop off; an emphatic particle
	新	新	新	xīn　　　sàn new; modern; up-to-date
断	斷	斷	斷	duàn　　　dyuhn　　　斷 break; snap; cut off; sever; interrupt; give up; abstain; quit
	方	方	方	fāng　　　fòng direction; orientation; ; place; region; locality; parallel; side by side; square; rectangle; cube; side; aspect
于	於	於	於	yú　　　yù　　　扵 at; in; on; with; by; to; with regard to
	施	施	施	shī　　　sì arrange; distribute; give; impose; flag waving; spread
	旁	旁	旁	páng　　　pòhng　　　方 side; beside; other
	旃	旃	旃	zhān　　　jīn a silk banner; felt
	旄	旄	旄	máo　　　mou an ancient flag decorated with yak tails; old

旅	旅	旅	lǔ léuih	travel; trip; journey; army; troops
斾	斾		pèi pui	pennant; banner; streamer; flag
旋	旋	旋	xúan syùhn	revolve; turn; return; come home; circle; loop; cycle; immediately
旌	旌		jing jìng	a banner or flag decorated with feathers; make clear; recognize; distinguish; honor; commend
旎	旎		nǐ nei	a fluttering flag; romantic
族	族	族	zú juhk	family; clan; tribe; nationality
旒	旒		liú lau	tassel; pennant
旖	旖		yǐ ji	a fluttering flag; romantic; charming; tender
旗	旗	旗	qí kèih	flag; banner; standard
旡	旡		jì gei 旡	when food is stuck in the throat; choke
既	既		jì gei	finished; since; already; then
日	日	日	rì yaht 国 囗	sun; daytime; daily; time; period; age; (*classifier for day*)
旦	旦	旦	dàn daan	dawn; daybreak; morning
早	早	早	zǎo jóu	morning; early
旬	旬	旬	xún chèuhn	decade; period of 10 days; period of time

日 2-4

旨	旨(seal)	旨(seal2)	zhǐ　　　jí　　　助 㫖 delicious food; fine; intention; purpose; goal
旮	旮(seal)		ga　　　go nook; corner
旯	旯(seal)		lá　　　lo nook; corner
旭	旭(seal)	旭(seal2)	xù　　　yuk dawn; rising sun; brilliant; radiant
旰	旰(seal)		gàn　　　gon sunset; dusk; evening
旱	旱(seal)	旱(seal2)	hàn　　　hóhn dry weather; drought; arid
旺	旺(seal)	旺(seal2)	wàng　　　wohng　　　暀 an occurrence bringing prosperity/wealth; bustling; filled with activity
昀	昀(seal)	昀(seal2)	yún　　　wan sunlight
昂	昂(seal)	昂(seal2)	áng　　　ngòhng　　　昂 raise; lift; elevated; high spirited
昃	昃(seal)		zè　　　jak　　　昗 late afternoon, evening; sunset; decline
昆	昆(seal)	昆(seal2)	kun　　　kwàn elder brother; decendants; simultaneously; later; many; numerous
昊	昊(seal)	昊(seal2)	hào　　　hou vast sky; heaven; summertime
昌	昌(seal)	昌(seal2)	chang　　　chèung sunlight; good; proper; right; beautiful; lovely; prosperous; flourishing
明	明(seal)	明(seal2)	míng　　　mìhng　　　朙 眀 bright; light; brilliant; clear; understand; tomorrow vision; sight; acute
昏	昏(seal)	昏(seal2)	hun　　　fàn　　　昬 dusk; dim; twilight; dizzy; faint; lose consciousness

易	易	易		yì　　　　yihk exchange; interchange; change; alter; modify; easy; simple; effortless
昔	荅	荅		xi　　　　sìk　　　　昝 former; ancient; past; sunset
昕	昕	昕		xin　　　　jan dawn; early morning
星	曐	曐		xing　　　　sìng　　　　曐 star; planet; heavenly body; celebrity; tiny; white; numerous and scattered; rapid; flying
昝	昝			zǎn　　　　jaan (dual pronoun); you and me; we two
春	萅	萅		chún　　　　chèun　　　　旾 旾 spring season; young; year; age; vitality; liveliness; energy; life; lust; passion; sexual desire
映	映	映		yìng　　　　yíng　　　　暎 reflect (light); mirror; shine; to project (movie); sunshine; sunlight; cover; hide
昧	昧	昧		mèi　　　　muih ignorant; stupid; foolish; conceal; dark; gloomy; venture; risk; violate; covet
昶	昶			chǎng　　　　chóng　　　　景 暢 畅 daytime; long; bright
是	是	是		shì　　　　sih be; is; yes; correct
昱	昱	昱		yù　　　　yuk bright light; sunlight; dazzling
昨	昨	昨		zúo　　　　jok yesterday; previously; past
昭	昭	昭		zhao　　　　chiu bright; luminous; illustrious
昴	昴			mǎo　　　　maau the pleiades (star cluster)
晁	晁	晁		cháo　　　　chìuh morning; dawn

日 6-7

	晃	晃(篆)	晃(篆)	huǎng　　fong bright; dazzling; sway; shake
时	時	時(篆)		shí　　sih　　昔 助 time; season; hour; era; age; period; opportunity; chance
	晌	晌(篆)		shǎng　　heung noon; midday; moment; unit of land
	晏	晏(篆)	晏(篆)	yàn　　aan late; tardy; sunny with clear sky; peaceful; tranquil; serene
晋	晉	晉(篆)	晉(篆)	jìn　　jeun　　晉晋 enter; advance; increase; promote; Jin dynasty
	耆	耆(篆)		qí　　kei aged; old; senior; tyrannical; detest; abhor
勖	勗	勗(篆)		xu　　juk advise; excite; exhort; encouragement
	晗	晗(篆)		hán　　ham pre-dawn
	晚	晚(篆)	晚(篆)	wǎn　　máahn evening; late
	晡	晡(篆)		bu　　bou late afternoon; early evening; 3 - 5 pm
	晦	晦(篆)	晦(篆)	huì　　fui last day of a lunar month; dark; night; unclear; obscure
	晤	晤(篆)	晤(篆)	wù　　ngh meet; interview
昼	晝	晝(篆)	晝(篆)	zhòu　　jau daytime; day; daylight
	晟	晟(篆)		chéng　　sing clear; bright; splendor; brightness
	晨	晨(篆)	晨(篆)	chén　　sàhn dawn, morning; daybreak

	景	景	景	jǐng　　gíng scenery; view; condition; situation; bright; luminous
	晾	晾	晾	liàng　　leuhng to dry in the sun; air-dry
	晰	晰	晰	xi　　sìk clear; distinct
	晴	晴	晴	qíng　　ching　　姓星晴精 clear; fine (*weather*)
	晶	晶	晶	jing　　jìng bright; radiant; crystal
	普	普	普	pǔ　　póu general; common; universal; popular
	智	智	智	zhì　　ji wisdom
	晷	晷	晷	guǐ　　gwai sundial
	暑	暑	暑	shǔ　　syú hot weather; heat; summer
暈	暈	暈	暈	yun　　wàhn faint; dizzy
晖	暉	暉	暉	hui　　fai sunshine; light, bright; radiant
	暌	暌		kúi　　kwai opposition; distant; separated; to part
	暖	暖	暖	nǔan　　nyúhn (*lyúhn*) warm
	暗	暗	暗	àn　　am　　闇晻陪 dark; secret; obscure; secret
	暇	暇	暇	xiá　　ha leisure; relaxation; spare time

日 9-14

	暄	暄	暄	xuan / hyun — warm; loose; genial; comfortable
	暝	暝	暝	míng / ming — dark; night; evening
畅	暢	暢	暢	chàng / cheung — unimpeded; uninhibited; unrestrained; smooth; comfortable
	暨	暨	暨	jì / kei (暨㬢) — initial appearance of sunrise; attain; reach; and; confines
晔	曄	曅	曄	yè / jip — bright; radiant; thriving
暂	暫	暫	暫	zàn / jaahm (蹔) — temporary
	暮	暮	暮	mù / mouh — dusk; evening; twilight; sunset
	暴	暴	暴	bào / bouh — violent; cruel; sudden; brutal; fierce; savage
昵	暱	昵		nì / nìk (嫟) — intimate; close; familiar
	暹	暹	暹	xian / chim — rise; advance; go forward; Siam
昙	曇	曇	曇	tán / taam — cloudy; overcast
晓	曉	曉	曉	xiǎo / hiú — dawn; know; understand
	暾	暾		tun / tan (燉) — morning sun; sun above the horizon
暧	曖	曖	曖	ài / oi — warm; obscure; clandestine
	曙	曙	曙	shǔ / chyúh — dawn; daybreak

	曛	纛		xun　　　fan twilight; sunset; dusk; night
	曜	曜	曜	yào　　　jiu daylight; sunlight; glorious
	曝	曓	曝	pù　　　buhk to expose or dry in the sun; expose; reveal
旷	曠	曠	曠	kùang　　　kong neglect; to skip (*class or work*); waste time; broad; vast; extensive; void; empty; wilderness
曦	曦	曦	曦	xi　　　hèi light of dawn; early sunshine
	曩	曩	曩	nǎng　　　nong previous; past
晒	曬	曬		shài　　　saai to shine on; to expose or dry in the sun
	曰	曰	曰	yue　　　yeuhk say; speak; be called
	曲	曲	曲	qu　　　kùk bent; twisting; curved; crooked; wrong
	曳	曳	曳	yè　　　yaih drag; pull; float in the wind; sway; tired; fatigued
	更	更	更	geng　　　gàng change; replace; take turns; rotate; experience; moreover
	曷	曷	曷	hé　　　hot what; why; where; when
书	書	書	書	shu　　　syù　　書 book; letter; document; writing; Chinese character; type style;
	曹	曹	曹	cáo　　　chòuh plaintiff and defendant; fodder; official; group; team; Zhou dynasty vassal state (*1046-221 BC*)
	曼	曼	曼	màn　　　maahn fine; long; extended

	最	冣	冣	zùi jeui 取寂 most; very; exceeding; extremely; -est
	替	暜	暜	tì tai substitute; replace
	曾	曾	曾	zeng jàng 曾 once; already; before; great-grandfather
会	會	會	會	hùi wuih 會 union; group; association; society; centre; town; occasion; match; conform; gather; assemble
	月	☽	月	yùe yuht moon; month
	有	有	有	yǒu yáuh to have; to be
	朊	朊		rǔan jyun protein; prion
	朋	朋	朋	péng pàhng friend; companion
	服	服	服	fú fuhk 舟 clothes; mourning dress; wear; put on; take; eat; submit; agree; accept; obey
	朔	朔	朔	shùo sok first day of a lunar month; new moon; beginning; North
	朕	朕	朕	zhèn jam I; my (used only by the emperor after the Qin Dynasty); omen
	朗	朗	朗	liǎng lóhng 朖 㫰 朤 bright; clear; distinct
	望	望	望	wàng mohng 朢 see; watch (from a vantage point); look at; observe; hope; expect; wish; desire; fame; reputation; location
	朝	朝	朝	zháo jiù 晁 朝 morning; breakfast; moment; short period; daytime; day; active; energetic; lively
	期	期	期	qí kèih 朞 稘 arranged time; date; engage; meet; gather; hope; expect; (classifier for time period or project stages); chance

	朦	朦	朦	méng mùhng dim; hazy; deceive; indistinct
胧	朧	朧	朧	lóng lung rising moon, hazy; cloudy; uncertain; unreliable
	木	木	木	mù muhk wood; wooden
	未	未	未	wèi meih not yet; not
	末	末	末	mò muht last; end; final stage; fine powder; insignificant; trivial; low-priority
	本	本	本	běn bún 本 this; root; origin; source; volume local
	札	札	札	zhá jaat letter; note; bill; correspondence
	朱	朱	朱	zhu jyù cinnibar; vermillion; scarlet; bright red
	朵	朵	朵	duǒ do 朵 flower or calyx of a plant; ear; move; (classifier for flowers, clouds, etc.)
	朽	朽	朽	xiǔ náu rotten; decayed
	朴	朴	朴	pò pok tree bark; stem; root; Chinese hackberry (Celtis sinensis)
	杉	杉	杉	shan chaam 樅 cedar; various species of pine and fir; (used in transliteration)
	材	材	材	cái chòih timber; wood; materials; talent
	村	村	村	cun chyùn village; hamlet
	杓	杓	杓	biáo biù ladle; dipper; spoon

木 3-4

	杈	杈		cha / cha — fork of a tree; pitchfork
	杖	杖	杖	zhàng / jéung — crutch; cane; walking stick; staff; wand; to flog
	杜	杜	杜	dù / douh — stop; keep out
	杆	杆	杆	gan / gòn — pole; staff; rod
	机	机		wù / ngat — sterility; low square stool
	杞	杞	杞	qǐ / gei — willow; medlar tree
	束	束	束	shù / chùk — tie up; restrain; bundle
	李	李	李	lǐ / léih — plum
	杏	杏	杏	xìng / hahng — apricot
	杳	杳	杳	yǎo / miúh — quiet; dark; gloom; vast, extensive; to disappear
	杲	杲	杲	gǎo / gou — white; brightness of the sun
	果	果	果	guǒ / gwó — 菓 fruit; results; sure enough; determined
东	東	東	東	dong / dùng — east; eastern; host; landlord
	杪	杪	杪	miǎo / miúh — branch; end of a twig; top of the tree
	枕	枕	枕	zhěn / jám — pillow; occipital bone

152

杭	杭	杭	háng suddenly	hong	
枋	枋	枋	fang sandalwood	fong	
杯	梧	槅	bei drinkware; cup; glass; mug	bui	梧盃
林	林	林	lín woods; forest; grove; group of similar things; circle; community	làhm	
析	析	析	xi analyze; divide; break apart; split wood	sìk	
杵	杵	杵	chǔ pestle	chyu	
杷	杷	杷	pǎ loquat; handle	pàh	
松	松	松	song pine tree	chùhng	枀 柗 崧 㭔
枚	枚	枚	méi shrub stalk; tree trunk; wooden peg; counting rod; (classifier for generic countable objects)	mùih	
枝	枝	枝	zhí branch; twig; (classifyer for long cylindrical objects)	jì	
板	版	版	bǎn board; plank	báan	
枘	枘		rùi tool handle; tenon	jeui	
枇	枇	枇	pí loquat	pèih	
杼	杼	杼	zhù shuttle of a loom; narrow; thin; a scrub oak	chyu	
枉	枉	枉	wǎng crooked; grievance; in vain	wóng	

柱	柱	柱		zhù　　　chyúh pillar; post; column; stand tall; stiff; bridge on a stringed instrument
枯	枯	枯		ku　　　fù withered; dry
枰	枰	枰		píng　　　ping chessboard; smooth board
枳	枳			zhi　　　chi orange (*citrus trifoliata*); thorn-hedge
枵	枵			xiao　　　hiu　　　飢餓 hollow stump of a tree; empty; hungry; hollow; thin (of silk)
柘	柘			zhè　　　che thorny tree; sugar cane
柏	柏	柏		bǎi　　　paak cypress; cedar
柑	柑	柑		gan　　　gàm　　　甘 Mandarin orange; tangerine
柙	柙			xiá　　　haap cage; pen for wild animals
柚	柚	柚		yòu　　　yáu pomelo
枸	枸	枸		gǒu　　　gau　　　构 Chinese wolfberry; an aspen found in Sichuan
柃	柃			líng　　　ling a shrub (*eurya japonica*)
柄	柄	柄		bǐng　　　bing handle of an implement; plant stem; mistake which can be used against someone; power; authority
柝	柝	柝		tùo　　　tok a watchman's wooden clapper or rattle
柞	柞	柞		zhà　　　jaa oak; to clear away trees

木 5

	柢	柢	柢	dǐ　　　dai root of a tree; foundation; origin
	柩	柩	柩	jiù　　　gau coffin containing a corpse
	柯	柯	柯	ke　　　o axe handle; stalk; bough; tan oak
拐	枴	枴	枴	guǎi　　　gwáai crutch; cane; staff
	柳	柳	柳	liǔ　　　láuh　　　柳柳柳柳 willow
	柿	柿	柿	shì　　　chí　　　柿柿 persimmon
栅	柵	柵	柵	zhà　　　chaak fence; palisade
	架	架		jià　　　ga frame; rack; stand; shelf; prop; (*classifier for planes, large vehicles and items*)
	某	某	某	mǒu　　　máuh certain; some; a particular person or thing
	柴	柴	柴	chái　　　chàaih firewood; bundle of sticks bound as fuel
	染	染	染	rǎn　　　yíhm to dye; infect; contagious
	柔	柔	柔	róu　　　yàuh mild; soft; supple; tender; gentle; act kindly
	柰	柰		nài　　　noi　　　奈 crabapple (*malus asiatica*); endure; how; why
	查	查	查	chá　　　chàh　　　查 examine; investigate; look into
	柬	柬	柬	jiǎn　　　gáan invitation; letter

155

木 6

桌	桌	桌	zhuo　　cheuk　　樟 槕 table; desk; stand
栗	栗	栗	lì　　leuht chestnut tree; chestnut
桕	桕		jiù　　kau tallow tree (*triadica sebifera*)
栓	栓	栓	shuan　　saan wooden peg; post
桔	桔	桔	jié　　gàt tangerine
校	校	校	xiào　　haauh school; college; university; compare; proofread
桁	桁	桁	héng　　hang roof crossbeam
栩	栩	栩	xǔ　　yihk pleased; lively; vivd; species of oak (*quercus serrata*)
株	株	株	zhu　　jyù tree stump; (*classifier for plants and viruses*)
栲	栲		kǎo　　haau mangrove
栳	栳		lǎo　　lou a round-bottomed basket made of willow or bamboo strips (*used only in* 栲栳)
核	核	核	hé　　haht　　槅 pit; seed; kernel; core; nucleus; nuclear
根	根	根	gen　　gàn base; basis; source; origin; foundation; ancestors
格	格	格	gé　　gaak pattern; standard; form; style; frame; personality; character; arrive; obstruct; hinder; investigate
桂	桂	桂	gùi　　gwai cassia cinnamon; cinnamon; laurel; osmanthus

	桃	桃	桃	táo　　tòuh peach (*tree and fruit*)
	栱	栱		guang　　gwong bamboo palm, broadleaf lady rhapis palm (*rhapis excelsa*)
	桅	桅	桅	wéi　　wàih ship mast
	框	框	框	kùang　　kwàang frame; framework; sill; restrain
	桉	桉		an　　on eucalyptus
	桎	桎		zhì　　jat fetters; shackles; foot iron; handcuffs
	桐	桐		tóng　　tùhng paulownia; (*trees related to the oil-tung tree*)
	桓	桓	桓	húan　　wun Chinese soapberry (*sapindus mukorossi*)
	栽	栽	栽	zai　　jòi to plant; cultivate
	桀	桀	桀	jié　　git chicken roost; Jie (*ancient Xia emperor*)
	案	案	案	àn　　on desk; file; record; court case; proposal; a wooden plate used to serve food
	桊	桊		jùan　　gyun a cow's nose ring
	桑	桑	桑	sang　　sòng　　桒 mulberry tree
	梁	梁	梁	liáng　　lèuhng beam; girder; ridge
条	條	條	條	tiáo　　tiùh　　樤 article; strip; stripe; item; article; clause; (*classifier for long and thin objects or animals*)

木 7

	梨			lí　　　　lèih pear	
梟	梟			xiao　　　hiu owl; brave; fierce; leader; to decapitate and hang the head	
	桴			fú　　　　fu rafter; ridgepole; drumsticks	
	桶			tǒng　　　túng bucket; barrel; pail; keg; tub	
	桷			júe　　　　gok rafter; crabapple (*malus toringo*)	
杆	桿			gǎn　　　gòn stick; rod; pole; club; lever; shaft	
	梓			zǐ　　　　jí Chinese catalpa (*catalpa ovata*); wood craftsman; hometown; printing block	
	梃			tǐng　　　ting club; stalk; straight	
	梅			méi　　　mùih plum	楳 槑
	梆			bang　　　bòng wooden cylinder; (*onomatopoeia*) rat-a-tat	
	梏			gù　　　　guk handcuffs; manacles; fetters; brace	
	梧			wú　　　　ng Chinese parasol tree (*firmiana platanifolia*)	
栀	梔			zhi　　　　jih gardenia	
	梗			gěng　　　gang spiny plant; stem; stalk	莖 茎
枧	梘			jiǎn　　　gaan bamboo water pipe	

158

	梢	梢	梢	sháo sàau pointed tip of a long item or branch; rudder
	梭	梭	梭	suo so weaver's shuttle; to and fro
	梯	梯	梯	tí tài ladder; steps; stairs; climb; lean against
	械	械	械	xiè haaih weapon; tool; implement; instrument
	梳	梳	梳	shu soh comb; brush
	梵	梵	梵	fàn faan lush; luxuriant; quiet; peaceful; undisturbed; (*Buddhism*) chant sutras; (*Hinduism*) Brahman
	棼	棼		fén fan roof beams; confused; disordered
	森	森	森	sen sam full of trees; dark; gloomy; cold; orderly; strict; rigid; rigorous
枣	棗	棗	棗	zǎo jóu jujube; date
	棘	棘		jí gik jujube tree; thorns; brambles; spines
	棒	棒	棒	bàng paang stick; club; truncheon; hefty; strong; terrific; smart; handsome; excellent; skillful
	棕	棕	棕	zong jung palm tree; palm fibre; light brown (*like a palm leaf sheath*)
	棉	棉	棉	mián mìhn 檰栭 cotton
	棋	棋	棋	qí kèih 棊碁櫀櫀 chess; strategy; plan; board game
	棍	棍	棍	gùn gwan stick; rod; bar; wand; scoundrel

木 8

枨	棖	棖		chéng　　　　chàahng doorpost; doorjamb
	棚	棚	棚	péng　　　　pàahng booth; shed; tent; awning; canopy
栋	棟	棟	棟	dòng　　　　duhng pillar; beam (*supporting a house*)
	棣	棣	棣	dì　　　　dai　　　　弟 (kerria japonica); cherry tree; younger brother
栈	棧	棧		zhàn　　　　jáan warehouse; storehouse; tavern; hotel; inn
	棰	棰		chui　　　　cheui　　　　箠 flog; whip
	棱	棱		léng　　　　lìhng angle; edge; ridge; corner
栖	棲	棲	棲	qi　　　　chài roost; perch; stay; dwell
	棵	棵	棵	ke　　　　pò (*classifyer for plants*)
	棹	棹	棹	zhào　　　　jaau　　　　桌 櫂 table; desk; stand; oar; to row
	棺	棺	棺	gwan　　　　gùn coffin
	椅	椅	椅	yi　　　　ji chair
	椋	椋		liáng　　　　leung a dogwood plant (*cornus hemsleyi*); starling
	植	植	植	zhí　　　　jihk plant; flora; cultivate; set up; establish
	椎	椎	椎	chúi　　　　chèuih vertebra; hammer; mallet; shiitake; small genus of beech (*castanopsis*)

木 8-9

桠	椏	丫		ya　　　　a　　　　丫桠 close; the forking of a tree branch; twig
	椐	𣐽		ju　　　　geui Japanese zelkova (*zelkova serrata*)
	椒	𣓉	𣖃	jiao　　　jiù Sichuan pepper; bell pepper; chili pepper; pepper
弃	棄	𠭖	𠭛	qì　　　　hei　　　　弃甭 abandon; give up; discard; reject
	棠	𣖎	𣖏	táng　　　tòhng crabapple tree; wild plum
	渠	𣲗	𣲘	qú　　　　keui ditch; canal; drain; large
业	業	𣎾	𣎿	yè　　　　yihp profession; occupation; business; trade; cause; property; estate
	椰	𣓷	𣓸	yé　　　　yèh coconut (*palm and fruit*)
	椴	𣓻		dùan　　　dyun poplar; aspen; lime tree
	椹	𣔉		zhen　　　jam　　　枯砧碪鍖 chopping board; mulberry tree fruit; mold and fungus grown on fallen/dead trees
	椽	𣔊		chúan　　chyùhn rafters; beams; supports
枫	楓	𣕚	𣕛	feng　　　fùng maple tree
	楔	𣕒	𣕓	xie　　　　sit wedge; gatepost
	楗	𣕔		jiàn　　　kin door bar; bolt lock
	楚	𣕕	𣕖	chǔ　　　chó pain; suffering; clear; distinct; neat; clean; tidy; bright; gorgeous; charming; medicinal deciduous bush (*vitex*)

木 9

	楝	楝	楝	liàn　　lin melia azedarach (*aka: melia japonica*); a type of mahogany tree
	楞	楞	楞	léng　　ling　　稜 edge; corner
	楠	楠	楠	nán　　naam machilus nanmu (*a tropical plant/tree*)
	楣	楣	楣	méi　　mèih door lintel; gate crossbeam
	楦	楦		xùan　　hyun shoe lasting machine; turn on a lathe
桢	楨	楨	楨	zhen　　ching hardwood; supports; posts
	楫	楫	楫	jí　　jip oar; paddle
杨	楊	楊	楊	yáng　　yèuhng willow; poplar; aspen
	椿	椿		chun　　cheun toon mahogany tree (*toona sinensis*); tree of heaven (*ailanthus altissima*); father (*figurative*); advanced age
	楂	楂		chá　　ja wooden raft; hew; to fell trees; hawthorn
	楮	楮	楮	chǔ　　chyúh mulberry; paper
	楷	楷	楷	kǎi　　kaai pistacia chinensis; upright
极	極	極	極	jí　　gihk extremely; utmost; pole; top
	楸	楸		qiu　　chau catalpa bungei and mallotus japonicus (*deciduous trees*); a go board
	楹	楹	楹	yíng　　jing pillar; column

162

	概	槩	糠	gài koi 概槩 outline; concept; in general; sum up; approximate
	榔	榔	榔	láng long betel-nut tree
	榍	榍		xiè sit (*classical Chinese*) threshold; doorstep; a type of tree described in ancient texts
	榆	榆	榆	yú jyu elm tree
	榕	榕	榕	róng jung ficus; banyan tree
	榛	榛	榛	zhēn jeun hazelnut; filbert; thicket; underbrush
	榜	榜	榜	bǎng bóng announcement; bulletin; placard; list of names
	榧	榧		fěi fei Chinese nutmeg yew (*torreya grandis*)
	榨	榨		zhà ja 搾 squeeze; press or extract juices; exploit; to force
杩	榪	榪		mà ma headboard
	榫	榫	榫	sǔn seun tenon (and mortise); fit into
	榭	榭	榭	xiè che pavillion; kiosk
	榱	榱		cuī cheui a rafter (*architecture*)
	榴	榴	榴	liú làuh pomegranate
	榷	榷	榷	què kok footbridge; toll; levy; monopoly; knock

	榻	榻	榻	tà　　　　taap couch; bed; cot
桤	榿	榿		qi　　　　kei alder tree
	槁	槀	槀	gǎo　　　gau wither; withered; rotten; dead
构	構	構	構	gòu　　　kau build; compose; construct; form; make; fabricate; organization; structure
枪	槍	槍	槍	qiang　　chèung gun; rifle; firearm; spear
	槎	槎		chá　　　chàh hew; fell trees; raft; time; occasion
	槌	槌	槌	chúi　　　chèuih hammer, mallet; strike; beat
	槐	槐	槐	húai　　　waai Chinese scholar tree (*styphnolobium japonicum*); Japanese pagoda tree; locust tree
杠	槓	杠	朾	gàng　　　gong lever; carrying pole; crowbar; (*mahjong*) "gong"; (*Cantonese*) wardrobe; trunk
	槔	槔		gao　　　gou water pulley; well sweep
	榘	榘		jǔ　　　　geui carpenter's square; ruler
荣	榮	榮		róng　　　wing glory; honor; flourish; prosper
	槊	槊		shùo　　　sok lance; pike
椠	槧	槧		qiàn　　　chim wooden tablet; writing surface; edition; publication; copy; a letter
桨	槳	槳	槳	jiǎng　　　chióng paddle; oar

木 11

乐	樂	樂	樂	yùe　　ngok　　樂 music; tune; melody; song; musical instrument; happy
	樊	樊	樊	fán　　faan railing; fence; enclosure
	模	模	模	mó　　mòuh pattern; model; mold; standard; example; copy; imitate
梁	樑	樑	樑	liáng　　lèuhng　　梁 roof beam; ridge
样	樣	樣	樣	yàng　　yeuhng　　㨾 様 kind; sample; type; pattern; appearance; form; shape; manner
标	標	標	標	biao　　biù specify; mark; label; sign
椁	槨	槨	槨	gǔo　　gwok outer coffin; vault
	槭	槭	槭	qi　　chik maple tree
	槲	槲		hú　　huk Mongolian oak (*quercus dentata*)
楼	樓	樓	樓	lóu　　làuh storied building; tower; floor; level
	槽	槽	槽	cáo　　chòuh livestock trough; groove; concave; depression; ditch; trench
	槿	槿		jǐn　　gan Chinese hibiscus (a rose)
桩	樁	樁	樁	zhúang　　jòng stake; post; pile; piling; (*classifyer for events*)
枞	樅	樅	樅	cong　　chung fir tree
	樗	樗		chu　　syu ailanthus glandulosa/altissima (a tree that is useless as timber)

165

木 11-12

枢	樞	樞	樞	shú	syù		
				hinge; pivot; central power; important point			
	樟	章	樟	zhang	chiong		
				camphor tree			
	樨	犀		xi	sai		
				sweet osmanthus (osmanthus fragrans); beaten or scrambled eggs			
桦	樺	樺	樺	hùa	wah		
				birch tree			
	樵	樵	樵	qiáo	chiùh		
				firewood; gather wood; woodcutter			
树	樹	樹	樹	shù	syuh	槸	
				tree; to plant; cultivate			
	樽	樽	樽	zun	jyùn	罇 墫	
				vessel for alcohol; goblet			
	樾	樾		yùe	jyut		
				tree shade			
	橄	橄	橄	gǎn	gaam		
				olive tree; olive			
	橇	橇	橇	qiao	cheui	鞽	
				sled; sleigh			
桡	橈	橈	橈	náo	naau		
				twisted piece of wood; radius (*forearm bone*); paddle			
桥	橋	橋	橋	qiáo	kiùh		
				bridge			
	橘	橘	橘	jú	gwàt	桔	
				tangerine			
	橙	橙	橙	chéng	cháang		
				orange			
	橛	橜		júe	gyut	橜	
				wood post; stake; peg			

机	機	檆	櫟	jī　　　gèi machine; device; craft; opportunity; cause
	橡	橡	櫾	xiàng　　　jeuhng　　樣样樣 oak tree; acorn
椭	橢	橢	橢	tuǒ　　　to oval-shaped; elliptical
	橫	橫	橫	héng　　　wàahng　　揎橫 horizontal; crosswise; traverse; fill; cover; broad; vast; crisscross; unreasonable; probably; anyway
朴	樸	樸	朴	pǔ　　　pok plain; simple; unpolished
	橐	橐		túo　　　tok　　橐 sack; bag; camel; tube for blowing fire
檩	檩	檩		lǐn　　　lam bole of a tree; purlin; cross beam
	檀	檀	檀	tán　　　tàahn sandalwood; hardwood
樯	檣	檣	檣	qiáng　　　chèuhng　　艢 mast; yardarm; boom
	檄	檄	檄	xí　　　hat order; dispatch; call to arms; urgency
柽	檉	檉		cheng　　　ching tamarisk tree; willow
	檎	檎		qín　　　kam small red apple; crabapple
	檑	檑		léi　　　leui large log covered in spikes (*defense weapon*)
档	檔	檔	檔	dàng　　　dong shelf for files; files; document; archives; frame; crosspiece
桧	檜	檜	檜	guì　　　kui Chinese cypress; juniper

木 13-15

检	檢	檢	檢	jiǎn gím examine; check; inspect
	檠	檠	檠	qíng king lamp stand; candlestick
	檫	檫		chá chaat sassafras tree
	檬	檬	檬	méng mung type of locust oracacia; "lemon"
槟	檳	檳	檳	bin ban betel nut; areca nut
柠	檸	檸	檸	níng ning "lemon"
槛	檻	檻	檻	jiàn haam fence; cage; railing
苘	檾	苘		qǐng king 苘 檾 abutilon (*flowering plant*); fibrous grass that is used for making clothes
凳	櫈	櫈		dèng dang stool; bench
台	檯	檯	檯	tái tòih desk; table; stage
柜	櫃	櫃		gùi gwaih closet; chest; cabinet; cupboard; wardrobe
橥	櫫	櫫		zhu jyu wood peg; post; stick
橹	櫓	櫓	櫓	lǔ lou 樐 艣 艪 艪 large shield; scull (*aft oar*)
榈	櫚	櫚		lú leui palm tree
栉	櫛	櫛	櫛	zhì jit comb; weed out; eliminate

椟	櫝	櫝	櫝	dú　　　　duk box; case; casket; cabinet; wardrobe; closet
橼	櫞	櫞		yúan　　　yùhn citron; cedrat; cedrate; citrus medica
栎	櫟	櫟		lì　　　　lik oak; railing; fight with; wrestle; scrape an implement to produce sound
橱	櫥	櫥	櫥	chú　　　chyùh cabinet; cupboard, wardrobe; closet
栌	櫨	櫨		lú　　　　lou sumac; loquat; smoke tree (*cashew family*)
枥	櫪	櫪		lì　　　　lik　　　　櫪 stable; type of oak
槠	櫧	櫧		zhu　　　jyu castanopsis (*an intermediate of oak and chestnut*)
榇	櫬	櫬	櫬	chèn　　　can coffin; tung tree (*vernicia fordii*)
栊	櫳	櫳		lóng　　　lung cage; bar; window; house; sparse
棂	櫺	櫺	櫺	líng　　　ling lattice; carved or patterned window sills
樱	櫻	櫻	櫻	yīng　　　jing cherry tree
栏	欄	欄	欄	lán　　　làahn railing; column; fence; hurdle; balustrade; animal pen; (*Cantonese*) wholesaler
榉	欅	欅		jǔ　　　　geoi　　　櫸 欅 梇 zelkova (*genus of elm*); beech
权	權	權	權	qúan　　　kyun　　　攡 権 power; authority; right; entitlement; scales; weigh; measure; judge; tentatively; for the time being
椤	欏	欏		lúo　　　lo horse-chestnut tree

栾	欒	欒		lúan　　　lyun goldenrain tree (*koelreuteria paniculata*); part of a cornice
榄	欖	欖	欖	lǎn　　　laam olive; olive tree
	欠	欠	欠	qiàn　　　him yawn; lacking; deficient; owe
	次	次	次	cì　　　chi time; order; second; next; sequence; inferior
	欣	欣	欣	xin　　　yàn happy; delighted; cheerful; joyful; admire
	欲	欲	欲	yù　　　yuhk want; wish; desire
	欷	欷		xi　　　hei sob; cry; sigh
	欹	欹		qi　　　kei interjection of a plea
	欺	欺		qi　　　hèi cheat; deceive; bully; excel; surpass
钦	欽	欽	欽	qin　　　yàm respect; admire
	款	款	款	kuǎn　　　fún　　　欵 money; style; entertain; signature; model; type; paragraph; section
	歃	歃		shà　　　saap drink; suck; to smear one's mouth with the blood of a sacrifice when taking an oath
	歆	歆		xin　　　jam like; admire; pleased; willingly; gladly; to quicken
	歇	歇	歇	xie　　　hit rest; relax; stop
	歉	歉	歉	qiàn　　　him apologize; regret; deficient; lacking; insufficient

歌	歌	歌	歌	ge song; sing; chant; praise	gò	謌	
欧	歐	歐	歐	ou Europe	ngàu		
叹	歎	歎	歎	tàn sigh	taan	歡	
	歙	歙		shè suck; an Anhui county	kap		
欤	歟	歟	歟	yú (*final particle to express admiration, doubt, surprise, or ask a question*)	jyu		
欢	歡	歡	歡	huan joy; glad; happy; pleased	fùn	驩	
止	止	止	止	zhǐ stop; halt; only	jí		
	正	正	正	zhèng straight; upright; proper; standardized; square; primary; main; pure; authentic; true; attractive; honest	jing	正	
	此	此	此	cǐ this; here	chí		
	步	步	步	bù walk; step	bouh		
	武	武	武	wǔ military; soldier; warrior; force; martial arts; wushu; valiant; brave; courageous; footstep; footprint	móuh		
	歧	歧	歧	qí fork; divide; different; divergent	kèih		
	歪	歪	歪	wai crooked; devious	wàai		
岁	歲	歲	歲	suì year; age; jupiter	seui	歲歳歲	
历	歷	歷	歷	lì calendar; experience; history; past; surpass; examine; observe; calculate; repeated; clear; distinct	lihk	歷厯	

止 14　歹 2-10

归	歸	歸	歸	gui　　　　gwài　　　　帰帰飯飯 return; come back to; revert; converge; submit; belong to
	歹			dǎi　　　　dáai bad; wicked; evil
	死			sǐ　　　　séi　　　　夘外虎危荒 to die; to kill; dead; inactive
	歿			mò　　　　mut die; alternative of to sink; have nothing (沒)
	殂			cú　　　　cou die; pass away
	殃			yang　　　　jeung misfortune; disaster; calamity; harm
	殄			tiǎn　　　　tin end; exterminate; extirpate
	殆			dái　　　　tóih perilous; dangerous; almost
	殉			xùn　　　　seun buried alive with the dead; die for a cause; martyrdom; pursue
	殊			shu　　　　syùh different; distinguished; special; extremely
	殍			piǎo　　　　piu　　　　莩 die of hunger; starve to death
	殖			zhí　　　　jihk produce; grow; spawn; increase
残	殘			cán　　　　chàahn ruin; cruel; disabled; damage; injure; kill
	殛			jí　　　　gik put to death; to imprison for life
殒	殞			yǔn　　　　wáhn die; perish; doom; loss; vanish; fall

172

歹 11-17　殳 5-11

殇	殤	殤	殤	shang　　seung tragedy; die young; national mourning
	殪	殪	殪	yì　　ji to die; kill; exterminate; take out; wipe out; murder
殚	殫	殫	殫	dan　　daan utmost; entirely; quite; exhaust; use up
殓	殮	殮	殮	liàn　　lim dress a corpse for burial; prepare body for coffin
殡	殯	殯	殯	bìn　　ban to lay a coffin in a memorial hall; to encoffin a corpse; to carry the body to the burial place or crematorium
歼	殲	殲	殲	jian　　chìm destroy; exterminate; annihilate
		殳	殳	shu　　syu (*an ancient Chinese weapon*); lance; handle of halberd
	段	段	段	dùan　　dyuhn section; paragraph; segment
	殷	殷	殷	yin　　yàn many; great; abundant; flourishing; blood red; sound of thunder; shake; tremble
杀	殺	殺	殺	sha　　saat kill; murder
壳	殼	殼	殼	ké　　hok shell; housing; husk; hull; skin; casing
毁	毀	毀	毀	hǔi　　wái ruin; destroy; damage; slander; defame
	殿	殿	殿	diàn　　dihn palace; temple; hall
殴	毆	毆	毆	ou　　ngàu beat; fight with fists; hit; strike; brawl
	毅	毅	毅	yì　　ngaih fortitude; firm; perseverance; resolve

173

毋 1-9　比 5　毛 7-11

毋			wú　　　mou do not, don't; not
母			mǔ　　　móuh mother; female
每			měi　　　múih lush; fluorish; each; every; often; frequently
毒			dú　　　duhk poison; poisonous; drug; toxin
毓			yù　　　juk give birth to; bring up; educate; nourish
比			bǐ　　　béi comparison; juxtaposition; contrast; metaphor; analogy; ratio; proportion
毖			bì　　　bei cautious; guard against; instruct; inform
毗			pí　　　bei help; assist; connect; adjoin; border
毛			máo　　　mòuh hair; wool; feather; small; gross
毫			háo　　　hòuh fine hair; measure of length (*100 micrometers*)
毯			tǎn　　　táam rug; carpet; blanket
毳			cùi　　　cheui fine fur or animal hair
毹			shu　　　syu rug
毽			jiàn　　　gin the shuttlecock used in the sport of jianzi
氅			san　　　saam shaggy; long haired

毛 12-18   氏 1-4   气 1-5

	氅	氅	氅	chǎng / chóng cloak; overcoat; down feathers
毡	氈	氈		zhan / jìn felt; felt underlay (*used in Chinese calligraphy*); blanket
	氍	氍		qú / keui fine wool cloth; a mat used by the emperor when worshipping gods
氏	氏	氏	氏	shì / sih clan; family; lineage; hereditary house; surname
	氐	氐	氐	di / dai foundation; root; Di (*an ethnic group*)
	民	民	民	mín / màhn people; citizens; folk; popular
	氓	氓	氓	máng / mong ruffian; hooligan; vagrant; rogue
气	氣	氣	氣	qì / hei steam; vapour; air; gas; weather; spirit
	氕	氕		pie / pit protium
	氘	氘		dao / dou deuterium
	氖	氖	氖	nǎi / naai neon (*chemistry*)
	氚	氚		chuan / chyun tritium
	氙	氙		xian / sin xenon
	氛	氛	氛	fen / fàn atmosphere; vapor
	氟	氟	氟	fú / fat fluorine

175

气 5-10　水 1

	氡	氡		dong radon	dung
气	氣	氣	氣	qì steam; vapor; air; gas; weather; spirit	hei
	氧	氧	氧	yǎng oxygen	yéuhng
	氦	氦	氦	hài helium	hoi
	氨	氨	氨	an ammonia	on
	氤	氤	氤	yin hanging fog; misty	jan
氢	氫	氫	氫	qing hydrogen	hìng
	氪	氪		kè krypton	hak
氩	氬	氬	氬	yà argon	aa
	氮	氮		dàn nitrogen	daam
	氯	氯	氯	lù chlorine	luhk
	氰	氰		qíng cyanide	ching
氲	氲	氲		yun heavy atmosphere; spirit of harmony; prosperity	wan
	水	水	水	shǔi water; liquid	séui 〰
	永	永	永	yǒng perpetual; eternal; permanent; forever	wíhng

水 1-3

凼	氹	凼		dàng　　tam　　　　氹壋 puddle; pool; pit; deep part of a river
	汆	氽		tǔn　　tan float; deep-fry; turn inside out
	氽	㕕		cuan　　chyun parboil; boil for short time; hot water kettle
	汀	汀	㓝	ting　　ting shore; sandbar; beach; bank; islet
	汁	汁	汁	zhi　　jàp juice; fluid; sauce
	求	求	裘	qiú　　kàuh beg; inquire; request; seek; look for
	汜	汜		sì　　chíh　　洍 creek; river branch; stagnant water
	汊	汊		chà　　cha　　汊 branching stream
	泛	汎	汜	fàn　　faan　　汛 氾 渢 drift on water; spread out; flood; overflow; superficial; extensive; general; broad; careless; reckless
	汐	汐	汐	xi　　sék morning and evening tides; night tides; ebb
	汔	汔		qì　　ngat to dry; nearly
	汕	汕	汕	shàn　　saan (of fish) moving; basket for catching fish; catch fish; rinse
	汗	汗	汗	hàn　　hohn sweat; perspiration; condensation on bamboo when put over fire; (internet slang) embarrassment
污	汚	汙	洿	wu　　wù dirty; stain; impure; polluted; rape; defile
	汛	汛	汛	xùn　　seun seasonal flood; high water; flood tides

汝	涿	涿		rǔ yúh you (*second-person pronoun*); Ru River (*a northern tributary of the Huai River*)
江	江	江		jiáng gòng Yangtze River; river
池	池	池		chí chìh pool; pond; moat; cistern
汞	氵頁	汞	澒鋉	gǒng hung mercury; quicksilver
沓	沓			tà daap repeated; crowded; wordy; talkative; diverse; meet; undisciplined; surge
汨	汨	汨	淠湏潣	mì mik Mi (*Luo*) River in Hunan; to sink
汩	汩			gu gwat confused; extinguished
汪	淮	淮		wang wong vast and deep (*bodies of water*); (*classifier for masses of liquids*); (*onomatopoeia*) woof; bark
沃	沃	沃		wò yùk fertile; lush; irrigate; soak
汰	汰	汰	汏汱溙	tài taai clean; wash; rinse; discard; eliminate through competition or selection; superfluous; excessive
汲	汲	汲		jí kap draw water from a well; imbibe; take in; absorb; guide; assist; nominate; recommend
汴	汴	汴		biàn bin name of a river in Henan
沖	衝	沖		chong chùng pour water on; rinse; flush; wash; infuse; rise; shoot up; (*of water*) dash against; collide with
沛	沛	沛		pèi pui abundant; full; copious; swift; sudden
沂	沂	沂		yí ji a river in southeast Shandong

	汶	汶	汶	wèn　　man　　浸	a river in Shandong
洶	汹	汹		xiong　　hung	(*of waves*) turbulent; tempestuous; roaring; tumultuous; agitated; violent
決	决	决	决	júe　　kyut　　决 吷	dredge; dig; burst; breach; determine; decide; contest; judge; execute; put to death; definitely; certainly
	汽	汽	汽	qì　　hei	steam; vapor; gas
	汾	汾	汾	fén　　fan	a river in Shanxi
	沁	沁	沁	qìn　　sam	soak into; seep in; percolate; ooze; exude; to draw water
	沅	沅	沅	yúan　　jyun	Yuan River in Hunan
	沆	沆	沆	hàng　　hong	ferry; fog; flowing; pool; lake
	沉	沉	沉	chén　　cam　　沈	sink; submerge; fall; subside; settle; suppress; neglect; hidden; weighty; dark; gloomy; deep; profound
	沌	沌	沌	dùn　　deun　　埻	disorderly; chaotic; ignorant
	沏	沏		qi　　chai	infuse; brew; to steep (*tea*)
	沐	沐	沐	mù　　muhk	bathe; shower; cleanse; receive
没	沒	沒	沒	méi　　muht	not; have not; disappear; drown; sink; die
	沔	沔	沔	miǎn　　min	(*archaic*) flood; overflowing; inundation
	沙	沙	沙	sha　　saa	sand; granular; hoarse; husky

水 5

沫	沫	沫	mò　　　　muht foam; suds; bubbles; froth
沬	沬	沬	mèi　　　　muih　　頮 湏 靧 the light of twilight; wash the face
沭	沭	沭	shù　　　　seut a river in Shandong
法	法	灋	fǎ　　　　faat law; rule; regulation; statute; standard; model; example; method; way; solution; imitate; emulate
沮	沮	沮	jǔ　　　　cheui stop; prevent; defeated; dejected; depressed; ruin; corrupt; glum; disheartened; threaten; intimidate
沱	沱		túo　　　　to small bay in a river; tearful; wailing; rainy; Tuojiang; Tuo River
沲	沲	沲	dùo　　　　- ripple; undulate
河	河	河	hé　　　　hòh　　蠹 river; canal; the Yellow River; (figurative) Milky Way
泅	泅	泅	qiú　　　　chàuh swim; swim under water; submerge; float; wade
泊	泊	泊	bó　　　　bok anchor a vessel; moor; berth; stay; (Cantonese) to park
油	油	油	yóu　　　　yàuh oil; grease; fat; lard; petroleum
治	治	治	zhì　　　　jih govern; regulate; administer; to treat; cure; kill; punish; discipline; research; socially stable
沼	沼	沼	zhǎo　　　　jiu marsh; pool; pond
沽	沽	沽	gu　　　　gu buy; sell; cheap; shoddy; poor quality
沾	沾	沾	zhan　　　　jìm overflowing; soak; moisten; benefit by association; influence; edify; stained; contaminated; touch; contact

沿	沿	沿	沿	yán yùhn 沿	follow; go along; continue
	況	況	況	kùang fong	condition; situation; furthermore
	沸	沸	沸	fèi fai	boiling
	泌	泌		mì bei	to secrete; seep out
	泐	泐	泐	lè lak 汋	write
	泓	泓		hóng wang	clear; deep pool
	泔	泔	泔	gan gam	water from washed rice; kitchen slops; swill
	泖	泖	泖	mǎo maau	still waters; a river in Jiangsu
	泗	泗	泗	sì si	nasal mucus; snivel; a river in Shandong
	泛	泛	泛	fàn faan	drift; float; careless; reckless; general; non-specific; extensive; flood
	泠	泠	泠	líng ling	cool; refreshing; mild; comfortable; sound of flowing water
	泡	泡	泡	pào póuh	foam; suds; bubbles; soak; steep; blister
	波	波	波	bo bò	waves; breaker; undulation
	泣	泣	泣	qì yàp	weep; sob
	注	注	注	zhu jyu	pour into; fill; concentrate; pay attention; (*gambling*) stake

泥	派	派		ní　　　　nàih mud; muddy; soil; sludge
泯	泯			mǐn　　　　man destroy; eliminate; perish; obliterate
泫	泫			xùan　　　　jyun weep; cry; shed tears; shine; glisten; flow; trickle
泮	泮			pàn　　　　pun disperse; fall apart; melt; dissolve
泱	泱	泱		yang　　　　ong great; expansive; boundless; agitated
泳	泳	泳		yǒng　　　　wing swim
泉	泉	泉		qùan　　　　chyùhn spring; fountain; an ancient coin
泰	泰	泰		tài　　　　taai　　太 large; great; extensive; extreme; greatest; excessive; exalted; honourable; excellent; safe; peaceful; stable
洄	洄			húi　　　　wui whirlpool; eddy
洋	洋	洋		yáng　　　　yèuhng multitudinous; vast; ocean; overseas; foreign; western; imported; modern; stylish; fashionable; novel; unusual
洌	洌	洌		liè　　　　lit pure; cleanse
洎	洎			jì　　　　gei until; when; soup; soak; pour water into a pot; arrive; reach
洗	洗	洗		xǐ　　　　sái wash; clean; purify; redress; to right; kill and loot; to sack; develop (*photo*); to clear; erase; (*cards*) to shuffle
洙	洙			zhu　　　　jyu a river in Shandong
洚	洚			jiàng　　　　gong flood; deluge; inundation

水 6

	洛			luò　　　lok a tributary of the Yellow River
	活			húo　　　wuht　　活 exist; life; lively; existence; provide food for; flexible; movable; adaptable; fluid
	洞			dòng　　　duhng hole; cave; opening; thorough; penetrating
	津			jīn　　　jèun ferry crossing; ford; bodily fluid; saliva; sweat; moisten
	洧			wěi　　　fui a river in Weishi county
泄	洩			xiè　　　sit leak; to vent; disperse; reveal; divulge; (archaic) waterfall
	洪			hóng　　　hùhng flood; vast; great
	洫			xù　　　gwik ditch; moat
	洮			táo　　　tou cleanse
	洱			ěr　　　nei a lake in Yunnan
	洲			zhōu　　　jàu continent; islet
	洳			rù　　　jyu damp; bog; marsh
	洵			xún　　　seun true; real; indeed
汹	洶			xiōng　　　hūng turbulent; tempestuous; roaring
	洹			húan　　　wun a river in Henan

洽	洽	洽	qià　　hàp in harmony with; discuss; blend with; penetrate; to cover
派	派	派	pài　　paai river tributary; group; faction; sect; branch; style; air; manner; send; dispatch; distribute; impose; censure
流	流	流	liú　　làuh　　㳅 汘 flow; current; drift; wander; class; grade; spread
浙	浙	浙	zhè　　chat　　淛 former name of the Qiantang River in Zhejiang
浚	浚	浚	jùn　　jeun dredge; deepen; unearth; enlighten; elucidate; deep; profound
浜	浜		bang　　bong small waterway; creek; stream; beach; sea coast
浞	浞		zhúo　　juk soak; steep in water
浣	浣		hùan　　wún wash; rinse
浦	浦	浦	pǔ　　póu river bank; shore
浪	浪	浪	làng　　lohng waves; billow; dissolute; stroll
浮	浮	浮	fú　　fàuh　　䍁 float; drift; swim
浩	浩	浩	hào　　houh vast; great; grand; numerous; abundant small port or harbor
浯	浯		wú　　ng name of a river in Shandong
浴	浴	浴	yù　　yuhk bath; bathe
海	海	海	hǎi　　hói sea; marine; ocean; overseas; abroad; abundance; infiniteness; numerous; unrestrained; casually

水 7-8

	浸	濅	濅	jìn jam 濅寖 soak; immerse
浃	浹	浹	浹	jia gaap saturate; drench; damp; wet
	浼	浼		měi mui 浼 request; ask a favor
	涅	涅	涅	niè nip 埿涅 black mud; melanterite; dye black; blacken; tattoo (*Buddhism*) abbreviation for nirvana (涅槃)
泾	涇	涇	涇	jing ging name of the Jing River
	涓	涓	涓	juan gyun brook; stream; tiny; negligible; choose; select; clean; to clear
	消	消	消	xiao siù dissolve; digest; consume; eliminate; vanish
	涉	涉	涉	shè sit ford a stream; wade across; experience; be involved
	涎	涎	涎	xián jin saliva
	涑	涑		sù chuk a river in Shansi
	涔	涔	涔	cén sam rainwater; stagnant water; flow together; overflow; stream; murky torrent; river in Shaanxi
	涕	涕	涕	tì tai tears; mucous
	涪	涪	涪	fú fau a river in Sichuan and Chongqing
	涫	涫		gùan gun to boil
	涮	涮		shùan syun rinse clean; cook or boil "hot-pot" style; to trick

185

涯	涯	涯	涯	yá — ngàaih shore; limit; border; horizon
液	液	液	液	yè — yihk liquid; fluid; sap; juice
涵	涵	涵	涵	hán — hahm soak; wet; immerse; tolerate; forgive; lenient; a culvert
涸	涸	涸	涸	hé — kok dry; dry up
涼	涼	涼	涼	liáng — lèuhng 凉 cool; cold; discouraged; disheartened
涿	涿	涿	涿	zhuo — duhk drip; dribble; trickle
淀	淀	淀	淀	diàn — din shallow water; swamp; precipitate; sediment
淄	淄	淄	淄	zi — ji a river in Shandong; black
淅	淅	淅	淅	xi — sik wash rice; (onomatopoeia) sound of rain; sleet
淆	淆	淆	淆	xiáo — ngaau confused; disarray; mixed up
淹	淹	淹	淹	yan — yím immerse; flooded; drown; soak; submerge; side; stay
淋	淋	淋	淋	lín — lam pour; drip; dribble; flow down at great speed; gush into; drench; soak
淌	淌	淌	淌	tăng — tong drip; trickle; flow down; alternative of to ford; wade (蹚)
淑	淑	淑	淑	shu — suhk virtuous; pure; kind-hearted; good; charming; beautiful; fair
凄	凄	凄	凄	qi — chai chilly; cold; sad; miserable

水 8

	淖	淖(篆)		nào　　　naau mud; slush
	淘	淘(篆)	淘(篆)	táo　　　tòuh wash; cleanse; eliminate; weed out; expend; consume; use up; naughty; mischievous
	淙	淙(篆)	淙(篆)	cóng　　chùhng gurgling sound of water
泪	淚	淚(篆)	淚(篆)	lèi　　　leuih tears; teardrop; weep; cry
	淡	淡(篆)	淡(篆)	dàn　　　daahm bland; tasteless; light in color; pale; indifferent; slack; dull; trivial; thin (liquid/gas); low in density
	淤	淤(篆)	淤(篆)	yu　　　jyu silt; mud; sediment; clog up
渌	淥	淥(篆)		lù　　　luk clear water; strain liquid
	淦	淦(篆)	淦(篆)	gàn　　　gam leak in a boat; a river in Jiangxi
净	淨	淨(篆)	淨(篆)	jìng　　jihng pure; clean; unspoiled; net weight; net amount
沦	淪	淪(篆)	淪(篆)	lún　　　leun sink into ruin; decline; fall; lost; submerged; small waves
	淫	淫(篆)	淫(篆)	yín　　　yim drench; decorate; spread; excessive; ostentatious; sinful; obscene; lewd; lascivious; depraved
	淬	淬(篆)	淬(篆)	cùi　　　cheui temper; dye; soak; quench; change; alter
	淮	淮(篆)	淮(篆)	húai　　wàaih a large river in China
	深	深(篆)	深(篆)	shen　　sàm　　　　溪 罙 deep; depth; profound; long time
	淳	淳(篆)	淳(篆)	chún　　jeun pure; honest; genuine; simple; unsophisticated

水 8-9

渊	淵	淵	淵	yuan　　　jyun　　　渕 䜌 開 囦 abyss; deep; gulf; profound
涞	淶	淶		lái　　　loi brook; ripple
	混	混	混	hùn　　　wan torrent; mix; blend; mingle; unite; make trouble; drift; muddy; careless; confused
浅	淺	淺	淺	qiǎn　　　chín shallow; light; easy; simple; superficial
	添	沾	添	tian　　　tìm　　　忝 add to; increase; give birth; again; more
	淼	淼		miǎo　　　miu wide expanse of water; flood; infinity
	清	清	清	qing　　　chìng　　　清 clear; clean; unstained; pure; distinct; apparent; upright; quiet; still
渌	淥	淥		lù　　　luk clear water; strain liquids
	渖	渖	渖	shěn　　　sam juice; liquid; water; leak; pour
	淠	淠		pì　　　pei luxuriant (of water plants)
	渚	渚	渚	zhǔ　　　jyu sandbank; islet
涣	渙	渙	渙	hùan　　　wun dissipate; dissolve; issue imperial edicts; overflowing; brimming; scattered; dispersed
	减	減	減	jiǎn　　　gáam reduce; decrease; subtract; diminish
	渝	渝	渝	yú　　　jyu change; go against; contrary; overflow; take off; remove; short for 重慶 (Chóngqìng)
	渠	渠	渠	qú　　　kèuih ditch; gutter; drain; canal; big

水 9

	游	游(篆)	游(篆)	yóu　　　yàuh　　遊沇 swim; travel
	渡	渡(篆)	渡(篆)	dù　　　douh cross a body of water; to ferry; carry; attend to; (*figurative*) to pull through difficult times
	渤	渤(篆)	渤(篆)	bó　　　but　　激 Bohai Sea; surging; swelling
	渥	渥(篆)	渥(篆)	wò　　　ak moisten; soak; great; deep; dye; enrich
涡	渦	渦(篆)	渦(篆)	wò　　　wò whirlpool; eddy; vortex; concavity
	澩	澩(篆)		xiè　　　sit dredge; get rid of; discharge; leak; disperse; a river in Shimen County, Hunan
测	測	測(篆)	測(篆)	cè　　　chàk estimate; measure; guage; predict; expect; speculate; suppose
	渭	渭(篆)	渭(篆)	wèi　　　wai a name of a river in Shanxi
	港	港(篆)	港(篆)	gǎng　　góng port; harbor; tributary of a large river or lake; airport; Hong Kong
	渴	渴(篆)	渴(篆)	kě　　　hot thirsty; parched; yearn; long for
	渺	渺(篆)	渺(篆)	miǎo　　miúh vague; remote; insignificant; small; tiny
浑	渾	渾(篆)	渾(篆)	hún　　　wahn turbid; muddy; whole; totally; flourishing, vigorous; still
	湃	湃(篆)	湃(篆)	pài　　　paai sound of waves; turbulent
	湄	湄(篆)	湄(篆)	méi　　　mei shore, bank
	湊	湊(篆)	湊(篆)	còu　　　chau gather; collect; assemble

水 9

	湍			tuan　　　tyun　　　湍 turbulent; rapids; rushing water
	湎			miǎn　　　min　　　酾 drunk
	湓			pén　　　pun　　　澎 overflow; rainstorm; shower; flowing water
	湔			jian　　　jin wash; cleanse; purge; rectify; refine
	湖			hú　　　wùh lake
	湘			xiang　　　seung a river originating from Dongting Lake; abbreviation of Hunan Province
	湛			zhàn　　　jaam deep; profound; clear; tranquil
浈	湞			cheng　　　cheng a river in Guangdong
	湟			húang　　　wong a river in Qinghai
	渣			zha　　　cha dregs; dross; sediment; particle; piece; scum; scrap
	渲			xùan　　　hyun render; add repeated washes of color
涌	湧			yǒng　　　yúng well up; gush out like water; rise; wave
	湫			qiu　　　jau pond; pool; puddle; cool; cold
	湮			yan　　　jan inundate; bury; cover up; sink; submerged; obscure; clog up; block
汤	湯			tang　　　tòng soup; hot or boiling water; broth; stock; decoction of medicinal herbs; dinner; meal

汍	潙	瀢		wéi gwai	a river in Shanxi
	溉	溉		gài goi	to water; irrigate; flood; wash
	滋	滋	滋	zi ji	grow; multiply; cause; increase
	溏	溏		táng tong	pond; pool; not hardened; semi-soft
	源	原	源	yúan yùhn	headwaters; headspring; fountainhead; source; origin; root
准	準	準	準	zhǔn jéun	rule; guideline; standard; follow; (prefix) quasi-, pene-, para-, sub-, semi-, demi-
	溘	溘	溘	kè hap	abruptly; suddenly; unexpectedly
	溢	溢	溢	yì yaht	overflow; excessive; brim over; flood; vigorous
	溫	溫	溫	wen wan	lukewarm; tepid; mild; soft; tender; gentle; irresolute; indecisive; weak; warm up; revise; review
	溜	溜	溜	liu lauh	slip; slide; slippery
沟	溝	溝	溝	gou kàu	ditch; gutter; drain
	溥	溥	溥	pǔ pou	big; great; vast; wide; extensive; widespread; universal
	溟	溟		míng ming	drizzling rain; dark; obscure
	漠	漠	漠	mò mohk	desert; aloof; indifferent
	溪	谿	溪	xi kài	stream; creek; brook; rivulet; unsophisticated

水 10

	溯	溯篆	溯古	sù / sou go upstream; go against a current; trace back; recall; retrospect
	溱	溱篆		qín / jeun an ancient river in Henan
	溲	溲篆		sou / sau 潚 urinate; soak; drench
	溴	溴篆	溴古	xiù / chau bromine
	溶	溶篆	溶古	róng / jung melt; dissolve
	溷	溷篆		hùn / wan toilet; privy; latrine; turbid; dirty; mixed; muddled; impure; confused
	溺	溺篆	溺古	nì / nihk 休夵 drown; indulge
	溻	溻篆		ta / taap wet
	溽	溽篆		rù / juk moist; humid; muggy; damp
	滁	滁篆		chú / chèuih a district in Anhui
	滂	滂篆	滂古	pang / pong torrential; rushing; pouring; flowing; gushing; spouting; spurting; voluminous
沧	滄	滄篆	滄古	cang / chong blue; dark green water; vast; cold; cool
灭	滅	滅篆	滅古	miè / miht extinguish; destroy; exterminate; obliterate
	滇	滇篆	滇古	dian / din a lake near Kunming, Yunnan
荥	滎	滎篆		xíng / jing a county in Henan; rising and dashing of waves

水 10-11

滑	滑	(seal)	(seal)	húa / waat; slip; slide; slippery; very smooth
	滓	(seal)	(seal)	zǐ / jí; sediment; dregs; residue
	滔	(seal)	(seal)	tao / tou; flood; inundate; overflow; rushing water; torrent
	滕	(seal)	(seal)	téng / tang; an ancient state in Shandong; water bursting forth
	滗	(seal)		běi / bei; drain; to filter
	漓	(seal)	(seal)	lí / lei; unkind; shallow
涤	滌	(seal)	(seal)	dí / dik; wash; sweep; clean up; eliminate; remove
滚	滾	(seal)	(seal)	gǔn / gwan; roll; turn; rotate; flash flood; boil; scalding hot; go away; to scram
沪	滬	(seal)	(seal)	hù / wu; weir; bamboo fence enclosure for catching fish; Shanghai
滞	滯	(seal)	(seal)	zhì / jaih; stagnation; sluggish; block up; obstruct; detain
渗	滲	(seal)	(seal)	shèn / sam; seep; soak through; ooze; infiltrate
	滴	(seal)	(seal)	di / dihk; drip; dribble; drop of liquid
浒	滸	(seal)		hǔ / wu; river bank; water's edge
	滹	(seal)		hu / fu; stream bank
满	滿	(seal)	(seal)	mǎn / múhn; full; filled; packed; complete; quite; brimming with; be full of; arrogant; conceited; satisfy

水 11

	演			yǎn　　　yín develop; evolve; deduce; perform; act; practice; exercise
渔	漁			yú　　　yùh fishing; fisherman
	漂			piao　　　più drift; float; bleach
	漆			qi　　　chàt　　　漆桼 paint; lacquer; varnish; lacquer tree; varnish tree; dark
	漉			lù　　　luk filter; strain; wet; dripping
	漏			lòu　　　lauh leak; drip; leave out; funnel; hourglass
渍	漬			zì　　　jik soak; steep; dye; stains; sodden; pickling; pickle
	漕			cáo　　　chòuh transport grain by water; canal transportation
沤	漚			òu　　　au prolonged soaking; prolonged suppression of feelings
汉	漢			hàn　　　hon Han dynasty; Chinese; fellow
涟	漣			lián　　　lin ripple; continuous weeping; a river in Hunan
	漤			lǎm　　　laam　　　灠 soak persimmons in hot water or lime water to remove tartness; soak vegetables in salt water to reduce flavor
	漩			xúan　　　syun eddy; whirlpool
	漪			yi　　　ji water ripples; swirling
	漫			màn　　　maahn　　　澫澷 overflow; brim over; flood; unrestrained; impromptu; spreading

	漭	㳽		mǎng　　mong vast; expansive
	濼	濼	濼	luò　　lok a river in northern Shandong
	漱	漱	漱	shù　　sau　　㵒 rinse; wash; gargle
涨	漲	漲	漲	zhàng　　jeung expand; increase; swell; rise
	漳	漳	漳	zhang　　jeung a river flowing from Shanxi to Hebei; a river in Fujian
	澴	澴		huàn　　waan indecipherable
渐	漸	漸	漸	jiàn　　jihm gradually; aggravate (an illness); worsen; dredge; open a path; omen; condition; prerequisite
	漾	漾	漾	yàng　　yeuhng overflow; swirl; ripple; tossed by waves
浆	漿	漿	漿	jiang　　jèung thick fluid; starch; broth; plasm; soy milk
颍	潁	潁		yǐng　　wing a river in Anhui
	溉			gài　　koi irrigate; water; pour
泼	潑	潑	潑	po　　put　　澄 splash; sprinkle; pour; wild; unreasonable; fierce; bold
	澄	澄	澄	chéng　　chìhng　　㵒 clear; clarify; to settle; purify
洁	潔	潔	潔	jié　　git clean; pure
	潢	潢		húang　　wong pond; lake; pool

水 12

	潘	潘	潘	pan / pun — rinsed rice water; a river that flows into the Han
潜	潛	潛	潛	qián / chìhm — submerged; hidden; conceal; secret; latent; stealthily; seclusion; concentrated effort
润	潤	潤	潤	rùn / yuhn — lubricate; moisten; enrich; freshen; sleek; profit
涧	澗	澗	澗	jiàn / gaan — brook, mountain stream 澗
	潦	潦	潦	lǎo / lóuh — flood; puddle; heavy rain; without care; neglect; unsuccessful
	潭	潭	潭	tán / taam — deep pool; lake; pit; deep; profound
	潮	潮	潮	cháo / chiùh — current; moist; rising tide; wet; popular; wave (figurative)
浔	潯	潯	潯	xún / chàhm — steep bank; waterside; Jiujiang city
溃	潰	潰	潰	kùi / kúi — overflow the banks; collapse; burst; defeated; routed; decompose; fester; ulcerate
	潲	潲		shào / saau — driving rain; sprinkle; spray; swill
	潸	潸	潸	shan / saan — tearful
	潺	潺	潺	chán / saan — sound of flowing water; trickle; flow
	潼	潼	潼	tóng / tung — high; lofty
涠	潿	潿		wéi / wai — still water
浇	澆	澆	澆	jiao / hiù — pour; to water; irrigate using a waterwheel; cast; mold

涝	澇	澇		lào　　　lòuh flood; inundated; torrent
	澈	澈	澈	chè　　　chit clear; understandable; thorough
	澉	澉		gǎn　　　gam wash
	澌	澌		si　　　si exhaust; disappear; wear out; drain dry
	澍	澍		shù　　　syu timely rain
	澎	澎	澎	peng　　　pàahng noise of rushing water; splatter; splash
渑	澠	澠	澠	miǎn　　　man a river in Shandong
	澡	澡	澡	zǎo　　　chou bathe; bath; tub
泽	澤	澤	澤	zé　　　jaahk marsh; pond; moist; damp; lustre; shine; grace; brilliant
	澧	澧	澧	lǐ　　　lai a river in northern Hunan
	澶	澶	澶	chán　　　sin still water; placid; tranquil
浍	澮	澮		kùai　　　kui ditch; gully; trench
	澳	澳	澳	ào　　　ou inlet; bay; dock; bank; (*abbreviation for Australia or Macau*)
	激	激	激	ji　　　gìk excite; stimulate; arouse
浊	濁	濁	濁	zhúo　　　juhk muddy; turbid

	澹	澹	澹	dàn　　　daam calm; indifferent to fame and fortune; quiet; tranquil; bland; insipid
	濂	濂	濂	lián　　　lim waterfall; a river in Hunan
浓	濃	濃	濃	nóng　　　nùhng thick; rich; dense
涩	澀	澀	澀	sè　　　sìk　　　澀 澁 涩 歮 rough; harsh; acrid; astringent; tart; obscure; stingy; miserly; hard to understand
湿	濕	濕	濕	shí　　　sàp wet; damp; moist; humid
泞	濘	濘	濘	nìng　　　ning mud; muddy; mire; stagnant
	濞	濞		pì　　　pei nasal mucus
济	濟	濟	濟	jì　　　jai　　　済 泲 help; aid; relieve; useful; cross a river; ferry
	濠	濠	濠	háo　　　hou moat; trench; ditch
	濡	濡	濡	rú　　　jyu immerse; moisten; wet; damp
涛	濤	濤	濤	tao　　　tou billows; large waves; sound of the sea
滥	濫	濫	濫	làn　　　laahm overflow; abusive; excessive; indiscriminate
	濮	濮	濮	pú　　　buk a county of Henan
	濯	濯	濯	zhúo　　　jok wash out; rinse; cleanse
潍	濰	濰	濰	wéi　　　wai a river in Shandong; a county in Shandong (Weifang)

滨	濱	顨	龖	bīn　　　bàn shore; coast; beach
溅	濺	濺	濺	jiàn　　　jin sprinkle; spray; spill; splash
泺	濼	濼		luò　　　lok a river in Shandong
滤	濾	濾	濾	lǜ　　　leui filter; strain; sieve
滢	瀅	瀅		yíng　　　jing　　瀅 clear and pure water; lucid; glossy
渎	瀆	瀆	瀆	dú　　　duk disrespectful; ditch; sluice; gutter; drain
泻	瀉	瀉	瀉	xiè　　　se purge; diarrhea
浏	瀏	瀏	瀏	liú　　　lau deep and clear water
	瀑	瀑	瀑	pù　　　buhk waterfall
沈	瀋	瀋	瀋	shěn　　　sám juice; liquid
濒	瀕	瀕	瀕	bīn　　　pan water's edge; be close to; border on; approach; near; on the verge of
濑	瀨	瀨	瀨	lài　　　laai swift current; rapids; (*Cantonese*) to pass urine or feces involuntarily
泸	瀘	瀘	瀘	lú　　　lou a river in Jiangxi
	瀚	瀚	瀚	hàn　　　hon vast; wide; extensive
	瀛	瀛	瀛	yíng　　　jing ocean; sea

水 16-19

沥	瀝			lì　　　　　lik drip; trickle; drip; drop; wine sediment; dregs
濴	濴			yíng　　　jing tiny stream; eddy; swirl
潇	瀟			xiao　　　siu　　　瀟 deep and clear water; a river in Hunan
	瀣			xiè　　　　haai sea mist; vapor
潴	瀦			zhu　　　　jyu　　　豬 猪 pool; pond; water hole
泷	瀧			lóng　　　lung raining; torrential; wet; soaked
潋	瀲			liàn　　　lim waves; ripples; trough; full of water; overflow
	瀹			yùe　　　jeuk boil; wash; cleanse; soak
	瀵			fèn　　　fan water overflowing from under the ground; spring
澜	瀾			lán　　　laan wave; ripple; overflowing
沣	灃			feng　　　fung a river in Shanxi
渿	灄			shè　　　sip a river in Hubei
	灌			gùan　　　gun irrigate; pour into; fill with liquid; install (software)
滩	灘			tán　　　tàan beach; shore; shoal
洒	灑			să　　　sá　　　洓 sprinkle; splash; scatter; throw

200

灏	灝	灝		hào　　　hou	vast; large; grand; expansive
	灞	灞	灞	bà　　　ba	a river in Shanxi
湾	灣	灣	灣	wan　　　wàan	bay; gulf; river bend
滦	灤	灤	灤	lúan　　　lyun	a river in Hebei
滟	灩	灩		yàn　　　jim　　灧	overflowing; billowing; wavy
	火	火	火	huǒ　　　fó	fire; flame; inferno; fiery; bright; brilliant; burn; torch; anger; rage; wrath
	灰	灰	灰	hui　　　fùi	gray color; ashes; dust
	灶	灶	灶	zào　　　jou	stove; furnace; kitchen
	灼	灼	灼	zhúo　　　cheuk	burn; scorch; clear; distinct; bright
	灸	灸	灸	jiǔ　　　gau	cauterize with moxa or mugwort; moxibustion
灾	災	災	災	zai　　　jòi　　　扏灾烖巛甾菑	disaster; misfortune; calamity
	炙	炙	炙	zhì　　　jek	roast; broil; toast; cauterize
	炅	炅		jiǒng　　　gwing	bright; shining; brilliant; heat
	炎	炎	炎	yán　　　yìhm	flame; blaze; hot; scorching
	炊	炊	炊	chui　　　cheui	cook; steam

炒	炒	炒		chǎo — cháau; pan fry; sauté; (*slang*) to fire; to sack
炔	炔			que — kyut; (*chemistry*) alkyne
炕	炕	炕		kàng — kong; brick oven; bake or dry by the heat of a fire; to toast
炮	炮	炮	砲	pào — paau; large gun; cannon; artillery; firecracker
炻	炻			shí — sehk; chinaware
炬	炬	炬		jù — geuih; torch; candle
炫	炫	炫		xùan — jyun; show off; boast; shine; dazzle; to puzzle; bravery
炯	炯	炯	烱	jiǒng — gwing; bright; brilliant; clear; obvious; flame; blaze
炱	炱		炲	tái — toi; soot
炭	炭	炭		tàn — taan; coal; charcoal
炳	炳	炳		bǐng — bing; bright; luminous; shine; remarkable; outstanding; prominent; striking; distinctive; ignite
炷	炷			zhù — jyu; wick of an oil lamp; candlewick; incense stick; burn incense
炸	炸	炸		zhà — ja; fry in oil; scald; explode
烀	烀			hu — fu; simmer
为	為	為	爲	wéi — wai; do; make; (*turn or transform*) into; to be; as (*the capacity of*)

	烈	煭	𤈷	liè　　　　lit fiery; violent; vehement; ardent; staunch; upright; merits; exploits; (*honorific*) person who dies for a cause
	烝	蒸		zheng　　jìng　　烝 rise; steam; vapor; many; numerous
乌	烏	烏	烏	wu　　wù　　乌 crow; raven; rook; black; dark
	烘	烘		hong　　hung bake; roast; dry by fire; (*figuratively*) showcase; highlight
	烙	烙	烙	lào　　lohk brand (*livestock*); to iron; pan-fry; burn; cauterize
	烤	烤	烤	kǎo　　hàau roast; bake; toast; dry using fire; heat oneself up
	烊	烊	烊	yáng　　jeung smelt; melt; molten
	烽	烽	烽	feng　　fung signal-fire; the tower where a signal-fire is lit
	焊	焊	焊	hàn　　hon weld; solder
烃	烴	烴		ting　　ting hydrocarbon
	焐	焐		wù　　ng warm something up
	焓	焓		hán　　ham enthalpy (*measurement of heat/energy content*)
	焉	焉	焉	yan　　yìn in; on; to; from; by; than; here; a kind of yellow bird found near the Yangtze and Huai Rivers
	烹	烹	烹	peng　　pàang cook; boil
无	無	無	無	wú　　mòuh　　橆 no; not; none; without

	焦	龘	覊	jiao　　jiù scorched; anxious	乾燋凋礁
	然	燃	顜	rán　　yìhn then; but; however; so; thus; in this manner; like this	燚
	煮	煑		zhǔ　　jyu cook; boil	煑
	焙	焙	焙	bèi　　bui bake; roast; heat over a fire	
	焚	焚	焚	fén　　fàhn burn	
	淬	淬	淬	cùi　　cheui to temper; to dye; soak; quench; change; alter	
	焯	焯		chao　　jeuk scald; blanch	
	焰	焰	焰	yàn　　yihm flame	焰 焰
	焱	焱		yàn　　yihm flames; spark	
茕	煢	煢		qióng　　king solitary; alone; desolate	惸煢
	煅	煅		dùan　　dyun refine; polish; forge metal; perfect one's skill	
炼	煉	煉	煉	liàn　　lihn refine; smelt; distill; condense	
	煊	煊		xuan　　hyun warm	
	煌	煌	煌	húang　　wong brilliant; bright; shining; luminous	
	煜	煜	煜	yù　　jap brilliant; bright; shining	

火 9-10

烟	煙	烟	烟	yan　　jin smoke; mist; vapour; tobacco (plant); tobacco product; cigarette; opium; soot; irritate the eyes by smoke
炜	煒	煒		wěi　　wai flaming; red and bright
	煤	煤	煤	méi　　mùih coal; charcoal
焕	煥	煥	煥	hùan　　wun flare; blaze; glowing; shining; lustrous; brilliant; radiate
	煞	煞	煞	sha　　saat kill; stop; halt; restrict
	煎	煎	煎	jian　　jìn pan fry; sauté
	煦	煦	煦	xù　　héui warm; kind; gentle; gracious; genial
	照	照	照	zhào　　jiu　　曌 曌 炤 shine; illuminate; reflect; contrast; compare; notify; sunlight; photo; license; according to; regardless
		煮	煮	zhǔ　　chú　　煮 cook; boil
	煨	煨	煨	wei　　wui simmer; stew
烦	煩	煩	煩	fán　　faan bother; to vex; troublesome
炀	煬	煬	煬	yáng　　yèuhng melt; smelt
		煸	煸	bian　　bin to stir-fry before broiling or stewing
		煲	煲	bao　　bou　　煲 包 (Cantonese) pot; kettle; cauldron; food in a pot; boil; cook; smoke a cigarette; do something for a long time
荧	熒	熒	熒	yíng　　jing luminous; fluorescent; shine; shimmer; dazzle

205

火 10-12

熙	煕	煕		xi / hei — bright; splendid; glorious 熙 熙 熙 熙 熙
熊	熊	熊		xióng / hùhng — bear (*mammal*); to scold; oppress; mean; malicious; merciless; (slang) a large, hairy man (*homosexual*)
熏	熏			xun / fàn — to smoke; fumigate 燻 爋
煽	煽	煽		shan / sin — fan a fire; incite; instigate; provoke
熄	熄	熄		xi / sìk — extinguish (*light or fire*); go out; (*Cantonese*) turn off; switch off
炝	熗	熗		qiàng / cheung — stir-fry (or boil in water or oil) then cook with a sauce
烨	燁	燁		yè / jip — bright; shine
	熔	熔	熔	róng / yùhng — melt; smelt; fuse; mold
	熠	熠		yì / jap — glow; smolder; bright; sparkling
	熟	熟	熟	shú / suhk — ripe; cooked; done; familiar with; acquainted with (*a concept*)
	熬	熬	熬	áo / ngòuh — cook over a fire; boil; extract something using heat; (*figurative*) endure; stay awake
热	熱	熱	熱	rè / yiht — hot; heat; fervent; kind; amiable; feverish; zeal; enthusiasm; trend; popular; fashionable; vogue
	熨	熨	熨	yùn / wahn — to iron; to press 尉 熨
	熵	熵		shang / seung — entropy
焖	燜	燜	燜	mèn / man — simmer; cook over a fire

火 12-13

炽	熾	熾	熾	chì　　chi intense fire; raging; flourishing; prosperous; burn
	熹	熹	熹	xi　　hei dim light; glimmer; warm; bright
	燃	燃	燃	rán　　yìhn burn; alight; ignite; to light; start (*debate*); raise (*hope*); (*slang*) awesome; cool; uplifting
	燕	燕	燕	yàn　　yin (*bird*) swallow; a swift
灯	燈	燈	燈	deng　　dang lamp; light; lantern
	燎	燎	燎	liáo　　liu burn; singe
炖	燉	燉	燉	dùn　　dahn to stew; simmer; braise; heat up
烧	燒	燒	燒	shao　　siù burn; cook; roast; fever
磷	燐	燐	燐	lín　　lèuhn phosphorus
	燔	燔		fán　　faan roast; burn
烫	燙	燙	燙	tàng　　tong hot; to warm; heat something up; burn; injury (*burn*); to blanch; (*Cantonese*) to iron
	燮	燮	燮	xiè　　sit harmonize; harmonious; to mediate
	燧	燧	燧	sùi　　seui flintstone; beacon fire; signal fire; torch
	燠	燠	燠	yù　　óu warm; warmth
毁	燬	燬	燬	hǔi　　wai blazing fire; burn up; burn down

207

	燥	燥	燥	zào　　　chou dry; parched; arid
灿	燦	燦	燦	càn　　　chaan brilliant; glittering; vivid; illuminating; bright; lustrous
烛	燭	燭	燭	zhú　　　jùk candle; taper; shine, illuminate
烩	燴	燴	燴	huì　　　wui ragout (*stew*); cook; braise; a Chinese dish consisting of fish grilled rare then thinly sliced
营	營	營	營	yíng　　　yìhng encampment; barracks; battalion; camp; activity; build; construct; operate; manage; seek; measure
烬	燼	燼	燼	jìn　　　jeun　　　尽 烬 cinders; ashes; embers; remnants
焘	燾	燾	燾	dào　　　dou illuminate everything (sun); cover; envelope; shelter; protect
	耀	耀	耀	yào　　　jiu　　　燿 shine; sparkle; dazzle; show off; flaunt; radiance; glorious
	燹	燹		xiǎn　　　sin fire; wild fire
	爆	爆	爆	bào　　　baau burst; explode; full; filled to capacity
烁	爍	爍	爍	shuò　　　seuk glisten; glimmer; bright; brilliant; hot; roast; broil
炉	爐	爐	爐	lú　　　lòuh fireplace; stove; oven; furnace
烂	爛	爛	爛	làn　　　laahn rotten; spoiled; decayed; decompose; broken; fragmented; shattered; bad; awful
	爝	爝		júe　　　jeuk (*archaic*) a torch made of bound reeds that was used for warding off evil spirits; a small torch or flame
	爨	爨		cùan　　　chyun cook; cooker; cookstove

	爪	爪	爪	zhuǎ　　jaau　　叉 claw; talon; paw; fingernail; (Hakka) to grab with claws
	爬	爬	爬	pá　　pàh crawl; creep; climb; ascend; get up; scramble
争	爭	爭	爭	zhéng　　jàng　　諍 dispute; fight; quarrel; contend; strive
	爰	爰	爰	yúan　　wun therefore; consequently
为	爲	爲	爲	wéi　　wàih　　為 do; make; (turn or transform) into; to be; as (the capacity of); (archaic) elephant
	爵	爵	爵	júe　　jeuk an ancient drinking vessel with three supporting feet; feudal title or rank; nobility
	父	父	父	fù　　fuh father
	爸	爸	爸	bà　　bà father; dad
	爹	爹	爹	die　　dè father; dad
爷	爺	爺	爺	yé　　yèh father; grandfather
	爻	爻	爻	yáo　　ngaau diagrams for divination; an I Ching hexagram
	爽	爽	爽	shuǎng　　song bright; clear; frank; straightforward; invigorating; joyful; healthy; deviate; mistake; violate; breach
尔	爾	爾	爾	ěr　　ji　　尒尔尒尔 you; your; so; this way; this; that; (flowers) exuberant; a final particle
	爿	爿	爿	pán　　baahn　　旁畔 piece of wood or bamboo (via chopping); thin piece; slice
床	牀	牀	牀	chúang　　chòhng bed; couch; bench

爿 13　片 4-15　牙　牛 2-5

墙	牆	牆	牆	qiáng　chèuhng wall
	片	片	片	piàn　pin slice; thin piece; flake; partial; incomplete; card; photo; movie; record; diaper
	版	版	版	bǎn　báan plank; printing blocks; form; page; edition; version; publishing
	牌	牌	牌	pái　pàaih board; plate; signboard; placard; sign; tablet; brand; trademark; nameplate; cards; dominoes; mahjong tile
	牒	牒	牒	dié　dip official document; certificate; credentials; genealogical records; indictment
	牖	牖	牖	yǒu　jau lattice window
牍	牘	牘	牘	dú　duk wooden tablets or bamboo slips for writing in ancient China; document; archive; letter; correspondence
	牙	牙	牙	yá　ngàh tooth; fang; ivory tusk
	牛	牛	牛	niú　ngàuh bovine; cow; bull; ox; buffalo; bison; yak; beef; stubborn; pigheaded; arrogant
	牟	牟	牟	móu　mau (*onomatopoeia*) moo; seek; obtain; exceed; increase; broad; great; longlasting; look; appearance; spear
	牝	牝	牝	pìn　pan female; ancient keyhole
	牢	牢	牢	láo　lou prison; jail; pen; enclosure; firm; fast; durable; dependable; reliable; animal used for sacrifice
	牧	牧	牧	mù　muhk to herd; tend; breed livestock; herdsman; herder; shepherd; govern; rule
	物	物	物	wù　maht thing; matter; everything excluding oneself; substance; content; choose; select; seek; look for
	牯	牯	牯	gǔ　gu bull; ox (*castrated*); cow

	牲	牲	牪	sheng　　sàng sacrificial animal; domestic animal
	特	特	犕	tè　　dahk　　牸 special; unique; distinguished; purposely; particular; very
	牾	牾		wú　　ng oppose; gore
	牿	牿		gù　　guk pen or shed for cattle
	犁	犂	犂	lí　　làih　　犂 plow; to plow
牽	牽	牽	牽	qián　　hìn pull; drag; involve; lead by the hand
	犀	犀	犀	xi　　sai rhinoceros; sharp; hard; well-tempered
	犄	犄	犄	ji　　gei animal horns; ox horn
	犍	犍		jian　　gin bullock; ox; castrate
	犏	犏		pian　　- yak; ox
	犒	犒	犒	kào　　hou to reward with food and drink; to feast; give a bonus; entertain victorious soldiers
犖	犖	犖	犖	lùo　　lok brindled ox; brindled in color
	犟	犟		jiàng　　giang　　勞 強 傚 stubborn
犢	犢	犢	犢	dú　　suhk calf; victim of sacrifice
牺	犧	犧	犧	xi　　hèi sacrifice; give up

犬 2-6

犬	犬	犬	quǎn / hyún dog
犯	犯	犯	fàn / faahn violate; offend; criminal; commit a crime
犰	犰		qiú / kau armadillo; Chinese mythological animal (犰狳)
犴	犴		àn / ngon　　　犴 狱 猂 狞 a wild dog from northern China; jail; prison
狀	狀	狀	zhuàng / johng form; appearance; shape; state; certificate; describe
狄	狄	狄	dí / dik the Di people; Zhou dynasty term for tribes from northern China; low servant
狂	狂	狂	kuáng / kòhng act aggressively; mad; insane; crazy; wildly arrogant; conceited; unruly; unrestrained; violent; ferocious
狃	狃		niǔ / nau adhere to; accustomed to; animal tracks
狍	狍		páo / paau roe deer
狗	狗	狗	gǒu / gau　　　豞 猗 dog; (derogatory) something or someone unpleasant
狐	狐	狐	hú / wùh fox
狒	狒		fèi / fei baboon
狎	狎	狎	xiá / haap be familiar with; disrespect
狙	狙	狙	jū / jeui ape; monkey; spy; watch for; to lie
狠	狠		hěn / hán cruel; hard-hearted; ruthless; vicious; severely; extreme

	狡	狡	狡	jiǎo　　gáau sneaky; cunning; sly; crafty
	狨	狨		róng　　yung marmoset
	狩	狩	狩	shòu　　sau winter hunting; imperial tour
	狳	狳		yú　　jyu armadillo; Chinese mythological animal (犰狳)
	狴	狴		bì　　bai a mythological tiger-like beast whose image was painted on prison doors; prison
	狸	狸	狸	lí　　lei raccoon dog; mangut; tanuki; leopard cat
	狷	狷	狷	juàn　　gyun rash; impetuous; impulsive; reserved; overcautious; upright (of character)
狭	狹	狹		xiá　　hahp narrow; limited; narrow-minded
	狼	狼	狼	láng　　lòhng wolf; cruel; pervert
	狺	狺		yín　　ngan snarling dogs
狈	狽	狽	狽	bèi　　bui legendary wolf-like animal with short forelegs and long hind legs; distressed; wretched; difficult position
	猁	猁		lì　　lei lynx
	猊	猊		ní　　ngai lion; wild beast; wild horse
	猓	猓	猓	guǒ　　gwo long-tailed monkey
	猜	猜	猜	cai　　chàai guess; doubt; conjecture; suspicion

犬 8-10

	猝			cù　　　chyut　　　卒 abruptly; suddenly
	猖			chang　　cheung mad; wild; reckless; unruly
	猗			yi　　　ji an exclamation of admiration
猙	猙			zheng　　jang hideous; fierce-looking; ferocious; a mythical red leopard-like creature with one horn
	猛			měng　　máahng ferocious; fierce; violent; bold; brave; powerful; vigorous; intense; (slang) awesome; spooky; suddenly
	猢			hú　　wu a monkey found in western China
	猥			wěi　　wai vulgar; low; cheap; wanton; obscene
	猩			xing　　sing ape; orangutan
	猱			náo　　naau　　夒 macaque
	猴			hóu　　làuh monkey; ape; naughty; clever
犹	猶			yóu　　yàuh　　猷 like; undecided; still; yet; as before; Jewish
	猷			yóu　　jau　　猶 plan; scheme; plan; plot; way
犸	獁			mǎ　　maa a long-tailed animal similar to a badger; mammoth
狲	猻			sun　　syun monkey
	猾			huá　　waaht sneaky; cunning; sly; crafty

214

犬 10-14

狮	獅	師		shi sì lion		師
	猿	猨	猨	yúan yùhn ape		猨
狱	獄	獄	獄	yù yuhk prison; jail; lawsuit; case		
	獐	獐	獐	zhang jeuhng water deer		
奖	獎	獎	獎	jiǎng jeung prize; reward; give an award to		獎 奨
	獒	獒		áo ngou mastiff; large dog		
	獗	獗	獗	jué kyut unruly; wild; violent; lawless		
	獠	獠		liáo liu to hunt; savage		
独	獨	獨	獨	dú duhk single; only; alone; independent		
	獬	獬		xiè haai a legendary 4-legged beast with a single curved horn on its head (like a unicorn)		
狝	獫	獫		xiǎn him a dog with a long snout		獵
狯	獪	獪		kùai kui cunning; sly; crafty		
	獯	獯		xun fan Scythian invaders in China during the Hsia dynasty		
狞	獰	獰	獰	níng ning ferocious; hideous; fierce-looking		
获	獲	獲	獲	hùo wohk obtain; catch; get; receive; win		

215

犬 15-19　玄 6　王 1-4

猎	獵	欜	欜	liè　　lihp to hunt
犷	獷	犷	犷	guǎng　　gwong fierce; rude; uncivilized
兽	獸	獸	獸	shòu　　sau beast; wild animal
獭	獺	獺	獺	tǎ　　chaat　　猯 otter
献	獻	獻	獻	xiàn　　hin offer; show; present; display
猕	獼	獼		mí　　mei macaque
	獾	獾		huan　　fun　　貛 badger
猡	玀	玀	玀	luó　　lo The Yi or Nuosuo (*aka Lolo*) are an ethnic group in China, Vietnam, and Thailand
	玄	玄	玄	xúan　　yìhn reddish black; dark; deep; profound
	率	率	率	shùai　　syùt frequency; rate; ratio
	王	王	王	wáng　　wòhng king; monarch; champion; emporer; grand; great
	玉	王	玉	yù　　yuhk　　禹 jade; nephrite; precious stone; gem; pure; beautiful; (*honorific*) your
	玎	玎		ding　　ding (*onomatopoeia*) jingling; tinkling
	玖	玖	玖	jiǔ　　gau black-colored jade; alternative form of nine (九)
	玟	玟	玟	mín　　man jade-like stone; beautiful jade; veins in jade

玫	玫	玫	méi　　　mùih rose; a type of gemstone	
玩	玩	玩	wán　　　wuhn　　販翫反仮 play; toy with; tease; have a good time; hang out	
玢	玢		bin　　　fan porphyrite	
玲	玲	玲	líng　　　ling tinkling of jade	
玳	玳	玳	dài　　　doi　　　瑇 tortoise shell	
玷	玷	玷	diàn　　　dim defect in jade; flaw in gem; flaw in character; blemish; stain	
玻	玻	玻	bó　　　bò glass	
珀	珀	珀	pò　　　paak amber	
珂	珂		ke　　　o inferior quality jade	
珈	珈		jia　　　gaa an ornament attached to a hairpin	
珊	珊	珊	shan　　　saan coral	
珍	珍	珍	zhen　　　jàn　　　鉁 precious; valuable; treasure	
珏	珏	珏	júe　　　gok two pieces of jade joined together	
珙	珙		gǒng　　　gúng precious stone	
珞	珞	珞	lùo　　　lok necklace	

217

珠	珠	珠		zhu jyù pearl; bead
珥	珥			ěr nei ear ornament; jade or pearl earring; stick; insert
珧	珧			yáo jiu 蚗 mother-of-pearl
班	班	班		ban bàan class; grade
琉	珋	琉		liú làuh 瑠 璃 sparkling stone; glazed; opaque
现	現	現	現	xiàn yihn present; current; appear; manifest; become visible; now
球	球	球		qiú kàuh ball; globe; sphere; orb
理	理	理		lǐ léih to polish jade; tidy up; manage; repair; prune; revise; review; reason; logic; truth; science; theory
琊	琊	琊		yá ye a place in eastern Shandong
琛	琛	琛		chen sam treasure; precious stone; gem
琢	琢	琢		zhúo doh gem-cutting; polish and cut jade
琥	琥	琥		hǔ fu amber
琦	琦	琦		qí kèih fine; admirable; extraordinary; jade; gem; precious stone; bizarre
琨	琨	琨		kun gwan high quality jade; jade ornament
琪	琪	琪		qí kèih fine jade; (connotation) flourishing flowers and plants; (metaphor) precious things

琬	琬			wǎn　　　jyun soft lustred jade; fine jade
琮	琮			cóng　　　chùhng rectangular jade vessel with circle-shaped interior
琰	琰			yǎn　　　jim glittering gems
琳	琳	琳		lín　　　lam beautiful jade; gem
琴	琴	琴		qín　　　kàhm lute; organ; piano
琵	琵	琵		pí　　　pei a Chinese guitar-like instrument; to pluck forward
琶	琶	琶		pá　　　paa a Chinese guitar-like instrument; to pluck backward
珐	珐	珐	珐	fà　　　faat enamel; cloisonné
珲	珲	珲	珲	hui　　　wan bright; glorious; splendid
玮	瑋	瑋		wěi　　　wai type of reddish jade; rare; valuable
	瑕	瑕	瑕	xiá　　　haa flaw; blemish; defect; spot
	瑚	瑚	瑚	hú　　　wu coral; virtuous person
	瑛	瑛	瑛	yīng　　　jing luster of jade; beautiful jade; jade-like stone
	瑜	瑜	瑜	yú　　　yùh a flawless gem or jewel
	瑗	瑗		yuàn　　　yun large ring of fine jade

王 9-11

	瑙	瑙	瑙	nǎo nou agate; cornelian
	瑞	瑞	瑞	ruì seuih jade token; good omen; auspicious
	瑟	瑟	瑟	sè sat ancient Chinese musical instrument
	瑁	瑁	瑁	mào mou 珇冒 fine piece of jade
琐	瑣	瑣	瑣	suǒ só trifling; petty; trivial; low
瑶	瑤	瑤	瑤	yáo jiu precious jade; fine; Yao (*Mien*) people
莹	瑩	瑩	瑩	yíng jing lustrous and transparent; jade-like stone; to polish; adorn
玛	瑪	瑪	瑪	mǎ maa agate; cornelian
	瑭	瑭	瑭	táng tong jade
琅	瑯	瑯	瑯	láng long white cornelian
	瑰	瑰	瑰	gui gwai 瓌瓌 rose; semi-precious stone; extraordinary; fabulous
	瑾	瑾	瑾	jǐn gan brilliance of gems; fine jade
	璀	璀	璀	cui chéui lustre of gems; glitter; shine
	璁	璁		cong chung jade-like stone
	璃	璃	璃	lí lèi glass; colored glaze

	璇	琁		xúan syun 璿 beautiful jade; star
琏	璉	槤		liǎn lin vessel for holding a grain offering
	璋	璋	璋	zhang jeung jade ornament
	璐	璐		lù lou beautiful type of jade
	璜	璜	璜	húang wong jade pendant of semi-circular-crescent shape
	璞	樸	璞	pú pok uncut jade
玑	璣	璣	璣	ji gei imperfect irregular pearl; ancient astronomical instrument
瑷	璦	璦	璦	ài oi fine quality jade; jasper
	璨	璨	璨	càn chaan luster of jade; beautiful jade; bright; beaming
	璩	璩	璩	qú keoi jade ring; earrings
环	環	環	環	húan wàahn ring; circle; loop; surround
	壁	壁	璧	bì bìk piece of jade
	璺	璺		wèn man crack (porcelain or stone)
玺	璽	璽	璽	xǐ saai 鉨 imperial seal; royal seal
琼	瓊	瓊	瓊	qióng king fine red jade; elegant; exquisite; beautiful; (abbreviation) Hainan

221

玉 16-19   瓜 5-17   瓦 6-11

珑	瓏			lóng　　　lung tinkling sound of a gem pendant; dragon-shaped jade
璎	瓔			ying　　　jing necklace made of precious stones
瓒	瓚			zàn　　　jaan impure jade; ceremonial ladle made of jade
瓜				gúa　　　gwà　　　苽 melon; squash; gourd
	瓞			dié　　　dit young melon
瓠				hù　　　wu calabash gourd; bottle gourd
瓢				piáo　　　piu a ladle made from a dried gourd
瓣				bàn　　　fáan melon seeds; flower petal; segment; section; piece; garlic clove
瓤				ráng　　　nong the flesh of fruits and nuts; (dialect) bad; weak
瓦				wǎ　　　ngáh　　　瓦 tile; earthenware
瓶				píng　　　ping　　　瓶 缾 bottle; vase; jar; flask
瓷				cí　　　chìh　　　甆 porcelain; chinaware
瓿				bù　　　bauh jar; pot; vase
甄				zhen　　　jan make pottery; potter's wheel; examine; discern; grade; distinguish; select the best
瓯	甌			ou　　　au small bowl; small cup; small tray (abbreviation) Wenzhou 溫州

瓦 11-13　甘 3-6　生 6-7　用 2

	甍	甍		méng　　　mang rafters supporting roof tiles
	甏	甏		bèng　　　paang　　瓨 罋 jar; jug; urn; pot
	甑	甑		zèng　　　jang cauldron; rice pot
	甓	甓		pì　　　　pik glazed tiles; bricks
瓮	甕	甕		wèng　　　ung pottery jar; urn
	甘	甘	甘	gan　　　　gàm sweet; voluntary; willingly
	甙	甙		dài　　　　doi glycoside
	甚	甚	甚	shèn　　　sàhm very; how; why; serious; extreme; extremely; considerably; exceed
	甜	甜	甜	tián　　　tim　　　甛 胡 酟 餂 sweet; sweetness; (*figurative*) pleasant; comfortable; happy
	生	生	生	sheng　　　sàng live; life; subsist; exist; grow; develop; give birth; to rear; offspring; student; fresh; raw; uncooked
产	產	產	產	chǎn　　　cháan give birth; produce; make; manufacture; product; property; wealth
	甥	甥	甥	sheng　　　sàng nephew; niece; son-in-law
	用	用	用	yòng　　　yuhng use; employ; operate; utility; usefulness; expenses; with; by; need
	甩	甩	甩	shuǎi　　　lat　　　㧿 swing; throw away; discard; fling; toss; abandon; leave behind; come off
	甫	甫	甫	fǔ　　　　fu begin; man; father; (*honorific*) title address for a man (*suffix placed after a man's courtesy name*)

甬	甬	甬	yong　　　jung bell handle; path with walls on both sides; ancient name for Ningbo, a city in Zhejiang, and its river
甭	甭		béng　　　búng don't; contraction of 不用; synonym of 不必
田	田	⊞	tián　　　tìhn field; farmland; cultivate
由	由	由	yóu　　　yàuh cause; reason; from; by
甲	甲	甲	jiǎ　　　gaap　　　𠇍 𠇍 鉀 armor; shell; nails (*finger and toe*); 1st heavenly stem (*1st day of a 10 day week - Shang Dynasty*)
申	申	申	shen　　　sàn　　　昌申伸 extend; stretch; explain; request; report; announce; express; repeatedly
町	町		tǐng　　　ting　　　圢 ridge or boundary between fields; field
男	男	男	nán　　　nàahm　　　叻伮 male; man; son; baron
甸	甸	甸	diàn　　　din suburbs of a capital; govern; crops
甾	甾		zi　　　zi steroid; calamity; disaster; ancient pottery for alcohol
畀	畀		bì　　　bei　　　鼻畁畀 give; pay; allow; let; for; to; by
界	界	界	jiè　　　gaai　　　阶 boundry; border; domain; realm; zone
畈	畈		fàn　　　faan farm; cropland; large field
畋	畋	畋	tián　　　tin　　　田佃甸 till land; cultivate; hunt
畎	畎	畎	quǎn　　　hyun　　　甽 drain between fields; irrigation; flow

	畏	𤰃	𤰞	wèi　　　　wai fear; dread
	畜	㽔		xù　　　　chuk　　畜 nourish; raise; rear; nurture; foster; cultivate; to submit; comply; tolerate; allow; to house; livestock
	留	畱	畱	liú　　　　làuh　　雷畄甾 stay; ask someone to stay; keep; save; retain; maintain
	畚	畚		běn　　　　bún bamboo or wicker scoop; dustpan
	畛	畛		zhěn　　　jan border; boundary; raised path
亩	畞	畮	畝	mǔ　　　　máuh　　畞畂畆畮 a Chinese acre
	畔	畔	畔	pàn　　　　buhn boundary path between fields; bank; shore; edge
毕	畢	畢	畢	bì　　　　bàt end; finish; conclude; completed; finished; all; completely
异	異	異	異	yì　　　　yih different; other; uncommon; unusual; special; strange; surprising; distinguish; separate; iso- (*isomers*)
	略	略	略	lùe　　　　leuhk　　畧 plan; strategy; summary; brief; omit; slightly; marginally; approximately; roughly; plunder; pillage
	畦	畦	畦	qí　　　　kwai unit of surface area; sections in a vegetable farm
画	畫	畫	畫	huà　　　　waahk　　畵画 paint; picture; draw; write; divide by a line
	番	番	番	fan　　　　fàan do in turns; take turns; repeat; (*classifier for actions, deeds*)
当	當	當	當	dòng　　　dang to bear; resist; should; suitable; when; be; same; this; when; during; undertake; to face; just at (*time or place*)
	畸	畸	畸	ji　　　　gei abnormal; odd, fractional, remainder

田 10-17　疋 7-9　疒 2-4

畅	暢	暢	暢	chàng / cheung — unimpeded; smooth; comfortable; uninhibited; unrestrained
	畿	畿	畿	ji / gei — imperial domain; area surrounding the capital
	疃	疃		tuǎn / tyun — hamlet; area outside a city
	疆	疆	疆	jiang / gèung — boundary; border; limit
畴	疇	疇	疇	chóu / chàuh — field; farmland; division in a field between different types of crops; to hill up; make equal
叠	疊	疊	疊	dié / dihp — pile up; fold up; stack
疋	疋	疋		pǐ / pàt — piece or bolt of cloth
疏	疏	疏		shu / sò — 疏 疎 踈 — careless; neglect; alienate; distant; sparse; dredge
疑	疑	疑		yí / yìh — doubt; question; suspect
疒	丬			chúang / chòhng — 疔 — sick
	疔	疔		ding / deng — boil; carbuncle; ulcer
	疙	疙	疙	ge / gaht — pimple; wart
	疚	疚	疚	jiù / gau — chronic disease; chronic illness; guilt; sorrow
	疝	疝	疝	shàn / saan — hernia; rupture
	疣	疣		yóu / jau — 肬 — wart; nodule; tumor; goiter; papule

疤	瘢		ba / ba — scar
疥	疥	疥	jiè / gaai — scabies
疫	疫	疫	yì / yihk — disease; epidemic; plague; pestilence
疲	疲	疲	pí / pei — weary; tired; exhausted; fatigued; weak
疳	疳	疳	gan / gam — rickets; childhood diseases
疴	疴		ke / o — malaria; illness; sickness; disease; pain
疵	疵		ci / chi — illness; defect; calamity; censure
疸	疸		dǎn / taan — jaundice; stomach disorders
疹	疹	疹	zhěn / chán — rash; measles; fever
疼	疼		téng / tang — pain; ache; sore; be fond of
疽	疽		ju / cheui — ulcer; carbuncle; abscess; gangrene
疾	疾	疾	jí / jaht — sickness; disease; illness
痂	痂	痂	jia / gaa — scab; crust
痃	痃		xúan / jin — indigestion; buboes; lymphatic inflammation
痄	痄		zha / jaa — mumps

疒 5-7

	病	病	病	bìng / bihng illness; sickness; disease; evil; fault; flaw; worry; anxious; criticize; denounce
	症	症	症	zhèng / jing indication or sign of disease; disease; illness
	痊	痊		quán / chyùhn cured; recovered
	痍	痍		yí / ji wound; bruise; sore
	痔	痔		zhì / ji hemorrhoids; piles
	痕	痕		hén / hàhn scar; mark; trace; (*Cantonese*) itchy
	痘	痘	痘	dòu / dauh smallpox; chickenpox
痉	痙	痙	痙	jìng / ging convulsions; fits; spasm
	痛	痛	痛	tòng / tung hurt; cause pain; sore; painful; ache; sorrowful; hate; abhor; lament; thoroughly; extremely
	痞	痞		pǐ / pei abdominal tumor; splenomegaly; hepatomegaly; stuffiness; dyspepsia; constipation; a ruffian
	酸	酸	酸	suan / syun sour; tart; acid; vinegar; grieved; sad; stingy; miserly; narrow-minded; pedantic; spoiled; rancid; ridicule
	痢	痢	痢	lì / leih dysentery
	痣	痣	痣	zhì / ji mole; birthmark
	痤	痤		cúo / chòh acne; carbuncle
	痦	痦		wù / ng mole

	痧	㾌		sha saa heatstroke; sunstoke; cholera; colic
	痰	㿏	痰	tán tàahm phlegm; sputum
	痴	㿉		chi chi foolish; stupid; dumb; silly; infatuated; crazy about; (*Buddhism*) delusion; ignorance
痺	痹	㿈		bì bei paralysis; numbness; rheumatism
	痼	㾓		gù gu chronic disease
	痿	㾊	痿	wěi wai paralysed; atrophy; impotent
	瘀	㿀	瘀	yu jyu bruise; hematoma; contusion
	瘁	㾽		cùi seui tired; weary; worn out; distressed; overworked
	痱	㾪	痱	fèi fai 痱 heat rash; prickly heat; ulcers
	麻	麻	麻	má màh 蔴 linen; flax; jute; short for measles (麻疹); pockmark; numb; senseless; paralysis; anesthesia
	瘃	㿃		zhú juk a painful, itchy swelling on the skin, caused by poor circulation in the skin when exposed to cold
	瘊	㾿		hóu hau wart; pimple
疯	瘋	㾼	瘋	feng fung insane; crazy; mad
	癩	㿗		là laat scabies; head-scald
疡	瘍	㿇	瘍	yáng jeung ulcer; sore; infection

疒 9-11

	瘐	瘐		yǔ　　　　yu die in prison from cold and hunger; treat with cruelty
瘓	瘓	瘓		huàn　　　wun numbness of the limbs
	瘕	瘕		jiǎ　　　　gaa asthma; disease of the bowels
疟	瘧	瘧		nüè　　　　ngohk malaria; intermittent fever and shivering
	瘙	瘙		sào　　　　sou scabies
瘗	瘞	瘞		yì　　　　ji bury; sacrifice; forfeit; inter; surrender
	瘠	瘠		jí　　　　jik barren; thin; lean; emaciated; poor; weak
疮	瘡	瘡	瘡	chuang　　chong sore; skin ulcer; boil; wound
	瘩	瘩	瘩	da　　　　daap　　　瘩 boil; scab
	瘢	瘢		ban　　　　baan scar; mark; fault; defect
	瘤	瘤	瘤	liú　　　　làuh tumor
	瘥	瘥		cúo　　　chòh sickness; illness; epidemic; plague; defect
	瘦	瘦	瘦	shòu　　　sau thin; skinny; slender; steep; reduce
	瘟	瘟	瘟	wen　　　wàn plague; epidemic; pestilence
	瘭	瘭		biao　　　biu felon; whitlow (infection under a fingernail or toenail cuticle)

疒 11-13

	瘰	瘰		luǒ lo scrofula; swelling
	瘳	瘳		chou chau heal; recover; convalesce
	瘴	瘴	瘴	zhàng chiòng malaria; quartan; mephitis; miasma; noxious vapor; pestilent vapor
	瘵	瘵		zhài jaai crippled; tubercular infection; wasting disease
	瘸	瘸	瘸	qúe ke limp; lame
瘘	瘺	瘺		lòu lau 瘦 atrium; anal fistula; recess; syrinx; tumor; sore
	瘼	瘼		mò mok sickness; distress
	癀	癀		húang wong anthrax of livestock; jaundice
疗	療	療	療	liáo liùh cure; heal; therapy; treatment
	癃	癃		lóng lung weakness; infirmity; retention of urine
痨	癆	癆	癆	láo lòuh 勞 撈 tuberculosis; pulmonary tuberculosis; (*traditional Chinese medicine*) internal injury via overstraining
痫	癇	癇		xián haan 癎 epilepsy; convulsions
瘅	癉	癉		dàn daan disease; suffering; distress; sick by overworking
	癌	癌	癌	ái ngàahm cancer; carcinoma
	癖	癖	癖	pǐ pik craving; disposition; addiction; habit; hobby; weakness for

231

疒 13-19   癶 4-7

疠	癘	癘篆	癘篆	lì　　　　lai sore; ulcer; boil; pestilence
	癜	癜篆		diàn　　　din erythema; leucoderma
瘪	癟	癟篆		biě　　　bit　　瘺 deflated; shrivelled; vexed
痒	癢	癢篆		yǎng　　　yéuhng itch; itching
疖	癤	癤篆		jié　　　jit pimple; sore; boil
癞	癩	癩篆	癩篆	lài　　　laai leprosy; favus; scabies; mange; coarse; uneven; rough; shoddy
癣	癬	癬篆	癬篆	xuǎn　　　sién　　癬 ringworm; tinea
瘿	癭	癭篆		yǐng　　　jing goitre; gall; burden; superfluous thing
瘾	癮	癮篆		yǐn　　　yáhn rash; addiction; craving; habit
痈	癰	癰篆		yong　　　jung carbuncle; sore; ulcer; abscess
瘫	癱	癱篆	癱篆	tan　　　taan paralysis; palsy; numbness
癫	癲	癲篆	癲篆	dian　　　din　　瘨 crazy; nuts; mad; display insane behavior
	癶	癶篆		bo　　　but two feet, legs
	癸	癸篆		guǐ　　　gwai 10th heavenly stem (*10th day of a 10 day week - Shang Dynasty*)
	登	登篆	登篆	deng　　　dàng go up; climb; mount; rise; publish; run (*story, ad, etc.*); succeed in imperial exams; ripen

发	發	發	發	fa faat 弢 發 發 彂 hair; send; issue; transmit; shoot; launch; depart; dispatch; expand; initiate; produce; become; express
	白	白	白	bái baahk white; clear; pure; plain; blank; easy to understand; bright; well-lit; eminent; prominent
	百	百	百	bǎi baak 佰百 hundred; numerous
	皂	皁	皂	zào jouh 皁 soap; black; short for acorn (皂斗) and Chinese honey locust tree - Gleditsia sinensis (皂荚)
	的	旳	旳	dì dìk (*possessive particle*); of; bright; clear; white; standard; criterion; archery target center; aim; objective; true
	皆	皆	皆	jie gàai all; each; every
	皇	皇	皇	huáng wòhng emperor; sovereign; ruler; superior; royal; imperial; magnificent
	皈	皈	皈	gu gwai follow; comply
	皋	皋		gao gou 皐皐皞皞 shore; land by a body of water; highland; marsh; pool; rice paddy; tall; high
	皎	皎	皎	jiǎo gaau white; bright; brilliant; clear
	皓	皓	皓	hào houh 暠皜 bright; luminous
	皖	皖	皖	wǎn wun alternative name for Anhui (安徽)
		晳	晳	xi sik pale skin; white
	皑	皚	皚	ái oi 溰 pure white; snow white
		皤	皤	pó po white; hoary; whitehaired; potbellied; paunchy

皮 5-10　皿 3-6

	皮			pí　　　pèih skin; leather; fur; hide; peel; rind; surface; outer; superficial
疱	皰			pào　　　paau blister; pimple; acne
	皴			cun　　　cheun chapped; cracked
皲	皸			jun　　　gwan chapped; cracked
皱	皺			zhòu　　　jau wrinkle; crease; fold
	皿			mǐn　　　míhng dish; vessel; utensil
	盂			yú　　　yùh spittoon; basin; cup; container for liquid
	盅			zhong　　　jùng small covered cup; handleless cup; goblet
	盆			pén　　　pùhn basin; pot; bowl; tub
	盈			yíng　　　yìhng fill; full; overflowing; surplus; excessive; waxing moon
	益			yì　　　yìk increase; add; gain; profit; benefit; advantage; more; further
	盍			hé　　　hap how; why; why not
	盎			àng　　　ong brimming; overflowing; an earthen vessel with a big belly and small mouth
	盒			hé　　　hahp box; case (*typically small with a lid*); (*classifier for boxes or cases*)
	盔			kui　　　kwai helmet; basin

	盛	盛	盛	shèng　　　sihng hold; contain; abundant; flourishing; prosperous
	盗	盗		dào　　　douh rob; robber; steal; theif; bandit; pirate
盏	盏	盏	盏	zhǎn　　　jáan small cup or container; (classifier for lamps and lanterns)
	盟	盟	盟	méng　　　màhng　　盟 treaty; alliance; pledge; oath; swear
尽	盡	盡	盡	jìn　　　jeuhn exhaust; finish; extreme; all
监	監	監	監	jian　　　gàam supervise; oversee; direct; prison; jail; incarcerate
盘	盤	盤	盤	pán　　　pùhn　　盤 tray; plate; dish; washbasin
	盥	盥	盥	gùan　　　gun wash; wash hands
卢	盧	盧	盧	lú　　　lou rice bowl; black; cottage; hut
荡	蕩	蕩	蕩	dàng　　　dong toss; swing; to rock; cleanse; wash away; root out; wipe out; slap with the palm of the hand
	目	目	目	mù　　　muhk　　目 圓 睅 eye; eyesight; look; view; to see; opinion
	盯	盯	盯	ding　　　ding　　丁 gaze upon; fix eyes upon; stare
	盱	盱		xu　　　heui open eyes wide; look up at; expand
	盲	盲	盲	máng　　　màahng blind
	直	直	直	zhí　　　jihk straight; linear; vertical; upright; straightforward; directly; honest; fair; deliberate

目 4-5

相	相	相	xiáng sèung evaluate by seeing for oneself; mutual; reciprocal; together; jointly; successively; towards; to; appearance
盹	盹	盹	dǔn deun doze; nap; nod
盼	盼	盼	pàn paan look; look forward to; hope for; long for; expect; bright; lucid
眄	眄		miǎn min look sideways; askance; ogle
眇	眇	眇	miǎo miu blind in one eye; minute; minuscule
眈	眈		dan daam stare; gaze intently
盾	盾	盾	dùn téuhn shield; support; assistance
省	省	省	shěng sáang omit; leave out; reduce, simplify; save, economize; palace; government department; province
眉	眉	眉	méi mèih eyebrows; brow
看	看	看	kàn hon see; watch; visit; predict
眩	眩	眩	xùan jyun dizzy; giddy; affected by vertigo; puzzled; bewildered
眙	眙		chì chi look; gaze at
眨	眨	眨	zhǎ jaap blink; wink; close one's eyes
眠	眠	眠	mián mìhn sleep; hibernate; dormant
真	真	真	zhen jàn true; genuine; actual; real; very; quite; clear; distinct; sharp; portrait; image; natural disposition

	眚	眚		shěng　　saang　　青 disease of the eye; cataract; eclipse; fault; negligence; disaster; catastrophe
	智	智		yuan　　jyun parched; inflamed eyelids
眦	眥	眥		zì　　jaai canthus (*the outer or inner corner of the eye, where the upper and lower lids meet*); eye sockets
	眷	眷	眷	juàn　　gyun　　睠 be fond of; take interest in; relatives
众	眾	眾	眾	zhòng　　jung　　乑 仦 people; multitude; masses; crowd; numerous; majority; various; common; everything; army; troops
	眵	眵		chi　　chi (*of the corner of the eye*) be injured or diseased; rheum (*substance in eyes after waking*)
	眭	眭		sui　　kwai evil look of deep-set eyes; a deep look
	眶	眶	眶	kùang　　hong eye-socket; rim of the eye; skin around the eyes
	眸	眸	眸	móu　　mau pupil (*eye*)
	眺	眺	眺	tiào　　tiu cast sidelong glances; look at; gaze
眼	眼	眼	眼	yǎn　　ngáahn eye; see; aperture; hole; opening; monitor; watch; sight; vision; (*classifier for actions of the eye*)
	睇	睇		dì　　tai　　眱睨 glance sideways; look; stare; look after; care for; believe; think
	睚	睚		yá　　ngaai corner of eye; stare
	睛	睛	睛	jing　　jìng eyeball; pupil
睁	睜	睜	睜	zheng　　jàng open one's eyes

目 8-9

睐	睐	睐	睐	lài / loi — sidelong glance; look sideways at; squint at
	瞧	瞧	瞧	sui / seui — stare at; look upward
	睥	睥	睥	pì / pai — look askance at, glare at
	睦	睦	睦	mù / muk — friendly; amiable; peaceful
	睨	睨	睨	nì / ngai — look askance at, glare at; squint
	睫	睫		jié / jit — eyelashes
	睬	睬	睬	cǎi / chói — to notice, pay attention to 保
	瞄	瞄	瞄	miáo / miùh — aim at; set sights on
	督	督	督	du / dùk — urge; supervise; direct
	瞀	瞀		mào / mau — look at closely; nearsighted; dim; indistinct vision
	睿	睿	睿	rui / haai — farsighted; astute; perspicacious; shrewd; clever; keen; emperor; Confucius
	睡	睡	睡	shùi / seuih — sleep; to sleep with (*sexual*); have the capacity for
	睹	睹	睹	dǔ / dou — see; look at; observe; witness 覩
	睽	睽	睽	kui / kwai — stare; to separate
	瞅	瞅		chǒu / cháu — see; look; gaze at 矁

238

	睾	帛	睪	gao　　　gou testicle
眯	瞇	眯	瞇	mi　　　mei squint; narrow one's eyes; take a nap; look furtively
	瞍	瞍		sǒu　　　sau blind person; senior; shrink
	瞌	瞌	瞌	ke　　　hahp nap; doze; sleepy
	瞎	瞎	瞎	xia　　　got blind; blindly; carelessly; at random
	瞑	瞑	瞑	míng　　　ming close one's eyes
	瞟	瞟	瞟	piǎo　　　piu glare at; cast a glance
瞞	瞞	瞞	瞞	mán　　　mùhn hide; conceal the truth; lie; conceal; deceive; eyes half closed
	瞠	瞠	瞠	cheng　　　chaang　　瞠 stare; gaze; glare at
	瞢	瞢		méng　　　mung alternative form of obscured eyesight (瞢); feel ashamed
	瞥	瞥	瞥	pie　　　pit quick glance; peek; glimpse
	瞧	瞧	瞧	qiáo　　　chiùh peep; to look at
	瞪	瞪	瞪	dèng　　　dahng stare; look at angrily; a hard look
	瞬	瞬	瞬	shùn　　　seun instant; wink; blink
	瞰	瞰	瞰	kàn　　　ham watch; spy; overlook; look down; bird's eye view

目 12-21　矛 4　矢 2-4

瞳 瞳 瞳			tóng　　　tung inexperienced; ignorant; pupil; sight; vision; view; see
瞵 瞵			lín　　　leun stare at
瞻 瞻 瞻			zhan　　　jìm look up; look forward to; look with reverence; observe
睑 瞼 瞼 瞼			jiǎn　　　gim eyelid
瞽 瞽			gǔ　　　gu blind; undiscerning
瞿 瞿			jù　　　geui shocked; scared; panic-stricken
矍 矍			júe　　　fok look about in fear or alarm
矗 矗			chù　　　chuk upright; erect; lofty
矚 矚 矚 矚			zhǔ　　　juk watch carefully; stare at; focus on
矛 矛 矛			máo　　　màauh spear; lance
矜 矜 矜			jin　　　ging to pity; feel sorry for; show sympathy
矢 矢 矢			shǐ　　　chí arrow; vow; to swear
矣 矣 矣			yǐ　　　yíh final particle expressing completion (*similar to* 了), or exclamation (*similar to* 啦)
知 知 知			zhi　　　jì know; knowledge
矧 矧			shěn　　　chán　　　弞 moreover; besides; also; gums; root of a tooth; big smile

240

矩	巨	矩		jǔ　　　géui carpenter's square; ruler (*measurement*); square (*shape*); rule; law
	矬	縒		cúo　　　chòh a dwarf, vertically short
	短	短		duǎn　　　dyún short (distance or time); brief; deficient; lacking; weakness; shortcoming; mistake
	矮	豫	矮	ǎi　　　ngái short; low; fall short
矫	矯	橋	矯	jiǎo　　　gíu to correct; rectify; straighten out; pretend; falsify; to fake; forge; pretentious; strong; powerful
	石	戶	石	shí　　　sehk rock; stone
	矸	肝		gan　　　gon cliff; rock; bottle
	矽	䂑	䂑	zi　　　jik silicon
	砂	淵	磯	sha　　　saa sand; gravel; gritty
	泵	愿	㲻	bèng　　　bam pump; to pump
	砉	砉		xu　　　waak　　　硅 noise of the separation of skin from bone
	砌	岮	幽	qì　　　chai build by laying bricks or stones; step (*stairs*); (*Cantonese*) to assemble
	砍	䃤	砍	kǎn　　　hám hack; chop; cut down; to fell; reduce; to weaken
	砑	岈		yà　　　ngaa grind; polish; roll with a stone roller
	砒	岘		pi　　　pei　　　砷 arsenic

石 4-6

研	研	研		yán　　yìhn　　研摰 grind; rub; sharpen; investigate; study; research
砘	砘			dùn　　deun stone roller; farm tool; roll a field with a stone roller after sowing
砝	砝	砝		fǎ　　faat balanced weight
砟	砟	砟		zhǎ　　ja　　磍 stone tablet; monument
砣	砣			túo　　to　　碢鉈 stone roller; heavy stone; steelyard weight; a plummet
砥	砥	砥		dǐ　　dai whetstone; grind; polish; smooth; level; even; temper oneself
砧	砧	砧		zhen　　jam　　碪椹 anvil; wood base for beating, chopping, cutting, or lethal sentence; stone base for beating clothes
砬	砬			lá　　laa large stone
砭	砭			bian　　bin acupuncture needle; stab with a needle; pierce; treat; cure; counsel; advise; constructive criticism
破	破	破		pò　　po break; smash; ruin; destroy; rout; banish; remove; dispel; cut open; expose
砰	砰	砰		peng　　paang sudden percussive sound; (*onomatopoeia*) bang
砷	砷	砷		shen　　san　　砒 arsenic
砸	砸			zá　　chap crush; press down; bash; smash; pound; throw; break; destroy; unsuccessful
砼	砼			tóng　　tung concrete
硐	硐			dòng　　dung cave; cavern; mine pit

	硒	硒		xi sai selenium
	硎	硎		xíng jing whetstone
硤	硤	硤		xiá haap a town in Hebei
砗	硨	硨		che che giant clam (*tridacna gigas*)
	硫	硫	硫	liú lau 瑠 sulfur
	硬	硬	硬	yìng ngaahng hard; stiff; inflexible; firm; obstinate; (*slang*) to become hard (an *erection*)
砚	硯	硯	硯	yàn jin inkstone
	硝	硝	硝	xiao siu niter (potassium nitrate); saltpeter; tan leather
	硼	硼	硼	péng pang boron; borax
	碉	碉	碉	diao diù room made of stone; stone house; pillbox (*military*)
	碇	碇		dìng ding 椗矴 anchor
	碌	碌	碌	lù luk busy; common; rough; uneven
	碎	碎	碎	sùi seui shattered; fragmented; shredded; small pieces; bits; fragments; talkative
	碑	碑	碑	béi bèi monument; stele
	碓	碓	碓	dùi deui pestle; pound with a pestle

石 8-10

碗	盌	䀜		wǎn　　　　wún　　　盌 瓮 椀 bowl
碘	㼐			diǎn　　　　din iodine
碚	陪			bèi　　　　pui suburb; (used in place names)
碰	䃔	䃔		pèng　　　pung　　　掽 踫 磅 collide; bump; knock; touch; meet by chance; bump into; test out; offend; provoke; (used in mahjong)
碧	碧	碧		bì　　　　bik green jade; blue-green
碟	𥓙			dié　　　　dihp　　　楪 疊 plate; dish; saucer; dish of food; disc; CD; DVD (classifier for dishes of food)
碡	𥓡			dú　　　　duk stone roller used to level fields
磁	磁	磁		cí　　　　chìh magnet; magnetic; alternative form of porcelain (瓷)
碣	碣	碣		jié　　　　kit large stone with inscriptions; stone tablet
硕	碩	碩	碩	shuò　　　sek large; big; great; eminent; beautiful; fine; firm; stable
砀	碭	碭		dàng　　　dong brilliantly colored stone with veined patterns; overflow; rush into; burst into; vast; expansive
	碲	碲		dì　　　　dai tellurium
	碳	碳		tàn　　　　taan carbon; carbon emission
	碴	碴		chá　　　　jaa chipped edge of a container; fragment (especially glass); fault; quarrel
确	確	確	確	què　　　　kok certain; sure; actual; real; true

244

码	碼	碼	碼	mǎ　　máh digit; number; programming code; pixelization; yard (*length*); (*colloquial*) to pile up; (*classifier for things*)
	碾	碾		niǎn　　nin grind; crush; stone roller
	磅	磅	磅	bàng　　bohng pound (*unit of mass*); weigh; scale; balance
	磉	磉		sǎng　　song stone plinth; pedestal; base of a pillar
	磋	磋	磋	cuo　　cho to polish; buff; scrutinize
	磕	磕	磕	ke　　hap　　礚 knock against a hard surface; dash against a stone; kowtow
	磊	磊	磊	lěi　　leui pile of rocks; pile up; large; tall; great
	磐	磐	磐	pán　　pun large rock; boulder
	磨	磨	磨	mó　　mòh grind; sharpen; rub; chafe; wear away; obliterate; wear out; wear down; erode; waste time; to pester
	磬	磬		qìng　　hing stone chimes; sounding stone; (*Buddhism*) inverted bell
砖	磚	磚	磚	zhuan　　jyun　　甎 brick; tile; paver
碛	磧	磧	磧	qì　　chik sand and gravel; rocks exposed at low tide; to crush
碜	磣	磣		chěn　　chám gritty; ugly
矶	磯	磯	磯	ji　　gei pound against a rock; submerged rock; jetty; eddy; levee; breakwater; enrage; offend
	磴	磴	磴	dèng　　dang stone steps on a cliff or hill; stone bridge with steps; stone bench; stone stool; (*classifier for steps or rungs*)

石 12-16

	磷			lín / leun phosphorus; ignis fatuus
	磺			huàng / wong sulphur; brimstone
硗	磽			qiao / kàuh stony soil; hard; infertile
	礁			jiao / jiu reef; shoal
	礅			dun / deun large stone; stone block
础	礎			chǔ / chó foundation; base; cornerstone
	礓			jiang / geung gravel; small stones
碍	礙			ài / ngoih　导 厚 obstruct; hinder; block; deter
	礞			méng / mung mineral
	礤			cǎ / chaat shredder; vegetable grater; grindstone; to rub; wipe; scrape
矿	礦			kuàng / kong　鑛 鉱 礦 卝 丱 mine; mineral; ore
砺	礪			lì / lai whetstone; to whet; sharpen; grind; sandstone
砾	礫			lì / lik gravel; pebbles
矾	礬			fán / faan alum; vitriol
砻	礱			lóng / lung　鑨 grind; hull (rice); whetstone

246

礴	礴		bó　　　bok fill; extend; to pound
示	示	示	shì　　　sih show; manifest; demonstrate; announcement
社	社	社	shè　　　séh association; company; society
祀	祀	祀	sì　　　ji　　　禩 worship; offer sacrifice
祁	祁	祁	qí　　　kèih large; numerous; ample; abundant; a county of Jinzhong, Shanxi
祈	祈	祈	qí　　　kèih pray; entreat; beseech; beg
祆	祆	祆	xian　　　hin the Zoroastrian god Ahura Mazda
祉	祉	祉	zhǐ　　　chí happiness; blessings; good luck; felicity
祚	祚	祚	zùo　　　jou throne; blessing; happiness
祖	祖	祖	zǔ　　　jóu ancestor; forebear; grandparent
祓	祓		fú　　　fat exorcise; remove evil; cleanse
秘	秘	秘	mì　　　bei mysterious; abstruse; secret; rare; scarce; to block; short for secretary (秘書) and Peru (秘魯)
祇	祇	祇	zhi　　　ji respect; look up to; revere
祛	祛		qu　　　keui　　　佉 expel; remove; disperse; dispel; exorcise
祐	祐		hù　　　wu blessing; happiness; prosperity

示 5-9

	祝	祝	祝	zhù　　jùk congratulate; express good wishes; exalt; chant; enchantment; incantation; mantra
	神	神	神	shén　　sàhn God; deity; spirit; soul; mind; expression; magic; psychic; countenance; supernatural
	祟	祟	祟	suì　　seui evil spirit; evil influence; haunt; cause mischief; sneaky; furtive
	祠	祠	祠	cí　　chìh ancestral temple; ancestral hall; offer sacrifice; spring sacrifice
	祢	祢		nǐ　　nei you; thou; (commonly written improperly as: 祢)
	祥	祥	祥	xiáng　　chèuhng luck; good omen; auspicious
	祧	祧		tiao　　tiu ancestral temple; ancestral hall
	票	票	票	piào　　piu ticket; coupon; bill; voting slip; bank note
	祭	祭	祭	jì　　jai make offerings to; sacrifice to; worship; ceremony where one offers a sacrifice to their ancestors
视	視	視	視	shì　　sih　　　眡 眎 眂 see; look; view; sight; inspect; examine; regard; consider; visit
	祺	祺	祺	qí　　kei auspicious; propitious; good luck; felicity; euphoria
禄	祿	祿	祿	lù　　luhk prosperity; blessing; happiness
	禁	禁	禁	jìn　　gam avoid; stop; prohibit; prevent; bear; endure; restrain; withstand; torment; torture; (Cantonese) durable
	禊	禊		xì　　hai purification ceremony
祸	禍	禍	禍	huò　　woh　　　旤 misfortune; disaster; calamity

	福	福	福	fú	fùk
				blessing; to bless; happiness; prosperity; good fortune	
祯	禎	禎	禎	zhen	jing
				lucky; auspicious; good omen	
御	禦	禦	禦	yù	yuh
				resist; defend; hold out against	
	禧	禧	禧	xǐ	hei
				favourable luck; good fortune; auspiciousness; blessings; congratulations	
禅	禪	禪	禪	chán	sim
				Buddhist doctrine; dhyana; deep meditation; contemplation; philosophical	
礼	禮	禮	禮	lǐ	láih
				ceremony; manner; politeness; etiquette; gift	
祷	禱	禱	禱	dǎo	tóu
				pray; prayer	
	禳	禳	禳	ráng	jèuhng
				pray or sacrifice to expel disaster; expel; drive off	
	内	内		róu	jau
				trample; animal track	
	禹	禹	禹	yǔ	jyu
				Yu the Great, an ancient king associated with the global flood and the foundation of the Xia dynasty	
	禺	禺	禺	yú	jyu
				area; district; time before noon (9–11 a.m.); a type of red-eyed monkey with a long tail	
	禽	禽	禽	qín	kàhm
				birds; fowl; poultry	
	禾	禾	禾	hé	wòh
				grain; rice plant; cereal	
	秃	秃	秃	tú	tùk
				bare; bald; stripped; hairless	
	秀	秀	秀	xiù	sau
				shoots of a plant; ear; bear fruit; blossom; beautiful; elegant; graceful; outstanding; extraordinary	

禾 2-5

	私	私	和	sí / sì self; personal; private; selfish; illegal or secret goods; smuggle; stealthily; secretly
籼	秈	秈		xian / sin non-glutinous long grain rice; indica rice
	秉	秉	秉	bǐng / bing grasp; hold; maintain; control; authority; preside over; persist; persevere
	秋	烁	秌	qiú / chàu autumn; fall
	科	科	科	ke / fò sort; class; kind; law; regulation; imperial examination; article; clause; rules; department; examine; punish
	秕	秕		bǐ / bei 粃 empty or unplump grain; bad; evil
	秒	秒	秒	miǎo / miúh tiny; insignificant; tip; end; instantly; (*classifier for time (seconds) and measuring angles or latitude/longitude*)
	秘	祕	祕	mì / bei mysterious; abstruse; secret; rare; scarce
	秭	秭		zǐ / ji billion; trillion; numerals that refer to various numbers, such as 10^9, 10^{12}, and 10^{24}
	租	租	租	zu / jòu rent; hire; charter; lease
	秣	秣	秣	mò / mut fodder; horse feed
	秩	秩	秩	zhì / diht rank; order; orderly; sequence; decade
	秫	秫		shú / sèuht glutinous grain/millet/rice; glutinous sorghum
	秤	秤	秤	chèng/píng ching/pìhng scale; scales steelyard
	秦	秦	秦	qín / chèuhn state of Qin; Qin dynasty

	秧	秧	秧	yang　　　yeung rice seedling; sprout; shoot; vine; stalk; transplant seedlings; grow; cultivate; raise
	移	移	移	yí　　　yìh　　　　　　 迻迻迻 move; change place; shift
	稂	稂		láng　　　long weeds; grass
秆	稈	稈	稈	gǎn　　　gón grain stalk; straw
税	税	稅	稅	shùi　　　seui tax; duty
	程	程	程	chéng　　　chìhng weights and measures; rules; regulations; standard; quota; time; schedule; agenda; journey; procedure
	稀	稀	稀	xi　　　hèi rare; unusual; scarce; sparse; dilute; thin
	稍	稍	稍	shao　　　sáau little bit; slightly; rather
	稠	稠	稠	chóu　　　chàuh dense; thick; viscous; often; frequently
	稔	稔	稔	rěn　　　nam to ripen; ripe; mature; crop; harvest; accumulate; know; usually; (classifier for crops grown in a year)
	稞	稞	稞	ke　　　fo wheat; barley; grain ready for grinding
	稗	稗		bài　　　bai　　　　　 稗 tare; barnyard grass; barnyard millet; insignificant; unofficial
	稚	稚	稚	zhì　　　jih young; immature; childish
种	種	種	種	zhǒng　　　júng　　　　 種 seed; kernel; cereal; clan; ethnic group; ethnicity; race; species; breed; kind; sort; type; guts; grit
称	稱	稱	稱	cheng　　　ching weigh; call; name; say; state; commend; name; address; appellation; designation; reputation

禾 10-17

	稷	稷	稷	jì　　　　jik foxtail millet (*setaria italica*); cereal god; minister of agriculture
	稼	稼	稼	jià　　　　gaa sow grain; grain sheaves
	稻	稻	稻	dào　　　douh　　　稲 paddy; rice
	稿	稿	稿	gǎo　　　góu　　　稾 draft; sketch; manuscript; grain stalk; straw; looks; appearance
	稽	稽	稽	ji　　　　kài　　　乩 examine; investigate; to check; delay; procrastinate; recriminate; argue; dispute
	穆	穆	穆	mù　　　　muk standing grain; right side position; reverent; solemn; majestic; peaceful; honest; profound and lasting
穌	穌	穌		su　　　　sou　　　鯂 Jesus; revive; rise again; resuscitate
积	積	積	積	ji　　　　jìk store up crops; accumulate; amass
颖	穎	穎	穎	yǐng　　　wihng clever; gifted; ear of grain; sharp point
	穗	穗	穗	suì　　　seuih　　　穂 繐 ear of grain; spike; tassel; fringe; snuff of a candle; elegant
穑	穡	穡	穡	sè　　　　sik harvest; reap; crops; cultivate; ear of grain; farming; farm labor; connect; hook together
秽	穢	穢		huì　　　　wai dirty; filthy; unclean; immoral; obscene; disgusting; revolting; infect
稳	穩	穩	穩	wěn　　　wán stable; firm; solid; steady; secure; (*slang*) excellent; amazing; fantastic
获	穫	穫	穫	huò　　　wohk harvest; reap
	穰	穰		ráng　　　jeung stalk of grain; bumper harvest

穴 2-7

穴	(seal)	(seal)	yúe / yuht — cave; cavern; hole; lair; (*Chinese medicine*) acupoint
究	(seal)	(seal)	jiù / gau — reach the limit; exhaust; intensive study; research; investigate; scrutinize; after all; actually; in fact
穸	(seal)		xi / jik 夕 — tomb; grave; death
穹	(seal)	(seal)	qióng / kung — elevated and arched; high and vast; dome structure; sky; fill up; to exhaust
空	(seal)	(seal)	kong / hùng 工 空 — empty; hollow; void; spacious; vast; quiet; still; secluded; fictitious; atmosphere; cosmos; in vain
穿	(seal)	(seal)	chuan / chyùn — penetrate; pierce; pass through; to string; to wear; to put on; (*placed after a verb to indicate fulfillment*)
窀	(seal)		zhun / jeun — tomb; grave; to bury; sepulcher; internment; resting place
突	(seal)	(seal)	tu / daht — suddenly; abruptly; dash forward; protrude; stick out
窄	(seal)	(seal)	zhǎi / jaak — narrow; tight space; narrow-minded
窆	(seal)		biǎn / bin — to bury; put a coffin in a grave; grave; tomb
窈	(seal)	(seal)	yǎo / jiu — profound; far-reaching; dim; gloomy; obscure; secluded; refined
窕	(seal)	(seal)	tiǎo / tiu — slender; quiet; modest; charming
窒	(seal)	(seal)	zhì / jaht 疾 — stop up; obstruct; smother; stutter; stammer; halting movements
窖	(seal)		jiào / gaau — pit; cellar; store in a cellar
窗	(seal)	(seal)	chuang / chèung — window　窓 窻 恖 囱 囪 囧

253

穴 7-13

	窘	窘	窘	jiǒng　　　kwan embarrassed; hard-pressed; distressed; awkward
	窟	堀		ku　　　gwat cave; hole; cellar; underground
	窠	窠	窠	ke　　　fo bird's nest in a cave; nest; simple dwelling; empty space; pit; hole
窥	窺	窺	窺	kúi　　　kwài to spy; watch; peep
窦	竇	竇	竇	dòu　　　dau hole; burrow; cavity; sinus
	窨	窨		yìn　　　jam　　　培 cellar, storeroom
	窬	窬		yú　　　ju hole in a wall
窭	窶	窶		jù　　　geui poor; rustic; impoverished
窝	窩	窩	窩	wo　　　wò den; cave; nest; hiding place
洼	窪	窪	窪	wa　　　wà hollow; swamp; depression; pit
窑	窯	窯	窯	yáo　　　yiùh　　　窑 窰 brick kiln; furnace; coal mine pit
穷	窮	窮	窮	qióng　　　kùhng to exhaust; constrained; limited; put to an end; dire straits; poor; destitute; impoverished
	窳	窳		yǔ　　　jyu dirty; useless; shoddy; lazy; corrupt; weak; powerless; cracked; flaw
窍	竅	竅	竅	qiào　　　kiu opening; hole; aperture
窜	竄	竄	竄	cuàn　　　chyún escape; run away; revise; edit; expel

穴 10-17　立 5-15　竹 2-3

窃	竊	竊	竊	qiè　　　　sit to steal; thief; acquire illegitimately; usurp; secretly; stealthily　竊竊竊
	立	立	立	lì　　　　lahp stand; establish; immediate
	站	站	站	zhàn　　　jaahm　　佔赶跕 firm stance; station; stop; halt
	章	章	章	zháng　　jèung chapter; section; composition; structure; regulations; constitution; seal; stamp; badge; medal; emblem
	竟	竟	竟	jìng　　　gíng finish; to end; finally, after all, at last; surprisingly; unexpectedly; whole; entire
	竦	竦		sǒng　　　sung revere; respect; honor; be in awe of
	竣	竣	竣	jùn　　　jeun complete; finish; abdicate
	童	童	童	tóng　　　tùhng child; juvenile; young servant
	靖	靖	靖	jìng　　　jing stable; peaceful; tranquil; pacify; stabilize; govern; administer; to plan; think of; respectful; prudent
	端	端	端	duan　　　dyun hold something level; end; tip; beginning; start; upright; erect; wipe out; destroy completely
	竭	竭	竭	jié　　　kit to shoulder; dry up; to drain; exhaust; use up
竞	競	競	競	jìng　　　gihng compete; strive; vie; contend
	竹	竹	竹	zhú　　　jùk bamboo; a musical instrument made of bamboo
	竺	竺	竺	dǔ　　　duk India; bamboo
	竽	竽	竽	yú　　　jyu an ancient Chinese wind instrument

255

竹 3-5

竿	竿		gan　　gon bamboo pole; stick; rod
笆	笂	㭔	ba　　baa bamboo fence
笈	粉		jí　　kap box for storing books; books; to carry
笊	㲵		zhào　　jaau ladle; strainer; colander; bamboo skimmer
笏	笏		hù　　fat a tablet held by someone having authority used to take notes or for ceremonial purposes
笑	笑	茓	xiào　　siu smile; laugh
笙	笙	笙	sheng　　saang a musical Chinese wind instrument consisting of vertical pipes made of reeds
笛	笛		dí　　dehk　　篴 flute; fife; whistle
笞	筈	筈	chi　　chi bamboo rod used for beatings
笠	笠	笠	lì　　lap Asian conical bamboo hat; (Cantonese) basket; cover with; slip on; put on a hat; flatter; to fool
笥	筍		sì　　ji hamper; wicker basket
笱	筍		gǒu　　gau basket for trapping fish; bamboo trap for fishing at the opening of a weir
笨	笨	笨	bèn　　bahn　　体 体 heavy; cumbersome; strenuous; stupid; foolish; silly; clumsy; awkward; inner part of bamboo
笪	笪		dá　　daat　　担 coarse mat made of bamboo; (Cantonese) (classifier for areas)
第	笫		zǐ　　dai mat made of thin bamboo strips; sleeping mat

	第	篇	箟	dì daih order; sequence; number; grade; degree
	笮	筰	筰	zé jaak narrow; confined; tight; boards that support roof tiles
	笳	笳		jia gaa reed leaf whistle
	笸	笸		pǒ po flat basket for grain
	筇	筇		qióng kung a species of bamboo; bamboo staff
	符	符	符	fú fùh tally; symbol; sign; mark; charm; to match; agree with; correspond; coincide
	笄	笄		ji gai 笄 hairpin; fifteen year old girl
	筅	筅		xiǎn sin bamboo brush; halberd
	策	策	策	cè chaak plan; scheme; to whip; urge
笔	筆	筆	筆	bǐ bāt pen; pencil; brush; write; compose
	等	等	等	děng dáng arrange bamboo slips neatly; rank; grade; class; sort; kind; type; equate; and so on
	筋	筋	筋	jin gàn tendon; sinew; muscle
	筏	筏	筏	fá fat raft
	筐	筐		kuang hòng bamboo basket or chest
	筒	筒	筒	tǒng túng section of thick bamboo; hollow tube; pipe; barrel; can; tin

竹 6-8

	筌	筌		qúan　　chyùhn bamboo fish trap
	答	答		dá　　daap　　畣 畗 reply; answer; promise; repay; requite
	筘	筘		kòu　　kau reed
笋	筍	筍	箰	sǔn　　séun bamboo shoot; tender; young
	筠	筠	筠	yún　　wan bamboo skin
笕	筧	筧	筧	jiǎn　　gaan bamboo water pipe
	筲	筲		shao　　saau bamboo basket for rice; bucket; pail
	筮	筮		shì　　sai divination with stalks of plants; divining rod
	筱	筱		xiǎo　　siu　　篠 篆 dwarf bamboo; thin bamboo
	筵	筵		yán　　yìhn banquet; feast
	筷	筷	筷	kùai　　faai chopsticks
节	節	節	節	jié　　jit　　卩 日 knot; node; joint; segment; link; integrity; spirit; ambition; particulars; season; festival; etiquette
	箅	箅		bì　　bei grate; grating; grid
	算	算	算	sùan　　syun　　祘 count; calculate; figure; plan; consider; guess; estimate; approximate; arrange; design
	箐	箐		jing　　jing to draw (pull) a bamboo bow or crossbow

	箕	箕	箕	jī　　　gei　　　甘笂笰匯 tool for removing chaff; dustpan
箏	箏	箏		zhēng　　jàng zither; guzheng (古箏)
箋	箋	箋	箋	jiān　　jīn annotation; commentary; stationery; letter; correspondence; note; memo
	箍	箍		gū　　　ku hoop; ring; to bind; encircle; (classifier for money: yuan; dollar; buck)
	箔	箔		bó　　　bok foil; tinsel; foil paper burnt as an offering; screen made of reeds; bamboo tray for raising silkworms
	管	管	管	guǎn　　gwún wind instrument; pipe; tube; duct; writing brush; manage; control; (classifier for tube-shaped objects)
	箬	箬		ruò　　　jeuk　　　篛 bamboo sheath; leaf of a type of bamboo; a type of disease in bamboo
	箭	箭	箭	jiàn　　jin arrow; a type of bamboo
	箱	箱	箱	xiáng　　sèung chest; box; trunk
	箸	箸	箸	zhù　　　jyu　　　楮筯 traditional Chinese word for chopsticks (now called 筷子 in most dialects for taboo reasons)
	篁	篁	篁	huáng　　wong bamboo forest; bamboo grove
范	範	範		fàn　　　faahn pattern; model; scope; boundary; rule; law
	箴	箴	箴	zhen　　jam admonish; warn
	篆	篆	篆	zhùan　　syun seal script; seal; official stamp
	篇	篇	篇	pian　　pìn chapter; page; piece of writing; sheet of paper; (classifier for written items and book leaves)

竹 9-11

篋	篋	篋		qiè　　　haap suitcase; case; rattan box
	篌	篌	篌	hou　　　hau ancient musical instrument; harp; type of bamboo
筑	築	築	築	zhù　　　jùk construct; build
笃	篤	篤	篤	dǔ　　　dùk sincere; honest; seriously ill
	篙	篙	篙	gau　　　gou pole used for punting boats; barge pole
	篚	篚		fěi　　　fei round or oval covered bamboo baskets with short legs
	篝	篝		gou　　　gau bamboo basket; bamboo frame; bamboo cage
	篡	篡	篡	cùan　　　saan usurp; seize
	篦	篦		bi　　　bei fine-toothed comb; comb with a fine-toothed comb; an ornament on ancient flags
	篪	篪		chí　　　chìh　　　笔箎篪鬵 bamboo traverse close-ended flute (*used in Chinese court music*)
	蓑	蓑		suo　　　so rain coat made of straw or grass
筛	篩	篩	篩	shai　　　sai sieve; strainer; sifter; to pour; warm up; rain; to strike a gong
	篥	篥		lì　　　leut bugle; horn
笔	篳	篳		bì　　　bat wicker or bamboo fence
	篷	篷	篷	péng　　　fùhng awning; sail; covering

		篾	𥳑	𥰠	miè / mit thin bamboo strips, splints, or slats; strips of reed or plant stalks (*i.e., sorghum*)
箦	簀	𥳑		zé / jaak bed mat; mat
	簇	𥳑	𥳑	cù / chuk swarm; crowd together; cluster; pile; (*classifier for bunched objects*)
	簌	𥳑	𥳑	sù / chuk sieve; dense vegetation; rustle; falling flower petals; flutter
篓	簍	𥳑	𥳑	lǒu / lau deep bamboo basket; gross; 144; twelve dozen
	簏	𥳑		lù / luk basket; box
	籪	𥳑		duàn / dyun bamboo fish trap
	簋	𥳑		guǐ / gwai square-shaped bamboo basket (*holds grain used in sacrifices and feasts*)
箪	簞	𥳑	𥳑	dan / daan round bamboo basket for cooked rice
	簟	𥳑		diàn / dim bamboo mat
简	簡	𥳑	𥳑	簡 jiǎn / gáan bamboo slip; letter; epistle; simple; uncomplicated; succinct; concise; brief; treat coldly; neglect; select
	簪	𥳑	𥳑	zan / jaam hairpin; clasp; wear in one's hair
篑	簣	𥳑	𥳑	kuì / gwai bamboo basket for carrying dirt and soil
	簦	𥳑		deng / dang large long-handled umbrella used for street stalls
	簧	𥳑	𥳑	huáng / wòhng reed (*of a musical instrument*); spring coil; sweet words

竹 12-19

箫	簫	簫	蕭	xiao　　siù　　簫 箾 籲 鑰 an ancient vertical end-blown bamboo flute (洞簫); pan-pipes
	簷	簷	簷	yán　　jim eaves of a house; brim
签	簽	簽	簽	qian　　chìm to sign; endorse; slip of paper
	簸	簸	簸	bǒ　　bo to winnow; toss; dustpan; to bump; to jerk; jolt
帘	簾	簾	簾	lián　　lim screen; blind; curtain
	簿	簿	簿	bù　　bouh book; account book; register; notebook
	籀	籀	籀	zhòu　　jau read; recite
	籍	籍	籍	jí　　jihk record; register; list; hometown; census
篮	籃	籃	籃	lán　　làahm basket; hamper; sports ring, basketball basket
筹	籌	籌	籌	chóu　　chàuh chip; tally; token; plan; stratagem; prepare; means; raise money or funds
箨	籜	籜		tùo　　tok bamboo sheath, bamboo shoots
籁	籟	籟		lài　　laai bamboo flute; pipe; various sounds
笼	籠	籠	籠	lóng　　lùhng bamboo implement for holding soil; bamboo animal cage; coop; bamboo container
签	籤	籤	籤	qian　　chim inscribed bamboo slips used for divination or drawing lots; slender pointed piece of wood; sticker; label
笾	籩	籩		biàn　　bin　　𩫡 bamboo container for food

篱	籬	籬	籬	lí　　　　　lei	bamboo fence
箩	籮	籮	籮	lúo　　　　lò	bamboo basket
吁	籲	吁	吁	yù　　　　jyu	appeal; plead; call
	米	米	米	mǐ　　　　máih	uncooked rice
	籽	籽	籽	zǐ　　　　ji	seed
	粉	粉	粉	fěn　　　　fán	powder
	粑	粑		ba　　　　ba	cake-like food
	粒	粒	粒	lì　　　　làp	particle; granule; (*classifier for small, round objects*)
	粘	粘		zhan　　　jìm	sticky; glutinous; adhere; to stick
	粕	粕	粕	pò　　　　pok	lees; dregs; sediments left after distilling liquor
	粗	粗	粗	cú　　　　chòu　　麤䉛鹿犐	rough; crude; coarse; vulgar; thick; bulky
	粞	粞		xi　　　　sai	ground rice; rice husk
	粥	粥	粥	zhou　　　jùk	congee; rice gruel; porridge; weak; feeble
妆	粧	粧	粧	zhuang　　jòng	beautify; dress up; adorn; use makeup
	粟	粟	粟	sù　　　　sùk	foxtail millet (*Setaria italica*); grains; paddy; unhulled rice; (*Cantonese*) short for corn (粟米)

米 6-10

粱	𥹆		zi　　　chi millet; grain offered in ritual sacrifice
粳	稉		jing　　　gang non-glutinous rice
粤	粤	粵	yùe　　　yuht Canton; Yue people; Baiyue people; Guangdong; Guangxi
梁	粱	粱	liáng　　　leung millet; exquisite staple food; sorghum
粲	粲		càn　　　chaan white rice; bright; radiant; beautiful; splendid; smiling; beaming; numerous
粽	糉	粽	zòng　　　júng leaf-wrapped rice dumpling
粹	粹	粹	cùi　　　seuih pure; unadulterated; essence
潾	粼		lín　　　leun limpid stream; clear
精	精	精	jing　　　jìng polished rice; energy; spirit; vigor; semen; fine; refined; pure; clear; bright; smart; proficient; expose
糈	糈		xǔ　　　seui sacrificial rice; rations; pay
糊	䊀	糊	hú　　　wùh porridge; paste; apply a mixture; muddled; unclear; (slang) to flop; (Cantonese) victory in mahjong
糅	糅		rǒu　　　nau blend; mix
糕	餻	糕	gao　　　gou cake; pastry
糖	糖	糖	táng　　　tòhng sugar; candy
糗	糗		qiǔ　　　chau cooked wheat or rice; become mush; (Mandarin) embarrassing; embarrassment

				Mandarin	Cantonese	Notes
	糙	糙	糙	cao	chou	unhusked; unshucked; unpolished rice; rough; coarse; crude; rude; impolite; unrefined
糁	糁	糁	糁	sǎn	saam 糁	rice grain; grain; cook soup with rice; disperse; paint
	糟	糟	糟	zao	jòu	sediment; alcohol dregs; preserve food in alcohol or alcohol dregs; awful; messy; terrible; rotten; decayed
	糠	糠	糠	kang	hòng 穅	chaff; husk; bran
	糨	糨		jiàng	jeung	starch; paste
	糜	糜	糜	mí	mei 縻 靡	mushy; rotten; to waste; spend extravagantly; damage
粪	糞	糞		fèn	fan	excrement; feces; dung; manure; apply manure to; clear away
粮	糧	糧	糧	liáng	lèuhng	food; grain; provisions; (Cantonese) salary
	糯	糯	糯	nùo	noh 稬 稌	glutinous; sticky; glutinous rice
粝	糲	糲		lì	lai	unpolished rice; brown rice
籴	糴	糴		dí	dek	buy in grain; alternative form of wash (滌)
粜	糶	糶		tiào	tiu	sell; sell grain
	糸	糸	糸	mì	mik 纟	thin silk
	系	系	系	xì	haih	system; faculty; department; college major; categorised as; classified as; be part of
纠	糾	糾	糾	jiu	dáu	丩乚乢弓纠 investigate; inspect; to correct; entwine; gather; amass; assemble; inform against; inform on

糸 3-4

纣	紂	紂	紂	zhòu — jau Shang dynasty emporer; crupper (*part of a saddle*)
纡	紆	紆	紆	yu — jyu winding; twisting; turning; depressed; downcast; entwine; wind around; encircle; hang; wear
红	紅	紅	紅	hóng — hùhng red; popular; in vogue
纪	紀	紀	紀	jì — géi to record; annals; historical account; age; century
纥	紇	紇	紇	hé — gat knot; inferior silk
纨	紈	紈		wán — jyun white silk; fine silk
约	約	約	約	yue — yeuk bundle up; bind; rope; cord; restrain; limit; meeting; appointment; treaty; covenant; frugal; concise; poor
纫	紉	紉		rèn — yahn sew; to thread (*a needle*); to stitch; to string
纺	紡	紡	紡	fǎng — fóng spin cloth; reel; weave
纷	紛	紛	紛	fén — fàn disturb; perturb; dispute; argument; disorderly; scattered; numerous
纹	紋	紋	紋	wén — màhn lines; stripes; streaks; wood grain; wrinkle; pattern; tatoo
纳	納	納	納	nà — naahp admit; receive; accept; take on; bring into; enjoy; delight in; give payment; sew stitches
纽	紐	紐	紐	niǔ — náu 鈕 button; frog-knot; handle; knob
纾	紓	紓		shu — syu loosen; relax; relieve
纱	紗	紗	紗	shá — sà gauze; muslin; yarn

纯	純	純	純	chún　sèuhn　屯 pure; clean; simple; unmixed; sincere
纰	紕	紕	紕	pi　pei spoiled silk; hem of a dress; mistake; error; carelessness
纸	紙	紙		zhǐ　jí　帋 paper; currency; banknote; bill
级	級	級	級	jí　kàp step; level; class; grade; rank
纭	紜	紜	紜	yún　wan numerous; disorderly; confused
	紊	紊	紊	wěn　man disorderly; chaotic; dysfunctional; confused
	素	素	素	sù　sou plain; simple; white; vegetarian food; formerly; normally; element; (*math*) prime
	索	索	索	suǒ　sok　索 rope; cable; climb; clamber; (*mahjong*) bamboo tile; search; inquire
扎	紮	紮	紮	zhá　jaat　紥 tie; bind; be stationed; be quartered (*of troops*); (*Cantonese*) be promoted in rank
绅	紳	紳	紳	shen　san ancient Chinese girdle worn by officials; to tie; bind; gentleman
	累	累	累	lěi　léuih pile up; accumulate ; repeated; numerous; involve; tired; continuous; persistent; overlap; grow
细	細	細	細	xì　sai small; little; tiny; fine; young
绂	紱	紱	紱	fú　fat silk ribbon; sash
统	統	統	統	tǒng　túng rule; govern; command; control; unite; unify
绁	紲	紲	紲	xiè　sit　緤 bridle; halter; to contract; draw in; reduce; shorten

绀	紺	紺	紺	gàn　　　gam purple; violet; blackish red
绋	紼	紼	紼	fú　　　fat heavy rope; rope of a bier (*a stand on which a coffin containing a corpse is placed before burial*)
绍	紹	紹	紹	shào　　　siuh continue; introduce; carry on
绐	紿	紿		dài　　　toi cheat; fool; pretend
绌	絀	絀	絀	zhúo　　　jyut deep red; sew; stitch; dismiss
终	終	終	終	zhong　　　jùng　　　終丹羿 end; ending; termination; (*euphemistic*) to die; reach the end of life; entire; all; eventually; finally
组	組	組	組	zǔ　　　jóu organize; section; group; weave; unite; team; (*classifier for sets and series*)
绊	絆	絆	絆	bàn　　　bun fetter; shackle; trip; stumble; hinder; restrain; (*figuratively*) trap
	紫	紫	紫	zǐ　　　jí purple; violet
	絮	絮	絮	xù　　　seui (*archaic*) coarse silk floss; cotton; cotton wadding; catkin; long-winded; bored; fed up; sick of something
绗	絎	絎		háng　　　hong sew with long stitches
结	結	結	結	jié　　　git knot; tie; solidify; to finish; bind; join; connect; to bear (*fruit*); stammering; stuttering
绝	絕	絕	絕	júe　　　jyuht break off; sever; discontinue; superb; peerless; matchless; extreme; utmost; absolutely; die; despair
绔	絝	絝		kù　　　fu pants; trousers; breaches
绞	絞	絞	絞	jiǎo　　　gaau twist; to wring; to wind; intertwine; grind; (*classifier for skeins of wools or thread*)

络	絡	絡	絡	luò　　　lok enmesh; wrap around; web; net
给	給	給	給	jǐ　　　kàp give; for; for the benefit of; to; by
绚	絢	絢	絢	xùan　　　hyun brilliant; gorgeous; shine; embellish; adorn; dazzle
绒	絨	絨	絨	róng　　　yùhng wool fabric; silk; cotton; velvet
丝	絲	絲	絲	sí　　　sì　　　絲絲糸 silk; items made from woven silk; fine thread; thin strip; trace; speck; (*music*) stringed instrument
绛	絳	絳		jiàng　　　gong crimson
绦	絛	絛		tao　　　tou　　　縧縚 silk braid; sash
绢	絹	絹	絹	jùan　　　gyun a stiff silk fabric that is thick and tough
绡	綃	綃		xiao　　　siu raw silk
绑	綁	綁	綁	bǎng　　　bóng to tie; bind; fasten
绨	綈	綈		tí　　　tai a kind of heavy silk; coarse greenish black pongee (*a soft unbleached silk from silkworms that feed on oak leaves*)
绥	綏	綏	綏	súi　　　sèui soothe; appease; pacify
经	經	經	經	jing　　　gìng　　　巠 control; manage; engage; principal; doctrinal; classical; norm; regulation; (*Chinese medicine*) blood vessel
绠	綆	綆		gěng　　　gang a well rope
综	綜	綜	綜	zong　　　jung assemble; synthesize; sum up; administer; proficient; to crease; (*classifier for threads or hair strands*)

糹 8

绿	綠	綠	綠	lù green; healthy	luhk
绻	綣	綣		quǎn affectionate; solicitous	hyun
	綦	綦		qí dark grey; variegated; superlative	kèih
绶	綬	綬	綬	shòu a silk ribbon attached to an official seal or medal	sau
维	維	維	維	wéi fasten; tie up; link; connect; maintain; preserve; safeguard; thick rope; cord; nook; recess; net; law	wàih
绯	緋	緋		fei red; scarlet; dark red; crimson	fei
绾	綰	綰	綰	wǎn string together; bind up	waan
绸	綢	綢	綢	chóu silk cloth; satin damask	chàuh 紬
纲	綱	綱	綱	gang guiding principle; essential part; program; outline; (taxonomy) class; main rope of a fishing net	gòng
网	網	网	網	wǎng net; web; network; enclose; internet	móhng 网 網 罒 丹
缀	綴	綴	綴	zhùi stitch up; connect; join; decorate	jeui
纶	綸	綸	綸	lún green ribbon or tassel; fishing line; thick rope; silk thread; emperor's order; govern; wide	leun
绺	綹	綹		liǔ skein; tuft; lock; wrinkle	lau
绮	綺	綺	綺	qǐ woven silk; beautiful; gorgeous	ji
绽	綻	綻	綻	zhàn burst open; split	jaan

绰	綽	綽	綽	chùo　　　cheuk ample; spacious; nickname
绫	綾	綾	綾	líng　　　ling a thin type of silk fabric resembling satin; damask
绵	綿	綿	綿	mián　　　mìhn　　緜 soft; downy; alternative form of cotton (棉)
绲	緄	緄		gǔn　　　kwan sew; hem; cord; woven belt; embroidered sash
绪	緒	緒	緒	xù　　　seui thread; end of a thread; beginning; mental state; mood; clue
缁	緇	緇	緇	zi　　　ji black silk; dark; darkness; Buddhist
紧	緊	緊	緊	jǐn　　　gán tense; tight; taut; firm; secure; strict; pressing; urgent; violent; heavy; critical; important; short of money
绱	緔	緔		shàng　　　seung　　鞝 to sole a shoe
缃	緗	緗		xiang　　　sèuhng yellow silk; light yellow
缄	緘	緘	緘	jian　　　gaam　　械 seal; close; bind; letter
缂	緙	緙	緙	kè　　　hak woof of a woven item
线	線	線	線	xiàn　　　sin　　綫 thread; wire; line; string; ray; route; path; boundary; clue; sign; secret agent; ideological or political line
缇	緹	緹	緹	tí　　　tai reddish color; red, brown
缗	緡	緡		mín　　　man money; string of coins; quantifier for a string of money that equals 1000 wén (文)
缉	緝	緝	緝	ji　　　chàp arrest; seize; catch; hem clothing

糸 9-10

缎	緞			duàn / dyun — satin
缓	緩			huǎn / wuhn — slow; delay; relaxed; leisurely
缔	締			dì / dai — associate; to form; connect; establish; suppress; restrain
缘	緣			yuán / yùhn 縁 — hem clothing; edge; brink; margin; climb up; ascend; implicate; cause; basis; because of; due to; rely on; fate
编	編			bian / pìn — put in order; arrange; weave; knit; write; compose; compile; edit; to join; fabricate
缅	緬			miǎn / min — distant; remote; short for Myanmar (緬甸)
纬	緯			wěi / wai — latitude; planet; weft; woof (*horizontal thread in woven fabric*); weave; to wrap
缑	緱			gou / gau — rope attached to a sword hilt; Gou mountain in Henan
缈	緲			miǎo / miu — indistinct
练	練			liàn / lihn — practice; train; drill; to perfect; exercise; boil and scour raw silk
缏	緶			biàn / bin — braid
萦	縈			yíng / jing — coil; wind around
缢	縊			yì / ai — die by hanging or strangulation
缝	縫			féng / fùhng 縫 — sew up; stitch; patch; mend
绉	縐			zhòu / jau — wrinkles; creases; crepe paper

縑	縑	縑	縑	jian　　gim　　慊 fine silk
缚	縛	縛	縛	fù　　bok tie; bind; fasten; tie up; attach
缜	縝	縝	縝	zhěn　　chán detailed; fine; closely woven
缟	縞	縞	縞	gǎo　　gou white raw silk; white; shine
縟	縟	縟		rù　　juk decorative; adorned; elegant
县	縣	縣	縣	xiàn　　yuhn county; district; an administrative division
缩	縮	縮	縮	suo　　sùk draw back; shrink; shorten; reduce; frugal; timid
纵	縱	縱	縱	zòng　　jung loose; relaxed; shoot an arrow; deliver; issue; let go; set free; free rein; indulge; let slip; jump up or over
缧	縲	縲	縲	léi　　leui a chain or rope used bind criminals
缦	縵	縵	縵	màn　　maan plain silk; plain; simple; unadorned
縶	縶	縶		zhí　　jap　　圖 restrain; to rein; control
缕	縷	縷	縷	lǔ　　léui thread; detailed; precise; (classifier for wisps, threads, or strands)
缥	縹	縹	縹	piǎo　　piu light blue; misty pretty; beautiful; handsome; to fly
	縻	縻		mí　　mei halter for ox; harness; tie up
	繁	繁	繁	fán　　fàahn numerous; complicated; luxuriant; lush

糸 11-13

	繇	繇		yáo　　　jiu reason; cause
总	總	總	總	zǒng　　　júng　　　惣揔捴總総 total; chief; all; collect; overall; altogether; always
绩	績	績	績	ji　　　jìk merit; achievement; accomplishment
绷	繃	繃	繃	beng　　　bang stretch; to strap; to brace; taut; spring up; bounce; strain one's muscles; to split
缫	繅	繅	繅	sao　　　sou reel silk from the cocoon
缪	繆	繆	繆	móu　　　mau a type of silk
缯	繢	繢	繢	hùi　　　kúi tie; bind; silk fabrics; silk products
缮	繕	繕	繕	shàn　　　sin repair; mend; renovate; keep; maintain; copy neatly; transcribe; prepare; firm; resolute
织	織	織	織	zhi　　　jìk weave; knit; organize; to form; unite; alternate; stagger
缭	繚	繚	繚	liáo　　　liu twist about; circulate; entangle
绕	繞	繞	繞	rào　　　yiú surround; bypass; entwine
绣	繡	繡	繡	xiù　　　sau　　　繍 embroider; embroidered clothing; gorgeous; rich and bright colors
缋	繢	繢		hùi　　　kui　　　繪 leftover embroidery
绎	繹	繹	繹	yì　　　jik unravel or unreel silk; interpret; explain
系	繫	繫	繫	xì　　　haih to tie; fasten; button up

274

绳	繩	繩	繩	shéng　　　sìhng　　　绳 繩 string; rope; cord; restrict; restrain
绘	繪	繪	繪	huì　　　kùi　　　絵 draw; sketch; paint
缳	繯	繯		huán　　　waan noose; tie; bind
缫	繰	繰		zǎo　　　jou reel silk from cocoons
缴	繳	繳	繳	jiǎo　　　giú to wind; entwine; hand over under compulsion; pay; disarm; capture weapons; cooperate; partner up
茧	繭	繭	繭	jiǎn　　　gaan　　　蠒 cocoon; callus; blister
继	繼	繼	繼	jì　　　gai　　　継 continue; maintain; carry on; succeed; follow; inherit
缱	繾	繾		qiǎn　　　hin attached to; inseparable; entangled
缤	繽	繽	繽	bin　　　ban flourishing; thriving; abundant
	纂	纂	纂	zuǎn　　　jyun edit; compile; topknot; chignon (*a roll or twist of hair*)
续	續	續	續	xù　　　juhk continue; carry on; succeed; (*internet slang*) to delete, block or censor
缬	纈	纈		xié　　　kit patterned silk; knot; to tie a knot
纩	纊	纊		kuàng　　　kwong　　　絖 纮 silk wadding; silk floss; silkworm cocoon
缠	纏	纏	纏	chán　　　juhk　　　纒 纏 纒 bind; tie; entwine; bother; pester; harass
缨	纓	纓	纓	ying　　　jing tassel; ribbon; chin strap; annoy; bother

糸 17-21　缶 3-17　网 3-4

纤	纖	纖	纖	xian　　　chim　　　　　纖紆臢孅縿 fine; delicate; graceful
	纛	纛		dào　　　dou large ancient Chinese army banner; ancient feather banner used on the emperor's carriage
缵	纘	纘		zǔan　　　jyun　　　　　纘 inherit; continue; carry on
缆	纜	纜	纜	lǎn　　　laam heavy-duty rope; cable
	缶	缶	缶	fǒu　　　fau　　　　　缶瓿 earthen pot or jar for holding alcoholic drinks; musical instrument for rituals
	缸	缸	缸	gang　　　gòng　　　　塯 earthen jar or vessel; crock; cistern
	缺	缺	缺	que　　　kyut lack; be short of; defect; weakness; deficient; imperfect; flawed; vacancy; gap; mean; wicked; stupid; dense
钵	缽	缽	缽	bo　　　but　　　　　盋 Buddhist monk's alms bowl; bowl; basin; earthenware or metal pot
	罄	罄	罄	qìng　　　hing empty; exhaust; run out; use up
	罅	罅		xià　　　laa crack; gap; rift; split; grudge
罂	罌	罌	罌	ying　　　aang　　　　罃甖 earthen small-mouthed jar; bottle
	罐	罐	罐	gùan　　　gwun　　　　鑵鏆 can; jar; tin; (classifier for canned items)
	网	网	网	wǎng　　　móhng　　　　四丹罔 net; web; network; enclose; internet
	罕	罕	罕	han　　　hón rare; scarce
	罘	罘		fú　　　fau net for catching rabbits; an ancient screen

网 5-19

	罡	罡		gang　　gong a group of stars in the "handle" of the Big Dipper
	罟	罟	罟	gǔ　　gu fish net; implicate
	罨	罨		yǎn　　jim fish net; medical compress
	署	署	署	shǔ　　chyúh public office; to sign; signature
	罩	罩		zhào　　jaau cover; wrap; hood; basket for catching fish; surpass
	置	置	置	zhì　　ji　　寘 to put; to place; to plant; establish; set up; set aside; set free; install; abandon; buy; purchase
	罪	罪		zuì　　jeui crime; sin; vice; fault; hardship; suffering
罚	罰	罰		fá　　faht　　罸 punish; penalty; fine; sentence
骂	罵	罵	罵	mà　　mah　　駡 傌 scold; chide; blame; curse; swear
罢	罷	罷	罷	bà　　bah cease; finish; stop; give up
	罹	罹	罹	lí　　lei suffering; misery; experience
	罾	罾		zeng　　jang large square fishing net
罗	羅	羅	羅	luó　　lòh net for catching birds; gauze; collect
罴	羆	羆		pí　　bei brown bear
羁	羈	羈	羈	ji　　gei bridle; halter; restrain; hold; control; stay; remain

羊 1-9

	羊	羊	羊	yáng　　yèuhng (*caprid*) goat; sheep
	芊	芊	芈	mie　　me　　哶 咩 baa! (*onomatopoeia, bleating of sheep*)
羌	羌	羌	羌	qiang　　gèung　　羗 Qiang people; ancient Chinese tribe; muntjac (*species of deer*)
美	美	美	美	měi　　méih　　媄羑嬭嬤 beautiful; pretty; attractive; good-looking; delicious; good; satisfactory; happy; praise; commend; USA
羔	羔	羔	羔	gao　　gòu lamb; young
羚	羚	麢	羚	líng　　ling antelope; lamb; young sheep
	羝	羝		di　　dai ram; male sheep or goat
	羞	羞	羞	xiu　　sàu disgraced; ashamed; shy
	群	羣	群	qún　　kwàhn group; crowd; flock; herd; pack; multitude; numerous; many; (*classifier for groups of people or animals*)
羟	羟	羟		qiǎng　　cheung hydroxide
	羧	羧		suo　　so carboxyl
羡	羨	羨	羨	xiàn　　sihn envy; admire; superfluous; surplus; affluence; surpass; exceed; abundant; plentiful; crooked; evil
义	義	義	義	yì　　yih　　羛 righteousness; justice; morality; meaning; implication
	羯	羯	羯	jié　　git castrated ram or buck goat; deer skin
	羰	羰		tang　　tong carbonyl

	羲	羲	羲	xi　　　　hei Fuxi, an ancient Chinese heroic ruler; breath; vapor
膻	羶	羶		shan　　　sin rank odor; the smell of mutton
	羸	羸		léi　　　　leui weak; lean; emaciated; exhausted
羹	羹	羹		geng　　　gàng　　　鬻 羮 焿 thick soup; vegetable soup; broth; (*Cantonese*) spoon
	羼	羼		chàn　　　chaan mix; blend
	羽	羽	羽	yǔ　　　　yúh feather; plume; wing; birds; fletching; banner; flag; feather fan; float (*for fishing line*)
	羿	羿	羿	yì　　　　ngai the name of a historic legendary archer (后羿)
	翁	翁	翁	weng　　　yùng elderly man; father; father of one's husband or wife; feathers of a bird's neck
	翅	翅	翅	chì　　　　chi　　　　翄 翨 wings; fins
	翎	翎	翎	líng　　　ling a stiff wing or tail feather of a bird; insect wing; arrow feather; official's hat feather (to display rank)
	翌	翌	翌	yì　　　　yihk　　　翊 next (*day or year*); bright; clear; assist; help; wing; flying
习	習	習	習	xí　　　　jaahp flapping wings; flutter; practice; review; study; learn; be used to; habit; custom; often; frequently
	翔	翔	翔	xiáng　　chèuhng soar; hover
	翕	翕		xi　　　　jap friendly; compliant
	翡	翡	翡	fěi　　　　fei a type of red kingfisher

	翟	翟		dí　　　　dik　　　狄 a long-tailed species of pheasant; pheasant plumes
	翠	翠	翠	cùi　　　　cheui blue kingfisher; kingfisher feathers (*for jewelry*); green jade; bluish-green; cyan; bright; distinct
	翥	翥		zhù　　　　jyu soar; hover
	翦	翦		jiǎn　　　　jin　　　剪 scissors; cut; clip; eliminate; annihilate
	翩	翩	翩	pian　　　　pin fly fast; flutter
	翮	翮	翮	hé　　　　hat quill; bird wing; bird; wind instrument
	翱	翱	翱	áo　　　　ngou　　　翱 翶 soar; roam; hover; spread wings and fly
	翰	翰	翰	hàn　　　　hon golden pheasant; fly high; long and stiff feather; writing brush; literary work; (*formal*) correspondence
	翳	翳	翳	yì　　　　ai shade; to shade; screen; to screen; nebula; hide; conceal; gloomy clouds
	翼	翼	翼	yì　　　　yihk wing; fin; military flank
	翻	翻	翻	fan　　　　fàan fly in a circle; soar; reverse; flip over; cross over; browse; change; alter; translate; interpret; decode
翘	翹	翹	翹	qiáo　　　　kiu rectrix tail feathers; lift; raise; expose; reveal; outstanding; extraordinary; dangerous; lush
	耀	耀	耀	yào　　　　yiuh　　　燿 shine; sparkle; dazzle; show off; flaunt; rays of light; radiance; glorious
	老	老	老	lǎo　　　　lóuh old; aged; elderly; experienced; overcooked; tough; very; quite; (*a term of endearment*)
	考	考	考	kǎo　　　　háau　　　丂 攷 examine; test; check; investigate; consider

者	峕	峕	zhě / jé — this; (suffix) -er; -ist; one who...; the things which...
耆	耆		qí / kei — man of sixty; aged; old; senior; tyrannical; detest; abhor
耄	耄		mào / mou — very old; senile; befuddled; confused
耋	耋		dié / dit — age of seventy or eighty; old age （耊）
而	而	而	ér / yìh — yet; moreover; and; then; but; nevertheless; to; you; your; (*particle indicating cause, purpose, or manner*)
耐	耐	耐	nài / noih — endure; durable; long time （耏）
耍	耍	耍	shuǎ / sá — frolic; play; perform; fiddle with; flourish; wield; show off; display; act; trick; fool; gamble
耒	耒	耒	lěi / leui — handle of a plow; plow
耕	耕	耕	geng / gàang — plough; till; cultivate （畊）
耘	耘	耘	yún / wan — to weed; to hoe
耗	耗	耗	hào / hou — consume; use up; waste; squander （耄耗）
耙	耙	耙	pá / pàh — rake; to rake （䎱耙）
耜	耜		sì / chíh — plowshare
耠	耠		huo / hap — till; dig
耦	耦	耦	ǒu / ngau — pair; couple (*regarding people*)

表 5-11　耳 2-5

耩	耩			jiǎng　　kau to plow; sow; the mechanized spread of seed and fertilizer
耨	耨			nòu　　nau　　鎒 an ancient tool used for weeding; a type of hoe; to hoe; to weed
耪	耪			pǎng　　póhng pull weeds and cultivate soil; to plow
耧	耬	耬		lóu　　lau drill for sowing grain
耳	耳	耳		ěr　　yíh ear; ear-like object; objects that are found on both sides; handle; knob; hear
	耵	耵		ding　　ding used in "earwax" (耵聹)
	耶	耶	耶	yé　　je alternative form of father (爺); particle indicating a questioning tone
	耷	耷		da　　daap large ears; droopy
耻	恥	恥	恥	chǐ　　chí shame; ashamed; humiliate; humiliation; disgrace
	耿	耿	耿	gěng　　gáng straightforward; bright; shining; honest; just; upright
	耽	耽	耽	dan　　daam delay; indulge; negligent; procrastinate
	聆	聆	聆	líng　　lìhng listen; hear; pay attention
	聊	聊	聊	liáo　　liùh depend on; chat; talk about; somewhat; slightly; at least; for the time being; tentatively
	聒	聒		guo　　kut noisy; clamorous
圣	聖	聖	聖	shèng　　sing　　𡉚 𦔻 holy; sacred; saint; noble; Confucius; master; emperor; king; an honorific form of address

	聘	聘	聘	聘	pìn / ping — an envoy; engage; employ; betroth; marry off a daughter
	聚	聚	聚	聚	jù / jeuih — gather; collect; congregate
闻	聞	聞	聞		wén / màhn — hear; listen; smell; detect; spread; transmit; famous; knowledge; expertise; news; message
联	聯	聯	聯		lián / lyùhn — unite; alliance; connect; join 聯聯聨聯
聪	聰	聰	聰		cong / chùng — quick at hearing; sense of hearing; intelligent; clever; bright; wise 聰聪
	聱	聱	聱		áo / ngou — not taking advice; uneven; bent and twisted; too complicated
声	聲	聲	聲		sheng / sìng — sound; noise; voice; tone; declare; reputation
耸	聳	聳	聳		sǒng / sung — deaf; urge on; rise up; raise up; erect; lofty; to reward; scare; frighten
聩	聵	聵			kùi / kui — deaf
聂	聶	聶	聶		niè / nip — whisper
职	職	職	職		zhí / jìk — duty; profession; occupation; position; office; post 戠職
聍	聹	聹			níng / ning — used only in "earwax" (耵聹)
听	聽	聽	聽		ting / tìng — listen; obey; allow; to smell; tin can; (classifier for canned drinks); (Cantonese) tomorrow; pick up the phone 聽聽
聋	聾	聾	聾		lóng / lùhng — deaf
	聿	聿	聿		yù / jyut — original form of pencil or brush (筆); then; and then; thereupon

聿 7-8　肉 2-4

肆	𦘒	肆	sì　　　　si　　　　𦘒四 impudent; undisciplined; profligate; shop; store; stall; alternative form of four (四) (*used to avoid forgery*)
肄	𦘒	𦘒	yì　　　　yih learn; study; practice
肅 肅	肅	肅	sù　　　　sùk　　　　肅 肅 solemn; reverential
肇	肈	肈	zhào　　　siu commence; start; begin; to found; originate
肉	𠕎	肉	ròu　　　　yuhk　　　宍 meat; flesh; body
肋	肋	肋	lèi　　　　lak rib; chest
肌	肌	肌	ji　　　　　gèi flesh; muscle; skin
肓	肓	肓	huang　　　fong region between heart and diaphragm; stubborn
肖	肖	肖	xiào　　　chiu resemble; imitate
肘	肘	肘	zhǒu　　　jáau elbow; upper part of a leg of pork
肝	肝	肝	gan　　　　gòn liver
肚	肚	肚	dù　　　　tóuh belly; abdomen; bowels; bulge; protrusion; tripe; animal stomach (*as food*); heart; mind
肛	肛	肛	gang　　　gong anus
股	股	股	gǔ　　　　gú thigh; haunches; share; portion; Pythagoras' theorem; (*mathematics*) longest side of a right triangle
肢	肢	肢	zhi　　　　jì　　　　胑 limbs; feet

肫	肫	肫	zhun　　jeun	gizzard; cheek; sincere
肥	肥	肥	féi　　fèih	fat; obese; fertile; (*derogatory*) benefit; advantage; gain
肪	肪	肪	fáng　　fòng	fat; grease
肱	肱	肱	gong　　gwang　　厷 ㄥ 厸	upper arm; (*figurative*) assistant
肽	肽		tài　　taai	peptide
肺	肺	肺	fèi　　fai	lungs
胼	胼		jǐng　　jeng	hydrazine
肩	肩	肩	jian　　gìn	shoulders; to bear
肯	肯	肯	kěn　　háng	consent; be willing; permit
育	育	育	yù　　yuhk	give birth; raise; bring up; rear; educate; nourish
胃	胃	胃	wèi　　waih　　图	stomach; gizzard of a fowl
背	背		bèi　　bui	(*anatomy*) back; backside; abandon; betray; disloyal; deviate; unlucky; recite; memorize; hard of hearing
胥	胥	胥	xu　　seui	all; together; mutual; (*historical*) an officer who was responsible for capturing thieves
胂	胂		shen　　san	arsine (*a compound of arsenic and hydrogen, a poisonous gas that smells like garlic*)
胛	胛	胛	jiǎ　　gaap	shoulder; shoulder blade

肉 5-6

胎	𦙄	𦝢	tai　　　tòi　　　孡 fetus; embryo; womb; source; origin
胖	𦙃	胖	pàng　　buhn　　膨胖 plump; fat
胙	𦙅		zuò　　　jou meat offered in sacrifice to one's ancestors
胗	𦙇		zhen　　　jan pustules; a rash or eruption; measles; various kinds of fever
胚	𦙈	胚	pei　　　pui embryo; unfinished
胝	𦙉	胝	chi　　　dai callous; corn
胞	𦙊	胞	bao　　　bàau womb; placenta; fetal membrane; blood (*family relationship*); cell (*biology*)
胡	胡	胡	hú　　　wùh wattle; dewlap; barbarian; foreign; short for 胡琴; ancient state of Hu; dark-skinned; great; senior; wild
胤	胤	胤	xǔ　　　yan heir; successor; progeny; posterity
胭	𦙋	胭	yan　　　jin rouge; cosmetics
胯	胯	胯	kùa　　　kwaa groin; crotch; hip
胰	胰	胰	yí　　　ji pancreas
胱	𦙌	胱	gwang　　gwong used only in bladder (膀胱)
胲	胲		gai　　　goi hydroxylamine (*an explosive inorganic derivative of ammonia*)
胳	𦙍	胳	ge　　　gaak armpit; arm

肉 6-7

	胴	胴	胴	chi　　　　dung torso; trunk; large intestine
	胸	匈		xiong　　　　hùng　　胷 匈 chest; thorax; breast; bosom; (*figurative*) mind; heart; thought
	胺	胺		àn　　　　on　　　餲 amine
	胼	胼	胼	pián　　　　pin used only in callus (胼胝)
	脂	脂	脂	zhi　　　　jì fat; grease; lard
	脆	脆	脆	cùi　　　　cheui　　臃 脺 胞 crsip; clear; brittle; fragile; frail
脉	脈	脈	脈	mài　　　　mahk　　蚚 pulse; veins; arteries; blood vessels; leaf vein; blood vessel-like network, like a mountain range
	脒	脒		mǐ　　　　mai amidine
	能	能	能	néng　　　　nàhng　　骯 able; capable; can; may; could; rather; energy; power; talent; talented person
	脊	脊	脊	jǐ　　　　jek spine; backbone; ridgeline; ridge; spine; ridge beam; book spine
胁	脅	脅		xié　　　　hip flank; coerce; threaten; armpit; underarm
	脖	脖	脖	bó　　　　buht　　預 膊 neck
	脘	脘		wǎn　　　　gun internal cavity of stomach
胫	脛	脛		jìng　　　　ging　　踁 shinbone; lower leg
	脞	脞		cǔo　　　　chòh minced meat; trifles (*a type of cake or fruit custard*)

肉 7-8

脫	脫	脫	脫	tuo　　tyut undress; take off; slip away; to strip; escape; avoid; omit; rapid; swift; fast; unaffected; free; at ease
	脬	脬		pao　　paau a bladder
	脯	脯	脯	pú　　pou breast; chest; candied fruit
	脲	脲		niào　　niu urea
脹	脹	脹	脹	zhàng　　jeung expand; increase in size; swell; bloated; puff up
	脾	脾	脾	pí　　pèih spleen; pancreas; temperament; disposition
	腆	腆	腆	tiǎn　　tin　　俱 prosperous; virtuous; make strong
	腈	腈		jing　　jing alternative form of lean meat (精); a cyanogen; nitrile
	腋	腋	腋	yè　　jik　　掖 armpit; underarm; (botany) axilla; axil
	腐	腐		fǔ　　fuh rotten; spoiled; decayed
	腑	腑	腑	fǔ　　fú viscera
	腓	腓	腓	féi　　fei calf (leg muscle); avoid; ill; wither; (plants) to die from diseases
	腔	腔	腔	qiang　　hòng cavity; hollow in body; (Chinese opera) tune; melody; speech accent
	腕	腕	腕	wǎn　　wún　　掔 wrist
	腙	腙		zong　　jung hydrazone

	腚	腚		dìng　　　ding (Mandarin) buttocks
	腠	腠		còu　　　chau tissue between the skin and the flesh
	腥	腥	腥	xing　　　sìng fishy smell
脑	腦	腦	腦	nǎo　　　nóuh　　　瑙 brain; mind; core
	腩	腩		nǎn　　　naam dip meat in condiments before roasting; dried meat; (Cantonese) belly meat; sirloin; tenderloin
肾	腎	腎	腎	shèn　　　san kidney; testicle; (Cantonese) gizzard
肿	腫	腫	腫	zhǒng　　　júng swell; swollen; swelling
	腮	腮	腮	sai　　　soi　　　顋 cheek; jaw
	腰	腰	腰	yao　　　yiù waist; loins; middle part; kidney
脚	腳	腳	腳	jiǎo　　　geuk foot; leg; base; foundation
	腴	腴		yú　　　jyu fat; plump; fertile land; rich; fat part of the belly; intestines of dogs and hogs; oil
肠	腸	腸	腸	cháng　　　chéung　　　膓 bowels; intestines; sausage; emotions
	腹	腹	腹	fù　　　fùk abdomen; belly; belly-shaped object; heart; mind; inside; interior
	腺	腺	腺	xiàn　　　sin gland
	腱	腱	腱	jiàn　　　gin tendon

肉 8-9

肉 10-12

	腿	䏗		tuǐ　　　　téui leg; thigh; base; foundation
	膀	䏖	䏖	bǎng　　　bóng　　　髈 upper arm; shoulder; wing
腽	腽	䐅		wà　　　　wat fat; fur seal blubber; (used only in 腽肭)
	膈	䐑	䐑	gé　　　　gaak diaphragm
	膊	䐇	䐇	bó　　　　bok upper arm; shoulder; upper body
	膂	䐒		lǚ　　　　leui　　　呂膋 backbone; spinal column
	膏	高	高	gao　　　　gòu fat; grease; oily; paste; cream; ointment; poultice; sleek; glossy; rich
肤	膚	膚	膚	fu　　　　fù skin; superficial; shallow
	膝	䣛	䏊	xí　　　　sàt　　　䣛 knee
胶	膠	膠	膠	jiao　　　gàau glue; adhesive; adhere; gum; resin; rubber; sticky; plastic; (internet slang) stupid; foolish
	膘	䐗	䐗	biao　　　biu　　　臕 fat (mainly livestock, derogatory when used of a person); concentrate one's attention on
	膜	䐞	䐞	mó　　　　mok membrane; film; placate
	膛	䐢	䐢	táng　　　tong chest; hollow space; cavity
	膣	䐤		zhì　　　jat vagina; (vulgar) female genitalia
	膨	䐩	䐩	péng　　　pàahng expanded; swollen; swell; bloated; inflated

肉 12-14

腻	膩	贕		nì　　　　　leih fatty; oily; greasy; meticulous; delicate; to disgust someone; be tired of; dirt; sticky; grimy; intimate
	膳	膳	膳	shan　　　　sin prepare food; offer food; meal
	臆	臆	臆	yì　　　　　jik chest; breast; bosom; thought
	臊	臊		sau　　　　sou having the smell of urine; embarrassed; to embarrass
	臌	臌		gǔ　　　　　gu dropsical swelling; puffy; bloated
脓	膿	膿	膿	nóng　　　　nung pus
胆	膽	膽	膽	dǎn　　　　　dáam gallbladder; inner container; liner (*thermos*); bladder (*ball*); guts; courage; bravery; strength; nerve
脍	膾	膾	膾	kùai　　　　kui traditional Chinese dish consisting of finely cut strips of raw fish or meat
脸	臉	臉	臉	liǎn　　　　líhm face; cheeks; facial expression; complexion; reputation; image
	臃	臃	臃	yong　　　　jung bloated; swollen
	膺	膺	膺	ying　　　　jing breast; chest; (*of horses*) breast strap; undertake; to bear; attack
	臀	臀	臀	tún　　　　tyun　　　臋 屍 屄 buttocks; bottom
	臂	臂	臂	bì　　　　　bei fore-arm
脐	臍	臍	臍	qí　　　　　chìh navel
膑	臏	臏	臏	bìn　　　　ban　　　髕 臏 kneecap; patella; cutting off kneecaps (*one of the* 五刑, *"Five Punishments"*)

肉 15-19　　臣 2-11　　自 4-5　　至 3-8

腊	臘	臘	臘	là　　　　laahp　　　　臈 dried meat; cured meat
胪	臚	臚	臚	lú　　　　lou arrange in order; display
脏	臟	臟		zàng　　　johng　　　臧 藏 viscera; guts; internal organs
脔	臠	臠		lúan　　　lyun small piece of meat; to cut meat into small thin pieces
	臣	臣	臣	chén　　　sàhn minister; official; statesman
	臥	臥	臥	wò　　　　ngoh lie down; crouch
	臧	臧	臧	zang　　　jong　　　 㱊 good; right; generous; to praise; commend
临	臨	臨	臨	lín　　　　làhm to overlook; descend; arrive; adjacent to; be faced with; confronted
	自	自	自	zì　　　　jih self, oneself; one's own; certainly, of course; personally; since; from; copy
	臬	臬	臬	niè　　　　jit archery target; ancient Chinese sundial-like device; provincial judge; standard; law; rule; door post
	臭	臭		chòu　　　chau foul smell; stinking
	皋	皋		gao　　　　gou　　　阜 皐 皋 皋 shore; land by a body of water; tall; high; marsh; pool; rice paddy
至	至	至	至	zhì　　　　ji reach; arrive; until; extreme; best; most
	致	致	致	zhì　　　　ji send; deliver; to present; cause; result in
台	臺	臺	臺	tái　　　　tòih　　　坮 tower; stage; platform; support; stand; base; station

292

臻	臻	臻	臻	zhen　　jeun	reach; arrive; attain; utmost; superior
	臼	臼	臼	jiù　　kau	mortar (*vessel used for grinding*); bone joint socket
	臾	臾	臾	yú　　jyu　　𠮿	moment, instant, short while
	舁	舁		yú　　jyu	carry on the shoulders
	舀	舀	舀	yǎo　　jiu　　抌 扷 㧵	to scoop; to ladle
	舂	舂	舂	chong　　jung	pound on grains to remove the husk; pestle; strike with a fist; beat
	舄	舄		xì　　sik　　舃	shoe; sole of a shoe; magpie
	舅	舅	舅	jiù　　kàuh	mother's brother; wife's brother; wife's father; husband's father
与	與	與		yǔ　　yúh	give; offer; agree; allow; permit; support; follow; associate with; to cope; compare; choose
兴	興	興	興	xing　　hìng　　兴	rise; thrive; prosper; flourish; popular; build; establish; promote; succeed; dispatch; advocate; encourage
舆	輿	輿	輿	yú　　jyu	cart; carriage; sedan chair; palanquin; public; populace; masses
举	舉	舉	舉	jǔ　　géui　　攑 挙 㪯	raise; lift up; recommend; action; deed; whole; entire
旧	舊	舊	舊	jiù　　gauh　　舊	old; ancient; past; worn
	舌	舌	舌	shé　　sit	tongue; tongue-shaped object; bell clapper
	舍	舍	舍	shè　　se　　舎	residence; cottage; lodging place; inn; hotel

舌 4-8　舛 6-8　舟 3-5

舐	𦧇	𦦙	shì　si　𦧇 𦦙 lick; to lap; stroke with the tongue
舒	𦧌	𦧌	shu　syù spread; comfortable
舔	𦧟	𦧠	tiǎn　tim　𠯠 lick; suck up to someone; to brownnose
舛	舛	舛	chǔan　chyun oppose; error; mistake; misfortune
舜	舞	舜	shùn　seun Emperor Shun; hibiscus syriacus
舞	舞	舞	wǔ　móuh dance; dancing; wield; brandish
舟	月	舟	zhou　jàu barge; boat; ship
舡	舡		gang　gong boat; ship; nautilus
舢	舢		shan　saan used only in sampan (舢板)
舨	舨	舨	bǎn　baan used only in sampan (舢舨) and an ancient warship (艨舨)
航	航	航	háng　hòhng sail; navigate; ship; boat; fly a plane
舫	舫	舫	fǎng　fong expensive boat; yacht
般	般		ban　bun sort; kind; class; like; similar to
舳	舳		zhú　juk stern of a ship; rudder
舴	舴		zé　jaak small boat

舟 5-14

舵	柁	舵		dùo　　　tòh　　　舵 軚 柁 helm; rudder
舶	舶	舶		bó　　　paak vessel; large oceangoing ship
舷	舷	舷		xián　　　jin　　　舷 edge; side of a ship
舸	舸			ge　　　go large boat; boat (*in general*)
船	船	船		chúan　　　syùhn　　　舩 watercraft; vessel (*ship, boat, hovercraft; submarine, etc.*); alcohol cup; carry by watercraft
舾	舾			xi　　　sai used only in equipment on a ship (*anchor, mast, ladder, plumbing, etc.*) (舾裝)
艄	艄			shao　　　saau stern of a ship/vessel
艇	艇	艇		tǐng　　　téng small boat; dugout; punt; barge
艋	艋	艋		měng　　　maang small boat
艘	艘	艘		sou　　　sau　　　樓艘 ship; (*classifier for boats, ships, vessels*)
舱	艙	艙		cang　　　chong cabin (*on ships, airplanes, etc.*)
	艚	艚		cáo　　　chòuh wooden cargo boat
	艟	艟		chong　　　chung ancient warship
舣	艤	艤		yǐ　　　ngai　　　檥 moor a boat
	艨	艨		méng　　　mung long and narrow boat-of-war

295

舟 14-16　艮 1-11　色 5-18　艹 2-3

舰	艦	艦篆	艦篆	jiàn　　　laahm battleship
舻	艫	艫篆		lú　　　lou　　艪 bow or prow of a boat
艮	艮	艮篆	艮篆	gèn　　　gan　　　㫔 seventh of eight Bagua trigrams; 52nd hexagram of the I Ching
	良	良篆	良篆	liáng　　　lèuhng good; virtuous; respectable
艰	艱	艱篆	艱篆	jian　　　gàan difficult; hard; distressing; dangerous
	色	色篆	色篆	sè　　　sik　　　卮殷 color; tint; hue; shade; expression; scenery; circumstance; kind; beauty; lust; sexual desire
	艴	艴篆		bó　　　fat a changed countenance; stern
艳	艷	艷篆	艷篆	yàn　　　jim　　　豔豓艶 plump; voluptuous; bright color; gorgeous; gaudy; romantic; envy; admire
	艹	艸篆		cǎo　　　chou　　　艸 grass
	艾	艾篆	艾篆	ài　　　ngaai Chinese mugwort (*artemisia argyi*); green; pale; elderly; end; stop; nurture; foster
	艽	艽篆		jiao　　　gaau wild; matted nesting grass of beasts and birds
	芑	芑篆		qǐ　　　gei white millet
	芝	芝篆	芝篆	zhi　　　ji sesame; a mushroom (*ganoderma lucidum*) used in Asian medicine
	芒	芒篆	芒篆	máng　　　mòhng awn (*the bristle of barley, oats, and grasses*); mango; zebra grass; edge of a knife; ray; beam
	芍	芍篆	芍篆	sháo　　　jeuk Chinese peony (*paeonia lactiflora*); water chestnut

	芎	芎		xiong　　　gung a type of herb	
	芊	芊		qian　　　chin vigorous and exuberant foliage	
	芋	芋	芋	yù　　　wuh　　芎 taro	
	苤	苤		dù　　　dou cyperus malaccensis; sedge grass	
	苄	苄		hù　　　ha a type of medicinal herb; mat woven from cattails	
芻	芻	芻	芻	chú　　　cho mow; cut grass; hay; fodder; ruminate	
	芘	芘		pí　　　bei used only in 芘苤; pyrene	
	花	花	花	hua　　　fà　　華蘤苍蕚 flower; blossom; pattern; fireworks; essence; cream; prostitute; spend (*money, time, etc.*); profligate	
	芙	芙	芙	fú　　　fu lotus; hibiscus	
	芰	芰	芰	jì　　　gei water chestnut	
	芟	芟	芟	shan　　　saam mow; cut; weed out; scythe	
	芡	芡		qiàn　　　him euryale ferox (*similar to a water lily*); cornstarch (*with water*); thicken a soup with starch; tempering (*spices*)	
	䓛	䓛		kou　　　kau onion; scallion stalk	
	芥	芥	芥	jiè　　　gaai broccoli; mustard greens; small grass; trivial	
	芩	芩		qín　　　kam a salt marsh plant	

艹 4-5

芪	芪		qí chi celery; used only in 芪母, 黃芪, and 北芪
芫	芫		yúan jyun 杬 daphne genkwa (*herb used in traditional Chinese medicine*)
芬	芬	芬	fen fàn fragrance; aroma
芳	芳	芳	fang fòng fragrant; flowers; plants; good reputation
芷	芷	芷	zhǐ ji angelica (*angelica dahurica*); a type of iris
芸	芸	芸	yún wan rue (*plant*)
芹	芹	芹	qín kan Chinese celery (*apium graveolens*)
芽	芽	芽	yá ngàh shoot; sprout; bud
芾	芾	芾	fěi fai flower; small; little; lush
芯	芯	芯	xin sam pith from the common rush (*juncus effusus*), used as lamp wick; core material (*of something*)
芮	芮		rùi jeui tiny; small; edge of a body of water
芴	芴		wù mat fluorene
芭	芭	芭	ba baa banana; fragrant grass
苑	苑	苑	yùan jyun pasture; park; garden; court; mansion
苞	苞	苞	bao baau 包 bulrush; root or stem of plants; luxuriant; profuse; bract; bud

苒	𦯯	苒	rǎn　　jim luxuriant growth; passing of time; fruit preserve; jam
苓	苓	苓	líng　　ling fungus; tuber; licorice
若	若	若	ruò　　yeuhk obedient; compliant; trim vegetables; choose; you; your; he; his; like; as if; in this way
苦	苦	苦	kǔ　　fú bitter; grievous; difficult; painful; hard; suffering; miserable; excessive
苫	苫		shàn　　sim rush or straw matting; cover with a straw mat
苔	苔	苔	tái　　tòih moss; lichen
苕	苕		tiáo　　tiu campsis grandiflora; vicia hirsuta; flower or ear of a reed
苗	苗	苗	miáo　　miùh seedling; shoot; sprout; offspring; symptom (trend); animal young (*of an animal*); short for vaccine (疫苗)
苛	苛		ke　　hò harsh; severe; exacting; cruel
苟	苟		gǒu　　gáu careless; frivolous; illicit; unprincipled; if; but; a type of grass; any; at all; at least; tentatively
茄	茄	茄	qié　　ké eggplant; (*Cantonese*) tomato
苠	苠		mín　　man bamboo skin
苡	苡		yǐ　　ji　　苢 barley
苣	苣		jù　　geui type of lettuce
苤	苤		pǐ　　pei kohlrabi (苤藍)

++ 5-6

苧	苧	𦫳		zhù chyu boehmeria nivea (*ramie*); China grass
苯	苯	苯		běn bun benzene
英	英	英		yīng yìng heroic; graceful; flower; petal; short for England or Britain
苜	苜	苜		mù muk clover
苴	苴			ju cheui seed-bearing hemp; coarse; rough; gunny; sackcloth; gunny sack; package; cattail bag; to patch; to mend
苷	苷			gan gam licorice; glycoside
苻	苻			fú fu type of herb, type of bamboo-like grass
茁	茁			zhúo jyut sprout; flourish; vigorous
茂	茂	茂		mào mauh exuberant; flourishing; dense
茅	茅	茅		máo màuh reeds (*imperata cylindrica*); thatched cottage; damaged; (*Cantonese*) not abiding by the rules
茆	茆	茆		mǎu maau species of grass, water mallows
茇	茇			bá bat root; thatched hut; remove; climb
茈	茈			zǐ chi gromwell; water chestnut; a plant yielding a red dye
茉	茉	茉		mò mut white jasmine
茗	茗	茗		míng ming 榠 tea buds; tea plant; late-picked tea; tea

	茚	🈀		yìn jan indene (*organic compound*)	
	莨	🈀		gèn gan Japanese buttercup; ranunculus	
	茨	🈀		cí chìh caltrop; puncture vine; tribulus terrestris	
	茫	🈀		máng mòhng vast; boundless; vague	汒
	茬	🈀		chá chaa harvest; stubble	
	茭	🈀		jiao gaau dry feed; oenanthe javanica; wild rice (*zizania aquatica*); a bamboo or reed cable	蔽
	茱	🈀	🈀	zhu jyu dogwood	
玆	兹	🈀	🈀	zí jì this; now; year; time; the present	兹
	茜	🈀		qiàn sin madder (rubia cordifolia); dark red; dye red	
	茴	🈀		húi wui fennel; aniseed	
	茵	🈀	🈀	yin jan cushion; matress	
	茶	🈀	🈀	chá chàh tea; beverage (*general*)	榛 荼
	茸	🈀	🈀	róng yùhng soft and downy; pilose; fine thin hair; antler of a young stag	
	茹	🈀	🈀	rú jyu eat; roots; vegetables; to bear; guess; soft; corrupted	
	茼	🈀		tóng tung garland chrysanthemum; crown daisy (*glebionis coronaria*)	

艹 6-7

	荀	𦬒	𦭐	xún　　　seun ancient state in China; a type of plant (mentioned in the classic Mountains and Rivers (山海經, 中山經)
	草	艸	𦯬	cǎo　　　chóu grass; straw; herbs; careless; sloppy; hasty; any green, leafy plant without bark; draft; sketch
	荃	荃	荃	quán　　　chyun calamus; pickled leaf mustard; fish tackle; fine cloth
	荏	荏	荏	rěn　　　jam perilla (*perilla frutescens*); a kind of large bean; soft; weak; yielding
	荑	荑		tí　　　ji tender bud; sprouts; tares
	荒	荒		huang　　　fòng wild; barren; wasteland; desert; uncultivated
	茘	茘	茘	lì　　　laih　　　荔 lichee; alternative name for iris lactea (馬蘭)
	荇	荇		xìng　　　hang　　　莕 banana plant
荆	荊	荊	荊	jing　　　ging thorns; bramble; cane; chaste tree or berry (*vitex agnus-castus*)
	莉	莉	莉	lì　　　lei white jasmine
	荷	荷	荷	hé　　　hòh lotus; water lily; short for Netherlands (荷蘭)
	荸	荸	荸	bí　　　but Chinese water chestnut
	荻	荻	荻	dí　　　dik amur silvergrass (*miscanthus sacchariflorus*)
	荼	荼	荼	tú　　　tou a type of bitter vegetable (*sonchus* or *lactuca*); white flower of cogon grass; pain; suffering
	荽	荽		sui　　　seui　　　荾 coriander

	莆	莆	莆	pú　　　pou　　　蒲 alternative form of 蒲; short for a city in Fujian (莆田)
	苺	苺		méi　　　mui moss; edible berries
庄	莊	莊	莊	zhuang　　　jòng　　　莊 grassy; village; hamlet; manor; main road; place of business; shop; dealer (*gamble*); solemn; serious
	莎	莎	莎	suo　　　so nutgrass (cyperus rotundus); a type of sedge grass used in the past for raincoats; to wither
	莒	莒	莒	jǔ　　　geui taro; herb; hemp-like plant; state of Ju (*Zhou dynasty*); Ju county (*Shandong*)
茎	莖	莖		jing　　　ging stem; stalk; tall and straight; pillar; penis; handle; (*classifier for strips or stalks of objects*)
	莘	莘	莘	shen　　　san long; numerous; the medicinal root of a marsh plant
	莛	莛		tíng　　　ting grass stalks
	莞	莞	莞	guan　　　gun long-stem watergrass; shichito matgrass; clubrush; a woven mat using this kind of grass; smile
	莠	莠	莠	yǒu　　　jau green foxtail (*setaria viridis*); green bristlegrass; wild foxtail millet; weeds; tares; undesirable; evil
荚	莢	莢		jiá　　　gaap pods of leguminous plants
苋	莧	莧	莧	xiàn　　　jin edible amaranth (*amaranthus tricolor*)
	莨	莨		làng　　　long herb; marsh grass; a yellowish catechu from an Asian woody vine (*uncaria gambir*) for tanning and dyeing
	莩	莩		fú　　　fu　　　殍 bulrush; membrane; die of hunger; starve to death
	莪	莪		é　　　ngo　　　蘁 incarvillea sinensis; alternative form of mushroom (菌)

艹 7

	莫			mò　　　　mohk　　　勿嗼麥賣甪 none; nothing; do not; don't; must not; particle indicating a rhetorical question
	茨			kǎn　　　　haam camphane (*camphor*); bornane
	莽			mǎng　　　mong thick weeds; luxuriant growth; (*toxic*) Japanese star anise (*illicium anisatum*); rude, impertinent; foolish
	萃			cùi　　　　seuih dense; thick; close-set; collect together; crowd
	菲			fei　　　　fei fragrant; luxurious; lush; humble; poor; unworthy; phenanthrene; the Philippines (*transliteration for Phi*)
	菀			wǎn　　　jyun exuberant; flourishing; luxuriant; thick; gloomy
	菁			jing　　　ching garlic chive flowers (*allium tuberosum*); flowers; brassica; turnip; betel nut
	菅			jian　　　gaan coarse grass (*themeda forskalii*)
	菇			gu　　　　gù　　　　菰 mushroom
	菌			jún　　　　kwán fungus; mushroom; bacteria; mold
	菏			hé　　　　ho　　　　渮 a river in Shandong
	菠			bo　　　　bo spinach and similar greens
	菹			ju　　　　jeui salted or pickled vegetables
	萍			píng　　　ping　　　苹 duckweed; wander; travel
华	華			húa　　　wàh China; Chinese; brilliance; magnificence; years; period; young; literary grace; prestige; status; resplendent

	菔	蕾		fú　　　　　fuk turnip
	菖	冒		chang　　　cheung iris; sweet flag; calamus
	菘	蒿		song　　　　sung Chinese cabbage (白菜)
	菜	蕐	茉	cài　　　　　choi vegetables; greens; food; course; dish
	菟	蕐	蒐	tù　　　　　tou dodder (*to tremble*); to crawl; to creep
	菊	蘜	蘜	jú　　　　　　gùk chrysanthemum
	菡	畜		hàn　　　　haam a lotus bud
	菩	蓄	蕃	pú　　　　　pòuh bodhisattva; herb; aromatic plant
	莨	崗		dàng　　　　dong henbane
	菰	藏	菰	gu　　　　　gu　　　苽 mushroom; Manchurian wild rice (*zizania latifolia*)
	菱	藏	菱	líng　　　　ling　　　薐 water caltrop; water chestnut (*trapa natans*)
	菽	朮	柔	shu　　　　suk　　　卡 beans and peas (*collectively*)
	萄	崗	崗	táo　　　　tou grape; a type of grass
	草	蕚		bì　　　　　bei straw raincoat; used in several plant names; alternative form of hide; conceal (蔽)
萇	萇	蕚	蕚	cháng　　　chèuhng starfruit; averrhora carambola

⺿ 8-9

莱	萊			lái　　　loi goosefoot; weed (wild grass); fallow field
	萋			qi　　　chai luxurious; lavish; abundant
	萌			méng　　　mang to bud; to sprout; germinate; begin; harbinger; omen; people; happen; occur; ignorant
	萎			wěi　　　wái wither; wilt; decay
	菡			dàn　　　daam lotus flower (not yet blossomed)
	萑			húan　　　wun reed; grass used for making mats
	萘			nài　　　noi naphthalene
	萜			tie　　　tip terpene
	著			zhúo　　　jyu attach; touch; wear; clothing; arrange; bear fruit; something to depend on; catch fire; love deeply
	萱			xuan　　　hyun daylily (hemerocallis flava); mother
莴	萵			wo　　　wo lettuce
	萸			yú　　　yu dogwood; cornelian cherry
	萼			è　　　ngok calyx
	落			lùo　　　lok fall; drop; leave out; leave behind; lag; write down; settle; (Cantonese) descend; get off (a vehicle)
	葆			bǎo　　　bou nurture; luxuriant growth; dense foliage; hide; conceal; alternative form of keep or preserve (保)

叶	葉	葉	蕭	yè　　yihp leaf; petal; wing; page; era; epoch
	葑	葑		feng　　fung turnip
荭	葒	葒		hóng　　hung prince's-feather (*amaranthus hypochondriacus*)
	葚	葚		shèn　　sam　　椹黮 mulberry fruit
万	萬	萬	萬	wàn　　maahn　　笔禸 ten thousand; numerous; myriad; a great number; original form of scorpion (蠆)
	葛	葛	葛	gé　　got kudzu (*pueraria lobata*); poplin; hemp cloth
	葡	葡	葡	pú　　pòuh grape; short for Portugal (葡萄牙)
	董	董	董	dǒng　　dúng to direct; director; govern; supervise
苇	葦	葦	葦	wěi　　wai reed; rush
	葸	葸		xǐ　　saai afraid; bashful; dread; unhappy; insecure
	葩	葩	葩	pa　　baa flower; beautiful; corolla; (*classifier for lamps*)
	葫	葫	葫	hú　　wu bottle-gourd; calabash
	葬	葬	葬	zàng　　jong inter; bury; burial place
	葭	葭		jia　　gaa reed plant
	葳	葳		wei　　wai luxuriant; flourishing

307

⺿ 9-10

荤	葷	葷	葷	hun　　　fan strong-smelling plants (*i.e. garlic*); meat or fish dishes; low-class; obscene; vulgar; dirty
	葺	葺		qì　　　cap thatch; fix; repair; pile up
	蒂	蔕		dì　　　dai　　蒂 peduncle or the stem of a plant
	蒈	蒈		kǎi　　　kaai carane (*a hydrocarbon*)
	葵	葵	葵	kúi　　　kwai　　葵 sunflower; helianthus; measure
	蓑	蓑		suo　　　so raincoat made of straw
	蒹	蒹		jian　　　gim reed (*phragmites australis*)
莳	蒔	蒔		shì　　　si transplant (*uproot and replant*); to plant; to set up
	蒙	蒙	蒙	méng　　　mùhng cover; conceal; deceive; cheat; suffer
	蒸	蒸	蒸	zheng　　　jìng evaporate; (*cooking*) to steam; ancient torch made of bamboo and wood; small pieces of firewood
	蒜	蒜		sùan　　　syun garlic
莅	蒞	蒞	蒞	lì　　　leih　　𧀎 attend; to arrive (*in an official function or ceremony*); manage
	蒡	蒡		bàng　　　bong burdock; herb
	蒯	蒯		kǔai　　　gwaai　　萄 a type of grass; a rush used to make various items
	蒲	蒲	蒲	pú　　　pou calamus; cattail

308

	蒴			shùo　　　sok capsule; pod; boil
	蕀			jí　　　jat furze (*a thorny evergreen shrub - ulex europaeus*); gorse
苍	蒼			cang　　　chòng dark blue; dark green; azure; greyish white; ashen
	蓉			róng　　　yùhng hibiscus
	蓖			bì　　　bei castor-oil plant (*ricinus communis*)
	蒽			en　　　jan anthracene
	蒿			hao　　　hou mugwort; artemisia
荪	蓀			sun　　　syun aromatic grass; iris
	蓁			zhen　　　jeun hazelnut
	蓄			xù　　　chùk　　稸 to save; stockpile; hoard; raise animals; cherish; wait for; preserve, dried cabbage or mustard greens
	蓊			wěng　　　jung lush; luxuriant; flourishing (*vegetation*)
盖	蓋			gài　　　goi　　乢 cover; conceal; apply; affix; overwhelm; surpass; construct; chatter; brag; shell (*animal*); thatch; canopy
	蓍			shi　　　si yarrow (*achillea millefolium*)
	蓓			bèi　　　pui flower bud
	蓐			rù　　　juk straw bed mat; rushes

艹 11

莼	蓴			chún　　seun edible water plant (*brasenia*)
	蓬			péng　　fung type of raspberry; fleabane; disheveled; Korean mugwort (*artemisia princeps*); flourishing; vigorous
莲	蓮			lián　　lìhn lotus (*nelumbo nucifera*); water lily
苁	蓯			cong　　chung a medicinal herb
	蓰			xǐ　　saai increase five-fold
	蓼			liǎo　　liu smartweed; polygonum; plant family polygonaceae
荜	蓽			bì　　bat bamboo or wicker fence; type of bean
	蓿			sù　　suk clover; lucerne
	蔌			sù　　chuk vegetables
	蔑			miè　　mit belittle; disdain; despise; extinguish; obliterate; small; lowly; nothing; none; red and swollen eye
	蔓			màn　　maahn vine; to creep; spread
	蔗			zhè　　je sugar cane
	蔚			wèi　　wai artemisia japonica; luxuriant; thick; ornamental
蒌	蔞			lóu　　lau artemisia stelleriana
	蔟			cù　　chuk a frame for silkworms to spin on

310

	蔡	蔡(seal)	蔡(seal)	cài　　choi a weed; tortoise used for divination
蒋	蔣	蔣(seal)	蔣(seal)	jiǎng　　jéung Warring States-era state in modern-day Henan; a surname
葱	蔥	蔥(seal)	蔥(seal)	cong　　chùng green onion; spring onion; scallion
茑	蔦	蔦(seal)		niǎo　　niu convolvulus plants; parasitic plants (*i.e. mistletoe*); ribes ambiguum
	蔫	蔫(seal)		nian　　jin listless; slow-tempered; sluggish
荫	蔭	蔭(seal)	蔭(seal)	yin　　jam　　蔭 shade of a tree; shadow; shelter; protect
	蔸	蔸(seal)		dou　　dau　　兜 root and stem of certain plants; clump; (*classifier for plants*)
荛	蕘	蕘(seal)		ráo　　jiu grass used as fuel; tinder
	蔽	蔽(seal)	蔽(seal)	bì　　bai cover; conceal; hide; summarize; sum up
荨	蕁	蕁(seal)		tán　　chàhm nettle
	蕃	蕃(seal)	蕃(seal)	fán　　faan luxuriant; lush; abundant; numerous; to breed; multiply
蒇	蕆	蕆(seal)		chǎn　　chín finish; complete; solve; to settle
	蕈	蕈(seal)	蕈(seal)	xùn　　cháhm mushroom; fungus; mold; mildew
	蕉	蕉(seal)	蕉(seal)	jiao　　jiù banana; plantain
芜	蕪	蕪(seal)	蕪(seal)	wú　　mou disused cropland; thickly-grown grass; overgrown with weeds

艹 12-13

	蕊	(seal)	(seal)	ruǐ / jeui — stamen; gynoecium; flower bud; (Taiwanese - classifier for flowers and eyes) 蕊榮紫蕋蘂
荡	蕩	(seal)	(seal)	dàng / dohng — wander; roam; to sway; wash away; clear away; unconstrained; flat; smooth; boundless
荞	蕎	(seal)		qiáo / kiu — buckwheat
莸	蕕	(seal)		yóu / yau — caryopteris divaricata (aka bluebeard)
	蕖	(seal)		qú / keui — lotus flower; tuber of a taro
	蕙	(seal)	(seal)	huì / wai — a species of fragrant orchid
	蕞	(seal)	(seal)	zùi / jeui — little; petty; small; tiny; miniature
姜	薑	(seal)	(seal)	jiáng / gèung — ginger
蒉	蕢	(seal)		kùi / gwai — amaranth (edible); straw basket
	蕤	(seal)		rúi / jeui — fringe; soft; delicate; drooping leaves
	蕨	(seal)	(seal)	júe / kyut — common bracken (pteris aquilina)
	蔬	(seal)	(seal)	shu / sò — vegetables; greens
荬	蕒	(seal)		mǎi / maai — used only in field milk thistle (苣蕒菜) and crepidiastrum sonchifolium (苦蕒)
蓣	蕷	(seal)		yù / jyu — yam
	蕹	(seal)		wèng / ung — water spinach (ipomoea aquatica)

	蕺	蕺		jí chap an herb used in traditional Chinese medicine to treat boils (*houttuynia cordata*)
	葓	葓		hóng hung budding
	蕾	蕾	蕾	lěi leui 蕾 flower bud
	薄	薄	薄	báo bohk thin; weak; feeble; poor; stingy
	薅	薅		hao hou 茠 to weed; pull out; eradicate; grab
	薇	薇	薇	wei mei royal fern (*osmunda regalis*); flowering fern
荟	薈	薈		huì wai luxuriant; flourishing; abundant; cloudy; overcast
蓟	薊	薊	薊	jì gai thistle (*cirsium* or *carduus*)
荐	薦	薦	薦	jiàn jin recommend; introduce; offer; to present; alternative for sacrum (荐)
芗	薌	薌		xiang heuhng fragrant smell of grain; aromatic
	薏	薏		yì ji heart of a lotus seed; Job's tears (*coix lacryma-jobi*)
蔷	薔	薔		qiáng chèuhng multiflora rose
	薛	薛	薛	xue sit 辥 type of marsh grass; name of a feudal state
	薜	薜	薜	bì bai 蘖 evergreen shrub (*ligusticum*)
	薟	薟		xian chim 蘝 spicy; pungent; vine

⺾ 13-14

	薤	韰		xiè　　　　haai Chinese onion (*allium chinense*); scallion; shallot
	薨	薨	薨	hong　　　　gwang (*of feudal lords / high officials*) pass away; die; (*onomatopoeia*) swarming; flocking; noisy
	薪	薪	薪	xin　　　　sàn salary; firewood
萧	蕭	蕭	蕭	xiao　　　　siù depression; lonely; mournful; dejected
萨	薩	薩	薩	sà　　　　saat short for bodhisattva
	薯	薯	薯	shǔ　　　　syùh　　　　茨 potato; sweet potato
	薹	薹	薹	tái　　　　toi type of sedge (*cyperus rotundus*); sedge (*carex*); brassica rapa
荠	薺	薺	薺	jì　　　　cháih shepherd's purse (*an edible weed, capsella bursa-pastoris*); caltrop
	藁	藁		gǎo　　　　gou straw; hay
	薰	薰	薰	xun　　　　fan　　　　薫蘍 fragrance of flowers; coumarou; tonka bean; cigarette; smoke
	薷	薷		rú　　　　jyu elsholtzia (*a plant genus in the Lamiaceae / mint family*)
蓝	藍	藍	藍	lán　　　　làahm blue; indigo plant (*indigofera tinctoria*)
荩	藎	藎		jìn　　　　jeun a type of weed; faithfulness; loyal
借	藉	藉	藉	jiè　　　　jihk pad; mat; pave; lean on; rely on; even if
	藏	藏	藏	cáng　　　　chòhng　　　　蔵臓 hide; conceal; to store; to lay

314

	藐	藐	藐	miǎo　　　miúh small; young; petty; look down on; think little of; view with contempt
	藕	藕	藕	ǒu　　　ngáuh lotus root; lotus rhizome
	藜	藜		lí　　　lai goosefoot plant
	藤	藤	藤	téng　　　tàhng vine; cane; rattan
药	藥	藥	藥	yào　　　yeuhk　　　药 藥 薬 medicine; drugs; pharmaceutical; to treat; cure; to poison
艺	藝	藝	藝	yì　　　ngaih skill; talent; craft; art
	藩	藩	藩	fan　　　faan fence; boundary; border; vassal state
薮	藪	藪	藪	sǒu　　　sau marsh; swamp; wild country; grove of trees or bushes
	蘑	蘑	蘑	mó　　　mo an edible mushroom
芦	蘆	蘆	蘆	lú　　　lou reed; rush; shepherd's purse root
蕴	蘊	蘊	蘊	yùn　　　wan accumulate; hold in store; contain; profoundness; profundity
蔼	藹	藹	藹	ǎi　　　ngói　　　藹 amiable; nice; kind; loving; lush; exuberant
蔺	藺	藺	藺	lìn　　　leun a rush used in making mats
	藿	藿		hùo　　　fok betony (*lophanthus rugosus*); heal-all
	藻	藻	藻	zǎo　　　jou algae; seaweed; literary embellishment; splendid; magnificent

蕲	蘄	蘄		qí　　　　kei variety of artemisia; bit (*for a horse*); ancient prefecture in Qichun, Hubei;
	蘅	蘅		héng　　　hang asarum blumei (*an unpleasantly fragrant plant with medicinal roots*)
苏	蘇	蘇	蘇	su　　　　sòu　　　　蕪 穌 perilla frutescens; firewood; take; get; tassel; alternative form of revive/regain consciousness (甦)
苹	蘋	蘋	蘋	píng　　　pìhng　　　蘋 apple; Chinese chestnut
茏	蘢	蘢		lóng　　　lung tall grass; water-weeds
	蘗	蘗		bò　　　　baak　　　　檗 stump; sprout
蔹	蘞	蘞		liǎn　　　lim wild vine (*vitis pentaphylla*)
	蘧	蘧		qú　　　　keui crimsonia (*dianthus superbus*); pleasantly surprised
兰	蘭	蘭	蘭	lán　　　　làahn orchid; elegant; graceful
藓	蘚	蘚	蘚	xiǎn　　　sin lichen; moss
	蘸	蘸		zhàn　　　jaam dip in; dunk; submerge in (*sauce, ink, etc.*)
	蘼	蘼		mí　　　　mei millet
萝	蘿	蘿	蘿	luó　　　　lo radish; creeping plants
蓠	蘺	蘺		lí　　　　lei algae (*gracilaria verrucosa*)
	虍	虍		hu　　　　fu tiger stripes; pattern on tiger fur

	虎	虎篆	虎古	hǔ　　　　fú tiger; brave; fierce	席 席 虤 麆 甝 彪 虓
	虐	虐篆		nüe　　　　yeuhk torture; cruel; tyrannical; oppressive; abusive; maltreat; disaster; calamity, catastrophe	
	虔	虔篆	虔古	qián　　　　kìhn sincere; devout; pious; reverent	
处	處	處篆	處古	chù　　　　chyu reside; dwell; situated in; virginity; chastity; punish; to discipline; get along with	
虚	虛	虛篆	虛古	xu　　　　hèui empty; hollow; false; unreal; worthless; vain	虗
虏	虜	虜篆		lǔ　　　　lóuh capture; imprison; plunder; rob; captive; enemy; prisoner of war; northern barbarian; slave; servant	
	虞	虞篆	虞古	yú　　　　jyu doubt; guess; suspect; anxious; worried; fear; danger; risk; deceive; capital of the state	驉
号	號	號篆	號古	hào　　　　houh name; alias; to command; shop; store; mark; symbol; number; a brass wind instrument; (internet) account	虠
亏	虧	虧篆	虧古	kui　　　　kwài lacking; deficient; deficit; treat unfairly; luckily; fortunately	
	虫	虫篆	虫古	chóng　　　　chùhng insect; worm; bug	
虬	虯	虯篆		qiú　　　　kau young horned dragon; twisted	
虹	虹	虹篆		hóng　　　　hùhng rainbow; (*figurative*) bridge	蝎
	虻	虻篆		méng　　　　mong horsefly; gadfly	䘃
	蚄	蚄篆		gè　　　　gat flea; dung beetle	
	虺	虺篆		hǔi　　　　wai venomous snake	

蚊			wén mosquito	màn	蟁 䘇 蚕 蠡 蠢 蠹 蠠
蚣			gong centipede	gung	
蚋			ruì gnat	jeui	
蚌			bàng clam	póhng	
蚍			pí large ant; small force (*i.e., an ant's strength*); high mallow (*plant*)	pei	
蚓			yǐn earthworm	jan	螾
蚪			dǒu tadpole	dau	
蚜			yá aphid; plant louse	ngàh	
蚧			jiè scale (*insect*)	gaai	
蚨			fú water beetle; money	fu	
蚤			zǎo flea	jóu	
蚩			chi worm; ignorant; stupid; rude; rustic	chi	
蛋			dàn egg; egg-shaped; ball; testicle	dáan	蛋 蜑
蚯			qiu earthworm	jau	
蚱			zhà grasshopper; locust; cicada	jaak	

318

蚴	(seal)		yǒu / yau — larva; tapeworm
蚵	(seal)	(seal)	kè / ho — oyster 蠔
蛀	(seal)	(seal)	zhù / jyu — moth eaten; decayed; insects that eat paper, clothes, and wood (*i.e., moth, termite, silverfish*)
蛄	(seal)	(seal)	gu / gu — mole cricket
蛇	(seal)	(seal)	shé / sèh — snake; serpent; snake-like; emperor; gentleman; illegal migration; (*Cantonese, poker*) straight 它 虵
蛉	(seal)	(seal)	líng / ling — dragonfly; sandfly; lacewing; libellulidae (*taxonomic family within the order odonata*)
蛆	(seal)	(seal)	qu / cheui — maggot; mosquito larva; wriggler; wiggler; despicable person
蚶	(seal)	(seal)	han / ham — ark clam
蚺	(seal)		rán / jim — anaconda; boa; python 蚦
蚰	(seal)		yóu / jau — centipede; millipede; earthworm
蛐	(seal)		qu / kuk — cricket
蛑	(seal)		móu / mau — marine crab
蛤	(seal)	(seal)	gé / gap — clam
蛞	(seal)	(seal)	kùo / fut — snail; slug; mole cricket
蛔	(seal)		húi / wui — tapeworm 蚘 蝈 痐 蚵

	蛘	详		yáng rice weevil	jeung	蛘蛘	
	蛙	蠹	䵷	wa frog	wà	䵷	
	蛛	珠	蛛	zhu spider	jyù	䵹	
	蛟	绞	蛟	jiao scaly dragon; flood dragon; aquatic reptile (*i.e., soft-shelled turtle, alligator*)	gaau		
	蛩	䖨		qióng cricket; locust; grasshopper; anxious	kung		
	蛭	䖝		zhì leech; bloodsucker	jat		
	蛸	䖝		xiao long-legged spider; octopus; a mantis chrysalis	siu		
	蛹	甬	蛹	yǒng chrysalis; pupa	jung		
蛺	蛺	䖅		jiá nymphalidae (*a family of butterflies*)	gaap		
蛻	蛻	䖅	蛻	tùi to shed skin; to change; exuvia; fossil	teui		
	蛾	䖅	蛾	é moth	ngòh		
	蜀	蜀	蜀	shǔ Sichuan	suk		
	蜂	䗬	蜂	feng hornet; wasp; bee; honey bee	fùng	蠭	
	蜊	䔲	蜊	lí clam; cockle; geoduck; mussel; shellfish	lei		
蜆	蜆	蜆	蜆	xiǎn basket clam (*corbiculidae*)	hín	蠇	

蜈	蜈	蜈	wú　　　　　ng centipede
蜉	蜉		fú　　　　　fau mayfly; wasp; large ant
蜍	蜍		chú　　　　chèuih　　蜍 toad
蜓	蜓	蜓	tíng　　　　ting dragonfly
蜃	蜃		shèn　　　　san large shellfish; clam; water spout; aquatic dragon with clam-like qualities
蜇	蜇		zhe　　　　　jit to sting (i.e., *bees, wasps, jellyfish*); to bite; sting (*pain*)
蜚	蜚		fěi　　　　　fei cockroach; gadfly; name of a mythical beast; alternate form of 飛
蜜	蜜	蜜	mì　　　　　maht honey; honey-colored; nectar; beeswax; sweet; mistress; young girl
蜞	蜞		qí　　　　　kei leech; sesarma crabs
蜢	蜢		měng　　　　máahng grasshopper; locust; catydid
蜣	蜣		diào　　　　geung dung-beetle
蜮	蜮		yù　　　　　wik　　蜮 mythical turtle-like creature; toad
蜱	蜱		pí　　　　　pei tick (*arachnid*)
蜴	蜴	蜴	yì　　　　　jik chameleon; lizard
蜷	蜷	蜷	qúan　　　　kyun curl up; creep like a worm

虫 8-9

	蜻	蜻	蜻	qing ching dragonfly	
	蜾	蜾		guǒ gwo potter wasp	
	蜿	蜿	蜿	wan jyun creep; crawl; meander	
	蜘	蜘	蜘	zhi ji spider	鼅 鼄
	蜥	蜥	蜥	xi sik lizard	
	蜩	蜩	蜩	tiáo tiu cicada; broad locust	
	蝓	蝓	蝓	yú jyu snail	
蚀	蝕	蝕	蝕	shí sik corrode; erode; an eclipse	
	蝗	蝗	蝗	húang wòhng locust; (*Hong Kong, derogatory*) swarms of migrants from the mainland	
	蝙	蝙	蝙	bian bin bat (*mammal*)	
	蝠	蝠	蝠	fú fùk bat (*mammal*)	
蜗	蝸	蝸	蝸	wo wò terrestrial snail	
	蝣	蝣		yóu jau mayfly (*ephemera strigata*)	
	蝤	蝤		qiú chàuh grub; larva; ephemera	
虾	蝦	蝦	蝦	xia hà shrimp; prawn; bend; to curve; flex	鰕

322

虫 9-10

	蝮			fù　　　　fuk venomous snake; viper
	蜂			kúi　　　　fui chain viper; Russell's viper (*vipera russelii siamensis*)
胡	蝴			hú　　　　wu butterfly
蛈	蝶			dié　　　　dihp butterfly
猬	蝟			wèi　　　　wai　　　猬 hedgehog
	蝽			chun　　　cheun stinkbug
	蝥			máo　　　　maau　　蟊 Spanish fly (*cantharis vesicatoria*); blister-beetle
虱	蝨			shi　　　　sat louse; bug; parasite
	蝌			ke　　　　fo tadpole
	螂			láng　　　　long　　　蜋 mantis; dragonfly; darning needle; dung beetle
蛳	螄			si　　　　si snail with spiral shell
	螃			páng　　　　pong crab
	螅			xi　　　　sik intestinal worm
	螋			sou　　　　sau earwig
	融			róng　　　　yùhng steam; melt; dissolve; mix; blend; fuse; harmonize; circulate

323

虫 10-11

	蓁	蓁(seal)		qín / cheun — a cicada with a square-shaped head
	螈	螈(seal)		yúan / jyun 蚖 — salamander; newt; axolotl
	螗	螗(seal)		táng / tong — cicada
蚂	螞	螞(seal)	螞(seal2)	mǎ / maa — (*prefix for insect names*); ant; leech
	螟	螟(seal)	螟(seal2)	míng / ming — bollworm; larva
萤	螢	螢(seal)	螢(seal2)	yíng / yìhng — firefly
	螫	螫(seal)		shè / sik — poison; poisonous insect; sting; stinger
	螯	螯(seal)		áo / ngou — pincer; claw; chela; nipper
蛰	蟄	蟄(seal)		zhé / jaht — hibernate; live in seclusion
	螽	螽(seal)		zhong / jung — grasshopper; katydid
	蟊	蟊(seal)		máo / maau 螯 — Spanish fly (*cantharis vesicatoria*); blister-beetle
	螬	螬(seal)		cáo / chòuh — scarab beetle grub
	螳	螳(seal)	螳(seal2)	táng / tong — mantis
	螵	螵(seal)		piao / piu — egg-case of a praying mantis
	螺	螺(seal)	螺(seal2)	lúo / lòh — aquatic snail; conch; whorl; swirl; spiral

324

螻	螻	螻	𤽄	lóu lau mole cricket (*gryllotalpa africana*)	
	蟆	蟆	蟆	má maa frog; toad	蟇
蝈	蟈	蟈	蟈	guo gwok green frog	
	蟋	蟋	蟋	xi sik cricket	
	螭	螭		chi chi hornless dragon; alternative form of mountain demon (魑)	彲
螨	蟎	蟎		mǎn mun a mite	
	蟑	蟑	蟑	zhang jeung cockroach	
	蟀	蟀	蟀	shùai sùt cricket	
	蟒	蟒	蟒	mǎng móhng python	
	蟓	蟓		xiàng jeung silkworm	
	蟛	蟛		péng paang land crab	
虮	蟣	蟣		jǐ gei louse eggs; wine foam	
蝉	蟬	蟬	蟬	chán sìhm cicada; thin silk; continuous; unending; cicada-shaped decoration	
	蟠	蟠	蟠	pán pun coil; coiling; curling; occupy	
	蟥	蟥		húang wong horseleech	

虫 12-14

	蟪			huì　　　　wai cicada (*platypleura kaempferi*)	
	蟺			shàn　　　sin　　　　蟬 earthworm	
蛲	蟯			náo　　　　jiu pinworm	
虫	蟲			chóng　　　chùhng　　　蚰 insect; worm; bug	
虿	蠆			chài　　　　chaai　　　蠚 venomous creature; scorpion	
	蟹			xiè　　　　háih　　　蠏 鱰 蚧 crab	
蛏	蟶			cheng　　　ching razor clam	
蚁	蟻			yǐ　　　　ngáih　　　螘 蛾 ant; small; wine foam or sediment; humble; inconsiderable; black	
	蠊			lián　　　　lim cockroach; mollusk	
	蟾			chán　　　sim toad	
	蠃			lǔo　　　　lo potter wasp	
蝇	蠅			yíng　　　yìhng fly; housefly	
蝎	蠍			xie　　　　kit scorpion	
蛴	蠐			qí　　　　cháih maggot; grub	
	蠕			rú　　　　jyu squirm; wriggle	

蝾	蠑			róng / wing salamander; newt	
	蠖			huò / wok inchworm; looper caterpillar	
	蠓			měng / mung midges; sandfly; mosquito	
蚝	蠔			háo / hòuh oyster	蚵
	蠛			miè / mit fly; flies	
蜡	蠟			là / laahp wax; candle	
蛎	蠣			lì / lai oyster	蛎
	蠡			lí / lai wood-boring insect; bore into wood	
	蠢			chǔn / chéun squirm; wriggle; stupid; foolish; clumsy; awkward	
蛊	蠱			gǔ / gu pest; vermin; noxious air; miasma; entice; bewitch; malevolent sorcery; affair; matter	
	蠲			juan / gyun remit; eliminate; cleanse; make clear; manifest; display	
蚕	蠶			cán / chàahm silkworm	蚕 螽 蠢 蚕 蠶
	蠹			dù / dou insects that eat paper, clothes, and wood (i.e., *moth, termite, silverfish*); vermin; moth-eaten; worm-eaten	
蛮	蠻			mán / màahn barbarous; savage; uncivilized; rough; rude; unreasonable; rash; hot-headed; uncouth; vulgar	满
	血			xuè / hyut blood; blood relations; kinship; firm; unyielding; ardent	

血 4　行 3-18　衣 2-3

	衄	衄		nù　　　nuk　　　衂 聏 衂 nosebleed; to bleed; defeated; shrink; cower; insult; humiliate; shame
	行	행	行	xing　　　haang walk; navigate; move; carry out; perform; behavior; occupation
	衍	衍	衍	yǎn　　　yín extend; spread out; overflow, spill over
术	術	術	術	shù　　　seuht art; craft; skill; technique; method; tactics; (obsolete) street; avenue
	街	街	街	jiē　　　gàai street; market; fair
	衙	衙	衙	yá　　　ngaa public office; official residence
卫	衛	衛	衛	wèi　　　waih　　　衞 protect; guard; defend; security guard
冲	衝	衝	衝	chong　　　chùng　　　衝 go straight ahead; rush; charge; dash; clash; collide; thoroughfare; important place
	衡	衡	衡	héng　　　hàhng cross yoke (i.e., for an ox); steel beam; to weigh; judge; measure; level; balanced; horizontal; tight; taut
	衢	衢	衢	qú　　　keui thoroughfare, highway junction, intersection
	衣	衣	衣	yi　　　yì clothes; garment; covering; skin; membrane
	初	初	初	chu　　　cho　　　礽 initial; inceptive; original; first; primary; elementary; basic; beginning; start
	表	表	表	biǎo　　　biú outer garment; surface; outside; exterior; external; superficial; table; form; list; to show; express; display
	衩	衩		chà　　　cha panties; open seam of a garment which allows freedom of movement
	衫	衫		shan　　　saam shirt; top; unlined garment; (Cantonese) clothing; clothes

328

衣 4-5

衽	衽	衽	rèn jam	lapel
被	被	被	bèi pei	bedding; quilt; blanket; to cover
衷	衷	衷	zhong chùng	middle; inner feelings; heart; from the bottom of one's heart
衰	衰	衰	shuai sèui 衰 衰	decline; fade; weaken; decrease in strength; detestable; make a grave mistake
袁	袁	袁	yúan jyun	robe; long clothing
衲	衲		nà naap	mend; sew; patch; line; quilt
衾	衾		qin kam	quilt; coverlet; quilt used to cover a corpse in a coffin
衿	衿		jin gam	gown; scholar
袂	袂		mèi mai	sleeves
袈	袈	袈	jia gaa	robe of a Buddhist monk
袋	袋	袋	dài doih	bag; sack; pouch; pocket; (*Cantonese*) put in a bag or pocket; (*classifier for bags of things*)
袞	袞	袞	gǔn kwan	ceremonial dress worn by the emperor
袤	袤		mào mau	longitude; length
袍	袍	袍	páo pòuh 袍	long Chinese gown, robe, cloak
袒	袒	袒	tǎn taan	bare; strip oneself naked to the waist; give unprincipled support; to shield

329

衣 5-7

	袖	袖	袖	xiù　　　jauh　　　褎褏褎 sleeve; tuck inside one's sleeve
	袢	袢		fán　　　faan white underwear; hot and suffocating; cloth made from kudzu
	被	被		bèi　　　pei bedding; quilt; blanket; to cover
	袷	袷		jiá　　　gaap　　　袷 lined garment
	袱	袱		fú　　　fuhk luggage in a sack
	裁	裁	裁	cái　　　chòih cut garments; cut into parts; dismiss; judge; decide
	裂	裂	裂	liè　　　lit to crack; break open; split; rend
	裉	裉		kèn　　　kang armpit of an upper garment; seam in a garment
裊	裊	裊	裊	niǎo　　　niu　　　嫋 curling upwards; wavering gently
	裎	裎		chéng　　　chìhng nude; take off clothes
	裒	裒		póu　　　pau　　　俘 collect; gather; assemble; reduce; decrease; subtract
	裘	裘	裘	qiú　　　kàuh fur coat
裝	裝	裝	裝	zhuāng　　　jòng　　　疢 baggage; luggage; clothes; dowry; style of bookbinding or packaging; pretend; to wrap; put into
	裟	裟	裟	sha　　　saa cassock or robe of a monk
	裔	裔		yì　　　yeuih offspring; descendant; posterity

衣 79

	裕	裕(seal)	裕(seal)	yù / yuh	wealthy; rich; abundant; plentiful
	裙	裙(seal)	裙(seal)	qún / kwàhn	skirt; dress; apron; petticoat
补	補	補(seal)	補(seal)	bǔ / bóu	repair; mend; fix; compensate; recompense; augment
里	裡	裡(seal)	裡(seal)	lǐ / leui	in; inside; interior; lining; during; within; (locational: here, there, where)
	裨	裨(seal)	裨(seal)	bì / bèi	advantage; aid; benefit; help; remedy; supplement; complement
	裸	裸(seal)	裸(seal)	luǒ / ló　　裸 羸 躶	bare; nude; naked; undress; strip; unclothed
	裹	裹(seal)	裹(seal)	guǒ / gwó	wrap; bind; encircle; confine; carry off
制	製	製(seal)	製(seal)	zhì / jai	make; manufacture; produce
	裳	裳(seal)	裳(seal)	shang / sèuhng	wear; put on
	裴	裴(seal)	裴(seal)	péi / pui　　裵	long flowing gown
	裰	裰(seal)		duo / jyut	to mend clothes
	裾	裾(seal)		ju / geui	lapel; hem; hemline; skirt
	褂	褂(seal)	褂(seal)	guà / gwá	Chinese-style unlined upper garment or jacket
	裼	裼(seal)		tì / tai	take off one's top; divest
	褊	褊(seal)	褊(seal)	biǎn / bin	tight-fitting clothing; narrow and small; crowded; deficient; narrow-minded; irritable; short-tempered

331

衣 9-11

	褐	褐	褐	hè　　　　　hot coarse-fiber cloth; poor; dull; brown
	褒	褒	褒	bao　　　　bou　　　　褒 褒 裒 praise; honor; commend; positive polarity; large; vast; wide
复	複	復	複	fù　　　　　fùk repeat; to double; overlap; complex; compound
	褓	褓	褓	bǎo　　　　bou swaddling cloth; infancy
	褪	褪		tùn　　　　tan take off (*clothes*); retreat; move; make available; withdraw; transfer; to shed (*hair*); discolour; fade
	褡	褡	褡	da　　　　 daap girdle; loincloth; pouch; bag
	褫	褫	褫	chǐ　　　　 chí to take off; to strip; deprive
	褥	褥		rù　　　　　yuhk mattress; cushion; bedding
裤	褲	褲		kù　　　　　fu pants; trousers
裢	褳	褳		lián　　　　lin pouch hung from a belt
	褵	褵		lí　　　　　lei bridal veil
	褶	褶	褶	zhě　　　　dip pleat; crease; fold; wrinkle; lined clothing; jacket
褛	褸	褸	褸	lǚ　　　　　leui lapel; collar; tattered; threadbare
	襁	襁		qiǎng　　　keung swaddling clothes
	褻	褻	褻	xiè　　　　 sit dirty; ragged; slight; insult; treat with disrespect

				Pinyin	Cantonese	Notes
	襄	襄(seal)	襄(seal)	xiang	seung	襄 aid; help; assist; rise to the occasion; undress
袄	襖	襖(seal)	襖(seal)	ào	óu	Chinese jacket; coat
	襟	襟(seal)	襟(seal)	jīn	kam	lapel; collar; front of a garment
	襞	襞(seal)	襞(seal)	bì	pik	fold clothes; folds or creases (*in cloth, the stomach, etc.*)
裆	襠	襠(seal)	襠(seal)	dang	dong	the crotch area; sleeveless garment; vest; waistcoat
褴	襤	襤(seal)	襤(seal)	lán	làahm	crotch or seat of pants; pants; ragged; torn
	襦	襦(seal)		rú	jyu	short coat; jacket; fine silk
袜	襪	襪(seal)	襪(seal)	wà	maht	socks; stockings 韈 韈 袜
衬	襯	襯(seal)	襯(seal)	chèn	chan	lining; inner garments; underwear; (*Cantonese*) to match clothing
袭	襲	襲(seal)	襲(seal)	xí	jaahp	attack; raid; follow a pattern; carry on as before; superpose; inherit; (*classifier for a suit or set of clothes*)
	襻	襻(seal)		pàn	paan	a loop; button loop; belt; band; fasten with rope or string
	西	西(seal)	西(seal)	xi	sài	west; western
	要	要(seal)	要(seal)	yào	yiu	want; must; wish; demand; ask; request; should; must
	覃	覃(seal)	覃(seal)	tán	taam	long; prolong; extend; deep
	覆	覆(seal)	覆(seal)	fù	fùk	覄 to cover; tip over; return; reply; overflow; capsize

見 4-18

见	見			jiàn　　　　gin see; visit; meet; opinion; appear
觅	覓			mì　　　　mihk　　覔 seek; hunt for; look for; search
规	規			gui　　　　kwài　　規䂓 regulation; rule; law; plan; arrange; exhort; admonish; advise
视	視			shì　　　　sih　　眡眎眎 see; look at; watch; view; inspect; examine; consider
觇	覘			chan　　　　chim peek; spy on; watch; investigate
觋	覡			xí　　　　hat wizard; shaman
觎	覦			yú　　　　jyu covet; long for; desire
亲	親			qin　　　　chàn　　親案 dear; intimate; beloved; parent(s); relatives; kiss; personally; accurate; true
觊	覬			jì　　　　gei covet; long for; desire
觏	覯			gòu　　　　kau meet or see unexpectedly; complete
觑	覷			qù　　　　cheui　　覰覻 peep; spy on; look; try to see with bad vision; squint as if one is nearsighted
觉	覺			júe　　　　gok　　覚竟覚 wake up; awaken to; become aware; to dawn on; think; sensation; feeling
览	覽			lǎn　　　　láahm　　覧 look at; inspect; perceive; to view; look around
觌	覿			dí　　　　dik to see; meet each other with courtesy; visit; to show; express
观	觀			guan　　　　gwùn　　観观 observe; watch; view; scrutinise; investigate; sightsee; enjoy; appearance; perspective; concept; outlook

	角	肏	斉	jiǎo　　gok　　角 horn; antler; point; angle; corner; cape; headland; role; character; actor; bugle; horn; contend; compete
	觖	觖		júe　　kyut dissatisfied; hypercritical
	觚	觚		gu　　gu goblet; jug; winecup
	解	解	解	jiě　　gaai　　解 untie; release; unfasten; loosen; split; separate; eliminate; solve; explain; understand
	觥	觥		gong　　gwang drinking vessel made of animal horn; large; sumptuous
	觳	觳		hú　　huk mean; frightened; ancient measuring tool
觞	觴	觴	觴	shang　　seung wine cup; drinking vessel; to toast; to drink
觯	觶	觶		zhì　　ji ceremonial drinking vessel; ornate goblet
触	觸	觸	觸	chù　　jùk touch; touched; come in contact with; to butt; to ram; to gore; affront; offend; stir up; invoke; cause
	言	言	言	yán　　yìhn say; speak; talk; explain; inquire; tell; speech; opinion; idea; decree; record; character; word; sentence; writing
	訇	訇		hong　　gwang (*onomatopoeia*); sound of a crash
计	計	計	計	jì　　gai calculate; to count; amount to; be concerned with; plan; plot; scheme; stratagem; gauge
讣	訃	訃	訃	fù　　fuh obituary; announcement of death
订	訂	訂	訂	dìng　　dihng draw up an agreement; arrange; engage; subscribe
讨	討	討	討	tǎo　　tóu beg; ask for; discuss; demand

言 3-4

讦	訐			jié — kit pry; expose a secret; accuse
讯	訊			xùn — seun inquire; investigate; trial; ask; to question; information; news; message
讧	訌			hòng — hung confusion; discord; strife; quarrel
训	訓			xùn — fan advise; instruct; teach; lecture; explain; scold; reprimand; rebuke; to train; submit to
讪	訕			shàn — saan mock; slander; ridicule
讫	訖			qì — gat bring to an end; complete; finish; conclude; finally; at last; exhaust
托	託			tuo — tok entrust; commit; rely on; depend on; pretext; to feign; assign responsibility
记	記			jì — gei remember; record; mark; keep in mind; chronicle
讹	訛			é — ngòh false; erroneous; mistaken; extort; blackmail
讶	訝			yà — ngah surprised; astonished
讼	訟			sòng — juhng dispute; accuse; argue; lawsuit; litigate
诀	訣			júe — kyut bid farewell; knack; trick of the trade; mnemonic chant; memory rhyme
讷	訥			nè — neut slow of speech; mumble; stammer; taciturn; speak little
访	訪			fǎng — fóng inquire; visit
设	設			shè — chit to set up; establish; plan; arrange; supposing

许	許	許	許	xǔ héui allow; permit; promise; betroth
诉	訴	訴	訴	sù sou 愬 tell; inform; relate; to vent
诈	詐	詐	詐	zhà ja deceive; cheat; defraud; swindle; pretend; feign; pretty; charming; dignified; haughty; proud
注	註	註	註	zhù jyu annotate; record; register; comment; note
诅	詛	詛	詛	zǔ jó curse; swear
评	評	評	評	píng pìhng criticize; comment; discuss; debate; judge; appraise
词	詞	詞	詞	cí chìh word; term; phrase; expression; speech; statement
诃	訶	訶	訶	he ho scold loudly; curse; verbal abuse
诊	診	診	診	zhěn chán diagnose; examine
诂	詁	詁	詁	gǔ gu exegesis; explanation
诋	詆	詆	詆	dǐ dái defame; slander; condemn; reproach
讵	詎	詎		jù geui (interjection used for expressing surprise)
诒	詒	詒		yí ji bequeath; to pass on
诏	詔	詔	詔	zhào jiu imperial decree; to decree; proclaim; foreign leader or king
诎	詘	詘		qu wat bend; stoop; crouch; yield

言 6

咏	詠			yǒng / wing chant; sing; hum; poetic description
	詈			lì / lei curse; scold; verbal abuse
	訾			zǐ / ji criticize; bad-mouth
	詹			zhan / jim　　　譫 talk too much; verbose; circumlocution
诩	詡			xǔ / héui boast; brag; flatter
询	詢			xún / sèun inquire; interrogate; consult with; ask about
诣	詣			yì / ngaih go to; reach; visit; call upon
试	試			chéng / sìhng test; examination; experiment; sincere; honest
诗	詩			shi / sì　　　訨 poem; poetry; ode; verse
诧	詫			chà / cha surprised; amazed; astonished; brag; show off; inform; cheat; deceive
诟	詬			gòu / gau abuse; scold; berate; insult; sense of shame
诡	詭			guǐ / gwái cunning; tricky; sly; deceitful; weird; bizarre
诠	詮			quán / chyùhn explain; expound; comment
诘	詰			jié / kit ask; enquire; question; interrogate; call to account; investigate; restrain
话	話			huà / wah　　　語 譮 speech; talk; dialect; spoken language; (*Cantonese*) say; refer to; talk about; scold; consider

338

该	該	諸	諸	gai — gòi contain; include; extensive; comprehensive; will be; should; ought to; need to; to deserve
详	詳	詳	詳	xiáng — chèuhng detailed; complete; thorough; explain; elaborate; serene; composed
侁	詵	詵		shen — san inquire; to question; numerous
诙	詼	詼	詼	hui — fui tease; joke with; ridicule; mock; humiliate
诖	詿	詿		gùa — gwaa error; mistake; disturb; deceive; mislead
诔	誄	誄		lěi — loi eulogize, eulogy
诛	誅	誅	誅	zhu — jyu execute; kill; put to death; punish; censure; to blame
诓	誆	誆		kuang — hong deceive; swindle; cheat; defraud; to coax; to fool
夸	誇	誇	夸	kua — kwà boast; praise; exaggerate; commend
诚	誠	誠	誠	chéng — sìhng sincere, honest; true; truly; indeed; very; if
认	認	認	認	rèn — yihng acknowledge; recognize; know; understand; confess; accept; undertake; agree; resign
诳	誑	誑	誑	kúang — gwong deceive; lie; delude; cheat; falsehood
	誓	誓	誓	shì — saih swear; oath; vow; pledge
志	誌	誌	誌	zhì — ji record; annals; memorize; mark; to show; colored spot on the skin
诞	誕	誕	誕	dàn — daan　誔 be born; birth; birthday; bear children; give birth to; absurd; ludicrous

诱	誘	誘	誘	yòu　　　yáuh teach; allure; induce; guide; pursuade; seduce; beguile; mislead
诮	誚	誚	誚	qiào　　　chiu criticize; scold; blame; ridicule; slander
语	語	語	語	yǔ　　　yúh speak; say; speech; language; expression; words; saying; proverb; (animal) chirp; hoot
诫	誡	誡	誡	jiè　　　gaai prohibit; warn; admonish; take precautions; guard against; (religion) commandments
诬	誣	誣		wu　　　mòuh false accusation; defame; deceive; hoodwink
误	誤	誤	誤	wù　　　mh mistake; mistaken; incorrect; delay
诰	誥	誥	誥	gào　　　gou inform; notify; admonish; to order; enjoin
诵	誦	誦	誦	sòng　　　juhng recite; praise; chant; recount
诲	誨	誨	誨	hùi　　　fui teach; instruct; encourage; induce
说	說	說	說	shuo　　　syut speak; say; explain; tell; persuade; discuss; scold
谁	誰	誰	誰	shéi　　　sèuih who; whom; someone; anyone; whoever
课	課	課	課	kè　　　fo lesson; course; classwork; examine; assess
谇	誶	誶	誶	sùi　　　seui speak ill of, vilify; defamatory; insult; offend; berate; interrogate
诽	誹	誹	誹	fěi　　　féi defame; slander; criticize
谊	誼	誼	誼	yì　　　yìh friendship

谆	諄	諄	諄	zhun　　　jeun earnest; patient
谈	談	談	談	tán　　　tàahm　　譚 chat; conversation; remark; discussion
诿	諉	諉	諉	wěi　　　wai shirk; give excuses; pass the buck, lay blame on others
调	調	調	調	tiáo　　　tiùh adjust; regulate; to train; to drill; tune or play an instrument; recuperate; mix; blend; harmonious; flirt
请	請	請	請	qǐng　　　chíng ask sincerely; invite; please; request; to treat; kindly
诤	諍	諍	諍	zhèng　　　jang　　爭 remonstrate; expostulate; admonish; quarrel; fight
诹	諏	諏		zou　　　jau consult; confer; select; choose; pick
诼	諑	諑		zhúo　　　jeuk slander; gossip; rumors; complain; grumble
谅	諒	諒	諒	liàng　　　leuhng forgive; excuse; pardon; believe; presume
论	論	論	論	lùn　　　leuhn debate; discuss; reason; argue; evaluate; recount; regard; consider; dialogue; discourse; theory; thesis
谄	諂	諂	諂	chǎn　　　chím　　諂讇 flatter; butter up; fawn over; cajole; toady
谀	諛	諛		yú　　　jyu flatter; cajole; toady; kind; gentle; meek
谍	諜	諜	諜	dié　　　dip espionage; spying; spy; agent; intelligence report
谝	諞	諞		pián　　　pin brag; boast; sweet but insincere speech
谐	諧	諧	諧	xié　　　hàaih harmonize; harmonious; coordinate; coordinated; congruous; joke; jest; persuade; advise

言 9

谏	諫			jiàn　　　gaan　　　　諫 remonstrate; admonish
谕	諭			yù　　　jyu instruct; tell; understand; know; make known; make clear; compare; order from above; imperial decree
谙	諳			an　　　am learn by heart; versed in, fully acquainted with; (*Sichuanese*) think; believe
谌	諶			chén　　　sam believe; sincere; honest; indeed
讽	諷			fěng　　　fung satirize; ridicule; recite
诸	諸			zhu　　　jyù many; each; every; all
谚	諺			yàn　　　yihn proverb; maxim; Korean hangul
谖	諼			xuan　　　hyun to cheat; bamboozle; forget
诺	諾			nùo　　　lok promise; approve; assent
谋	謀			móu　　　màuh plan; plot; scheme; stratagem; device; devise; seek; work for; consult
谒	謁			yè　　　jit visit; pay respects; to state; inform; report; accuse; request; name card
谓	謂			wèi　　　waih say; call; tell
谔	諤			è　　　ngok honest speech; straightforward
谛	諦			dì　　　dai examine; scrutinise; careful; attentive; principle; basis; essence; (*Buddhism*) truth
诨	諢			hùn　　　wan joke; jest

讳	諱	諱(seal)	諱(seal)	huì　　　wai avoid mentioning; regard as taboo; to fear; to dread
誊	謄	謄(seal)	謄(seal)	téng　　　tàhng copy; transcribe
诌	謅	謅(seal)		zhou　　　jau talk nonsense; make up a story
谎	謊	謊(seal)	謊(seal)	huǎng　　　fòng lie; falsehood, untruth
谜	謎	謎(seal)	謎(seal)	mí　　　maìh　　　誅謎 riddle; puzzle; enigma; mystery
谧	謐	謐(seal)	謐(seal)	mì　　　mat calm; quiet; still
谥	謚	謚(seal)		shì　　　si posthumous title or name
谑	謔	謔(seal)		xùe　　　jeuk crack a joke; banter; to tease
谡	謖	謖(seal)		sù　　　suk to rise; raise
谤	謗	謗(seal)	謗(seal)	bàng　　　bong (*archaic*) openly criticize; slander; defame; to vilify
谦	謙	謙(seal)	謙(seal)	qián　　　hìm humble; modest
讲	講	講(seal)	講(seal)	jiǎng　　　góng speak; tell; talk; say; inform; discuss; lecture
谢	謝	謝(seal)	謝(seal)	xiè　　　jeh excuse oneself; apologise; decline; renounce; resign; leave; warn; thanks; gratitude; to wane; to wither
谣	謠	謠(seal)	謠(seal)	yáo　　　yiùh　　　謠 sing without instruments; folk song; ballad; false rumour
	謇	謇(seal)		jiǎn　　　hin stutter; boldly speaking

言 11-12

	謦	謦		qǐng　　　　hing speak softly
谬	謬	謬	謬	miù　　　　mauh false; error; exaggeration; erroneous
谪	謫	謫	謫	zhé　　　　jaak blame; disgrace; demote; charge; punish
讴	謳	謳		ou　　　　au sing; folk song; ballad
谨	謹	謹	謹	jǐn　　　　gán careful; respectful; prudent; cautious; reverent
谟	謨	謨	謨	mó　　　　mou　　　謩 scheme; plan; be without
谩	謾	謾		màn　　　　maan deceive; insult; slight; disrespect
证	證	證	證	zhèng　　　　jing prove; proof; evidence; testify; verify
谲	譎	譎	譎	júe　　　　kyut deceitful; lying; imposter; untruthful
讥	譏	譏	譏	jí　　　　gèi ridicule; satirize; jeer; mock; admonish; interrogate
谮	譖	譖		zèn　　　　jam　　　譜 slander
谱	譜	譜	譜	pǔ　　　　pou register; list; table; manual; musical score; grasp; foundation; confidence
识	識	識	識	shí　　　　sìk know; knowledge; recognize; realize; aware; distinguish; discriminate
谯	譙	譙	譙	qiáo　　　　chiu blame
谭	譚	譚	譚	tán　　　　tàahm　　　談 chat; conversation; remark; discussion

344

	警	警	警	jǐng　　gíng warn; admonish; alert; alarm; siren; vigilant; intuitive; sharp; witty; police
	譬	譬	譬	pì　　pei analogy; metaphor; inform; explain; understand
谵	譫	譫	譫	zhan　　jim　　嚪 talkative; delirium; incoherent speech; drivel; raving
译	譯	譯	譯	yì　　yihk translate; interpret; decode; decipher
议	議	議	議	yì　　ji talk over; discuss; to comment; criticize; critique; opinion; suggestion; parliament; legislative assembly
谴	譴	譴	譴	qiǎn　　hin reprimand; scold; abuse; denounce; censure
护	護	護	護	hù　　wuh safeguard; protect; defend; shelter
誉	譽	譽	譽	yù　　yuh praise; reputation; fame
谫	譾	譾		jiǎn　　jin　　譾 shallow; stupid
读	讀	讀		dú　　duhk read; study; peruse; read aloud; tell; pronounce
变	變	變	變	biàn　　bin　　彰 change; transform; alter; turn into; flexible with matters; accommodate to circumstances
雠	讎	讎		chóu　　chàuh　　讐 enemy; rival; opponent; feud; collate; proofread
谗	讒	讒		chán　　chàahm　　譖 slander; defame; vilify; speak maliciously of others; libel
让	讓	讓	讓	ràng　　yeuhng　　譲 yield; give away; concede; allow; cause; permit
谰	讕	讕		lán　　laan　　譋 嚹 calumniate; false charge; slander; refuse to admit; disavow

言 17-20　谷 10　豆 3-21　豕

谶	讖	讖	讖	chèn　　　chaam prophecy; foretelling
赞	讚	贊	讚	zàn　　　jaan　　　讃 praise; eulogize; commend
谠	讜	讜	讜	dǎng　　　dong　　　讜 upright; honest; person who speaks candidly
谳	讞	讞		yàn　　　jit decide; judge; verdict; decision; decide judicially
	谷	谷	谷	gǔ　　　gùk valley; ravine; gorge; mountain stream; predicament; difficult position
	豁	豁	豁	huò　　　kut open; clear; exempt; remit
	豆	豆	豆	dòu　　　dauh　　　荳 bean; bean-shaped; legume; pea
岂	豈	豈	豈	qǐ　　　héi how; possibly; perhaps
	豇	豇		jiang　　　gong cowpea
	豉	豉		chǐ　　　sih　　　豉枝尗皷䜴餕 fermented bean
	豌	豌		wan　　　wun pea
竖	豎	豎	豎	shù　　　syuh　　　伛豎 erect; vertical; upright; perpendicular; attendant; boy servant
丰	豐	豐	豐	fēng　　　fùng abundant; fruitful; luxuriant; bountiful; plenty; well-developed; plump; great; enhance; enlarge
艳	豔	豔	豔	yàn　　　yihm　　　豓艷 charming; pretty; bright and beautiful color; gaudy; romantic; envy; admire
	豕	豕	豕	shǐ　　　chí pig; hog; boar; swine

	豚	豚	豚	tún　　tyun　　㹠 piglet; suckling pig; dolphin; porpoise	
	象	象	象	xiàng　　jeuhng elephant; ivory; tusk; shape; figure; emblem; phenomenon; appearance; sign; law; principle	
	豢	豢		huàn　　waan feed livestock	
	豪	豪	豪	háo　　hòuh strong, superior; brave, heroic, chivalrous; great; extraordinary	
	豫	豫	豫	yù　　jyu　　　　豬 豬 猪 relaxed; comfortable; at ease; content; short for Hénán (河南)	
猪	豬	豬	豬	zhū　　jyù pig; hog; boar; swine; a lazy and contemptible person; (*Cantonese*) virginity	
	豳	豳	豳	bin　　ban a Zhou-dynasty state	
	豸	豸		zhì　　jaai legless insect; larva; legendary animal	
	豺	豺	豺	chái　　chàaih　　犲 dhole (*cuon alpinus*)	
	豹	豹	豹	bào　　paau leopard; panther	
	貂	貂	貂	diao　　diù sable; mink; marten; ermine	
	貉	貉	貉	hé　　hok raccoon dog	
	貅	貅		xiu　　yau brave; fierce; courageous; female counterpart of 貔; (Chinese mythology) female panther-like feline	
	貊	貊	貊	mò　　mak　　狛 leopard; ancient tribe in northeastern China	
	貌	貌	貌	mào　　maauh facial appearance; facial features; looks; outward appearance; expression; countenance; superficial	

	貓	貓	貓	mao　　　　màau cat; to hide; loaf around; (*Cantonese*) get drunk; non-productive and negative person; (*Hokkien*) stingy
	貔	貔		pí　　　　pei fox; leopard; panther; panther-like feline
	貘	貘		mò　　　　mak　　　　獏 tapir; giant panda
贝	貝	貝	貝	bèi　　　　bui shell; cowrie; money; currency
贞	貞	貞	貞	zhēn　　　　jìng virtuous; pure; chaste; loyal; faithful
负	負	負	負	fù　　　　fuh load; burden; rely on; carry; bear; negative (math or situation); ungrateful; betray; repudiate
贡	貢	貢	貢	gòng　　　　gung pay tribute; gift; select or recommend talented persons for the imperial court
财	財	財	財	cái　　　　chòih　　　　財 wealth; property; valuables; riches; money
贩	販	販	販	fàn　　　　fáan sell; trade; to deal in; to traffic; peddler; hawker; street merchant
败	敗	敗		bài　　　　baai lose a game; defeat; fail; decay; destroy
贬	貶	貶	貶	biǎn　　　　bin abase; lower; vilify; censure; criticize
贫	貧	貧	貧	pín　　　　pàhn poor; needy; impoverished; destitute; inadequate; insufficient; lacking; garrulous; talkative
贪	貪	貪	貪	tan　　　　tàam greedy; embezzle; be fond of; insatiable desire; pursue something excessively or inappropriately
货	貨	貨	貨	huò　　　　fo merchandise; goods; currency; commodities; products
责	責	責	責	zé　　　　jaak demand; demand to; order to; blame; reproach; interrogate; punish by beating; duty; responsibility

贯	貫	貫	貫	guàn gwan string of one thousand coins; go through, penetrate; one's native place
贵	貴	貴	貴	guì gwai 貴 expensive; costly; precious; valuable; superior; noble; (*honorific for deity, person, or establishment*) your
买	買	買	買	mǎi máaih buy; purchase; bribe; persuade
贸	貿	貿	貿	mào mauh commerce; trade; barter; mixed; rashly
贺	賀	賀	賀	hè hoh congratulate; send a present
贲	賁	賁	賁	bì bei adorn oneself; honor with one's presence
费	費	費	費	fèi fai 廢 cost; spend; fee; bill; charge; dues; consume; exhaust; squander; waste; lose; loquacious; garrulous; verbose
贳	貰	貰		shì sai borrow; pardon; loan; lease; lend; rent; buy on credit
贰	貳	貳	貳	èr yih 二 two
贷	貸	貸	貸	dài taai lend with interest; borrow
贮	貯	貯	貯	zhù chyúh store up; save; stockpile; hoard; put food in a container
贶	貺	貺		kuàng fong give; grant; bestow
贴	貼	貼	貼	tiē tip paste to; stick on; be attached to
贻	貽	貽	貽	yí ji give as a present; hand down; leave behind; bequeath
赂	賂	賂	賂	lù lou bribe; bribery; to present a gift; money and goods

貝 6-8

贿	賄	賄	賄	huì　　　kúi bribe; wealth; property; to give belongings
赅	賅	賅	賅	gai　　　goi complete; comprehensive; include; to give belongings
贼	賊	賊	賊	zéi　　　chaahk　　賊 damage; to corrupt; to ruin; destroy; harm; injure; slander; murder; thief; bandit; robber; villain; traitor
赁	賃	賃		lìn　　　jam rent; wage
资	資	資	資	zí　　　jì money; fund; wealth; capital; expense; cost; resources; qualifications; certificate; material; grain; aid
贾	賈	賈	賈	jiǎ　　　gá merchant; to trade
赀	貲	貲	貲	zi　　　ji estimate; count; property; wealth
宾	賓	賓	賓	bin　　　bàn　　　賓 賓 guest; visitor; object
赈	賑	賑	賑	zhèn　　　jan relieve; aid the distressed; succor
赇	賕	賕		qiú　　　kau bribe
赊	賒	賒	賒	she　　　sè　　　賒 賒 buy or sell on credit; forgive; distant; far; long time; long-standing; sparse; rare; slow
赓	賡	賡	賡	geng　　　gang continue; go on doing; compensate; make up for
赋	賦	賦	賦	fù　　　fu　　　賦 bestow; give; compose or sing; spread; disseminate; collect; impose; levy; taxation; revenue; endowment
赐	賜	賜	賜	cì　　　chi give from superior to inferior; give as a favor; bestow
赉	賚	賚		lài　　　loi reward; bestow; confer; grant

貝 8-11

贤	賢	賢	賢	xián yìhn 賢政賢臣 virtuous; kind; good; clever; wise; judicious; worthy; able; capable
卖	賣	賣	賣	mài maaih 賣賣 sell; betray; sell out; spare no effort; do one's best; show off; (Cantonese) to publish news
质	質	質	質	zhì jat 質質 substance; matter; quality
赏	賞	賞	賞	shǎng séung 贈 reward; to present as a gift; bestow; grant; enjoy; appreciate; admire; praise
账	賬	賬	賬	zhàng jeung 帳 account; bill; debt
赌	賭	賭	賭	dǔ dóu gamble; bet; wager
赔	賠	賠	賠	péi pùih compensate; pay damages; indemnify, lose; apologize; suffer financial loss
赕	賧	賧		tǎn daam 倓 pay for atonement; money for atonement
贱	賤	賤	賤	jiàn jihn cheap; lowly; poor; inferior; base; despicable; obnoxious; (humble) my; despise; detest
赖	賴	賴	賴	lài laaih rely; depend on; accuse falsely; blame; shameless; impudent; brazen; disavow; deny
赚	賺	賺	賺	zhuàn jaahn earn; gain; profit; gain an unfair advantage
赙	賻	賻	賻	fù fu contribute to funeral expenses; financial gift for covering funeral costs
购	購	購	購	gòu kau buy; purchase; hire
赛	賽	賽	賽	sài choi compete; contend; contest; race; match
赜	賾	賾		zé jaak deep; profound; mysterious; abstruse; difficult to comprehend; concealed

351

貝 11-17　赤 4-9

贅	贅	贅	贅	zhùi　　jeui unnecessary; superfluous; redundant
赞	贊	贊	贊	zàn　　jaan　　　　贊 assist; praise; help; support; agree
赠	贈	贈	贈	zèng　　jahng give a gift; bestow
赡	贍	贍	贍	shàn　　sihn support; provide for; aid; sufficient; rich, elegant
赢	贏	贏	贏	yíng　　jing win; triumph; beat; to defeat; triumph over; profitable gain
赆	贐	贐		jìn　　jeun　　　　賮贐 farewell present
赃	贓	贓	贓	zang　　jong　　　　臟賍贓 plunder; booty; loot; stolen goods; accept or take a bribe
赝	贗	贗		yàn　　ngaan counterfeit; fake; false; forged
赎	贖	贖	贖	shú　　suhk redeem; to ransom
赣	贛	贛		gàn　　gam　　　　贑灨 Gan river; alternative name for Jiangxi (江西)
	赤	赤	赤	chì　　chek　　　　㷊 red; brown; bare; naked; loyal; empty
	赦	赦	赦	shè　　se forgive; pardon
	赧	赧	赧	nǎn　　naan blush; turn red
	赫	赫	赫	hè　　haak bright red; luminous; distinguished; eminent; glorious; show off; angrily; furiously; short for hertz (赫茲)
	赭	赭	赭	zhě　　je ochre; burnt ochre; reddish brown; dye red; bare; punish

	走	歨	𧺆	zǒu　　jáu　　辵 walk; run; go; leave; go away; flee; visit; call on; pass away; die; from; through
	赳	赳	赳	jiu　　dáu grand; valiant; brave
	赴	赴	赴	fù　　fuh attend; go to; visit; join
	起	起	起	qǐ　　héi rise; stand up; start; initiate; prepare; extract; remove; (*particle after verbs indicating upward movement*)
	趁	趂	趂	chèn　　chan　　趂 趂 賺 chase; pursue; follow; accompany; take advantage of an opportunity; avail oneself; to earn; have a lot of
	趄	趄		ju　　cheui reclined; inclined; slanting; hesitate
	超	超	超	chao　　chiù jump over; leap over; transcend; exceed; overtake; surpass; super; hyper; far; distant
	越	越	越	yùe　　yuht　　邺 pass over; exceed; surpass; overstep; transgress; propagate; relax; to rob; seize by force; turn around
	趑	趑		zi　　chi walk with difficulty; cannot move; falter
	趔	趔		liè　　lit stagger; stumble; to reel; not progressing
赶	趕	趕	趕	gǎn　　gón overtake; catch up with; hurry; rush; try to catch (bus, train); chase away; avail oneself of an opportunity
赵	趙	趙	趙	zhào　　jiuh an ancient city-state in Shanxi region; an ancient state during the Warring States period; run
	趣	趣	趣	qù　　cheui interest; delight; amusing; inclination; objective; purport; intention; action; conduct; charm; appeal
	趟	趟	趟	tàng　　tong take a journey; time; occasion; (*classifier for journeys or occasions*)
趋	趨	趨	趨	qú　　chèui hasten; hurry; be attracted to

走 19　足 2-5

趲	趲	趲	zǎn　jyun go in a hurry; hasten; urge
足	足	足	zú　jùk　昱呈 foot; leg; walk; tread; step; fulfill; stop; cease; enough; sufficient; abundant; affluent; entirely; very; quite
趴	趴		pa　paa to lie on one's stomach; resting the upper body on a surface
趵	趵		bào　paau jump; well up; spring forth; kick
跶	跶		ta　taat tread down on the back of one's shoes; tread on; slipshod
趼	趼		jiǎn　gin　繭跉鱗 callous; thick patch of skin
趾	止	趾	zhǐ　jí toe; foot; footprint
趺	趺	趺	fu　fu instep; top of the foot; foot of a mountain; pedestal of a stone tablet; sit cross-legged; footprint
跌	跌	跌	die　dit fall down; drop
跆	跆	跆	tái　toi instep; trample
跋	跋	跋	bá　baht fall; toss; throw; trample; step on; go by foot; climb; base of a candle; postscript; epilogue
跎	跎	跎	túo　to stumble
跏	跏		jia　gaa walk with feet pointing inwards; sit cross-legged; squat
跑	跑	跑	pǎo　páau run; flee; walk; stroll; rush about; leak; evaporate; go away; run a computer program; popular
跗	跗		fu　fu tarsus; instep

蹣	蹣	蹣	shan　　　saan limp; stagger
跛	跛	跛	bǒ　　　bái　　　柀 lame; crippled
距	距	距	jù　　　kéuih apart; away from; distance; spur (*of a cock, pheasant, etc.*)
跬	跬		kuǐ　　　kwai　　　頤起 half a step; short step; near; brief
跨	跨	跨	kuà　　　kwà　　　𠀋 step across; cross over (*a wall etc.*); transgender; transition (*gender*)
跪	跪	跪	guì　　　gwaih to kneel
路	路		lù　　　louh road; route; street; path; pattern; arrangement; way; method; journey; kind; type
跳	跳	跳	tiào　　　tiu jump; leap; hop; pass over; skip; bypass; palpitate; pulsate; jump (*into or from*) resulting in death
跺	跺	跺	duò　　　do to stamp one's feet; stomp
跟	跟	跟	gen　　　gàn heel (*foot, shoe, or sock*); follow; (*woman*) to marry; with; as (*comparison*); to; with; and
迹 跡	跡	跡	jì　　　jik mark; track; trace; footprint
跣	跣		xiǎn　　　sin barefoot
跤	跤	跤	jiao　　　gaau　　　腳骹 tumble; fall
跫	跫		qióng　　　kung trampling; sound of footsteps
跇	跇		xúe　　　chyut circle; whirl; spin; walk back and forth; turn back; tied up; entangled in a matter

足 7-9

	踉	踉		liàng　　leung hop; jump; urgently; in a hurry
	踝	踝	踝	húai　　wa　　　　踝 髁 ankle
	踔	踔		chuo　　cheuk get ahead; stride; excel
	踏	踏	踏	tà　　daahp step on; trample; tread on; investigate onsite
	踢	踢	踢	tí　　tek kick
践	践	踐	踐	jiàn　　chíhn trample; tread upon; ascend the throne; inherit; implement; carry out; abide by; experience; orderly
	踟	踟	踟	chí　　chìh hesitate; undecided; embarrassed
	踞	踞	踞	jù　　geui crouch; squat; to sit; occupy; lean on
	踣	踣		bó　　baak　　　　仆 fall forward; fall prone; fall prostrate; exhibit a corpse; overturn; be defeated
	踮	踮		diǎn　　dim　　　　站 惦 to tiptoe
	踩	踩	踩	cǎi　　cháai step on; trample on; (*Cantonese*) belittle; denigrate; criticize; (*internet*) dislike
	蹀	蹀		dié　　dip step; stamp; tread; skip
踊	踴	踴	踴	yǒng　　yúng jump upwards; leap
	踵	踵	踵	zhǒng　　dung heel; follow; visit; call on
	踹	踹		chùai　　cháai kick; run; tread upon; stomp on; to dump a partner; to ditch

356

	踽	踽		jǔ geui to walk alone; self-reliant; hunchbacked
	蹁	蹁		pián pin walk with a limp; splayfoot
	蹂	蹂	蹂	róu jau trample under foot; tread on
	蹄	蹄	蹄	tí tàih 蹏 hoof; pork leg
	踱	踱	踱	dúo dohk stroll; pace; walk slowly; walk barefoot; stupid; dull
	蹊	蹊	蹊	xi hai footpath; trample on; to cross; traverse; footprint; path; way
	蹈	蹈	蹈	dǎo dou trample; stomp; tread on; jump into; devote oneself; follow
	蹋	蹋	蹋	tà taap kick; alternative form of step on; trample (踏)
	蹉	蹉	蹉	cuo cho slip and fall; to err; make a mistake
跄	蹌	蹌		qiàng cheung error; mistake; slip; failure; stagger
	蹇	蹇		jiǎn gin 謇 lame; crippled; difficult; hard; unlucky; dull; stupid; dumb; arrogant; haughty; stutter
	蹙	蹙	蹙	cù chuk 顣 knit one's brows; approach; close in on; force; compel; shrink; contract; urgent; critical
跸	蹕	蹕	蹕	bì bat 僻 clear the way; make room for the emperor; emperor's carriage; emperor's halting place; stand unsteadily
跖	蹠	蹠		zhí jik sole of the foot; plantar
蹒	蹣	蹣	蹣	pán pun limp; hobble; cripple

足 11-13

	蹦	蹦	蹦	bèng　　　bang hop; jump
踪	蹤	蹤	蹤	zóng　　　jùng trace; footprint; track
	蹩	蹩		bié　　　bit sprain; limp
	蹬	蹬	蹬	deng　　　dang step on; tread; press down or out with one's feet; to wear
	蹭	蹭		cèng　　　sang rub against; be smeared with; shuffle; drag the feet; dawdle; delay; procrastinate; freeload; scrounge
	蹯	蹯		fán　　　faan paw; animal track
	蹲	蹲	蹲	dun　　　dèun sit; stay; squat
	蹴	蹴	蹴	cù　　　juk kick; tread on; trample; leap; solemn
	蹶	蹶	蹶	júe　　　kyut　　　蹷 tumble; fall down; run; fail; step on; tread on; rapidly; suddenly
跷	蹺	蹺	蹺	qiao　　　hiu　　　蹻 raise one's foot
	蹼	蹼	蹼	pǔ　　　buk webbed; the membrane between the toes of birds
	躁	躁	躁	zào　　　chòu short temper; impetuous; irritable
	躇	躇	躇	chú　　　chyuh　　　躆 hesitate; falter; undecided
	躅	躅	躅	zhú　　　juk flutter; falter; hesitate; step on; footprint; walk carefully
趸	躉	躉		dǔn　　　dan wholesale

踌	躊	蠹	蹋	chóu / chàuh hesitate; waver; falter; pace back and forth; smug; self-satisfied	
跃	躍	躍	躍	yùe / yeuk leap; jump	趯
跻	躋	躋	躋	ji / jai ascend; go up; rise; high; steep	
	躐	躐		liè / lip stride over; step across; overstep; overpass	
踯	躑	躑	躑	zhí / jik hesitating; doubtful; waver; hesitate; irresolute	
跞	躒	躒		lì / lik walk; move	
踬	躓	躓		zhì / ji stumble; totter; trip; fall through; frustrated	
	躔	躔		chán / chìhn tread; footprint; track; to move in orbit; follow; imitate; rut; path	
蹰	躕	躕		chú / chyùh hesitate; waver; falter	蹰 跦
跹	躚	躚		xian / sin wander around; walk; revolve	
	躞	躞		xiè / sit walk	
蹿	躥	躥		cuan / chyun leap; jump; spurt out	
蹑	躡	躡	躡	niè / nihp to tiptoe; chase; tread; step lightly	
躏	躪	躪	躪	lìn / leun trample on; oppress; overrun	
	身	身	身	shen / san body; pregnancy; oneself; in person; I; me; life; social status; moral character; (classifier for suits of clothes)	

身 3-11　車 1-5

	躬	躬	躬	gong　　　gùng body; oneself; in person; personally; stoop
	躭	躭	躭	dan　　　dàam delay; hinder; indulge; negligent
	躲	躲		duǒ　　　dó　　　　躱 躱 hide; avoid; evade
	躺	躺	躺	tǎng　　　tóng lie flat; recline
躯	軀	軀	軀	qu　　　kèui human body; trunk
	車	車	車	che　　　chè vehicle; car; cart; chariot; to machine, shape with a lathe; tailor or sew using a sewing machine
	軋	軋	軋	yà　　　gaat crush by weight; grind; squeeze in; (onomatopoeia)
	軌	軌	軌	guǐ　　　gwái rail; track; rut
	軍	軍	軍	jun　　　gwàn army; military; soldiers; troops
	軒	軒	軒	xuan　　　hin　　　衛 high; lofty; airy; small veranda with windows; ancient Chinese curtained carriage; window; door
	軔	軔	軔	rèn　　　jan brake; a block that keeps a wheel from moving
	軟	軟	軟	ruǎn　　　yúhn　　　輭 soft; flexible; pliable; gentle; mild; weak; feeble
	軛	軛	軛	è　　　aak　　　軶 yoke; collar; restrain; control
	軻	軻	軻	ke　　　o axle
	軸	軸	軸	zhóu　　　juhk axis; axletree; pivot; keyboard key switch

360

軹	軹		zhǐ　　ji an axle end; divergent
軼	軼	軼	yì　　jat scattered; lost; surpass; excel; alternative form of leisurely (逸)
軫	軫		zhěn　　jan cross board at rear of a carriage; tuning peg of a stringed instrument
輇	輇		qúan　　chyùhn cart wheel with no spokes; shallow
軾	軾	軾	shì　　sik horizontal wooden bar in front of a sedan chair
較	較	較	jiào　　gaau compare; comparatively; relatively; obvious; clear
輅	輅		lù　　lou chariot; carriage; carriage pull-bar
載	載	載	zài　　joi ide; carry; hold; loaded with; bear the weight of; support; hold up; be charged with; to come into effect
輊	輊	輊	zhi　　ji low; short; lower rear portion of cart
輒	輒	輒	zhé　　jip then; at once; always; luggage rack on a chariot
輔	輔	輔	fǔ　　fuh assist; cheekbone; wooden bars that prevent a carriage from overturning
輕	輕	輕	qíng　　hìng　　軽 lightweight; small; slight; insignificant; portable; rash; frivolous; skittish; giddy; easy; humble; gentle
輜	輜	輜	zi　　ji carriage that has a curtain; military supply carriage
輛	輛	輛	liàng　　leuhng (*classifier for wheeled vehicles*)
輞	輞	輞	wǎng　　mong exterior rim of a wheel

車 8-10

輟	輟	輟	chuò　　jyut stop; suspend; halt; cease
輥	輥	輥	gǔn　　gwan revolve; stone roller
輦	輦	輦	niǎn　　lin handcart; imperial carriage; transport by carriage
輩	輩	輩	bèi　　bui generation; lifetime; people of a certain kind or class
輝	煇	煇	hui　　fāi brightness; splendid; lustre; brilliance; radiance; shine upon
輪	輪	輪	lún　　lèuhn wheel; edge; rim; round of talks or performances; take turns; Chinese zodiac 12 year cycle
輸	輸	輸	shu　　syù transport; carry; haul; lose; defeated; donate; contribute
輯	輯	輯	jí　　chàp gather up; collect; edit; compile; (*classifier for a volume of literary work*)
輳	輳	輳	còu　　chau hub of a wheel; converge around
輻	輻	輻	fú　　fuk wheel spokes
輾	輾		zhǎn　　jín turn over; roll; alternative form of to crush flat with a wheel or run over (碾)
轅	轅	轅	yúan　　jyun axle; magistrate's office
轂	轂		gǔ　　guk　　轂 hub of a wheel; wheel; chariot; cart
轄	轄	轄	xiá　　hat govern; control; jurisdiction; rule; manage; wheel linchpin
輿	輿	輿	yú　　jyu cart; carriage; sedan chair; palanquin; public opinion

轆	轆		lù　　　　luk　　　　轆轤碌 well pulley; windlass; potter's wheel; rolling; turn over; to squash; throw; toss; swing; (Cantonese) tire
轉	轉	轉	zhǔan　　　jyún　　　搏摎返 rotate; roll; turn; revolve; to wind; entwine; circuitous; change; shift; alter; contemplate; reconcile
轍	轍	轍	zhé　　　　chit wagon ruts; wheel tracks; path; way; method; have no recourse; rhyme
轎	轎	轎	jiào　　　　giú sedan chair; bamboo carriage; palanquin
轔	轔	轔	lín　　　　leun sound of rumbling of wheels; wheel; threshold; doorsill; doorstep
轟	轟	轟	hong　　　gwàng rumble; explode; blast; shoo away; expel; vigorous; (onomatopoeia) bang; boom
轡	轡		pèi　　　　bei bridle; reins
轢	轢		lì　　　　lik run over with a vehicle; vandal; to bully someone
轤	轤		lú　　　　lou windlass; capstan; pulley
辛	辛	辛	xīn　　　　sàn　　　　亲 spicy; pungent; hard; laborious; toilsome; suffering; hardship; misery; bitter; 8th heavenly stem
辜	辜	辜	gu　　　　gu crime; wrong; sin; to let down
辣	辢	辢	là　　　　laaht spicy; hot; peppery; pungent; hot; cruel; vicious
办 辦	辦	辦	bàn　　　　baahn deal with; to handle; manage; take care of; prepare; process; obtain; to set up; bring to justice; punish
辨	辨	辨	biàn　　　　bihn distinguish; differentiate; discriminate
舌辛 辭	辭	辭	cí　　　　chìh　　　　嗣辝辞辞 diction; phraseology; speech; words; depart; dismiss; discharge; to fire; resign; apologize; excuse

辛 13-14　辰 3-6　辵 3-4

辟	關	關		pì　　　　　pik to open up; settle; develop; death sentence (大辟) (one of the 五刑, "Five Punishments")
辮	辮	辮	辮	biàn　　　　bin braid; plait
辩	辯	辯	辯	biàn　　　　bihn　　　辡 debate; to argue; to discuss; braid-like object; alternative form of distinguish; differentiate (辨)
	辰	辰	辰	chén　　　　sàhn　　　辰辰辰匢厊 vibrate; time; day; season; heavenly body; stars
	辱	辱	辱	rù　　　　　yuhk disgrace; shame; discredit; humiliate; insult; abuse
农	農	農	農	nóng　　　　nùhng land cultivation; farming; agriculture; farmer; grower; catholic nun
辵	辵	辵		chuò　　　　cheuk walk; walking
	巡	巡	巡	xún　　　　chèuhn patrol; walk a beat; mark; line; (classifier for lines or for rounds of drinks during a banquet)
	迄	迄	迄	qì　　　　　ngaht until; up to; as yet
	迅	迅	迅	xùn　　　　seun quick; rapid; swift
	迂	迂	迂	yu　　　　　jyu circuitous; round about; pedantic; far; wide; slow; evil; exaggerated
	近	近	近	jìn　　　　　gahn near; close range; intimate; close (affection); approximately; approach; make a profit; earn
	迕	迕		wǔ　　　　　ng obstinate; perverse
	迓	迓		yà　　　　　ngaa receive; greet a visitor; to welcome
	返	返	返	fǎn　　　　fáan　　　仮翻番 return to; go back to; give back

迎			yíng　　　　yìhng	receive; welcome; greet; meet; flatter; to face; go against; forge ahead
迢			tiáo　　　　tiu	far; distant
迨			dài　　　　doi	until; by the time
迦			jia　　　　gaa	(*used in transliteration*)
迤			túo　　　　ji	winding; twisting movement or course
迪			dí　　　　dik　　廸	enlighten; guide; employ; implement; put into practice; comply; advance; progress
迫			pò　　　　bīk	compel; coerce; force; imminent; urgent; (*Cantonese*) crowded; packed; jostle; shove
迥			jiǒng　　　　gwing　　逈	distant; far; remote; drastically different; far different; tall; totally; completely
迭			dié　　　　dit	alternate; change; repeatedly; again and again; in time; timely; frequently
迮			zé　　　　jaak	urgent; haste; pressure; coerce; press
述			shù　　　　seuht　　唓	follow; adhere to; observe; obey; to state; narrate; recount; works; writings; account; recount
迷			mí　　　　màih	get lost; to confuse; bewilder; bewitch; to charm; infatuate; obsessed; crazy about; fan of
送			sòng　　　　sung　　遜	see someone off; send; dispatch; deliver; give; offer; to gift; lose; sacrifice
逆			nì　　　　yihk	greet; meet; welcome; accept; disobey; oppose; resist; opposite; adverse; unfavourable; rebel; traitor
迸			bèng　　　　bing	gush out; burst; to split; to crack

辵 6-7

追	追	追		zhui　　　jèui chase; pursue; follow; overtake; hunt; to track; seek; woo; to court; recall; recollect
退	退	退		tùi　　　teui retreat; withdrawl; step back; move backwards; leave; recede; fade; to ebb; to refund; cancel; call off
逃	逃	逃		táo　　　tòuh escape; flee; run away; evade; abscond; dodge
回	迴	回	回	húi　　　wùih　　　廻 迴 return; go back; revolve; rotate; circular; winding; crooked
逅	逅	逅		hòu　　　hau unexpected meeting
逗	逗			dòu　　　dauh amuse; tease; funny; ridiculous; amusing; to tempt; to allure; loiter; remain
逍	逍	逍		xiao　　　siu ramble, stroll, jaunt, loiter; leisurely; easygoing
透	透	透		tòu　　　tau penetrate; disclose; pass through; to show; reveal; disclose; thoroughly; completely
逐	逐	逐		zhú　　　juhk chase; pursue; gradually; expel; one by one; every
逑	逑			qiú　　　kau spouse; match; unite; pair; collect
途	途	途		tú　　　tòuh　　　涂塗 road; passage; path; method; way; career; course
速	速	速		sù　　　chùk fast; swift; speedy; quick; quickly; invite; incur
逖	逖	逖		tì　　　tik far; distant; kept at a distance
逡	逡			qun　　　seun retreat; withdraw; fall back
逝	逝	逝		shì　　　saih to die; pass away

	逛	遷		guàng　　　kwaang stroll; roam; wander
	逞	遲		chěng　　　chíng　　　呈 brag; show off; succeed; achieve something bad; indulge oneself
	逕	迳	遲	jìng　　　ging　　　徑 small path; go to; to reach; flow through; directly; diameter
	造	達	譜	zào　　　jouh　　　艁 make; build; manufacture; produce; create; invent; fabricate; era; period; (*classifier for harvest*)
这	這	遙	遲	zhè　　　jéh　　　迒遞即遮者拓 this; this one; these; at this moment; right away; at once; here
	逢	逢	達	féng　　　fùhng meet with; encounter; chance meeting; whenever; pander to; (classifier for periods of time)
	逋	逋		bu　　　bou flee; abscond; owe; delay; evade
	通	通	通	tong　　　tùng pass through; travel through; allow passage; make sense; logical; expert; can; may
连	連	連	連	lián　　　lìhn man-drawn carriage; join; connect; to link; ally with; involve; implicate; continuous; successively
进	進	進	遙	jìn　　　jeun advance; move forward; enter; receive; admit; recruit; give; offer advice; score a goal; eat; drink
	逭	逭		huàn　　　wun avoid; evade; escape from
	逮	逮	逮	dài　　　daih seize; catch; until; throw; to cast
	逯	逯		lù　　　luk walk carefully
	逸	逸	逸	yì　　　yaht escape; flee; break loose; reclusive; leisurely; indulgent
	逵	逵	逵	kúi　　　kwai thoroughfare; crossroads

辵 8-9

	逶	蹊	逶	wei　　　wai winding; curving; swagger
遁	遁	遁		dùn　　　deuhn escape; hide; conceal; flee; evade
周	週	周	周	zhou　　　jàu week; circumference; turn; cycle; revolve; anniversary
过	過	過		guò　　　gwo go across; go over; pass through; passing time; surpass; excess in degree or amount; (*past tense*)
	遏	遏	遏	è　　　aat stop; suppress; to curb; to check; snap something off; break something
	遇	遇	遇	yù　　　yuh meet; come across; encounter; to treat
运	運	運	運	yùn　　　wahn move; revolve; transport; convey; carry; to ship; use; utilize; fortune; luck; fate
	逼	逼	逼	bi　　　bìk compel; to force; to bother; extort; approach; press on; narrow; (*Cantonese*) crowded; packed
	逾	逾	逾	yú　　　jyu go over; pass over; exceed; go beyond
	遂	遂	遂	suì　　　seuih fulfill; satisfy; comply; complete; succeed; then; consequently; thereupon; proceed; promote
	遄	遄		chúan　　　chyùhn immediately; soon; at once; quickly; hurry
	遊	遊	遊	yóu　　　yàuh　　　遊 travel; tour; wander; roam; play; walk; associate with; persuade; convince; move freely
	遍	遍	遍	biàn　　　pin　　　徧 everywhere; all over; throughout; (*classifier for an event occurrence*)
	遐	遐	遐	xiá　　　haa far; distant; durable; advanced; old
	遑	遑	遑	húang　　　wong free time; leisure; hasty; how; how can (*rhetorical*); alternative form of fearful (惶) and hesitation (徨)

| | | | | qiú　　　　chàuh
strong; unyielding; forceful |
|---|---|---|---|---|
| | 道 | �道 | | dào　　　　douh　　　導衜衟
way; path; road; method; principle; to say; utter;
(*classifier for long things, barriers, meals, questions, orders*) |
| 达 | 達 | 達 | 達 | dá　　　　daaht　　　达
lead to; reach; arrive; achieve; attain; understand;
convey; general; common; optimistic; everywhere |
| 违 | 違 | 違 | 違 | wéi　　　　wàih
disobey; violate; apart; seperated by; leave; depart;
go away; avoid |
| 遥 | 遙 | 遙 | 遙 | yáo　　　　yiùh
far; distant; remote |
| | 遘 | 遘 | 遘 | gòu　　　　gau　　　冓
meet unexpectedly, encounter; come across |
| | 遛 | 遛 | 遛 | liù　　　　lau
stroll; saunter; walk around |
| 逊 | 遜 | 遜 | 遜 | xùn　　　　seun
humble; modest; inferior; abdicate; give up the throne;
flee; escape; evade |
| 递 | 遞 | 遞 | 遞 | dì　　　　daih　　　遰遞
take turns; alternate; hand over; deliver; transmit;
successively; posthouse; (*Cantonese*) lift; raise |
| | 遢 | 遢 | 遢 | ta　　　　taap
careless; negligent; slipshod; being a jerk |
| | 遣 | 遣 | 遣 | qiǎn　　　　hín
dispatch; banish; exile; send |
| 远 | 遠 | 遠 | 遠 | yuǎn　　　　yúhn　　　远
far; distant; remote; profound;
(*comparative intensifier*) much; by far |
| | 遨 | 遨 | 遨 | áo　　　　ngou　　　敖傲
roam; ramble; excursion; travel for pleasure;
spin; rotate |
| 适 | 適 | 適 | 適 | shì　　　　sìk　　　啻
proceed; towards; submit; comply; fitting; proper;
appropriate; comfortable; obtain; restrict; assuming |
| | 遮 | 遮 | 遮 | zhe　　　　jè　　　庶
to block; obstruct; hide; conceal;
(*Cantonese*) umbrella; parasol |

辵 11-13

	遭	遭	遭	zao / jòu — come across; encounter; meet; suffer; (*classifier for a number of occurrences of events, times, or turns*)
	遵	遵	遵	zun / jèun — follow; go along; obey; comply
迁	遷	遷	遷	qián / chìn — ascend; promote; relocate; migrate; change; shift; transfer; banish; exile; disperse; die
	遴	遴	遴	lín / leun — select; choose; pick
选	選	選	選	xuǎn / syún — choose; pick; select; elect; election
遗	遺	遺	遺	yí / wàih — lose track of; omit; abandon; annul; forget; to lack; bequeath; emit; involuntary discharge
辽	遼	遼	遼	liáo / liùh — distant; far; Liao or Khitan dynasty
迟	遲	遲	遲	chí / chìh — late; tardy; slow; delay 遲遞遲
	避	避	避	bì / beih — avoid; escape; dodge; prevent; keep away
	邂	邂	邂	xiè / haai — unexpected meeting; encounter
	遽	遽	遽	jù / geui — suddenly; unexpectedly; at once; be afraid
	邀	邀	邀	yao / yiù — solicit; seek; wait for the arrival of someone; meet; intercept; invite; welcome
迈	邁	邁	邁	mài / maai — stride; take a step; pass by; surpass; old; mile; kilometer per hour
	邃	邃	邃	sùi / seui — remote; distant; deep; mysterious; profound; detailed
还	還	還	還	huán / wàahn — return; give back; do or give something in return; eye for an eye; tit for tat

迩	邇	邇	邇	ěr　　ji	(archaic) near; close
	邈	邈		miǎo　　miu	far; distant; remote; slight
边	邊	邊	邊	bian　　bìn	edge; side; border; boundary; (suffix for locality) 邊
	邋	邋	邋	la　　laap	tattered clothes; rags; slovenly
逻	邏	邏	邏	luó　　lo	patrol; inspect; watch; vigil; guard
逦	邐	邐	邐	lǐ　　lei	winding; continuous and meandering
	邑	邑	邑	yì　　yàp	state; country; nation; capital; city; town; area; district; original form of miserable (悒)
	邙	邙		máng　　mong	Mount Mang, a mountain Luoyang, Henan
	邛	邛		qióng　　kung	Ming dynasty county in Sichuan province; a mound; fatigue; sickness; distress
	邕	邕	邕	yong　　jung	former name for Nanning (in Guangxi)
	邢	邢	邢	xíng　　jing	name of ancient state in modern-day Hebei province
	那	那	那	nà　　náh	that; those; then; in that case; so
	邦	邦	邦	bang　　bòng	nation; country; sovereign state
	邪	邪	邪	xié　　chèh	evil; depraved; vicious; perverse; unnatural; disaster; calamity; (traditional Chinese medicine) pathogenetic
	邱	邱	邱	qiu　　yàu	mound; dune; hill; ugly; bad

邑 5-7

邰	𨚫		tái / toi a state in modern Wugong County, Shaanxi
邳	𨛬		pi / pei a department in the State of Lu (*modern Shantung*)
邴	𨞣		bǐng / bing happy; joyous; pleased; a city in the ancient state of Song
邵	𨛯	𨚽	shào / siu name of various places in ancient China; short for Shàoyáng (邵陽); Thao people (*Taiwanese aborigines*)
邶	𨛥	𨛥	bèi / bui an ancient state south of present-day Tangyin, Henan
邸	𨛮	𨛮	dǐ / dai lodging house; official residence
邯	𨛗		hán / hon Hándan (邯鄲), a city in southwestern Hebei; various
耶	𨛕	𨛕	yé / yèh alternative form of father (爺); (*particle indicating a questioning tone*)
郎	𨛳	𨛳	láng / lòhng 郎 an official's title; (*laudatory*) man; (*term of endearment by a wife for her husband*) darling; love
郅	𨛨		zhì / jat most; extremely
邾	𨛯		zhu / jyu ancient name for the state of Zou (鄒); an ancient county in modern Huanggang, Hubei
郊	𨛺	𨛺	jiao / gàau suburbs; outskirts; open space; countryside
郝	𨜂	𨜂	hǎo / gok a place in modern-day Shanxi
郛	𨜁		fu / fu suburbs; outer walls of a city
郡	𨜗	𨜗	jùn / gwahn an administrative subdivision of imperial China; commandery; prefecture; county; district

郏	郟	郟		jiá gaap county in Henan
	郢	郢	郢	yǐng jing capital city of the former State of Chu
	郭	郭	郭	guo gwok outer city wall; outer part of a city
	郫	郫		pí pei a former county of Chengdu, Sichuan
邮	郵	郵	郵	yóu yàuh postal; mail; post office
	部	部	部	bù bouh part; division; section; department; ministry; (*classifier for works of literature, film, and vehicles*)
	都	都	都	du dòu metropolis; large city; capital city; establish a capital; also; all; graceful; elegant
	郾	郾	郾	yǎn jin historical town in Yingchuan; alternative form of "Yan, historical Chinese state and kingdom" (燕)
	鄄	鄄		jùan gyun a place in Shandong
郓	鄆	鄆		yùn wan a prefecture in Shandong
乡	鄉	鄉	鄉	xiáng hèung 鄉 鄕 village; town; countryside
	鄂	鄂	鄂	è ngok state in Henan; short for Hubei (湖北); forehead; tool to capture animals
邹	鄒	鄒	鄒	zou jau an ancient Chinese state during the Zhou dynasty
邬	鄔	鄔		wu wu (*used in various place names*)
郧	鄖	鄖		yún wan name of an ancient country in Hubei; a county of Shiyan, Hubei; name of a place in Jiangsu

邑 11-19

	鄙	鄙	鄙	bǐ péi 啚 mean; ignoble; vile; despise; hold in contempt; remote place; march; (*humble*) my
	鄞	鄞	鄞	yín ngan county in Zhejiang
	鄢	鄢		yan jin name of a district in Henan
	鄣	鄣		zhang jeung name of ancient city in Jiangsu
郸	鄲	鄲		dan daan county in Hebei
郑	鄭	鄭	鄭	zhèng jehng a former state in Henan
	鄯	鄯		shàn sin a Gansu district during the Tang dynasty
邻	鄰	鄰	隣	lín lèuhn 隣 neighbor; neighborhood; neighboring; adjacent
	鄱	鄱	鄱	pó bo county and lake in Jiangxi
邓	鄧	鄧	鄧	dèng dang name of an ancient kingdom
郐	鄶	鄶		kùai kui an ancient state in Henan
邺	鄴	鄴	鄴	yè jip a place in Henan
	酃	酃		líng ling the spirit of a being; divine; efficacious
	酆	酆		feng fung 鄷 a Zhou dynasty state in Shaanxi
郦	酈	酈	酈	lì lik a place in Henan

374

酉	酉	酉	yǒu　　　jau　　　丣 alcoholic drinking vessel; rooster (*Chinese zodiac*); between 5:00 and 7:00 PM; math unit
酋	酋	酋	qiú　　　yàuh tribal chief; chieftain
酊	酊		dǐng　　　ding tincture; intoxicated
酎	酎		zhòu　　　jau saké; richly fermented alcoholic drink
酐	酐		gan　　　gon anhydride
酌	酌	酌	zhúo　　　jeuk pour an alcoholic beverage; alcohol and a meal; consider; discretionary
配	配	配	pèi　　　pui to match; join; deserve; allocate; create a medical prescription; a dish served to accompany rice
酏	酏		yí　　　yih watery congee; elixir; millet wine
酒	酒	酒	jiǔ　　　jáu wine; liqour; alcoholic beverages in general
酗	酗	酗	xù　　　jyu　　　酌 酖 drunk; roaring drunk; become violent under the influence of alcohol
酞	酞		tài　　　taai phthalein (*organic compound*)
酚	酚		fen　　　fan carbolic acid; phenol
酡	酡		túo　　　to flushed from drinking alcohol; flushed; rubicund
酢	酢		zùo　　　jok vinegar
酣	酣	酣	han　　　ham enjoy drinking alcohol; carefree manner; joyfully to the fullest; intense fighting; fierce

酉 5-8

酤	酤		gu / gu an alcoholic drink that is fermented for one night; to buy an alcoholic drink
酥	酥	酥	su / sòu flaky pastry; crispy; shortbread; weak; limp; soft; butter; alcohol
酩	酩	酩	mǐng / ming 佲 drunk; intoxicated; tipsy
酪	酪	酪	lào / lok curdled milk, cream, cheese; fruit juice; koumiss (*fermented drink from mare's milk*)
酬	酬	酬	chóu / chàuh 酧 醻 propose a toast; toast; reward; repay; payment; remuneration; friendly exchange; realize; fulfill
酮	酮		tóng / tung ketone (*organic chemistry*)
酷	酷	酷	kù / huhk cruel; oppressive; extreme; brutal; savage; (*Mandarin slang*) cool; awesome
酲	酲		chéng / chìhng hangover; uncomfortable
酴	酴	酴	tú / tou leaven; yeast; wine
酵	酵	酵	jiào / hàau ferment; yeast; dough with yeast
酶	酶		méi / mui enzyme; alternative form of yeast (媒)
酸	酸	酸	suan / syùn sour; tart; grieved; sad; stingy; narrow-minded; pedantic; spoiled; rancid; ridicule; (*Cantonese*) vinegar
酹	酹		lèi / laai pour out a libation; sprinkle; sparge
醇	醇	醇	chún / sèuhn 醕 rich alcoholic drink; alternative form of pure (純); (*organic chemistry*) alcohol
醅	醅		pei / pui unstrained liquor or rice wine; mash

				Pinyin	Jyutping	
	醉	醉	醉	zùi	jeui	醉
				become drunk; intoxicate; fascinated; enchanted; crazy about; addicted; marinate in cooking wine		
腌	醃	醃	醃	yán	yip	
				marinate; to pickle; to salt		
	醋	醋	醋	cù	chou	酢
				vinegar; jealousy; envy; bitterness		
	醌	醌		kun	kwan	
				quinone		
	醍	醍		tí	tai	
				essential oil of butter; a pink or light red wine		
	醒	醒	醒	xǐng	síng	
				sober up; awaken; be awake; to decant (*wine*); (*Cantonese*) clever; intelligent; sharp		
	醐	醐		hú	wu	
				purest cream		
	醛	醛		qúan	chyùhn	
				aldehyde		
	醚	醚		mí	mai	
				ether		
丑	醜	丑	丑	chǒu	cháu	
				ugly; homely; hideous; shameful; disgraceful		
酝	醞	醞	醞	yùn	wán	
				to brew; ferment an alcoholic beverage; wine		
	醢	醢		hǎi	hoi	
				mince; minced pickled meat		
	醪	醪		láo	lou	
				alcohol with dregs; alcoholic beverage; dirty; sweet pudding-like dish in Chinese cuisine (醪糟)		
医	醫	醫	醫	yi	yì	
				medicinal; medicine; doctor; cure; to treat		
酱	醬	醬	醬	jiàng	jeung	
				sauce; any jam or paste type food		

酉 12-20   釆 5-13   里 2-4

	醯	醯		xi　　　hei vinegar; pickle; acid
	醭	醭		bú　　　buk the white mold growing on the surface of vinegar or alcohol; scum
	醮	醮	醮	jiào　　　jiu religious service; Taoist or Buddhist ceremony
	醴	醴	醴	lǐ　　　lai sweet wine; sweet spring water
	醺	醺	醺	xun　　　fan drunk; intoxicated
酿	釀	釀	釀	niàng　　　yeuhng to brew; ferment; wine; liquor; make honey (*of bees*); lead to; result in
衅	釁	釁		xìn　　　jan　　　衅釁 blood rite (*sacrificial blood is smeared upon the object*); crack; dispute
酾	釃	釃		shi　　　si to filter alcohol; pour alcohol or tea into drinkware; branch off a river
酽	釅	釅	釅	yàn　　　jin (*of beverage*) thick; strong; concentrated; dark color
	釆	釆		cǎi　　　choi distinguish; discriminate
	釉	釉	釉	yòu　　　jau glaze
释	釋	釋	釋	shì　　　sìk explain; elucidate; release
	里	裏	裡	lǐ　　　léih li (*a half kilometer - mainland China*); neighborhood; urban village; lane (*Hong Kong*)
	重	重	重	zhòng　　　chúhng heavy; grave; serious; severe; considerable (*amount*); important
	野	野	野	yě　　　yéh　　　壄墅埜壄壄 countryside; field; wilderness; region; boundary; out of office; simple; plain; feral; rough; informal

	量	量	量		liáng lèuhng measure; estimate; evaluate
厘	釐	厘			lí lèih centimeter; cash; regulate; unit of monthly or annual interest
	金	金	金		jin gàm gold; metal; money; noble; rich; imperial
钇	釔	釔			yǐ jyut yttrium (rare earth element - atomic #39)
钌	釕	釕			liǎo liu ruthenium (atomic #44)
钉	釘	釘	釘		ding dèng 盯 叮 gold slab; nail (spike); body piercing; to monitor; lamp; (Cantonese slang) die
针	針	鍼	針		zhen jàm needle; pin; tack; injection; acupuncture; poke; (Cantonese) spy; informer; probe
钊	釗	釗	釗		zhao chiu encourage; endeavor; strive
钋	釙	釙	釙		po pok polonium
	釜	釜	釜		fǔ fú 釜 pot; pan; cauldron; kettle
钎	釬	釬			hàn hon solder; metallic sheath or sleeve
钍	釷	釷			tǔ tou thorium
钓	釣	釣	釣		diào diu to fish; fishhook; go after; tempt; lure
钒	釩	釩	釩		fán faan vanadium
钗	釵	釵	釵		chai chaai ornamental hairpin

金 3-4

钏	釧	釧	釧	chùan / chyun bracelet; armlet
扣	鈕	鈕	鈕	kòu / kau button; buckle
钕	釹	釹		nǔ / neui neodymium
钛	鈦	鈦		tài / taai titanium
钦	欽	欽	欽	qin / jam respect; respectful; admire
钣	鈑	鈑	鈑	bǎn / baan metal plate; sheet of metal
钠	鈉	鈉	鈉	nà / naap sodium
钯	鈀	鈀		bǎ / paa palladium
钧	鈞	鈞	鈞	jun / gwan ancient unit of measure equivalent to 15 kilograms; (polite) you; your; potter's wheel; tone; tune
钙	鈣	鈣	鈣	gài / koi calcium
斜	斜	斜		tǒu / dau wine flagon; large wine vessel
钝	鈍	鈍	鈍	dùn / duhn dull; blunt; dim-witted; stupid
钤	鈐	鈐	鈐	qián / kim official seal; affix a seal to; tea-curing tool; stratagy; plot; plan; tactic
钞	鈔	鈔	鈔	chao / chàau paper money; banknotes; alternative form of copy (抄)
钪	鈧	鈧		kàng / kong scandium

金 4-5

钚	鈈	鈈		bù　　　　bat plutonium
钮	鈕	鈕	鈕	niǔ　　　náu　　　纽 button; knob
钳	鉗	鉗	鉗	qián　　　kìhm pliers; tongs; pincers; crustacean claw
钼	鉬	鉬		mù　　　　muk molybdenum
钲	鉦	鉦		zheng　　jing an ancient Chinese percussion instrument similar to a gong used to recall troops from battle
巨	鉅	巨	巨	jù　　　　geuih steel; iron; huge; large; great
刨	鉋	鉋	鉋	bào　　　pàauh carpenter's plane
钩	鉤	鉤	鉤	gou　　　ngàu hook; barb; sickle
钶	鈳	鈳		e　　　　o　　　鈳 columbium niobium
铈	鈰	鈰		shì　　　si cerium
铃	鈴	鈴	鈴	líng　　　lìhng bell; chime
钴	鈷	鈷	鈷	gǔ　　　　gu cobalt
钺	鉞	鉞		yuè　　　jyut ancient Chinese battle axe; broad-axe; halberd
钹	鈸	鈸	鈸	bó　　　　bat cymbals
铍	鈹	鈹	鈹	pí　　　　pei beryllium

钰	鈺	鈺		yù　　　　juk rare treasure; solid metal
钸	鈽	鈽	鈽	bu　　　　bou plutonium
铀	鈾	鈾		yóu　　　　jau uranium
钿	鈿	鈿	鈿	diàn　　　din hairpin; gold inlay; filigree
钾	鉀	鉀	鉀	jiǎ　　　　gaap potassium
铊	鉈	鉈		shi; ta　　si; taa　　　鉈 鉈 鎉 spear; lance thallium
铉	鉉	鉉	鉉	xùan　　　jyun device for carrying a tripod ding cauldron (鼎)
铋	鉍	鉍	鉍	bì　　　　bit bismuth
铂	鉑	鉑	鉑	bó　　　　bok platinum; alternative form of foil (箔)
铆	鉚	鉚	鉚	mǎo　　　maau mortise (wood) ; rivet (metal); exert strength
铅	鉛	鉛	鉛	qian　　　yùhn　　　鈆 lead; pencil lead
铬	鉻	鉻	鉻	gè　　　　gok chromium
铭	銘	銘	銘	míng　　　mìhng inscribe; engrave; inscription; unforgettably; remember forever
铜	銅	銅	銅	tóng　　　tùhng copper; bronze; brass
铢	銖	銖	銖	zhu　　　　jyu ancient unit of currency equal to 100 grains of millet; Thai baht (currency)

铰	鉸	鋏	鋏	jiǎo gaau scissors; cut with scissors; to ream; hinge
银	銀	銀	銀	yín ngàhn silver; silver-colored, lustrous, shiny; cash, money, currency; (*classifier for money*)
铳	銃	銃		chòng chung an old type of pistol; blunderbuss; (*Taiwanese*) gun; firearm
銎	銎	銎		qiong kung the handle hole in the blade of an axe
铣	銑	銑	銑	xiǎn sín cast iron; lustrous metal; shining metal; small chisel
铨	銓	銓	銓	qúan chyùhn weigh; measure; to select officials
铫	銚	銚		yáo jiu a large hoe
衔	銜	銜	銜	xián hàahm 啣 街 bit (*horse*); hold in mouth; bite; gag; accept; connect; join together; combine; link up; title (*of an official*)
铑	銠	銠		lǎo lou rhodium
铷	銣	銣		rú jyu rubidium
铱	銥	銥		yi ji iridium
铵	銨	銨		ǎn on ammonium
铯	銫	銫		sè sik cesium
铐	銬	銬	銬	kào kaau shackles; to shackle; manacles; to manacle
锑	銻	銻	銻	ti tài antimony

金 7

锐	銳	銳	銳	ruì / yeuih sharp; keen; acute; pointed
销	銷	銷	銷	xiao / siù fuse; smelt; melt; sell; expend; cancel; write off; bolt
锄	鋤	鉏	鋤	chú / chòh hoe; to hoe; dig; remove; get rid of; eradicate
锈	銹	銹	鏽	xiù / sau rust
锉	銼	鋝	銼	cùo / cho carpenter's file; file smooth
铝	鋁	鋁	鋁	lǔ / léuih aluminum
锒	鋃	鋃		láng / long lock; ornament; lanthanum
焊	銲	焊	焊	hàn / hon solder; weld; leg armor; greaves
锌	鋅	鋅	鋅	xin / san zinc
钡	鋇	鋇	鋇	bèi / bui barium
	鋈	鋈		wù / juk silver plating
铤	鋌	鋌		dìng / ting ingot; bars of metal; copper or iron ore; hurry; walk fast
铗	鋏	鋏		jiá / gaap sword hilt; dagger; tongs
锋	鋒	鋒	鋒	feng / fùng pointed edge; cutting edge; vanguard; pioneer; a weather front
锊	鋝	鋝		lùe / lyut 6 oz; an ancient measurement of weight

锓	錂	鋟		qian	chim
				carve	
锇	鋨	鋨		é	ngo
				osmium	
铖	鋮	鋮		chéng	sing
				used for a person's name	
铺	鋪	鋪	鋪	pu	pòu
				spread out; arrange; display; pave; to tile; to lay; (*classifier for games or matches*)	
锆	鋯	鋯		gào	gou
				zirconium	
锂	鋰	鋰	鋰	lǐ	lei
				lithium	
锯	鋸	鋸	鋸	jù	geui
				saw (*tool*); to saw; amputate	
钢	鋼	鋼	鋼	gang	gong	鋥
				steel; hard; strong; tough	
锕	錒	錒		a	aa
				actinium	
锢	錮	錮	錮	gù	gu
				pour metal into cracks; confine; imprison; chronic illness	
表	錶	錶	錶	biǎo	biù
				a watch; pocket watch; wristwatch; gauge; meter; instrument	
锞	錁	錁		kè	fo
				gold or silver ingot	
录	錄	錄	錄	lù	luhk	録
				copy; write down; record; report	
锥	錐	錐	錐	zhui	jèui
				awl; drill; to bore; cone	
锟	錕	錕	錕	kun	kwan
				an ancient sword	

金 8-9

锱	錙	錙	錙	zī　　　　　jī 8 oz; an ancient measurement of weight
铮	錚	錚	錚	zhēng　　　　jaang (*onomatopoeia*) metal objects being struck; ancient bell-shaped percussion instrument used for marching
锛	錛	錛		bēn　　　　ban adze; cut with an adze; dent the edge of a knife
锬	錟	錟		tán　　　　taam long spear
锭	錠	錠	錠	dìng　　　　ding spindle; ingot-shaped tablet; (*classifier for ingot-shaped objects*)
钱	錢	錢	錢	qián　　　chìhn　　　錢 coin; money; cash; currency; cost; fund; expense
锦	錦	錦	錦	jǐn　　　　gám brocade; tapestry; embroidered; bright and beautiful
锡	錫	錫	錫	xī　　　　sek　　　　鑞 tin; stannum; bestow; confer
错	錯	錯		cuò　　　　cho　　　錯 逪 剒 鑐 wrong; erroneous; incorrect; bad; poor; inferior; substandard; make a mistake; blunder; error; fault
锰	錳	錳	錳	měng　　　maang manganese
锤	錘	錘	錘	chúi　　　chèuih hammer; mace (*weapon*); hammer into shape; steelyard weight; (*slang*) proof
锹	鍬	鍬		qiāo　　　chiù　　　鐰 spade; hoe
锲	鍥	鍥		qiè　　　　kit sickle; cut; carve; engrave
锚	錨	錨	錨	máo　　　màauh anchor
锸	鍤	鍤		chā　　　　chaap spade; shovel; marking pin

金 9

锴	鍇	鍇(篆)		kǎi　　　kaai high quality iron
锗	鍺	鍺(篆)		zhe　　　je germanium
锶	鍶	鍶(篆)		si　　　si strontium
锤	鎚	鎚(篆)	錘(篆)	chúi　　　chèuih hammer; mallet; club
锅	鍋	鍋(篆)	鍋(篆)	guo　　　wo cooking pot; pan; wok; blame; fault
链	鍊	鍊(篆)	鏈(篆)	liàn　　　lihn　　　煉 smelt; refine; to temper; cultivate; measure one's words; polished speech
镀	鍍	鍍(篆)	鍍(篆)	dù　　　douh to plate (*cover a metal object with a thin coating of a different metal*)
锷	鍔	鍔(篆)	鍔(篆)	è　　　ngok high; lofty; edge of knife
铡	鍘	鍘(篆)		zhá　　　jaat hand hay cutter; straw cutter; fodder chopper; cut with a hay or straw cutter
	鍪	鍪(篆)		móu　　　mau iron pot; iron pan; metal cap
锻	鍛	鍛(篆)	鍛(篆)	duàn　　　dyun to forge; to shape metal; to temper; refine
锾	鍰	鍰(篆)	鍰(篆)	húan　　　waan money; ring
键	鍵	鍵(篆)	鍵(篆)	jiàn　　　gihn key; keyboard; to type; door bolt, lock bolt; bond (*chemistry*)
镁	鎂	鎂(篆)		měi　　　mei magnesium
钟	鍾	鍾(篆)	鐘(篆)	zhong　　　jung　　　鐘 vessel for alcohol; percussion instrument; concentrate one's attention; love at first sight; unit of capacity

金 10-11

镇	鎮	鎮	鎮	zhèn / jan guard; garrison; to calm; sedate; suppress; repress; subdue; to cool (*food or drinks*); town; township
锁	鎖	鎖	鎖	suǒ / só lock; to lock; fasten
镍	鎳	鎳	鎳	niè / nip nickel (*element*)
镑	鎊	鎊	鎊	bàng / bohng pound (*currency*)
	鎏	鎏		liú / lau gold leaf
枪	槍	槍	槍	qiang / chèung spear; lance; pike; gun; pistol; firearm; shooter; collide; (*classifier for gunshots*)
镉	鎘	鎘	鎘	gé / gaak cadmium
钨	鎢	鎢	鎢	wu / wu tungsten; wolfram
鎣	鎣	鎣		yíng / jing polish
镏	鎦	鎦		liú / lau / 鎦 traditional Chinese gilding process involving gold dissolved in mercury, which is painted on metal
铠	鎧	鎧		kǎi / loi armor; chain mail
镒	鎰	鎰	鎰	yì / jat unit of weight equivalent to 20 or 24 liang (*taels* 兩)
镓	鎵	鎵		jia / gaa gallium
镐	鎬	鎬	鎬	gǎo / góu pickaxe; pick
镝	鏑	鏑	鏑	dí / dik arrowhead; barb of an arrow; head of a javelin; dysprosium

镛	鏞	鏞		yong　　　jung a large bell used as a musical instrument
铩	鎩	鏾		sha　　　saat long spear; lance; to wreck; devastate; clip the wing of a bird
镞	鏃	鏃	鏃	zú　　　juk arrowhead; barb; sharp; swift; quick
链	鏈	鏈	鏈	liàn　　　lin chain; wire; cable; (unit of length equal to 22 yards)
錾	鏨	鏨		zàn　　　jaam chop; chisel; engrave; cut
	鏖	鏖		áo　　　ou fight to the end, engage in a fierce battle; fierce; clamorous
镆	鏌	鏌		mò　　　mok ancient legendary sword name (aka: 莫邪)
铿	鏗	鏗	鏗	keng　　　hang strike; beat; stroke; jingling of metal
镗	鏜	鏜	鏜	tang　　　tong　鐣 small copper drum; (onomatopoeia) drum or gong sound
锵	鏘	鏘	鏘	qiang　　　cheung tinkle, tinkling of small bells; clang, jingle
镘	鏝	鏝	鏝	man　　　maan trowel
铲	鏟	鏟	鏟	chǎn　　　cháan spade; shovel; scoop; root out; destroy
镖	鏢	鏢	鏢	biao　　　biu dart; spear; harpoon; valuables sent with an armed escort
镂	鏤	鏤	鏤	lòu　　　lau engrave; carve; inlay; tattoo
镜	鏡	鏡	鏡	jìng　　　geng mirror; reflecting glass; lens; scope; glasses; reflect; perceive; use for reference; draw lessons from; clear

金 11-13

锵	鏘	鏘		qiǎng　　　keung sulfuric acid; money; string of coins; wealth
旋	鏇	鏇	鏇	xùan　　　syùhn lathe; whirl
铙	鐃	鐃	鐃	náo　　　naau large cymbals; disturb; argue; debate
镦	鐓	鐓		dun　　　deun upsetting; alternative form of castrate (騸)
镣	鐐	鐐		liào　　　liu fetters; leg irons
铧	鏵	鏵		húa　　　waa spade; ploughshare
镡	鐔	鐔		tán　　　taam dagger; small sword
镫	鐙	鐙		dèng　　　dang stirrup; oil lamp
锏	鐧	鐧		jiàn　　　gaan iron protection for a wooden wheel axle
钟	鐘	鐘	鐘	zhong　　　jung bell; clock; time (*measured in hours and minutes only*); (*Cantonese*) hour
铛	鐺	鐺	鐺	dang　　　dong (*onomatopoeia*) clank; clang; metallic sound; woman's earring
镭	鐳	鐳	鐳	léi　　　leui radium
镌	鐫	鐫	鐫	juan　　　jyun engraving tool; carve; engrave; keep in the heart; demote; dismissal of an official
镰	鐮	鐮	鐮	lián　　　lìhm　　　劇 鎌 鎌 scythe; sickle
镯	鐲	鐲	鐲	zhúo　　　juk　　　錠 ridgid bracelet; bangle

铁	鐵	鐵	鐵	tiě / tit — 鐵 銕 iron (*metal*); arms; weapon; strong; solid; firm; ironclad; hard; ruthless
	鐾	鐾		bèi / bai — 錍 sharpen a knife
铎	鐸	鐸	鐸	duó / dok large ancient bell
鉴	鑑	鑑		jiàn / gaam examine; inspect; reflect; mirror
铸	鑄	鑄	鑄	zhù / jyu — 鋳 melt; cast; coin; mint
镔	鑌	鑌		bin / ban wrought iron; high-quality iron
镬	鑊	鑊		huò / wok cauldron; (*Cantonese*) problem; trouble; blame
铄	鑠	鑠	鑠	shuò / seuk melt by heat; weaken; fine; glorious; alternative form of bright/brilliant (爍)
镳	鑣	鑣		biao / biu — 驃 horse bit; alternative form of dart (鏢)
	鑫	鑫		xin / jam prosperity; wealth; nickname for Kim Jong-un
镧	鑭	鑭		lán / laan lanthanum
钥	鑰	鑰	鑰	yào / yeuhk bolt; lock; key (*object or figurative*); strategic place
	鑲	鑲	鑲	xiang / sèung insert; inlay; set; mount; fill
镊	鑷	鑷	鑷	niè / nip tweezers; forceps; pincers; to nip by tweezers
锣	鑼	鑼	鑼	luó / lòh gong

钻	鑽	鑽	鑽	zuan　　　　jyun　　　　鑽鉆 to drill; to bore; intensive study; go through; get into; pierce; secure personal gain
銮	鑾	鑾		lúan　　　　lyun carriage bell; emporer's carriage
凿	鑿	鑿	鑿	záo　　　　jok chisel; to bore; cut a hole; to chisel; dig; break ground; beat forcefully
长	長	長	長	cháng　　　　chèuhng; jéung long; length; everlasting; permanent; constantly; frequently; straight; upright; merit; excel; grow
门	門	門	門	mén　　　　mùhn door; gate; entrance; opening; portal; valve; switch; knack; tradition; class; category; phylum; division
闩	閂	閂		shuan　　　　saan bolt; latch; crossbar; (Cantonese) to close; switch off; turn off
闪	閃	閃	閃	shǎn　　　　sím flash; lightning; flash; sparkle; shine; dodge; evade; twist; sprain
闭	閉	閉	閉	bì　　　　bai　　　　閇 close; shut; obstruct; block up
问	問	問	問	wèn　　　　maan ask; inquire; send regards; greet; show concern; interrogate; interfere; intervene; meddle
阎	閆	閆	閆	yán　　　　jim village gate
开	開	開	開	kai　　　　hòi open; unlatch; unfasten; start; begin; open up; to boil; to write out; to book a room; operate; drive
闶	閌	閌		kang　　　　kong door
闵	閔	閔	閔	mǐn　　　　man mourn; grieve; urge on; incite
闳	閎	閎	閎	hóng　　　　wang gate; barrier; wide; vast; expand
闷	悶	悶	悶	mèn　　　　mun gloomy; depressed; melancholy; bored; stuffy

闰	閏	閏	閏	rùn　　jeun	intercalary (*i.e., leap day or leap year*); extra; surplus
闲	閒	閒	閒	xián　　hàahn	vacant; unoccupied; unused; carefree; trivial; extraneous; tranquil; calm; leisure; free time
间	間	閒	閒	jiān　　gàan	among; between; moment; a little while; instant; room; chamber; section of a room
闸	閘	閘		zhá　　jaahp　牐	sluice; switch; (*Cantonese*) gate; to dam; to block; obstruct
闹	鬧	鬧	鬧	nào　　naau　鬧	noisy; create a disturbance; to occur (*of a disaster, or other negative event*); (*Cantonese*) to scold
闻	聞	聞	聞	wén　　man	hear; listen; detect; to smell; spread; transmit; well-known; famous; knowledge; expertise; news
阂	閡	閡	閡	hé　　ngoi	cut off; blocked or separated; prevent
阀	閥	閥		fá　　faht	contribution; powerful and influential group; clique; family status; valve
闺	閨	閨	閨	gui　　gwài	boudoir; lady's chamber; small arched gate
闽	閩	閩	閩	mǐn　　man　閩	Min people and language (*ancient ethnic group*); Min river (*in Fujian, China*)
阁	閣	閣	閣	gé　　gok	chamber; pavilion; cabinet; mezzanine
闾	閭	閭	閭	lǘ　　leui	gate of a lane or alley; neighborhood; hamlet; lane; alley; village consisting of twenty-five families
阅	閱	閱	閱	yuè　　yuht	inspect; examine; review; read; peruse; to experience; to go through
阃	閫	閫		kǔn　　kwan	threshold; doorsill; doorstep; women's quarters; women; (*honorific*) wife
阆	閬	閬		láng　　long	dry moat outside a castle wall; (*of a door*) high; spacious

門 8-10

阍	閽	閽		hun　　　fan doorkeeper; gatekeeper; guard the gate; palace gate
阊	閶	閶		chang　　cheung gate of heaven; main gate of a palace
阉	閹	閹		yan　　　jim castrate; eunuch
阗	閼	閼		yan　　　jin block; shut; obstruct; stop up; conceal
阈	閾	閾		yù　　　wik threshold; separated; confined
阎	閻	閻	閻	yán　　　jim　　　閻閈 village gate
阔	闊	闊	闊	kùo　　　fut　　　濶 broad; wide; rich; wealthy; extravagent; empty; impractical
闱	闈	闈	闈	wéi　　　wai side door of a palace; parents' bedroom; women's quarters; imperial examination hall or room
阕	闋	闋	闋	què　　　kyut to stop; to end; (*classifier for songs and poems*)
阑	闌	闌	闌	lán　　　laan door screen; railing; fence; to exhaust; use up; end; finish; late
阒	闃	闃		qù　　　gwik alone; quiet; still
阗	闐	闐	闐	tián　　　tin fill up; (*used for place names in Xinjiang*)
闯	闖	闖	闖	chuǎng　　chóng　　　闯 rush in; enter abruptly; burst in; break through; to charge
阖	闔	闔	闔	hé　　　hap　　　閤 door; all of; whole; entire; to close; to shut
阙	闕	闕	闕	què　　　kyut a watchtower on both sides of a palace gate; palace

394

关	關	關	關	guan gwàan 関 关 close; shut; lock up; detain; turn off; implicate; border control; checkpoint; video game level; family relation
阚	闞	闞		kàn ham approach; be near to; alternative form of watch; spy; overlook (瞰)
阐	闡	闡	闡	chǎn chín explain; clarify; elucidate
辟	闢	闢		pì pìk open; settle; develop
闼	闥	闥		tà taat door; gate
	阜	阜	自	fù fauh mound of earth; abundant
	阡	阡	阡	qian chin footpath
	阮	阮	阮	ruǎn jyun Chinese long-necked fretted lute; a small state during the Shang Dynasty
	阪	阪	阪	bǎn baan 坂 岅 hillside; farmland; slope
	防	防	防	fáng fòhng 埅 embankment; dam; fortress; stronghold; to block; prevent; guard against; defend; protect
	阱	阱	阱	jǐng jihng 穽 䆤 坓 trap; pit
	附	附	附	fù fuh adhere; to stick; rely on; augment; increase; boost; attach; enclose; be close to
	阻	阻	阻	zǔ jó obstruct; obstacle; barrier; hinder; impede
	阼	阼		yán jou steps leading up to the Eastern gate or throne
	阽	阽		diàn dim approach; close to danger

	阿	阿	阿	e　　　　　ah　　　　啊 prefix used in someone's first or last name to express familiarity or friendliness
	陀	陀	陀	túo　　　　to steep bank; rough terrain
	陂	陂	陂	bei　　　　bei hillside; slope of a hill; pool; pond; bank of a pond
	限	限	限	xiàn　　　　haahn boundary; limit; line; threshold; place a limit on
	陋	陋		lòu　　　　lauh plain; ugly; vulgar; coarse; unrefined; humble; mean; limited in knowledge; shallow
	陌	陌	陌	mò　　　　mak street; path; road; footpath between fields going east to west
	降	降		jiàng　　　gong　　　夅 fall; drop; descend; decrease; to lower; (honorific) visit; bestow; confer; reduce; (music) flat; give birth
升	陞	陞	陞	sheng　　　sing promote; rise; ascend
	陔	陔		gai　　　　goi step; terrace; ledge
	陟	陟		zhì　　　　jik climb; ascend; ascend to heaven; promote; (an archaic euphemism of a monarch)
	陡	陡	陡	dǒu　　　　dau steep; sloping; abruptly; suddenly; deep; extensive
陉	陘	陘	陘	xíng　　　　jing defile; mountain pass; slope; edge of a kitchen stove
	陛	陛		bì　　　　bai flight of steps; (specifically) steps to the throne
陕	陝	陝	陝	shǎn　　　sím The Shan Pass in Shanzhou, Henan (where the Yellow River flows into the North China Plain); Shan County
	院	院	院	yùan　　　　yún courtyard; yard; public or government building; court; institution; academy; hospital; (Sichuanese) go around

阜 7-9

阵	陣	陣	陣	zhèn　　jahn　　陳 short moment of time; military column; (*classifier for short periods of an event*)
	除	除	除	chú　　chèuih remove; get rid of; exclude; be assigned to a new post; except; (*math*) to divide; division
阴	陰	陰	陰	lù　　luhk　　全队 cloudy; overcast; hidden; secret; negative; the moon; shade; shadow; (*yin*) female; treacherous; deceitful
	陷	陷	陷	xiàn　　hahm　　陷陷各埳 sink; plunge; captured; breach; break through; trap; to frame; fault; defect; drawback
	陪	陪	陪	péi　　pùih accompany; go with; help; assist
	陬	陬	陬	zou　　jau corner; cranny; nook; niche
陈	陳	陳	陳	chén　　chàhn　　敶 exhibit; display; explain; old; ancient
	陲	陲	陲	chúi　　seui frontier; border
	陴	陴	陴	bì　　pei parapet
	陶	陶	陶	táo　　tòuh pottery; ceramics; make pottery; cultivate; educate; to mould; contented; happy
	陵	陵	陵	líng　　ling mound; hill; royal tomb; to mount; ascend; surpass; override; bully and humiliate; encroach on; invade
陆	陸	陸	陸	lù　　luhk land; continent; mainland; short for mainland China (中國); short for army (陸軍)
阶	階	階	階	jie　　gàai　　堦 stair; step; rank; degree; level; seniority; order of precedence; phase; stage; (*music*) scale; (*math*) degree
阳	陽	陽	陽	yáng　　yèuhng sun; light; positive; open; overt; (yang) male; south side of mountain or north side of river
	隅	隅	隅	yú　　jyu corner; nook; edge; border; remote

陧	陧	陧		niè　　　nip disorder; dangerous condition of the State
	隍	隍	隍	huáng　　wong dry moat; dry ditch; a guardian deity of a Chinese village, town, or city
	隆	隆	隆	lóng　　lùhng　　隆 abundant; prosperous; thriving; profound; protruding; swollen; (*onomatopoeia*) of thunder or explosion
	隈	隈		wei　　wui cove; bay; inlet
队	队	隊	隊	duì　　deuih group; team; army unit; line; queue; (*classifier for people or objects in groups or rows*)
	隋	隋	隋	suí　　chèuih Sui dynasty
	隔	隔	隔	gé　　gaak separate; partition ; to block; obstruct; pull something apart; every other
陨	陨	隕	隕	yǔn　　jyun fall; slip; let die
	隗	隗		wěi　　ngai high; lofty; collapse; to fall
	隘	隘	隘	ài　　aai　　隘埊陊陋 narrow; confined; a strategic and dangerous pass
	隙	隙		xì　　gwìk　　阠隟 crack; crevice; gap; free time; take advantage of an opportunity; enmity; resentment; grudge
际	際	際	際	jì　　jai border; boundary; juncture; between; moment; associate; on the occasion of; one's lot in life
	障	障	障	zhàng　　jeung block; separate; cut off; obstruct; to shield; barricade; obstacle; barrier; impediment
	隧	隧	隧	suì　　seuih subway; tunnel; underground passage
随	隨	隨	隨	suí　　chèuih　　遀遃 follow; listen to; submit; accompany; subsequently; then; (*Northern Mandarin, of people*) resemble a parent

险	險	嶮		xiǎn　　hím　　　碊 perilous; treacherous; dangerous; hazardous; risk; narrow pass; strategic point; steep; rugged
	隰	隰		xí　　jaahp low wet land ; newly cultivated field
隐	隱	隱	隱	yǐn　　yán　　隐 hidden; cover; shield; conceal; cover up; profound; indistinct; subtle; delicate; secretly; inwardly
	隳	隳		hui　　fai　　陸憞 destroy; wreck; overthrow
陇	隴	隴	隴	long　　lung a mountain in Gansu; name of an ancient province; to flourish
	隶	隸	隸	lì　　li　　隸逮 scribe; attached
	隹	隹		zhui　　jeui short-tailed bird; (*original form of "to be"* (唯))
	隻	隻	隻	zhi　　jek one bird; single; alone; unique; (*math*) odd; (*classifier for nouns and animals*)
	隼	隼		sǔn　　jeun falcon; aquiline
	雀	雀	雀	què　　jeuk　　鴬 sparrow; small bird
	集	集	雧	jí　　jaahp　　雧雦 collect; collection; gather; assemble; set; episode
	雁	雁	雁	yàn　　ngaahn　　鴈 wild goose
	雄	雄	雄	xióng　　hùhng　　雄 male; masculine; powerful; strong; grand; hero; influential person or state
	雅	雅	雅	yǎ　　ngáh elegant; graceful; refined; proper; standard; usually; often; very much; extremely; friendship; (*polite*) your
	雎	雎		ju　　jeui osprey; fishhawk; hold back

	雉	雉	雉	zhì　　　ji pheasant; crenellated wall; ancient Chinese measuring unit approximately 1 meter long and 1/3 meter high
隽	雋	雋		jùn　　　chyúhn meaningful; thought-provoking; outstanding; talented
	雍	雍	雍	yong　　　jung　　　邕 harmony; union; harmonious; alternative form of obstruct (壅) and hold (擁)
	雒	雒		lùo　　　lok dreadful; black horse with white mane; alternative form of Luoyang (洛)
	雌	雌	雌	cí　　　chì female (*of animals and plants*)
	雕	雕	雕	diao　　　diù　　　彫琱 engrave; inlay; carve; carving
虽	雖	雖	雖	sui　　　seui　　　錐雖 although; even if; despite
双	雙	雙	雙	shuang　　　sèung　　　㕠雙霜 two; two-fold; pair; twice; double; twin; (*classifier for a pair of objects*)
杂	雜	雜	雜	zá　　　jaahp　　　雜襍襍 miscellaneous; mixed; confused; assorted; extra; irregular
鸡	雞	雞	雞	ji　　　gài　　　鷄 chicken; hen; rooster; fowl; poultry; (*slang*) female prostitute; (*Cantonese*) whistle
雏	雛	雛	雛	chú　　　chò　　　鶵 young bird; chick; fledgling
离	離	離	離	lí　　　lèih leave, depart; go away; separate; away from; alternative form of suffering (罹)
难	難	難	難	nàn　　　nàahn difficult; distress; disaster
	雨	雨	雨	yǔ　　　yúh　　　宋雨冈罒 rain; (*figuratively*) friend; teaching; instruction
	雩	雩		yú　　　jyu　　　雩 sacrificial ceremony with prayer and dancing for rain

	雪	雪	雪	xuě　　　syut	snow; wipe away; to clean; ice; product containing ice; (*Cantonese*) refrigerate
	雯	雯		wén　　　man	a multicolored cloud
云	雲	雲	雲	yún　　　wahn	clouds; many; numerous
	零	零	零	líng　　　lìhng　　囹 僗 夌 雺 霝 霗 霝	drizzle; fragmentary; fraction; scattered; remainder; zero
	雷	雷	雷	léi　　　lèuih　　畾 畾 靁 雷 雷 雷 雷	lightning; thunder; explosive device; astonishment; land or naval mine; surprise; (*slang*) shocking content
电	電	電	電	diàn　　　dihn	lightning; electricity; battery; romantic attraction; phone call; telegram; fast; speedy
	雹	雹	雹	báo　　　bok	hail
	需	需	需	xu　　　sèui	await; need; require; should; ought to; must; necessities
	霈	霈		pèi　　　pui	torrential rain, heavy rain, flow of water
	霄	霄	霄	xiao　　　siu	sky; heaven; clouds; mist; night (*same as* 宵)
	霆	霆		tíng　　　ting　　霣 陳	sudden peal of thunder; thunderbolt; thunderclap
	震	震	震	zhèn　　　jan	thunder; lightning strike; tremble; shake; jolt; quake; excited; shocked; invigorate; power; prestige; tremble
	霍	霍	霍	hùo　　　fok	quickly; suddenly; lightning
	霏	霏		fei　　　fei　　霏	falling snow
	霓	霓	霓	ní　　　ngai　　蜺 蛪	secondary rainbow

雨 8-16

	霖	霖	霖	lín　　　lam continuous heavy rain; long spell of rain, copious rain
	霎	霎		shà　　　saap light rain, drizzle; instant, suddenly; moment; passing
	霞	霞		xiá　　　hàh　　　遐 light and clouds at sunrise and sunset; afterglow; mist; rosy clouds; colorful; vapor
	霜	霜	霜	shuang　　sèung frost; ice; (*medicine*) cream
雾	霧	霧	霧	wù　　　mouh fog; mist; vapor; fine spray; blurry
	霪	霪		yín　　　jam　　　霪 long and heavy rain
	霰	霰		xiàn　　　sin hail; sleet; graupel (*popcorn snow*)
	露	露	露	lù　　　louh dew; fog; mist; syrup; nectar; juice; expose; disclose; reveal
	霹	霹	霹	pi　　　pìk thunderclap; crashing thunder
	霸	霸	霸	bà　　　ba dominate; overlord; tyrant; despot; hegemony; powerful; awesome; impressive
霁	霽	霽		jì　　　jai clear up after rain; cease being angry; bright; sunny
	霾	霾		mái　　　maai misty; foggy; hazy; dust storm
霭	靄	靄		ǎi　　　oi mist; haze; cloudy sky; calm; peaceful
雳	靂	靂		lì　　　lik thunderclap; crashing thunder
灵	靈	靈	靈	líng　　　lìhng　　　灵靈霛霊棂 spirit; soul; deity; efficacious; keen; quick; nimble

青 5-8　非 7-11　面 14　革 4-5

青	青	青	qing　　　cheng　　　宵青青岙峇峇岑 blue; blue-green; green; black (*of hair, cloth, silk, etc.*); luxuriant; exuberant; young; spring
	靖	靖	靖	jìng　　　jing stable; peaceful; tranquil; pacify; stabilize; govern; administer; to plan; think of; respectful; prudent
靚	靚	靚		jìng　　　jihng invite; dress up; gentle and refined; fair and quiet; bright; beautiful; gorgeous; magnificent
	靛	靛	靛	diàn　　　din indigo (*dye and color*)
靜	靜	靜	靜	jìng　　　jihng quiet; silent; devoid of noise; still; motionless; gentle
非	非	非		fei　　　fèi not be; is not; not; wrong; incorrect; reproach; blame; used to insist on something; must
	靠	靠	靠	kào　　　kaau lean on; recline; depend on; rely on; trust; confidence; come near to; approach; keep to a certain side
	靡	靡	靡	mǐ　　　mei fall down; extravagant; beautiful; splendid; no; not
	面	面	面	miàn　　　mihn face; side; surface; plane; aspect; dimension; short for interview (面試); (*Cantonese*) dignity; reputation; face
靥	靨	靨	靨	yè　　　yip dimple
	革	革	革	gé　　　gaap leather; animal hide; leather armour; change; alter; reform; remove; expel
	靳	靳		jìn　　　gan stingy; strap on a horse's breast
	靴	鞾	靴	xue　　　hèu　　　鞾鞾鞮靴鞾鞾屐 boots
	靶	靶	靶	bǎ　　　baa target; mark; bridle
鼗	鞀	鞀		táo　　　tou　　　靴 hand-held pellet drum

革 5-17　韋 3

	鞅	鞅		yang　　　jeung leather strap over horse's neck	
	鞍	鞌	鞥	án　　　òn saddle	
	鞋	鞵	鞋	xié　　　hàaih　　鞵 shoes; footwear	
巩	鞏	鞏	鞏	gǒng　　　góng fasten using a leather band; firm; secure; strengthen; alternative form of post (栱) and afraid (恐)	
	鞘	鞘	鞘	qiào　　　chiu scabbard; sheath; tube-shaped container used to carry valuables	
	鞠	鞠	鞠	ju　　　guk　　毬 bow; bend; to rear; raise; nourish; ball	
	鞫	鞫		ju　　　guk interrogate; to question; criminal case; exhaust; poverty	
	鞣	鞣		róu　　　yau tanning; soften	
	鞭	鞭	鞭	bian　　　bìn whip; flog; animal penis; string of firecrackers	
	鞲	鞲		gou　　　gau leather arm guard	
缰	韁	繮		jiang　　　geung bridle; reins	
鞑	韃	韃		dá　　　taat Tartars	
鞯	韉	韉		jian　　　jin saddle blanket	
韦	韋	韋	韋	wéi　　　wáih soft leather; tanned leather	
韧	韌	韌	韌	rèn　　　yahn strong; tough; tenacious; robust; sturdy; (*Cantonese*) hard	

404

韩	韓	韓	韓	hán　　hòhn　　埠 fence or puteal surrounding a well; ancient kingdom of the Zhou Dynasty; short for Korea (韓國)
韪	韙	韙		wěi　　wai right; properly; correctly; propriety; suitable
韬	韜	韜	韜	tao　　tou sheath; scabbard; bow case; art of war; military strategy; hide; conceal
韫	韞	韞		yùn　　wan contain; hold in store; hide; conceal; red or orange color; bow case
	韭	韭	韭	jiǔ　　gau　　韮 scallion; leek; chives
	音	音	音	yin　　yàm sound; voice; tone; pitch; (*music*) note; pronunciation; syllable; news; tidings
	章	章	章	zhang　　jeung chapter; section; composition; structure; regulations; constitution; charter; seal; stamp; badge; medal
	竟	竟	竟	jìng　　ging finish; end; finally; after all; at last; unexpected; surprising; whole; entire
	韶	韶	韶	sháo　　siu name of music composed by emperor Shun; ancient music; splendid; beautiful; carry forward; carry on
韵	韻	韻	韻	yùn　　wáhn sweet music; melodious tune; rhyme; appeal; charm; taste; articulate
响	響	響	響	xiǎng　　héung　　嚮 窨 make noise ; loud and clear; resonant; famous; reputable; sound; echo; news; (*classifier for sounds*)
页	頁	頁	頁	yè　　yihp sheet of paper; page; (*classifier for pages*)
顶	頂	頂	頂	dǐng　　díng top; peak; crown; support from below; substitute; talk back; head strike; confront; exceeding
顷	頃	頃	頃	qǐng　　king　　頑 unit of area equal to 100 mǔ (畝) or 6.67 hectares; short while; just now; a moment; about; circa (*after dates*)
项	項	項	項	xiàng　　hohng neck; nape of neck; item; sum of money; (*math*) term; (*classifier for items, tasks, principles, etc.*)

頁 3-6

頇	頇			han / hon large face; flat face; stupid; bald
順	順			shùn / seuhn 慎 慎 做 follow; go along; obey; submit; smooth; successful; pilfer; cisgender
须	須			xu / sèui must; have to; should; halt; bring to an end
顼	頊			xu / juk grieved; anxious
颂	頌			sòng / juhng laud; acclaim; praise; hymn; ode
頎	頎			qí / kei tall and slender
頏	頏			hang / hong fly downward; scoot; neck; throat
预	預			yù / yuh pre- ; beforehand; take part in; (*Cantonese*) foresee; expect; anticipate; prepare;
顽	頑			wán / wàahn obstinate; stubborn; recalcitrant; ignorant; naughty; mischievous
颁	頒			bán / bàan confer; bestow; grant; award; present; publish; promulgate
顿	頓			dùn / deuhn pause; arrange; to handle; deal with; stamp your foot; kowtow; suddenly; abruptly
颇	頗			po / pó leaning to one side; oblique; very; rather
领	領			lǐng / líhng neck; collar; main point; lead; guide; get; receive; understand; grasp
颏	頦			ke / hoi chin
颌	頜			hé / hap mouth; jaw

颉	頡	頡	頡	xié	git	
				fly upward; soar; contest; to rob		
颐	頤	頤	頤	yí	ji	頤 匝
				chin; jaw; cheek; nourish; maintain one's health		
头	頭	頭	頭	tóu	tàuh	頭
				head; top; tip; first; end; hair; hairstyle; chief; boss; leader; remnant		
颔	頷	頷		hàn	háhm	
				chin; jaw; jowl; neck; to nod		
颊	頰	頰	頰	jiá	gaap	頰
				cheek		
颓	頹	頹		túi	tèuih	頽 頺 穨
				fall; drop; collapse; decline; degenerate; decay; feeble; dilapidated; dejected; depressed; down; listless		
频	頻	頻	頻	pín	pàhn	
				frequently; again and again; incessant; (*physics*) short for frequency (頻率)		
颈	頸	頸	頸	jǐng	géng	
				neck		
颗	顆	顆	顆	ke	fó	
				(*classifier for small round objects*)		
题	題	題	題	tí	tàih	
				forehead; title; question; quiz; problem; to sign; write; inscribe; alternative form of mention (提)		
额	額	額		é	ngaahk	額
				forehead; top part; tablet; plaque; amount; quantity; number		
颚	顎	顎	顎	è	ngok	
				jaw; palate; mandible		
颜	顏	顏	顏	yán	ngàahn	
				color; face; countenance; facial expression; prestige, dignity		
颛	顓	顓	顓	zhuan	jyun	
				good; honest; simple; respectful		
愿	願	願	願	yùan	yuhn	
				desire; want; wish; ambition		

頁 10-18　風 4-5

颡	顙	顙		sǎng　　song　　賴 forehead; kowtow
颠	顛	顛	顛	dian　　din　　顛 top; crown; peak; summit; fall; topple; upset; inverted; to bump; to jerk; jolt
类	類	類	類	lèi　　leui class; group; kind; category
颟	顢	顢		man　　mun dawdling; thoughtless; careless
颢	顥	顥	顥	hào　　hou luminous; white; hoary
顾	顧	顧	顧	gù　　gu　　顧 look back; look at; visit; patronize; consider; look after; take care of; attend to; care for
颤	顫	顫	顫	chàn　　jin shake; vibrate; tremble; shiver
显	顯	顯	顯	xiǎn　　hín　　㬎 显 顕 prominent; conspicuous; visible; appear; manifest; display
顰	顰	顰		pín　　pan　　嚬 frown; knit one's eyebrows
颅	顱	顱	顱	lú　　lou skull; head; forehead
颧	顴	顴		qúan　　kyun cheek bones
颞	顳	顳		niè　　nip temple (*head*)
风	風	風	風	feng　　fùng　　風凬凮凨飌䫻 air; atmosphere; custom; conduct; discipline; demeanor; news; affection; promiscuous; ungrounded
飒	颯	颯	颯	sà　　saap (*onomatopoeia*) sound of wind; bleak; melancholy
飑	颮	颮		biao　　biu squall; whirlwind

408

刮	颳	劜	劜	gua　　　gwat blow; blowing of the wind
飓	颶	颶	颶	jù　　　geuih hurricane; cyclone; typhoon
飕	颼	颼	颼	sou　　　sau sound of wind; blowing wind
飘	飄	飄	飄	piao　　　più　　　　颰 to drift; float; snowfall; whirlwind
飙	飆	飆		biao　　　biù　　　猋 颮 颮 颮 颮 飆 whirlwind; wind; move or rise intensely; (Mandarin) do something difficult or requiring skill
飞	飛	飛	飛	fei　　　fèi to fly; hover; flutter; disappear; fast; swift; very; unfounded; unexpected; (Cantonese) skip; disregard
	食	食	食	shí　　　sihk eat; have a meal; food; take in; (Cantonese) drink; to smoke; capture; (mahjong) short for win (食糊)
饥	飢	飢	飢	ji　　　gei　　　　饑 hunger; hungry; starving; famine
飧	飧	飧	飧	sun　　　syun　　　　飱 evening meal; supper; cooked food
饪	飪	飪	飪	rèn　　　jam　　　　餁 胚 恁 恁 cook thoroughly
饫	飫	飫		yù　　　jyu full of food; surfeited; satiated; confer; sick of food; disgusted with
饬	飭	飭	飭	chì　　　chik put in order; readjust; rectify; instruct; cautious; careful; prudent; alternative form of decorate (飾)
饭	飯	飯	飯	fàn　　　faahn any cooked grain; cooked rice; food; meal
饮	飲	飲	飲	yǐn　　　yám　　　　歙 飲 㳄 㵫 beverage; (Cantonese) to drink; attend a banquet; keep in the heart; alternative form of hidden (隱)
饨	飩	飩	飩	tún　　　tan wonton; stuffed dumpling

409

食 5-8

饱	飽	馢	䭃	bǎo　　báao full after a meal; satisfied; replete; abounding; plump; embezzle
饲	飼	馢	䭃	sì　　jih　　食飤卟 feed; nourish; to rear; support one's parents (elders); (Taiwanese) support a mistress
饴	飴	馢	䭃	yí　　ji syrup or candy made from malt or rice; soft candy; very sweet
饰	飾	馢	䭃	shì　　sìk decorate; decorations; adorn; adornments; ornament; cover up; deceive; to polish
饼	餅	馢	䭃	bǐng　　béng　　餠 biscuit; cookie; pastry; pancake-shaped object; (Cantonese, classifier for video cassettes)
养	養	養	䭃	yǎng　　yéuhng raise; to rear; bring up; support; give birth to; (Sichuanese, formal) you
饵	餌	馢	䭃	ěr　　nei　　粥 food; food made of rice dough; medicine; eat; feed; bait (fish and animals); lure
饷	餉	馢	䭃	xiǎng　　heung　　饟 entertain with food and beverage; pay and rations for soldiers and government officials
饺	餃	馢	䭃	jiǎo　　gáau wonton; stuffed dumpling
馁	餒	馢	䭃	něi　　neui hungry; starving; famished; peckish; discouraged; rotten fish; putrid
	餐	餐	餐	can　　chàan　　湌飡喰餐 food; cuisine; eat; (classifier for meals or occurrences of an event)
饽	餑	馢		bo　　but steamed bun; cake; pastry; surface bubbles in tea
余	餘	余	䭃	yú　　yùh over; surplus; remainder; excess; spare; time after an event; alternative form of I (余); (obsolete) salt
饿	餓	馢	䭃	è　　ngoh hungry; starving
饯	餞	馢	䭃	jiàn　　chin give a farewell party; see off; send off; preserve fruit in honey or syrup

馄	餛	䭝	䭝	hún / wan wonton; stuffed dumpling
馅	餡	䭡	䭡	xiàn / haam filling for dumplings
馆	館	䭧	䭧	guǎn / gwún 舘 dwelling; accommodation; restaurant; shop; building or place for cultural activities; private school; factory
	饕	䭲		tiè / tit gluttonous; hyperphagic; greedy; gourmand; ravenous; voracious
糖	餳	糖	糖	xíng / chìhng sugar; syrup; malt sugar; sticky
馍	饃	䭿		mó / mo 饝 bread; steamed bun (*no filling*)
馏	餾	䭮	䭮	liù / lau distill; distillation
馐	饈	䭴		xiu / sau food; meal; eat; offer; delicate
饩	餼	䭩		xì / hei grain; grain ration; fodder; sacrificial victim; livestock; raw meat; provisions; (*Cantonese*) to feed animals
馊	餿	䭹	䭹	sou / sau spoiled food that smells
馒	饅	䭽	䭽	mán / maan mántou (饅頭); steamed bun (*no filling*); steamed dumpling
饥	饑	䭢	䭢	ji / gèi 飢 crop failure; famine; poor harvest year
馑	饉	䭤	䭤	jǐn / gan time of famine or crop failure
馔	饌	䭵		zhuàn / jaan food; feed; support; provide for; fine meats; delicacy
馓	饊	䭳		sǎn / san fried round cake made of wheat flour

饶	饒	饒	饒	ráo yiùh forgive; mercy; abundant; plentiful; (Mandarin) give as a giveaway or extra
馈	饋	饋		kùi gwai to send gift; transport; to ship; offer food to a superior
	饔	饔		yong jung cooked food (especially meat); breakfast
飨	饗	饗		xiǎng heung banquet; feast; sacrificial offering
	饕	饕		tao tou gluttonous, gourmand; greedy, covetous
餍	饜	饜		yàn jim full; satiated; satisfied
馋	饞	饞		chán chàahm gluttonous; greedy; lewd; lecherous; rapacious
馕	饢	饢		náng nong naan (bread)
	首	首	首	shǒu sáu 甞 百 head; chief; leader; start; first; best; highest; prime; primary; side; direction; (classifier for songs and poems)
	馗	馗		kúi kwai 頯 cheekbone; path; road; intersection; thoroughfare
	馘	馘		gúo gwok 聝 severed ear of an enemy (tally for military merit); killed enemy; dead enemy
	香	香	香	xiang hèung 馨 fragrant; delicious-smelling; popular; perfume; incense; deep sleep; (figurative) woman; (Cantonese) die
	馥	馥	馥	fù fuk fragrance; scent; aroma
	馨	馨	馨	xin hìng 馫馨 fragrant; widespread fragrance; widespread renown and reputation
马	馬	馬	馬	mǎ máh 馬 傌 影 影 影 碼 horse; horse-shaped; (chess) knight; big/large (prefix for nouns); (Mandarin) to bully

冯	馮	馮	馮	féng　　　fung gallop; because of; by means of
驭	馭	馭	馭	yù　　　jyu control; drive; ride; manage
驰	馳	馳	馳	chí　　　chìh speed; gallop; chase; spread afar; long for; eager for
驯	馴	馴	馴	xùn　　　seun tame; to tame; docile; obedient
驮	馱	馱	馱	túo　　　to　　　駄 carry on the back; load carried by a pack animal
驳	駁	駁	駁	bó　　　bok (*horse's fur*) variegated; mixed; heterogenous; impure; refute; rebut; transport by barge; barge; suddenly
驶	駛	駛	駛	shǐ　　　sái drive (*vehicle*); sail (*vessel*); fly (*aircraft*); (*Cantonese*) alternative form of need to (使)
骀	駘	駘		tái　　　toi an old horse; tired; exhausted; jade
驹	駒	駒	駒	ju　　　keui colt; foal; fleet; swift; sun
驻	駐	駐	駐	zhù　　　jyu (*troops and diplomats*) be stationed; be posted; halt; stop
驵	駔	駔		zǎng　　　chóng excellent horse; powerful horse; noble steed
驸	駙	駙	駙	fù　　　fu side horse; prince consort
驼	駝	駝	駝	túo　　　tòh　　　駞 camel; humpbacked; hunchbacked; carry on the back
驷	駟	駟	駟	sì　　　si vehicle drawn by four horses; horse; drive; to ride; (*classifier for horses and vehicles drawn by four horses*)
驽	駑	駑	駑	nú　　　nou tired; old horse; old; weak

馬 5-10

驾	駕			jià　　　ga drive; to sail; to fly; giddyup; cart; carriage; emperor's carriage; (*figurative*) emperor
骂	罵			mà　　　ma　　　　　駡傌 chide; scold; blame; to curse; swear
骈	駢			pián　　pin　　　　　駍 two horses side by side; side by side; parallel; antithetical
骇	駭			hài　　　hoih terrify; frighten; hack a computer
骆	駱			luò　　　lok white horse with a black mane; camel
骏	駿			jùn　　　jeun excellent horse; noble steed
骋	騁			chěng　　ping　　　　騯 gallop; run; give free rein to; released from constraint; put to use; showcase
骒	騍			kè　　　fo mare
骓	騅			zhui　　jeui piebald horse; the name of Xiang Yu's (*an ancient warlord*) horse
骑	騎			qí　　　ke ride (*i.e., horse, bicycle*); sit astride; (*vulgar*) to ride; to mount
骐	騏			qí　　　kei　　　　　騹駬 piebald horse; excellent horse
骗	騙			piàn　　pin　　　　　騗 deceive; to fool; swindle; cheat out of; defraud
骛	騖			wù　　　mou disorderly gallop; rush about; pursue; run
骞	騫			qian　　hin raise; hold high; fly; soar
骘	騭			zhì　　　jat　　　　　隲 stallion; promote

414

馬 10

腾	騰	騰		téng　　　tàhng gallop; run; prance; soar; rise
骚	騷	騷	騷	sao　　　sòu　　　騷 harass; bother; annoy; disturb; agitate; sad; grieved; coquettish; flirty; provocative
驺	騶	騶		zou　　　jau stablemaster; groom; coach driver; calvary escort
骟	騸	騸		shàn　　　sim geld; spay; castrate
骡	騾	騾	騾	luó　　　lèuih mule
骠	驃	驃	驃	biao　　　biu white horse; charger; steed; swift; valiant; brave
驱	驅	驅	驅	qu　　　kèui　　　駆駈 run quickly; expel; disperse; drive; urge on; to spur; short for destroyer (驅逐艦)
骖	驂	驂		can　　　chaam two flanking horses of a charioteer's 3-horse team; horse (*generic*)
蓦	驀	驀	驀	mò　　　mak suddenly; quickly; abruptly; leap over
骜	驁	驁		ào　　　ngou noble steed; untamed; person of outstanding talent; alternative form of arrogant (傲)
惊	驚	驚	驚	jing　　　gìng fear; frighten; frightening; to scare; scary; afraid; (*animals*) startled; shy
骄	驕	驕	驕	jiao　　　giù haughty; proud; arrogant; large horse
骣	驏	驏		zhàn　　　chán horse without a saddle
骁	驍	驍	驍	xiao　　　hiu an excellent horse; brave; valiant
骅	驊	驊		húa　　　waa name of a legendary fine horse; chestnut horse

415

驿	驛	驛	驛	yì　　　jik postal horse; relay station for posting horses; (*Taiwanese*) train station; bus stop
验	驗	驗	驗	yàn　　　yihm　　　䮞 test; examine; inspect; verify
骤	驟	驟	驟	zhòu　　　jaauh　　　骓 駎 逫 驟 gallop; run; sudden; abrupt; frequent; repeated; a fast horse
驴	驢	驢	驢	lú　　　lòuh　　　驴 驉 驢 donkey; ass
骥	驥	驥	驥	jì　　　gei horse which can travel 1000 li in a day; good horse; proficient person
骧	驤	驤		xiang　　　seung gallop; run; raised head; hold high
骊	驪	驪	驪	lí　　　lei pure black horse; Mount Li in Shaanxi; ancient Chinese tribe
	骨	骨	骨	gǔ　　　gwàt　　　𩨂 bones; skeleton; frame; framework; moral character
肮	骯	骯	骯	ang　　　hòng dirty; filthy
	骰	骰		tóu　　　tau die (polyhedron used in games); dice
	骱	骱		gà　　　haai a joint between bones
	骶	骶		dǐ　　　dai sacrum; coccyx
	骷	骷		ku　　　fu skeleton
	骺	骺		hóu　　　hàuh epiphysis; rounded end of a long bone
	骼	骼		gé　　　gaak bones; skeleton

	骸	骸(seal)	骸(seal2)	hái　　haai　　骹　skeleton of a dead person; body
	髀	髀(seal)		bì　　bei　thigh; thighbone
	髁	髁(seal)		ke　　fo　thigh bone; hipbone; kneecap; condyle
	髂	髂(seal)		qià　　kaa　ilium
髅	髏	髏(seal)		lóu　　lau　skull; cranium
	髒	髒(seal)		zang　　jòng　dirty; filthy
	髑	髑(seal)		dú　　duk　顕　skull
	髓	髓(seal)	髓(seal2)	suǐ　　seui　髓　bone marrow; essence; substance
体	體	體(seal)	體(seal2)	tǐ　　tái　軆躰　body; state of a substance; style; form; genre; structure; typeface; three-dimensional; principle
髌	髕	髕(seal)		bìn　　ban　臏　kneecap; patella
髋	髖	髖(seal)		kuan　　fun　hip; hibone
高	高	高(seal)	高(seal2)	gau　　gòu　高　tall; high; of high level; above average; high place; loud; altitude; (honorific) your
	髟	髟(seal)		biao　　biu　hair; long hair; shaggy
	髡	髡(seal)		kun　　kwan　髠髨　shave a man's head as punishment (ancient China); Buddhist monk; trim branches off a tree
发	髮	髮(seal)	髮(seal2)	fà　　faat　髪頢　hair; vegetation

髟 4-15　鬥

	髦	髦		máo　　　mou (*hair*) bangs; mane; forelocks; fashionable
	髭	髭		zi　　　ji　　　顛齔 mustache
	髯	髯		rán　　　jim beard; whiskers
	髫	髫		tiáo　　　tiu a child's hair style; a child's tuft of hair; youngster
	髻	髻		jì　　　gai　　　髻 hair worn in a bun; coiled hair; topknot
	髹	髹		xiu　　　yau lacquer
	鬃	鬃		zong　　　jung　　　騣 駿 mane; bristle; coarse hair
松	鬆	鬆	鬆	song　　　sùng loose; loosen; relax; useless; dried minced meat; (*Cantonese*) leave
	鬈	鬈		qúan　　　kyun wavy; curly hair
胡	鬍	鬍	胡	hú　　　wùh beard; mustache; whiskers
	鬏	鬏		jiu　　　chau hair bun; chignon; coiffure
	鬚	須	須	xu　　　sòu　　　須 beard; whisker; whisker-like; antenna; feeler
鬢	鬢	鬢		bìn　　　ban hair on the temples
	鬣	鬣		liè　　　lip horse mane; fin; human whiskers
斗	鬥	鬥	鬥	dòu　　　dau fight; struggle; contend; compete with; strive; chaotic, disorderly; encounter; confront; piece together

418

闹	鬧	鬧(seal)	鬪(seal)	nào naauh 鬧 be noisy; create a disturbance; (*of negative events*) to occur; (*Cantonese*) scold
哄	鬨	鬨(seal)	鬨(seal)	hòng hung fight; combat; cause a commotion or disturbance
阋	鬩	鬩(seal)		xì jik 鬩 feud; fight; quarrel
阄	鬮	鬮(seal)		jiu kau lots (*items used for making decisions*); to draw lots
		鬯(seal)	鬯(seal)	chàng cheung 凶凼 a type of ancient Chinese sacrificial spirit; sacrificial wine; alternative form of unhindered (暢)
郁	鬱	鬱(seal)	鬱(seal)	yù wàt 鬱欝欎欝欝欝欝欝 lush; luxuriant; exuberant; profuse; deep; profound; stagnate; depressed; sad; gloomy; resent; type of plum
	鬲	鬲(seal)		lì lik 瓾厤 cauldron with three hollow legs; tripod
	鬻	鬻(seal)		yù juk 賣 sell; vend; to use; usurp; alternative form of nourish (育)
	鬼	鬼(seal)	鬼(seal)	guǐ gwái ghost; apparition; spirit; devil; demon; stealthy; tricky; furtive; sinister; ghastly; clever; traitor
	魁	魁(seal)	魁(seal)	kúi fùi first; leading; chief; leader; best; monstrous; dipper; spoon
	魂	魂(seal)	魂(seal)	hún wàhn 寬 soul; spirit; the soul which goes to heaven (*contrary to the pò* (魄)); mood; national morale
	魄	魄(seal)	魄(seal)	pò paak the soul which does not leave the body after death; soul; spirit; vigor; body; illuminated part of the moon
	魃	魃(seal)		bá baat drought demon
	魅	魅(seal)		mèi meih 鬽魁魖 legendary evil spirit; demon; captivate; to charm; seduce
	魈	魈(seal)		xiao siu elf; a mischievous mountain spirit

	魍	魍		wǎng　　　　mong elf; sprite; demon; mountain spirit; trick
	魎	魎		liǎng　　　　leung sprite; pixie; fairy; monster
	魏	魏	魏	wèi　　　　ngai State of Wei (*Warring States period*); high; tall; palace watchtower
	魑	魑		chi　　　　chi　　　蟲飍禍 mountain demon resembling a tiger; evil spirit
	魔	魔	魔	mó　　　　mò (*Buddhism*) mara (*spectre*); demon; evil spirit; harmful; magic; unnatural; crazy; delusional, obsessed; idolatry
魇	魘	魘		yǎn　　　　jim nightmare; bad dream
鱼	魚	魚	魚	yú　　　　yùh　　　　魚 fish
鲁	魯	魯	魯	lǔ　　　　lou foolish; stupid; rash; rude; vulgar
鲂	魴	魴		fáng　　　　fong bream (*a fresh water fish*)
鱿	魷	魷		yóu　　　　jau cuttlefish; squid
鲅	鮁	鮁		bà　　　　bat Spanish mackerel
鲆	鮃	鮃		píng　　　　ping flounder
鲋	鮒	鮒		fù　　　　fu carp, silver carp (*carassius auratus*)
鲍	鮑	鮑	鮑	bào　　　　bàau abalone; salted fish
鲐	鮐	鮐		tái　　　　toi　　　台 mackerel; old person

鮎	鮎	鮎		nián　　nim　　鯰 catfish (*order siluriformes*); sheatfish
鮚	鮚	鮚		jié　　git clam; oyster
鮞	鮞	鮞		ér　　ji caviar; roe
鮪	鮪	鮪		wěi　　fui tuna; Chinese paddlefish; Chinese swordfish (*psephurus gladius*)
鮫	鮫	鮫		jiao　　gaau shark
鮭	鮭	鮭		gui　　gwai blowfish; salmon (*spheroides vermicularis*)
鮮	鮮	鮮	鮮	xian　　sìn　　𩺰 鱻 鮮 fresh; new; recent; live fish; fresh food; clear; vivid; brightly coloured; delicious; tasty; special; peculiar
鯀	鯀	鯀		gǔn　　gwan a giant fish; father of Yu the Great
鯁	鯁	鯁		gěng　　gang fish bone; honest; upright; blunt; unyielding
鯇	鯇	鯇		hùan　　waan　　鯶 grass carp (*ctenopharyngodon idella*)
鯉	鯉	鯉	鯉	lǐ　　léih common carp; messenger; letter; correspondence
鯊	鯊	鯊		sha　　sà shark; small fish
鯽	鯽	鯽		jì　　jik crucian carp (*carassius auratus*)
鯡	鯡	鯡		fei　　fei herring
鯔	鯔	鯔		zi　　ji flathead mullet (*mugil cephalus*)

魚 8-9

鯖	鯖	鯖		qing / ching mackerel; black carp (*mylopharyngodon piceus*)
鯛	鯛	鯛		diao / diu sea bream; porgy
鯝	鯝	鯝		gù / gu Taiwan shovel-jaw carp (*onychostoma barbatulum*); fish guts
鯢	鯢	鯢		ní / ngai giant salamander (*cryptobranchus japonicus*)
鯤	鯤	鯤		kun / kwan 卵 fish roe; fry; spawn; (*Chinese mythology*) a large fish that transforms into a roc (鵬)
鯧	鯧	鯧	鯧	chang / cheung pomfret; butterfish; pompano
鯨	鯨	鯨		jing / king 鱷 鯨 whale; great; huge
鯪	鯪	鯪		líng / ling common carp; mud carp (*cirrhinus molitorella*); pangolin; mythological fish with a human-like face
鯫	鯫	鯫		zou / jau small fish; meagre; mean; stupid
鯰	鯰	鯰		nián / nim catfish; sheatfish
鯗	鯗	鯗		xiǎng / jeung 鯗 dried fish
鰈	鰈	鰈		dié / dip righteye flounder; flatfish; sole
鰉	鰉	鰉		húang / wong sturgeon; kaluga (*huso dauricus*)
鰍	鰍	鰍		qiu / chau 鰌 loach
鰒	鰒	鰒		fù / fuk abalone; sea ear

鰓	鰓	𩶢		sai	sòi	
				fish gills		
鰣	鰣	𩷲		shí	si	
				reeves' shad; hilsa herring		
鳐	鰩	𩺊		yáo	jiu	
				ray; skate		
鰥	鰥	𩽀		guan	gwàan	
				widower		
鳎	鰨	𩸕		tǎ	taap	鰏
				common sole		
鳍	鰭	𩸦		qí	kei	
				flipper; fin		
鲦	鰷	𩻂		tiáo	tiu	
				Korean sharpbelly (*hemiculter leucisculus*); chub		
鳔	鰾	𩹉		biào	biu	
				swim bladder; air bladder; fish glue; isinglass; glue with fish glue; gather; bring together; bet; contend		
鲣	鰹	𩸙		jian	gin	
				skipjack tuna; bonito; great eel; type of shark		
鳗	鰻	𩹌		mán	maan	鯙 鰐
				eel		
鳕	鱈	𩼣		xùe	syut	
				codfish		
鰳	鰳	𩻝		lè	lak	
				Chinese herring; shad		
鲢	鰱	𩻞		lián	lin	
				silver carp (*hypophthalmichthys molitrix*); any fish of the genus hypophthalmichthys		
鳘	鰵	𩼀		mǐn	máhn	
				codfish		
鳌	鰲	𩸀		áo	ngou	鼇
				large mythological sea turtle		

魚 12-16　鳥 2

鱉	鱉	鱉	鱉	bie　　　bit　　　　鼈鼈 soft-shell turtle
鳜	鱖	鱖		gùi　　　kyut mandarin fish
鳟	鱒	鱒		zun　　　jyun barble fish
鳝	鱔	鱔		shàn　　sin　　　　鱣 eel
鳞	鱗	鱗	鱗	lín　　　lèuhn　　　鮻 鯩 scale (*i.e. fish, reptiles*); scaly; creatures with scales
鲟	鱘	鱘		xún　　　cam sturgeon
鲎	鱟	鱟		hòu　　　hau horseshoe crab; king crab; clumsy; ungraceful
鳢	鱧	鱧		lǐ　　　　lai　　　　鮦 鱱 snakehead; blotched snakehead (*channa maculata*)
鲚	鱭	鱭		jì　　　　cai anchovy
鳄	鱷	鱷		è　　　　ngok crocodilian; crocodile; alligator
鲈	鱸	鱸		lú　　　　lou　　　　鲈 鱸 bass; perch
鲡	鱺	鱺		lí　　　　lei eel; Japanese eel
鸟	鳥	鳥	鳥	niǎo　　liúh bird; (*slang*) pay attention; heed; take notice of; (*vulgar, Taiwan*) unpleasant; inferior; objectionable
凫	鳧	鳧		fú　　　　fu mallard duck; wild duck; alternative form of swim (浮)
鸠	鳩	鳩	鳩	jiu　　　kau　　　　鴡 pigeon; dove (*family columbidae*); gather; assemble

凤	鳳	鳳	鳳	fèng　　fuhng　　　鳳凤风 Chinese phoenix (*male*)
鸢	鳶	鳶	鳶	yuan　　jyun　　　戴鳾 black kite (*milvus migrans*); kite (*toy*)
鸣	鳴	鳴	鳴	míng　　mìhng cry of a bird; chirp (*also of insects*)
鸩	鴆	鴆	鴆	zhèn　　jam　　　酖 poisonous; to poison; mythical Chinese bird with poisonous feathers (*resembles the secretary bird*)
鸨	鴇	鴇		bǎo　　bou bustard; procuress; female brothel-keeper
鸦	鴉	鴉	鴉	ya　　ngà　　　鵐 crow; raven
鸳	鴛	鴛	鴛	yuan　　yùn male mandarin duck
鸯	鴦	鴦	鴦	yang　　yèung female mandarin duck
鸵	鴕	鴕	鴕	túo　　to ostrich
鸱	鴟	鴟		chi　　chi scops owl; horned owl
鸲	鴝	鴝		qú　　keui mynah bird
鸪	鴣	鴣	鴣	gu　　gu species of Taiwan pigeon; partridge
鸭	鴨	鴨	鴨	ya　　ngaap duck; male prostitute
鳾	鳾	鳾		ér　　ji swallow (*migratory bird*)
鸿	鴻	鴻	鴻	hóng　　hung　　　鴻 swan; letter; epistle; big; large; huge; strong; powerful; energetic

鳥 6-8

鸺	鵂	(seal)		xiu / jau — horned owl (*scops chinensis*); bird of ill omen
鸽	鴿	(seal)	(seal)	ge / gaap — pigeon; dove; (*internet slang*) humorous
鸹	鴰	(seal)		gua / kut — crow; raven
鹆	鵒	(seal)		yù / juk — mynah bird
鹄	鵠	(seal)	(seal)	hú / huk — swan; white
鹃	鵑	(seal)	(seal)	juan / gyùn — cuckoo
鹁	鵓	(seal)		bó / but — wood pigeon
鹈	鵜	(seal)		tí / tai — pelican
鹅	鵝	(seal)	(seal)	é / ngòh — domestic goose 鵞 䳘 鵞
鹉	鵡	(seal)	(seal)	wǔ / mou — parrot 䳇
鹌	鵪	(seal)	(seal)	an / am — quail 䳺 鶉 鵪
鹏	鵬	(seal)	(seal)	péng / paang — an enormous legendary bird; roc
鹎	鵯	(seal)		bei / bei — bulbul
鹊	鵲	(seal)	(seal)	què / jeuk — magpie
鸫	鶇	(seal)		dong / dung — thrush

鳥 8-11

鶉	鶉	鶉	鶉	chún quail	cheun	䳉
鶘	鶘	鶘		hú pelican	wu	
鶚	鶚	鶚		è osprey; fishhawk	ngok	
鶩	鶩	鶩		wù domestic duck; duck	mou	鶩鶩
鶯	鶯	鶯	鶯	ying oriole; greenfinch; warbler	ngàng	鸎
鶿	鶿	鶿		cí cormorant	chìh	
騫	騫	騫	騫	qian raise; hold high; fly; soar	hin	
鶴	鶴	鶴	鶴	hè crane; white	hohk	鶴鶴雀
鶻	鶻	鶻		gǔ falcon	gwat	
鶼	鶼	鶼		jian a Chinese mythical bird with one eye and one wing	gim	
鷂	鷂	鷂	鷂	yào sparrow hawk; harrier; kite	jiu	
鷓	鷓	鷓	鷓	zhè partridge	jeh	
鷗	鷗	鷗	鷗	ou seagull	ngàu	鴎
鷙	鷙	鷙		zhì bird of prey; vulture; fierce; cruel; brutal; violent	ji	
鷚	鷚	鷚		liù anthus	lau	

				Mandarin	Cantonese	Other
鷥	鷥	鷥		sī	si	heron; egret
鷦	鷦	鷦		jiāo	jiu	wren
鷯	鷯	鷯		liáo	liu	wren
鷳	鷳	鷳		xián	haan	a silver pheasant badge (*worn by government officials of the 5th rank*)
鷸	鷸	鷸		yù	jyut	snipe; sandpiper; kingfisher
鷲	鷲	鷲		jiù	jau	eagle; condor; vulture 就
鷺	鷺	鷺	鷺	lù	lou	heron; egret
鷹	鷹	鷹	鷹	yīng	yìng	eagle; falcon; hawk 雁
鸕	鸕	鸕		lú	lou	cormorant
鸚	鸚	鸚	鸚	yīng	jing	parrot; parakeet
鸛	鸛	鸛	鸛	guàn	gun	crane (*grus japonensis*); stork
鸝	鸝	鸝		lí	lei	black-naped oriole
鸞	鸞	鸞	鸞	luán	lyun	a benevolent mythical bird related to the Chinese Phoenix (鳳凰); (*aka "simurgh" in Persia*); imperial
卤	鹵	卤		lǔ	lou	saline soil; natural salt; halogen
咸	鹹	咸	咸	xián	hàahm	salt; salted; salty; briny; stingy; miserly; (*Cantonese*) short for pornographic (鹹濕) 醎

鹵 10-13　鹿 2-12　麥 4

鹺	鹾	𪉸		cúo　　　chòh　　　醝 salt; salted
碱	鹼	𪉟	𪉷	jiǎn　　　gaan　　　城 鱇 礆 鹸 sodium carbonate; alkali; base (*soluble or non*); soap
盐	鹽	𪉩	鹽	yán　　　yìhm　　　壏 塩 盬 盦 salt; table salt; food pickled with salt; sweat stain; salt efflorescence
鹿	鹿	鹿	鹿	lù　　　luhk deer
麂	麂	麂		jǐ　　　gei muntjac
麈	麈	麈		zhǔ　　　jyu species of deer; stag
麇	麇	麇		jun　　　gwan hornless deer; collect
麋	麋	麋		mí　　　mei moose; elk
麒	麒	麒		qí　　　kei legendary auspicious animal called a qílín (麒麟); female unicorn
麓	麓	麓	麓	lù　　　luk foot of a hill; foothill
丽	麗	麗		lì　　　laih　　　麗 丽 𠠎 beautiful; lovely; pretty; fair; elegant; graceful; adhere; alternative form of a pair (儷)
麝	麝	麝		shè　　　seh musk deer; musk
麟	麟	麟		lín　　　lèuhn　　　䴢 legendary auspicious animal called a qílín (麒麟); female unicorn; big deer
麦	麥	麥	麥	mài　　　mahk wheat; barley; oats
麸	麩	麩	麩	fu　　　fu　　　䴭 麱 wheat bran; panned gold; gold dust

麥 4-9　麻 3-4　黃 13　黍 3-5　黑 5

	麴	䴜	麴	qu　　　kuk　　　柚 yeast; leaven; alcoholic beverage
面	麵	麵	麵	miàn　　mihn noodles (*normally a Japanese shinjitai character*)
	麻	麻	麻	má　　　màh　　　蔴 hemp; linen; mourning garment; imperial edict; chaotic; coarse; rough; pockmark; numb; anesthesia
么	麼	麼	麼	me　　　mo　　　广 (*particle after the first clause of a compound sentence to show tactfulness; suffix for pronouns or adverbs*)
	麾	麾		hui　　　fai pennant; flag; banner; signal; give orders; rejoice
	黃	黃	黃	huáng　　wòhng yellow; (*colloquial*) pornographic; lewd; fizzle out
黌	黌	黌	黌	hóng　　hung school (*old usage*)
	黍	黍	黍	shǔ　　　syú proso millet; (*dialectal*) sorghum; corn; maize
	黎	黎		lí　　　　láih black; numerous; crowded; almost; dawn; Li people (*largest ethnic minority in Hainan*)
	黏	黏	黏	nián　　nìm sticky; glutinous; adhesive; adhere; to stick
	黑	黑	黑	hei　　　hàk　　　黒 黙 black; dark; night; illegal; clandestine; secret; shady; sinister; evil; to mock; libel; (*computing*) hack
	黔	黔	黔	qián　　kim black; name of an ancient prefecture located in Chongqing and Guizhou; short for Guizhou (貴州)
	默	默	默	mò　　　mahk silent; quiet; keep still; secretly; covertly; write from memory
	黛	黛		dài　　　doi a dark pigment used to paint eyebrows in ancient times; black; women's eyebrows
	黜	黜		chù　　　cheut dismiss; demote; downgrade; discard; reject; abolish

	黝	黝		yǒu　　　jau dark green; black
点	點	點	點	dím　　　diǎn　　點丶 dot; speck; point; drop; o'clock; dot stroke (丶); select; to tap; ignite; a little; (Cantonese) dip in; misguide
	點	點		xiá　　　hat sly; cunning; shrewd; artful
	黟	黟		yi　　　ji black wood; ebony
	黢	黢		qu　　　cheut black
	黪	黪		cǎn　　　chan greyish black
	黧	黧		lí　　　lai yellowish black; dark
党	黨	黨	黨	dǎng　　　dóng　　攩 political party; Chinese Communist Party; league; community; fellow member; gang; faction
	黥	黥		qíng　　　king facial tattoo (one of the 五刑, "Five Punishments"); tattooed person; carve
	黯	黯		àn　　　am dim; dark; black; sullen; dreary
霉	黴	黴		méi　　　mei　　霉黴 mold; mildew; must; dirty face; dingy; dark
黩	黷	黷		dú　　　duk tarnish; insult; blacken; be rash; dishonour; defile; corrupt; soiled
	黹	黹		zhǐ　　　ji　　絺 embroidery; needlework
	黻	黻		fú　　　fat special pattern of embroidery (an embroidered figure resembling 亞 - a symbol for knowing right from wrong)
	黼	黼		fǔ　　　fu embroidered official or sacrificial robe

黽 4-12　鼎 2　鼓　鼠 4-10　鼻 2-3

黽	黽	黽		měng　　　maang toad; strive; endeavour
黿	黿	黿		yúan　　　jyun　　　魵鱉黿 Asian giant softshell turtle (*pelochelys cantorii*)
鼉	鼉	鼉		túo　　　to　　　鼉 large reptile; water lizard
鼎	鼎	鼎	鼎	dǐng　　　díng ancient ritual bronze cauldron (*3-legs*); throne; monarchy; great; just (*at this time*); meanwhile
	鼐	鼐		nài　　　naai incense tripod; a large dǐng (鼎)
鼓	鼓	鼓		gǔ　　　gú drum; beat a drum; perform; sound an instrument; beat; clap; blast air for smelting; incite; bulge
鼠	鼠	鼠		shǔ　　　syú　　　鼠鼡 rat; mouse; rodent; cowardly; timid; (*traditional Chinese medicine*) scrofula; (*Cantonese*) sneak; stealthy
鼢	鼢	鼢		fén　　　fan mole; zokor (*an Asiatic burrowing rodent*)
鼬	鼬	鼬		yòu　　　jau Japanese weasel (*mustela itatsi*)
鼯	鼯	鼯		wú　　　ng flying squirrel (*petaurista leucogenys*)
鼴	鼴	鼴		yǎn　　　jin type of insectivorous shrew; mole
	鼷	鼷		xi　　　hai mouse
	鼻	鼻	鼻	bí　　　beih nose; snot; protrusion; handle; (*geography*) cape; founding; initial; beginning; original; to smell; kiss
	鼽	鼽		qiú　　　kau clogged or congested nose
	鼾	鼾		han　　　hòhn　　　哻 snore; snoring

				ji　　　　　chi
	齹	齹		red sores on the nose
齐	齊	齊	齊	qí　　　　　chàih　　　齊𠧧亝㠫 even; uniform; same; identical; complete; together; simultaneously; be level with; along a line
斋	齋	齋		zhai　　　jàai show piety before offering sacrifices; solemn; earnest; vegetarian; fasting; (*Cantonese*) plain; dull; boring; dry
赍	齎	齎		ji　　　　　jai　　　　賫齏 give; grant; to present; bring; carry; take in both hands and offer to
齑	齏	齏		ji　　　　　jai　　　　韲䪢 break into pieces; pulverize; hash; finely chopped; pickled vegetables
齿	齒	齒	齒	chǐ　　　　chí　　　　齒𪗰𪘀𠚕 teeth; sawtoothed; age (*of something*); juxtapose; place side by side; utter; mention; employ; take in
龀	齔	齔		chèn　　　chan　　　齓 process of losing baby teeth and getting adult teeth
龇	齜	齜		zi　　　　　chi to bare; show the teeth; crooked teeth
龃	齟	齟		jǔ　　　　jeui uneven or irregular teeth; discord
龄	齡	齡		líng　　　lìhng age; length of time; duration; instar (*arthropod*)
龆	齠	齠		tiáo　　　tiu process of losing baby teeth and getting adult teeth; young
龊	齣	齣	齣	chu　　　　chèut (*classifier for all forms of entertainment shows*); act; stanza; occasion; drama; play; trouble; hassle
龅	齙	齙		bao　　　baau projecting teeth; exposed teeth
龈	齦	齦		yín　　　ngan gums
龊	齪	齪		chuò　　　chuk　　　齱 cautious; careful; meticulous; narrow; small; dirty

齒 7-9　龍 6　龜　龠

齬	齬	齬		yǔ　　　　　jyu irregular or uneven teeth; discord; disagree
齷	齷	齷		wò　　　　　ak narrow; small; dirty
齲	齲	齲		qǔ　　　　　geui tooth decay; cavity
龙	龍	龍	龍	lóng　　　　lùhng　　　　龍 龓 龖 龘 竜 dragon; emperor; sovereign; king; hero; clear-minded; (*Cantonese*) goal; queue; money; snake meat
龚	龔	龔	龔	gong　　　　gung follow; obey; alternative form of supply (供) and respectful (恭)
龛	龕	龕		kan　　　　 ham　　　　 龕 shrine; idol niche
龟	龜	龜	龜	gui　　　　 gwài turtle; tortoise; cuckold
	龠	龠		yùe　　　　 yeuhk　　　　龠 flute; pipe; fife; recorder; an ancient unit of volume

Indices

Cantonese (Pinyin)
Mandarin (Yale)

Cantonese (Pinyin)

a 4, 61, 161
à 45
aa 176, 385
aai 42, 398
àai 43, 125
aak 360
aan 12, 146
aang 276
aat 107, 118, 130, 368
aau 59, 123
ah 36, 38, 396
ai 272, 280
ak 33, 38, 120, 189, 434
am 96, 147, 342, 426, 431
ám 61, 130
au 113, 194, 222, 344
ba 66, 201, 227, 263, 402
bá 121
bà 35, 37, 92, 209
baa 86, 256, 298, 307, 403
baahk 92, 233
baahn 209, 363
baai 123, 126, 129, 348
báai 137
baaih 115, 140
baak 8, 9, 233, 316, 356
baan 120, 230, 294, 380, 395
báan 153, 210
bàan 141, 218, 406
baang 51
báao 410
baat 19, 126, 419
baau 28, 78, 208, 298, 433
bàau 29, 286, 420
bah 277

Cantonese (Pinyin)

bahn 256
baht 100, 121, 354
bai 213, 251, 311, 313, 391, 392, 396
bái 355
baih 94, 98, 140, 141
bàk 29
bam 241
ban 17, 58, 75, 136, 168, 173, 275, 291, 347, 386, 391, 417, 418
bán 40
bàn 68, 101, 141, 199, 350
bang 50, 274, 358
bàng 89
bat 50, 260, 300, 310, 357, 381, 420
bàt 1, 225, 257
bauh 222
be 45
bei 29, 31, 37, 70, 75, 95, 174, 181, 193, 224, 229, 247, 250, 258, 260, 277, 291, 297, 305, 309, 349, 363, 396, 417, 426
béi 12, 101, 174
bèi 109, 243, 331
beih 14, 370, 432
béng 410
bihn 11, 363, 364
bihng 2
bìhng 228
biht 23
bik 244
bìk 65, 112, 221, 365, 368
bin 30, 31, 98, 104, 178, 205, 242, 253, 262, 272, 322, 331, 345, 348, 364
bín 119
bìn 371, 404
bing 12, 62, 85, 133, 154, 202, 250, 365, 372
bíng 1
bìng 19, 21
bit 114, 232, 358, 382, 424

Cantonese (Pinyin)

bìt 103
biu 74, 230, 290, 389, 391, 408, 415, 417, 423
biú 328
biù 101, 151, 165, 385, 409
bo 59, 135, 262, 304, 374
bò 181, 217
bohk 313
bohng 245, 388
bok 5, 31, 131, 139, 180, 247, 259, 273, 290, 382, 401, 413
bong 184, 308, 343
bóng 163, 269, 290
bòng 94, 158, 371
bou 8, 43, 60, 62, 92, 106, 146, 205, 306, 332, 367, 382, 425
bóu 11, 62, 83, 331
bouh 126, 148, 171, 262, 373
buhk 199
buhn 8, 34, 123, 225, 286
buht 27, 134, 287
bui 43, 77, 109, 131, 153, 204, 213, 285, 348, 362, 372, 384
buk 198, 358, 378
bùk 31
bun 31, 132, 268, 294, 300
bún 151, 225
búng 126, 224
but 189, 232, 276, 302, 410, 426
caau 91
cahn 48
càhng 14
cai 424
cam 179, 424
can 41, 169
cap 308
cha 120, 152, 177, 190, 328, 338
chà 33, 86, 91
chaa 47, 301

chaahk 350
chàahm 114, 327, 345, 412
chàahn 172
chàahng 160
chaai 15, 51, 131, 326, 379
cháai 356
chàai 213
chàaih 155, 347
chaak 20, 59, 123, 155, 257
chaam 90, 117, 138, 151, 346, 415
cháam 114
chaan 208, 221, 264, 279
cháan 223, 389
chàan 410
chaang 51, 134, 239
cháang 166
chaap 130, 386
chaat 24, 54, 82, 137, 168, 216, 246
cháau 38, 202
chàau 121, 380
chàh 132, 155, 164, 301
cháhm 311
chàhm 83, 196, 311
chàhn 64, 397
chàhng 85
chai 23, 54, 56, 82, 179, 186, 241, 306
chài 71, 160
cháih 314
chàih 326, 433
chàk 112, 189
chám 82, 245
chàm 10
chan 333, 353, 431, 433
chán 122, 227, 240, 273, 337, 415
chàn 334

Cantonese (Pinyin)

chap 118, 242, 313

chàp 271, 362

chat 184

chàt 1, 194

chau 48, 50, 162, 189, 192, 231, 264, 289, 292, 362, 418, 422

cháu 1, 238, 377

chàu 122, 130, 250

chàuh 55, 94, 110, 180, 226, 251, 262, 270, 322, 345, 359, 369, 376

che 154, 163, 243

ché 1, 120

chè 69, 360

chèh 141, 371

chek 84, 352

cheng 190, 403

chèuhn 103, 143, 250, 364

chèuhng 63, 76, 96, 118, 167, 210, 248, 279, 305, 313, 339, 392

cheui 45, 88, 160, 163, 166, 174, 180, 187, 201, 204, 227, 280, 287, 300, 319, 334, 353

chéui 34, 73, 130, 220

chèui 15, 38, 133, 353

chèuih 97, 102, 127, 129, 131, 160, 164, 192, 321, 386, 387, 397, 398

cheuk 28, 31, 53, 118, 142, 156, 201, 271, 356, 364

cheun 162, 234, 323, 324, 427

chéun 327

chèun 145

cheung 12, 44, 73, 94, 110, 148, 206, 214, 226, 278, 305, 357, 389, 394, 419, 422

chéung 129, 289

chèung 13, 76, 144, 164, 253, 388

cheut 107, 430, 431

chèut 22, 433

chi 18, 40, 45, 49, 50, 64, 66, 94, 96, 107, 154, 170, 207, 227, 229, 236, 237, 256, 264, 279, 298, 300, 318, 325, 350, 353, 420, 425, 433

chí 10, 71, 108, 155, 171, 240, 247, 282, 332, 346, 433

chì 400

chih 59

chíh 8, 71, 107, 177, 281

chìh 99, 111, 124, 178, 222, 244, 248, 260, 291, 301, 337, 356, 363, 370, 413, 427

chìhm 196

chíhn 356

chìhn 97, 359, 386

chìhng 37, 60, 110, 116, 195, 251, 330, 376, 411

chik 24, 35, 101, 140, 165, 245, 409

chìk 118, 142

chim 64, 148, 164, 262, 276, 313, 334, 385

chím 341

chìm 173, 262

chin 6, 24, 120, 297, 395, 410

chín 188, 311, 395

chìn 30, 370

ching 57, 147, 162, 167, 176, 250, 251, 304, 322, 326, 422

chíng 124, 341, 367

chìng 188

chiong 166

chióng 164

chiòng 231

chip 71

chit 86, 103, 134, 197, 336, 363

chiu 11, 26, 87, 106, 109, 145, 284, 340, 344, 379, 404

chiú 112

chiù 353, 386

chiùh 115, 166, 196, 239

chìuh 145

cho 89, 125, 245, 297, 328, 357, 384, 386

chó 11, 116, 161, 246

chò 23, 400

chòh 228, 230, 241, 287, 384, 429

chohng 95

chòhng 94, 209, 226, 314

choi 16, 80, 305, 311, 351, 378

chói 101, 128, 238

chòih 119, 151, 330, 348

Cantonese (Pinyin)

chong 25, 70, 113, 192, 230, 295

chóng 97, 110, 145, 175, 394, 413

chòng 12, 49, 309

chou 53, 101, 128, 197, 208, 265, 296, 377

chóu 302

chòu 136, 263, 358

chòuh 149, 165, 194, 295, 324

chú 205

chúhng 378

chùhng 102, 153, 187, 219, 317, 326

chuk 131, 185, 225, 240, 261, 310, 357, 433

chùk 11, 152, 309, 366

chùn 58

chung 20, 104, 115, 165, 220, 295, 310, 383

chúng 82

chùng 17, 178, 283, 311, 328, 329

chyu 153, 300, 317

chyuh 358

chyúh 17, 148, 154, 162, 277, 349

chyùh 169, 359

chyúhn 400

chyùhn 15, 19, 77, 161, 182, 228, 258, 338, 361, 368, 377, 383

chyun 2, 83, 138, 175, 177, 208, 294, 302, 359, 380

chyún 47, 104, 111, 254

chyùn 91, 151, 253

chyut 45, 123, 135, 214, 355

cok 33

cou 172

cung 29, 34

dá 120

daahm 187

daahn 8, 100

daahp 356

daaht 369

daai 93, 118

dáai 172
daaih 67
daam 176, 198, 236, 282, 306, 351
dáam 291
dàam 136, 360
daan 47, 100, 115, 134, 143, 173, 231, 261, 339, 374
dáan 318
dàan 2, 31
daap 132, 178, 230, 258, 282, 332
daat 53, 106, 256
dahk 211
dahm 45
dahn 207
dahng 239
daht 22, 253
dai 61, 73, 93, 109, 155, 160, 175, 242, 244, 256, 272, 278, 286, 308, 342, 372, 416
dái 95, 122, 337
dài 8
daih 99, 257, 367, 369
dak 103
dàk 103
dan 65, 358
dang 22, 52, 90, 118, 168, 207, 225, 245, 261, 358, 374, 390
dáng 257
dàng 232
dau 254, 311, 318, 380, 396, 418
dáu 121, 141, 265, 353
dàu 18
dauh 228, 346, 366
de 49
dè 209
dehk 256
deih 58
dek 265
deng 226

Cantonese (Pinyin)

dèng 379
deuhn 56, 368, 406
deuht 39, 69
deui 18, 83, 114, 116, 243
dèui 62
deuih 398
deun 179, 236, 242, 246, 390
dèun 53, 140, 358
diăn 431
dihk 140, 193
dihn 9, 64, 173, 401
dihng 80, 335
dihp 226, 244, 323
diht 250
dik 50, 76, 193, 212, 280, 302, 334, 365, 388
dìk 233
dim 95, 110, 128, 217, 261, 356, 395
din 69, 186, 192, 224, 232, 244, 382, 403, 408
dín 19
dìn 91
ding 5, 216, 235, 243, 282, 289, 375, 386
díng 405, 432
dìng 1, 35
dip 46, 62, 130, 210, 332, 341, 356, 422
dit 60, 92, 222, 281, 354, 365
diu 35, 36, 99, 126, 379, 422
diù 2, 21, 22, 243, 347, 400
do 22, 41, 42, 59, 111, 151, 355
dó 360
dò 67
doek 44
doh 65, 218
dohk 357
dohng 312
doi 87, 217, 223, 365, 430

doih 6, 102, 329

dok 391

dong 18, 54, 79, 167, 235, 244, 305, 333, 346, 390

dóng 136, 431

dou 24, 34, 51, 103, 175, 208, 238, 276, 297, 327, 357

dóu 13, 63, 88, 131, 351

dòu 22, 373

douh 70, 83, 95, 110, 152, 189, 235, 252, 369, 387

duhk 174, 186, 215, 345

duhn 380

duhng 27, 114, 160, 183

duk 169, 199, 210, 244, 255, 417, 431

dùk 238, 260

dung 21, 40, 59, 87, 107, 176, 242, 287, 356, 426

dúng 116, 307

dùng 21, 152

dyuhn 142, 173

dyun 142, 161, 204, 255, 261, 272, 387

dyún 241

fa 29

fà 297

faahn 212, 259, 409

fàahn 22, 92, 273

faai 14, 53, 64, 104, 258

faan 94, 159, 165, 177, 181, 205, 207, 224, 246, 311, 315, 330, 358, 379

fáan 34, 222, 348, 364

fàan 225, 280

faat 180, 219, 233, 242, 417

fahn 7, 23

fáhn 69

fàhn 65, 204

faht 2, 7, 9, 277, 393

fai 97, 147, 181, 229, 285, 298, 349, 399, 430

fài 103, 130, 362

faih 37

Cantonese (Pinyin)

fan 38, 74, 105, 115, 149, 159, 179, 200, 215, 217, 265, 308, 314, 336, 375, 378, 394, 432

fán 263

fàn 28, 144, 175, 206, 266, 298

fat 44, 56, 61, 99, 106, 110, 175, 247, 256, 257, 267, 268, 296, 431

fàt 105, 123

fau 25, 185, 276, 321

fáu 37

fauh 61, 395

fàuh 184

fe 45

fei 69, 109, 163, 212, 260, 270, 279, 288, 304, 321, 401, 421

féi 30, 141, 340

fèi 119, 403, 409

fèih 285

fo 251, 254, 323, 340, 348, 385, 414, 417

fó 67, 201, 407

fò 250

fòhng 70, 119, 395

fok 26, 137, 138, 240, 315, 401

fong 21, 29, 93, 107, 139, 146, 153, 181, 284, 294, 349, 420

fóng 7, 101, 266, 336

fòng 58, 113, 142, 285, 298, 302, 343

fu 24, 25, 40, 52, 74, 77, 81, 95, 96, 119, 123, 158, 193, 202, 218, 223, 268, 297, 300, 303, 316, 318, 332, 350, 351, 354, 372, 413, 416, 420, 424, 429, 431

fú 12, 43, 134, 142, 288, 299, 317, 379

fù 11, 39, 68, 78, 141, 154, 290

fuh 6, 15, 209, 288, 335, 348, 353, 361, 395

fùh 2, 121, 257

fuhk 7, 29, 103, 150, 330

fuhng 68, 425

fùhng 260, 272, 367

fui 41, 47, 68, 108, 109, 146, 183, 323, 339, 340, 421

fùi 108, 201, 419

fuk 67, 79, 305, 323, 362, 412, 422

fùk 93, 249, 289, 322, 332, 333

Cantonese (Pinyin)

fun 216, 417
fún 170
fùn 82, 171
fung 12, 21, 43, 200, 203, 229, 307, 310, 342, 374, 413
fùng 83, 88, 161, 320, 346, 384, 408
fut 319, 394
ga 16, 81, 155, 414
gá 350
gà 14, 27, 50
gaa 40, 50, 53, 75, 83, 217, 227, 230, 252, 257, 307, 329, 354, 365, 388
gaai 5, 46, 84, 85, 98, 117, 224, 227, 297, 318, 335, 340
gàai 9, 14, 233, 328, 397
gaak 48, 64, 156, 286, 290, 388, 398, 416
gaam 84, 166, 271, 391
gáam 188
gàam 235
gaan 72, 158, 196, 258, 275, 304, 342, 390, 429
gáan 129, 155, 261
gàan 296, 393
gàang 281
gaap 48, 68, 87, 129, 185, 224, 285, 303, 320, 330, 373, 382, 384, 403, 407, 426
gaat 84, 360
gaau 72, 140, 233, 253, 268, 296, 301, 320, 355, 361, 383, 421
gáau 131, 138, 213, 410
gàau 4, 290, 372
gahn 364
gaht 226
gai 100, 257, 275, 313, 335, 418
gài 400
gam 52, 135, 181, 187, 197, 227, 248, 268, 300, 329, 352
gám 111, 140, 386
gàm 6, 154, 223, 379
gan 62, 97, 165, 220, 296, 301, 403, 411
gán 271, 344
gàn 92, 142, 156, 257, 355

447

Cantonese (Pinyin)

gang 42, 60, 95, 158, 264, 269, 350, 421

gáng 282

gàng 149, 279

gap 319

gàp 105

gat 123, 266, 317, 336

gàt 36, 156

gau 40, 60, 67, 75, 100, 139, 154, 155, 164, 201, 212, 216, 226, 253, 256, 260, 272, 338, 369, 404, 405

gáu 2, 3, 299

gauh 293

ge 50

gei 7, 25, 37, 52, 72, 81, 95, 104, 127, 143, 152, 182, 211, 221, 225, 226, 245, 259, 277, 296, 297, 325, 334, 336, 409, 416, 429

géi 91, 95, 266

gèi 22, 61, 167, 284, 344, 411

geih 70, 120

geng 389

géng 407

geoi 86, 169

gèuhng 16

geui 35, 135, 161, 164, 240, 254, 299, 303, 331, 337, 356, 357, 370, 385, 434

géui 241, 293

gèui 85

geuih 19, 91, 117, 202, 381, 409

geuk 289

geung 72, 246, 321, 404

gèung 226, 278, 312

giang 211

gihk 162

gihm 16

gihn 7, 14, 387

gihng 255

giht 14

gik 4, 118, 159, 172

gìk 136, 197

Cantonese (Pinyin)

gim 26, 135, 240, 273, 308, 427
gím 168
gìm 19
gin 63, 98, 132, 174, 211, 289, 334, 354, 357, 423
gìn 61, 285
ging 18, 25, 27, 100, 102, 115, 136, 140, 185, 228, 240, 287, 302, 303, 367, 405
gíng 64, 147, 255, 345
gìng 5, 269, 415
gip 24, 27
git 157, 195, 268, 278, 407, 421
giu 35, 76, 90, 103, 134, 140
giú 241, 275, 363
giù 415
giuh 135
go 43, 144, 295
gò 171
goh 42
goi 59, 191, 286, 309, 350, 396
gói 139
gòi 339
gok 36, 137, 158, 217, 334, 335, 372, 382, 393
gon 94, 135, 144, 241, 256, 375
gón 251, 353
gòn 3, 94, 152, 158, 284
gong 86, 164, 182, 269, 277, 284, 294, 346, 385, 396
góng 189, 343, 404
gòng 25, 88, 120, 178, 270, 276
got 25, 239, 307
gou 37, 152, 164, 233, 239, 260, 264, 273, 292, 314, 340, 385
góu 252, 388
gòu 278, 290, 417
gu 15, 38, 40, 50, 56, 139, 180, 210, 229, 240, 277, 291, 305, 319, 327, 335, 337, 363, 376, 381, 385, 408, 422, 425
gú 8, 34, 284, 432
gù 71, 78, 304

449

Cantonese (Pinyin)

guhk 10, 84
guhng 19
guk 55, 128, 158, 211, 362, 404
gùk 305, 346
gun 12, 185, 200, 235, 287, 303, 428
gún 80
gùn 20, 160
gung 98, 124, 297, 318, 348, 434
gúng 217
gùng 10, 19, 27, 80, 91, 99, 108, 139, 360
gur 26
gwa 32, 38, 82, 128
gwá 331
gwà 222
gwaa 25, 339
gwaai 106, 308
gwáai 122, 155
gwàai 3
gwaan 113, 133, 136
gwàan 395, 423
gwaat 24
gwahn 372
gwaht 13
gwai 30, 57, 78, 79, 110, 147, 156, 191, 220, 232, 233, 261, 312, 349, 412, 421
gwái 26, 338, 360, 419
gwài 172, 393, 434
gwaih 168, 355
gwan 2, 159, 193, 218, 234, 349, 362, 380, 421, 429
gwàn 36, 58, 360
gwang 285, 314, 335
gwàng 363
gwat 88, 128, 178, 254, 409, 427
gwàt 166, 416
gwik 183, 394
gwìk 398

gwing 20, 119, 201, 202, 365
gwo 117, 213, 322, 368
gwó 152, 331
gwok 57, 88, 94, 132, 165, 325, 373, 412
gwong 97, 157, 216, 286, 339
gwòng 18
gwun 276
gwún 259, 411
gwùn 334
gyun 73, 125, 157, 185, 213, 237, 269, 327, 373
gyún 32, 127
gyùn 426
gyut 166
ha 147, 297
hà 42, 322
haa 67, 219, 368
hàahm 22, 41, 383, 428
haahn 396
hàahn 393
haai 200, 215, 238, 314, 370, 416, 417
hàai 78, 130
haaih 116, 159
hàaih 341, 404
haak 46, 54, 80, 352
haam 46, 134, 168, 304, 305, 411
haan 73, 114, 231, 428
haang 328
hàang 58
haap 39, 127, 154, 212, 243, 260
haau 77, 84, 156
háau 91, 124, 280
hàau 38, 42, 140, 203, 376
haauh 139, 156
hah 1, 97
hàh 402

Cantonese (Pinyin)

hahm 28, 89, 116, 135, 186, 397
háhm 407
hàhm 38
hahn 108
hàhn 228
hahng 94, 152
hàhng 107, 328
hahp 11, 30, 36, 88, 213, 234, 239
haht 156
hai 19, 30, 69, 248, 357, 432
haih 11, 265, 274
háih 326
hak 176, 271
hàk 18, 24, 430
ham 22, 58, 59, 114, 118, 146, 203, 239, 319, 375, 395, 434
hám 241
hàm 62
hán 65, 102, 115, 212
hang 5, 37, 42, 44, 110, 156, 302, 316, 389
háng 285
hap 191, 234, 245, 281, 394, 406
hàp 108, 184
hat 27, 167, 280, 334, 362, 431
hàt 3
hau 62, 229, 260, 366, 424
háu 34
hauh 36, 102
háuh 33
hàuh 10, 46, 416
hei 16, 43, 51, 53, 76, 86, 113, 114, 118, 161, 170, 175, 176, 179, 206, 207, 249, 279, 378, 411
héi 47, 346, 353
hèi 92, 149, 170, 211, 251
hek 35
heoi 52

hèu 403
heuhng 313
heui 33, 57, 235
héui 205, 337, 338
hèui 65, 317
heung 36, 54, 146, 410, 412
héung 5, 405
hèung 373, 412
hihp 31
him 170, 215, 297
hím 399
hìm 343
hin 111, 114, 216, 247, 275, 343, 345, 360, 414, 427
hín 320, 369, 408
hìn 127, 211
hing 32, 245, 276, 344
hìng 17, 176, 293, 361, 412
hip 106, 112, 113, 125, 287
hit 170
hiu 52, 154, 158, 358, 415
hiú 148
hiù 16, 55, 196
ho 49, 54, 59, 304, 319, 337
hò 39, 299
hoh 349
hòh 9, 180, 302
hohk 78, 427
hohn 126, 177
hóhn 144
hòhn 81, 405, 432
hohng 92, 405
hòhng 294
hoi 4, 26, 49, 63, 113, 176, 377, 406
hói 22, 184
hòi 392

Cantonese (Pinyin)

hoih 80, 414
hok 173, 347
hon 32, 109, 194, 199, 203, 236, 280, 372, 379, 384, 406
hón 23, 276
hong 30, 153, 179, 237, 268, 339, 406
hóng 114
hòng 96, 257, 265, 288, 416
hot 47, 149, 189, 332
hou 54, 144, 198, 201, 211, 281, 309, 313, 408
hóu 70
hòu 49, 54, 65
houh 184, 233, 317
hòuh 174, 327, 347
huhk 376
hùhng 183, 206, 266, 317, 399
huk 141, 165, 335, 426
hùk 43
hung 88, 128, 178, 179, 183, 203, 307, 313, 336, 419, 425, 430
húng 77, 107
hùng 18, 22, 29, 253, 287
hyun 24, 28, 64, 148, 162, 190, 204, 224, 269, 270, 306, 342
hyún 212
hyùn 47, 56
hyut 327
ja 3, 162, 163, 202, 242, 337
jà 41
jaa 39, 98, 131, 132, 135, 154, 227, 244
jaahk 79, 132, 136, 137, 197
jaahm 148, 255
jaahn 351
jaahp 279, 333, 393, 399, 400
jaai 231, 237, 347
jàai 433
jaak 36, 253, 257, 261, 294, 318, 344, 348, 351, 365
jaam 190, 261, 316, 389

Cantonese (Pinyin)

jáam 142

jaan 135, 138, 145, 222, 270, 346, 352, 411

jáan 160, 235

jaang 386

jaap 39, 44, 236

jaat 119, 124, 151, 267, 387

jaau 160, 209, 256, 277

jáau 92, 121, 284

jaauh 416

jahn 397

jahng 352

jahp 29

jaht 227, 253, 324

jai 24, 26, 89, 124, 129, 198, 248, 331, 359, 398, 402, 433

jái 6

jài 136

jaih 193

jak 5, 144

jàk 14, 24

jam 66, 70, 150, 161, 170, 185, 242, 254, 259, 302, 311, 329, 344, 350, 380, 391, 402, 409, 425

jám 105, 152

jàm 141, 379

jan 6, 32, 37, 62, 67, 81, 98, 105, 125, 145, 176, 190, 222, 225, 286, 301, 309, 318, 350, 360, 361, 378, 388, 401

jàn 217, 236

jang 88, 214, 223, 277, 341

jàng 16, 65, 115, 128, 150, 209, 237, 259

jap 109, 125, 204, 206, 273, 279

jàp 61, 177

jat 75, 157, 290, 309, 320, 351, 361, 372, 388, 414

jau 8, 32, 38, 40, 41, 44, 46, 68, 80, 87, 91, 129, 139, 146, 190, 210, 214, 226, 234, 249, 262, 266, 272, 303, 318, 319, 322, 341, 343, 357, 373, 375, 378, 382, 397, 415, 420, 422, 426, 428, 431, 432

jáu 353, 375

jàu 183, 294, 368

jauh 80, 84, 330

Cantonese (Pinyin)

je 13, 46, 61, 282, 310, 352, 387

jé 71, 281

jè 48, 369

jeh 71, 343, 427

jéh 367

jehng 374

jek 89, 133, 201, 287, 399

jeng 285

jéng 4

jeuhn 16, 235

jeuhng 6, 15, 30, 167, 215, 347

jèuhng 249

jeui 34, 150, 153, 212, 270, 277, 298, 304, 312, 318, 352, 377, 399, 414, 433

jéui 39, 51

jèui 366, 385

jeuih 65, 90, 95, 140, 283

jeuk 55, 69, 200, 204, 208, 209, 259, 296, 341, 343, 375, 399, 426

jeun 11, 88, 146, 163, 184, 187, 192, 208, 253, 255, 285, 293, 309, 314, 341, 352, 367, 393, 399, 414

jéun 21, 191

jèun 183, 370

jeung 90, 93, 102, 138, 172, 195, 203, 215, 221, 229, 252, 265, 288, 320, 325, 351, 374, 377, 398, 404, 405, 422

jéung 1, 69, 129, 152, 311, 392

jèung 83, 100, 101, 195, 255

ji 11, 19, 26, 32, 39, 40, 41, 49, 53, 58, 72, 100, 104, 106, 117, 133, 143, 147, 160, 173, 178, 186, 191, 194, 209, 214, 228, 230, 247, 250, 256, 263, 270, 271, 277, 286, 292, 296, 298, 299, 302, 313, 322, 335, 337, 338, 339, 345, 349, 350, 359, 361, 365, 371, 383, 386, 400, 407, 410, 418, 421, 425, 427, 431

jí 35, 77, 83, 124, 144, 158, 171, 193, 267, 268, 354

jì 2, 139, 153, 240, 284, 287, 301, 350

jih 9, 77, 91, 158, 180, 251, 292, 410

jihk 13, 67, 81, 93, 160, 172, 235, 262, 314

jihm 195

jihn 25, 351

jihng 187, 395, 403

jiht 118, 127

Cantonese (Pinyin)

jik 43, 48, 61, 68, 90, 98, 99, 116, 128, 194, 230, 241, 252, 253, 274, 288, 291, 321, 355, 357, 359, 396, 416, 419, 421

jìk 32, 252, 274, 283

jim 17, 20, 33, 68, 75, 116, 128, 201, 219, 262, 277, 296, 299, 319, 338, 345, 392, 394, 412, 418, 420

jìm 31, 84, 180, 240, 263

jin 18, 43, 70, 75, 88, 118, 132, 142, 185, 190, 199, 205, 227, 243, 259, 280, 286, 295, 303, 311, 313, 345, 373, 374, 378, 394, 404, 408, 432

jín 15, 362

jìn 175, 205

jing 55, 63, 74, 75, 76, 106, 138, 139, 162, 169, 171, 192, 199, 200, 205, 219, 220, 222, 228, 232, 243, 249, 255, 258, 272, 275, 288, 291, 344, 352, 371, 373, 381, 388, 396, 403, 428

jíng 141

jìng 14, 93, 103, 143, 147, 203, 237, 264, 308, 348

jip 55, 79, 128, 132, 148, 162, 206, 361, 374

jit 32, 42, 51, 74, 168, 232, 238, 258, 292, 321, 342, 346

jiu 26, 51, 72, 76, 94, 103, 131, 149, 180, 205, 208, 218, 220, 246, 253, 274, 293, 311, 326, 337, 378, 383, 423, 427, 428

jiù 36, 122, 150, 161, 204, 311

jíu 28

jiuh 34, 353

jo 44, 47

jó 8, 91, 337, 395

joh 27, 44, 58, 96

johk 137

johng 9, 134, 212, 292

joi 20, 361

jòi 41, 157, 201

joih 57

jok 9, 105, 145, 198, 375, 392

jong 66, 69, 117, 292, 307, 352

jòng 165, 263, 303, 330, 417

jou 201, 247, 275, 286, 315, 395

jóu 143, 159, 247, 268, 318

jòu 250, 265, 370

jouh 14, 233, 367

Cantonese (Pinyin)

ju 254

juhk 11, 143, 197, 275, 360, 366

juhng 7, 11, 336, 340, 406

juk 4, 28, 71, 146, 174, 184, 192, 229, 240, 273, 294, 309, 358, 382, 384, 389, 390, 406, 419, 426

jùk 55, 125, 208, 248, 255, 260, 263, 335, 354

jung 46, 48, 65, 108, 113, 159, 163, 192, 224, 232, 237, 269, 273, 288, 291, 293, 309, 320, 324, 371, 387, 389, 390, 400, 412, 418

júng 251, 264, 274, 289

jùng 2, 80, 105, 234, 268, 358

jyu 2, 7, 10, 12, 15, 19, 35, 52, 56, 70, 72, 73, 89, 96, 123, 129, 163, 168, 169, 171, 181, 182, 183, 187, 188, 198, 200, 202, 204, 213, 229, 249, 254, 255, 259, 263, 266, 280, 289, 293, 301, 306, 312, 314, 317, 319, 322, 326, 333, 334, 337, 339, 341, 342, 347, 362, 364, 368, 372, 375, 382, 383, 391, 397, 400, 409, 413, 429, 434

jyú 2

jyù 151, 156, 218, 320, 342, 347

jyuh 8

jyuht 268

jyun 20, 55, 60, 64, 74, 116, 129, 150, 179, 182, 188, 202, 219, 236, 237, 245, 266, 275, 276, 298, 304, 322, 324, 329, 354, 362, 382, 390, 392, 395, 398, 407, 424, 425, 432

jyún 134, 363

jyùn 83, 166

jyut 23, 53, 127, 166, 268, 283, 300, 331, 362, 379, 381, 428

jyùt 31

kaa 40, 417

kaai 162, 308, 387

kàat 32

kaau 383, 403

kàhm 219, 249

kàhn 28

kahp 33

kai 68, 89, 139

kái 45

kài 191, 252

kam 52, 136, 167, 297, 329, 333

kan 298

kang 330

kap 86, 171, 178, 256

kàp 38, 267, 269

kat 41

kàt 41

kau 9, 17, 35, 81, 91, 120, 132, 156, 164, 212, 258, 282, 293, 297, 317, 334, 350, 351, 366, 380, 419, 424, 432

kàu 191

kàuh 177, 218, 246, 293, 330

ke 8, 231, 414

ké 299

kĕ 35

kehk 26, 85

kei 20, 58, 86, 146, 148, 164, 170, 248, 281, 316, 321, 406, 414, 423, 429

kèi 88

kéih 7

kèih 19, 68, 143, 150, 159, 171, 218, 247, 270

keoi 221

keui 27, 161, 175, 247, 312, 316, 328, 413, 425

kèui 12, 30, 90, 122, 360, 415

kéuih 122, 355

kèuih 188

keuk 32

keung 332, 390

khán 9

kìhm 381

kìhn 317

kim 380, 430

kin 128, 161

king 168, 204, 221, 405, 422, 431

kìng 15

kit 77, 124, 130, 137, 244, 255, 275, 326, 336, 338, 386

kiu 47, 254, 280, 312

kiùh 15, 166

kòhng 212

koi 1, 112, 118, 163, 195, 380

Cantonese (Pinyin)

kok 65, 108, 112, 163, 186, 244
kong 4, 7, 121, 137, 149, 202, 246, 380, 392
ku 259
kùhng 254
kui 16, 115, 167, 197, 215, 274, 283, 291, 374
kúi 196, 274, 350
kùi 275
kuk 319, 430
kùk 149
kung 253, 257, 320, 355, 371, 383
kut 123, 282, 346, 426
kwà 60, 339, 355
kwaa 124, 286
kwaang 367
kwàang 157
kwàhn 278, 331
kwai 67, 90, 129, 147, 225, 234, 237, 238, 308, 355, 367, 412
kwài 254, 317, 334
kwáih 112
kwàih 138
kwan 56, 108, 125, 126, 254, 271, 329, 377, 385, 393, 417, 422
kwán 304
kwàn 59, 144
kwok 97
kwong 66, 275
kyùhn 124
kyun 169, 321, 408, 418
kyut 3, 21, 26, 52, 77, 121, 133, 179, 202, 215, 276, 312, 335, 336, 344, 358, 394, 424
kyùt 33
là 45
laa 46, 242, 276
laahm 198, 296
láahm 334
làahm 262, 314, 333
laahn 208

Cantonese (Pinyin)

láahn 116
làahn 138, 169, 316
láahng 21
laahp 58, 292, 327
laaht 363
laai 199, 232, 262, 376
làai 123
laaih 351
laak 50
laam 44, 73, 89, 170, 194, 276
láam 138
laan 141, 200, 345, 391, 394
laap 371
laat 24, 229
làauh 134
lahk 28
láhm 21
làhm 153, 292
lahp 255
lai 119, 126, 197, 232, 246, 265, 315, 327, 378, 424, 431
laih 10, 17, 28, 33, 302, 429
láih 249, 430
làih 211
lak 3, 5, 181, 284, 423
lam 98, 116, 167, 186, 219, 402
lap 256
làp 263
lat 223
lau 51, 89, 143, 199, 231, 243, 261, 270, 282, 310, 325, 369, 388, 389, 411, 417, 427
lauh 191, 194, 396
láuh 133, 155
làuh 26, 163, 165, 184, 214, 218, 225, 230
le 40
lei 11, 42, 72, 75, 86, 193, 213, 263, 277, 302, 316, 320, 332, 338, 371, 385, 416, 424, 428

Cantonese (Pinyin)

lèi 220
leih 23, 36, 228, 291, 308
léih 152, 218, 378, 421
lèih 158, 379, 400
lek 35
leon 88, 90
leuhk 225
leuhn 10, 36, 57, 341
lèuhn 13, 207, 362, 374, 424, 429
leuhng 5, 147, 341, 361
léuhng 12, 19
lèuhng 157, 165, 186, 265, 296, 379
leuht 102, 156
leui 37, 44, 75, 167, 168, 199, 245, 273, 279, 281, 290, 313, 331, 332, 390, 393, 408
léui 273
leuih 114, 187
léuih 10, 66, 85, 143, 267, 384
lèuih 136, 401, 415
leuk 128
leun 127, 187, 240, 246, 264, 270, 315, 359, 363, 370
léun 32
leung 160, 264, 356, 420
leut 260
li 399
lihk 27, 171
líhm 291
lìhm 97, 390
lihn 204, 272, 387
lìhn 115, 310, 367
lihng 6
líhng 90, 406
lìhng 8, 160, 282, 381, 401, 402, 433
lihp 216
liht 23
lik 54, 66, 169, 200, 246, 359, 363, 374, 402, 419

Cantonese (Pinyin)

lim 141, 173, 198, 200, 262, 316, 326

lin 137, 162, 194, 221, 332, 362, 389, 423

ling 21, 34, 38, 56, 63, 112, 123, 154, 162, 169, 181, 217, 271, 278, 279, 299, 305, 319, 374, 397, 422

lip 359, 418

lit 182, 203, 330, 353

liu 51, 82, 97, 133, 207, 215, 274, 310, 379, 390, 428

liuh 141

líúh 424

liùh 16, 82, 135, 231, 282, 370

líuh 3

lo 133, 144, 169, 216, 231, 316, 326, 371

ló 331

lò 263

loeng 64

lòh 277, 324, 391

lohk 203

lohng 184

lóhng 150

lòhng 96, 213, 372

loi 102, 188, 238, 306, 339, 350, 388

lòih 9

lok 183, 195, 199, 211, 217, 269, 306, 342, 376, 400, 414

long 45, 163, 220, 251, 303, 323, 384, 393

lou 10, 52, 54, 66, 72, 79, 90, 98, 156, 168, 169, 199, 210, 221, 235, 292, 296, 315, 349, 361, 363, 377, 383, 408, 420, 424, 428

louh 355, 402

lóuh 135, 196, 280, 317

lòuh 28, 197, 208, 231, 416

luhk 19, 176, 248, 270, 385, 397, 429

lúhng 138

lùhng 54, 262, 283, 398, 434

luk 118, 187, 188, 194, 243, 261, 363, 367, 429

lung 66, 151, 169, 200, 222, 231, 246, 316, 399

lyuhn 3

lyúhn 147

Cantonese (Pinyin)

lyùhn 79, 138, 283
lyun 77, 90, 170, 201, 292, 392, 428
lyún 117
lyut 27, 126, 384
ma 77, 163, 414
mà 49, 75
maa 214, 220, 324, 325
maahn 113, 149, 194, 307, 310
máahn 146
màahn 327
maahng 78
máahng 214, 321
màahng 235
maai 312, 370, 402
maaih 31, 351
máaih 349
màaih 60
maak 136
maam 93
maan 64, 273, 344, 389, 392, 411, 423
maang 295, 386, 432
maau 87, 145, 181, 300, 323, 324, 382
màau 348
maauh 347
màauh 240, 386
mah 50, 277
máh 245, 412
màh 229, 430
mahk 65, 287, 429, 430
mahn 23, 45
máhn 38, 115, 139, 423
màhn 141, 175, 266, 283
màhng 235
maht 29, 210, 321, 333
mai 40, 99, 287, 329, 377

Cantonese (Pinyin)

maìh 343
máih 263
màih 365
mak 51, 347, 348, 396, 415
màk 49
man 87, 111, 123, 179, 182, 197, 206, 216, 221, 267, 271, 299, 392, 393, 401
màn 318
mang 223, 306
mat 81, 298, 343
mau 42, 115, 210, 237, 238, 274, 319, 329, 387
mauh 32, 33, 300, 344, 349
máuh 155, 225
màuh 300, 342
me 40, 278
mei 72, 74, 81, 89, 189, 216, 239, 265, 273, 313, 316, 387, 403, 429, 431
meih 39, 151, 419
méih 84, 278
mèih 103, 162, 236
mh 43, 340
mihk 334
mihn 403, 430
míhn 18, 20, 27
mìhn 159, 236, 271
mihng 39
míhng 234
mìhng 36, 144, 382, 425
miht 192
mik 20, 178, 265
min 73, 79, 179, 190, 236, 272
ming 20, 148, 191, 239, 300, 324, 376
mit 261, 310, 327
miu 129, 188, 236, 272, 371
miú 97
miuh 70
miúh 152, 189, 250, 315

Cantonese (Pinyin)

miùh 238, 299
mo 315, 411, 430
mó 133
mò 133, 420
mòh 245
mohk 82, 93, 191, 304
mohng 150
móhng 70, 270, 276, 325
mòhng 4, 104, 296, 301
mok 25, 231, 290, 389
mong 110, 175, 195, 304, 317, 361, 371, 420
mou 74, 76, 97, 114, 117, 142, 174, 220, 281, 311, 344, 414, 418, 426, 427
mouh 20, 28, 64, 93, 133, 148, 402
móuh 10, 71, 115, 122, 171, 174, 294
mòuh 91, 165, 174, 203, 340
muhk 151, 179, 210, 235
muhn 109
múhn 193
mùhn 11, 239, 392
muhng 67
mùhng 151, 308
muht 151, 179, 180
mui 74, 185, 303, 376
múi 71
muih 145, 180
múih 174
mùih 153, 158, 205, 217
muk 238, 252, 300, 381
mun 115, 126, 325, 392, 408
mung 116, 168, 239, 246, 295, 327
mut 121, 172, 250, 300
nàahm 224
nàahn 400
naahp 266
naai 175, 432

Cantonese (Pinyin)

náaih 2, 69
naam 46, 56, 162, 289
naan 352
naap 38, 329, 380
naat 127
naau 78, 166, 187, 214, 390, 393
naauh 419
nàauh 134
náh 42, 371
nàh 125
nahm 31
nàhng 287
nai 59
nàih 182
nam 251
nàp 22
nau 70, 120, 212, 264, 282
náu 151, 266, 381
nauh 39
nei 71, 106, 143, 183, 218, 248, 410
néih 8, 108
nèih 84, 100
neui 380, 410
néuih 69
neut 336
ng 37, 49, 82, 104, 158, 184, 203, 211, 228, 321, 364, 432
nga 7, 86
ngá 45
ngà 425
ngaa 241, 328, 364
ngaahk 407
ngàahm 87, 231
ngaahn 399
ngáahn 237
ngàahn 407

Cantonese (Pinyin)

ngaahng 243
ngaai 237, 296
ngáai 23
ngàaih 88, 186
ngàak 130
ngaan 352
ngaap 425
ngaat 122
ngaau 89, 186, 209
ngáauh 41
ngah 336
ngáh 222, 399
ngàh 210, 298, 318
ngàhn 383
ngaht 364
ngai 32, 55, 89, 213, 238, 279, 295, 398, 401, 420, 422
ngái 241
ngaih 14, 173, 315, 338
ngáih 326
ngak 46
ngam 46
ngan 60, 213, 374, 433
ngàng 427
ngat 17, 54, 86, 152, 177
ngau 281
ngáu 50
ngàu 29, 171, 173, 381, 427
ngáuh 14, 315
ngàuh 210
ngh 109, 146
ńgh 4, 7, 30
ngo 73, 76, 87, 303, 385
ngoh 292, 410
ngóh 117
ngòh 12, 320, 336, 426

ngohk 87, 112, 230
ngohn 87
ngòhng 144
ngoi 67, 393
ngói 315
ngoih 246
ngòih 37
ngok 53, 165, 306, 342, 373, 387, 407, 424, 427
ngon 212
ngou 49, 97, 140, 215, 280, 283, 324, 369, 415, 423
ngouh 15
ngòuh 206
nia 126
niang 73
nihk 192
nihm 105
nìhn 94
nihng 137
nìhng 82
nihp 359
nik 132
nìk 30, 148
nim 44, 60, 122, 127, 421, 422
nìm 430
nin 245
nín 134
ning 54, 168, 198, 215, 283
nip 130, 185, 283, 388, 391, 398, 408
niu 77, 84, 288, 311, 330
no 17, 73
noh 116, 265
nòh 125
nòhng 55
noi 155, 306
noih 19, 20, 68, 281

Cantonese (Pinyin)

nong 139, 149, 222, 412
nou 78, 99, 220, 413
nouh 106
nóuh 27, 112, 289
nòuh 69
nuhng 98
nùhng 198, 364
nuk 105, 107, 328
nung 16, 53, 291
nyúhn 147
nyun 76
o 73, 85, 155, 217, 227, 360, 381
oh 42
oi 60, 75, 112, 148, 221, 233, 402
ói 53
òi 41
ok 62, 109
on 124, 132, 157, 176, 287, 383
òn 79, 404
ong 182, 234
ou 63, 69, 74, 90, 116, 197, 389
óu 207, 333
òu 39
pa 106
paa 219, 354, 380
pàahng 160, 197, 290
paai 12, 184, 189
pàaih 127, 210
paak 45, 92, 122, 154, 217, 295, 419
paan 137, 236, 333
paang 106, 159, 223, 242, 325, 426
pàang 203
paau 39, 95, 202, 212, 234, 288, 347, 354
páau 354
pàau 123

pàauh 23, 381

pàh 119, 153, 209, 281

pàhn 348, 407

pàhng 114, 150

pai 238

pài 120

pan 52, 199, 210, 408

pang 101, 243

pàt 30, 226

pau 126, 330

pauh 29

pei 1, 6, 39, 57, 61, 74, 76, 84, 92, 95, 96, 188, 198, 219, 227, 228, 241, 267, 299, 318, 321, 329, 330, 345, 348, 372, 373, 381, 397

péi 374

pèi 122

pèih 153, 234, 288

pek 26, 53

pìhng 59, 94, 250, 316, 337

piht 2

pik 136, 223, 231, 333, 364

pìk 16, 395, 402

pin 280, 287, 341, 357, 368, 414

pìn 259, 272

ping 3, 71, 72, 121, 124, 154, 210, 222, 283, 304, 414, 420

pit 134, 175, 239

piu 26, 50, 75, 172, 222, 239, 248, 273, 324

più 194, 409

po 35, 233, 242, 257

pó 406

pò 160

pòh 73

póhng 282, 318

pòhng 98, 103, 142

pok 52, 135, 151, 167, 221, 263, 379

pong 3, 192, 323

Cantonese (Pinyin)

pou 56, 191, 288, 303, 308, 344
póu 147, 184
pòu 385
pouh 29
póuh 122, 181
pòuh 305, 307, 329
pùhn 234, 235
pui 9, 12, 59, 143, 178, 244, 286, 309, 331, 375, 376, 401
pùih 61, 102, 351, 397
pun 23, 182, 190, 196, 245, 325, 357
pung 244
put 195
sá 45, 200, 281
sà 31, 266, 421
saa 179, 229, 241, 330
saah 48
saai 85, 149, 221, 307, 310
sáai 102
saam 100, 174, 265, 297, 328
sáam 133
sàam 1, 33
saan 14, 71, 78, 140, 156, 177, 196, 217, 226, 260, 294, 336, 355, 392
sàan 23, 86, 125
saang 237, 256
sáang 236
saap 58, 170, 402, 408
saat 24, 134, 173, 205, 314, 389
saau 42, 196, 258, 295
sáau 251
sàau 125, 159
sahm 5
sàhm 223
sahn 113
sàhn 146, 248, 292, 364
sahp 30, 123

Cantonese (Pinyin)

saht 82

sai 1, 28, 51, 74, 166, 211, 243, 258, 260, 263, 267, 295, 349

sái 182, 413

sài 333

saih 53, 339, 366

sak 53, 63

sam 33, 77, 86, 105, 159, 179, 185, 188, 193, 218, 298, 307, 342

sám 82, 199

sàm 103, 187

san 73, 81, 242, 267, 285, 289, 303, 321, 339, 359, 384, 411

sàn 8, 39, 142, 224, 314, 363

sang 136, 358

sàng 211, 223

sàp 198

sat 220, 323

sàt 68, 80, 290

sau 34, 48, 49, 51, 131, 137, 192, 195, 213, 216, 230, 239, 249, 270, 274, 295, 315, 323, 384, 409, 411

sáu 79, 119, 412

sàu 12, 49, 139, 278

sauh 34, 44, 66, 127

sàuh 5, 111

se 32, 126, 199, 293, 352

sé 82

sè 4, 350

seh 83, 429

séh 247

sèh 319

sehk 202, 241

sei 55

séi 172

sek 244, 386

sék 177

seon 92, 102, 107

seuhn 406

Cantonese (Pinyin)

sèuhn 43, 267, 376

seuhng 84, 102

séuhng 1

sèuhng 17, 50, 93, 271, 331

seuht 328, 365

sèuht 250

seui 40, 93, 171, 207, 229, 238, 243, 248, 251, 264, 268, 271, 285, 302, 340, 370, 397, 400, 417

séui 176

sèui 269, 329, 401, 406

seuih 65, 100, 220, 238, 252, 264, 304, 368, 398

séuih 110

sèuih 59, 340

seuk 24, 208, 391

seun 11, 56, 87, 163, 172, 177, 183, 239, 294, 302, 310, 336, 364, 366, 369, 413

séun 258

sèun 338

seung 173, 190, 206, 271, 333, 335, 416

séung 111, 351

sèung 15, 44, 64, 96, 236, 259, 391, 400, 402

seut 180

sèut 117

shyun 37

si 48, 52, 63, 84, 87, 97, 99, 181, 197, 284, 294, 308, 309, 323, 343, 378, 381, 382, 387, 413, 423, 428

sí 9, 35, 85

sì 35, 93, 105, 134, 142, 215, 250, 269, 338

sién 232

sih 4, 6, 10, 66, 145, 146, 175, 247, 248, 334, 346

síh 92

sìh 29

sihk 409

sìhm 325

sihn 46, 136, 278, 352

sihng 25, 60, 235

sìhng 3, 117, 121, 275, 338, 339

sik 49, 75, 186, 233, 252, 293, 296, 322, 323, 324, 325, 361, 383
sìk 99, 107, 108, 110, 124, 145, 147, 153, 198, 206, 344, 369, 378, 410
sim 25, 74, 249, 299, 326, 415
sím 392, 396
sin 76, 119, 132, 175, 197, 206, 208, 250, 257, 271, 274, 279, 289, 291, 301, 316, 326, 355, 359, 374, 402, 424
sín 383
sìn 6, 18, 421
sing 28, 63, 71, 106, 111, 146, 214, 282, 385, 396
síng 377
sìng 30, 145, 283, 289
sip 117, 138, 200
sit 85, 120, 161, 163, 183, 185, 189, 207, 255, 267, 293, 313, 332, 359
siu 27, 52, 81, 200, 243, 256, 258, 269, 284, 320, 366, 372, 401, 405, 419
siú 83
siù 185, 207, 262, 314, 384
siuh 18, 268
so 42, 43, 73, 126, 159, 260, 278, 303, 308
só 119, 220, 388
sò 48, 226, 312
soh 159
sòh 15
soi 289
sòi 423
sok 48, 131, 150, 164, 267, 309
song 77, 209, 245, 408
sóng 132
sòng 47, 48, 157
sou 48, 61, 63, 75, 112, 127, 140, 192, 230, 252, 267, 274, 291, 337
sòu 131, 316, 376, 415, 418
suhk 34, 65, 78, 86, 186, 206, 211, 352
sùhng 88
suk 67, 305, 310, 320, 343
sùk 81, 263, 273, 284
sung 79, 89, 104, 109, 113, 255, 283, 305, 365

Cantonese (Pinyin)

súng 114
sùng 418
sùt 325
syu 96, 107, 117, 137, 165, 173, 174, 197, 266
syú 147, 430, 432
syù 121, 149, 166, 294, 362
syuh 166, 346
syùh 172, 314
syùhn 143, 295, 390
syun 109, 129, 185, 194, 214, 221, 228, 258, 259, 308, 309, 409
syún 131, 370
syùn 78, 80, 376
syut 44, 340, 401, 423
syùt 108, 133, 216
tà 6, 70, 79
taa 382
tàahm 229, 341, 344
tàahn 65, 167
taai 67, 112, 178, 182, 285, 349, 375, 380
taam 128, 148, 196, 333, 386, 390
táam 174
tàam 348
taan 50, 58, 104, 171, 202, 227, 232, 244, 329
táan 58
tàan 138, 200
taap 48, 63, 164, 192, 357, 369, 423
taat 135, 354, 395, 404
tàhng 315, 343, 415
tai 25, 54, 85, 150, 185, 237, 269, 271, 331, 377, 426
tái 417
tài 159, 383
tàih 46, 62, 130, 357, 407
tam 177
tan 148, 177, 332, 409
tàn 37

tang 193, 227
tau 4, 366, 416
tàu 14
tàuh 120, 407
tek 356
téng 295
téuhn 236
teui 320, 366
téui 290
tèui 127
tèuih 407
teun 100
tihk 25
tìhn 64, 224
tíhng 125
tìhng 5, 14, 96, 98
tik 104, 113, 366
tìk 110
tim 105, 108, 128, 223, 294
tìm 188
tin 172, 224, 288, 394
tìn 67
ting 74, 158, 177, 203, 224, 303, 321, 384, 401
tìng 98, 283
tip 306, 349
típ 92
tit 391, 411
tiu 13, 237, 248, 253, 265, 299, 322, 355, 365, 418, 423, 433
tiù 9, 124
tiùh 157, 341
to 59, 70, 167, 180, 242, 354, 375, 396, 413, 425, 432
tò 121
tòh 295, 413
tòhng 43, 61, 63, 161, 264
toi 38, 202, 268, 314, 354, 372, 413, 420

Cantonese (Pinyin)

tòi 286
tóih 105, 172
tòih 122, 168, 292, 299
tok 96, 120, 122, 154, 167, 262, 336
tong 17, 92, 132, 186, 191, 207, 220, 278, 290, 324, 353, 389
tóng 13, 140, 360
tòng 190
tou 18, 36, 44, 45, 62, 69, 183, 193, 198, 269, 302, 305, 376, 379, 403, 405, 412
tóu 57, 249, 335
tóuh 284
tòuh 57, 63, 85, 102, 127, 157, 187, 366, 397
tsak 51
tsin 85
tùhng 36, 157, 255, 382
tùk 249
tung 10, 56, 101, 126, 196, 228, 240, 242, 301, 376
túng 158, 257, 267
tùng 367
tyùhn 57, 86
tyun 133, 190, 226, 291, 347
tyut 288
ùk 85
ung 223, 312
wa 356
wà 254, 320
waa 52, 390, 415
waah 41, 42
waahk 26, 118, 225
waahn 94, 108
wáahn 125
wàahn 221, 370, 406
wàahng 167
waaht 214
waai 164
wàai 171

Cantonese (Pinyin)

waaih 66
wàaih 117, 187
waak 241
waan 57, 80, 82, 195, 270, 275, 347, 387, 421
wàan 100, 201
waat 124, 141, 193
wah 72, 166, 338
wàh 31, 304
wahn 189, 206, 368, 401
wáhn 17, 172, 405
wàhn 29, 147, 419
wàhng 79
wai 31, 47, 55, 72, 83, 89, 93, 107, 113, 189, 196, 198, 202, 205, 207, 214, 219, 225, 229, 252, 272, 307, 310, 312, 313, 317, 323, 326, 341, 343, 368, 394, 405
wái 8, 71, 173, 306
waih 46, 109, 285, 328, 342
wáih 404
wàih 44, 57, 93, 110, 157, 209, 270, 369, 370
wan 112, 113, 144, 176, 188, 191, 192, 219, 258, 267, 281, 298, 315, 342, 373, 405, 411
wán 252, 377
wang 90, 99, 181, 392
wat 290, 337
wàt 85, 419
wihk 60
wihng 252
wíhng 176
wik 321, 394
wing 164, 182, 195, 327, 338
wo 62, 306, 387
wò 189, 254, 322
woh 248
wòh 39, 249
wohk 215, 252
wohng 144
wóhng 101

Cantonese (Pinyin)

wòhng 103, 111, 216, 233, 261, 322, 430
wok 327, 391
wong 178, 190, 195, 204, 221, 231, 246, 259, 325, 368, 398, 422
wóng 153
wòng 22
wu 21, 57, 87, 106, 119, 125, 193, 214, 219, 222, 247, 307, 323, 373, 377, 388, 427
wù 49, 177, 203
wuh 4, 119, 297, 345
wùh 66, 99, 190, 212, 264, 286, 418
wuhn 47, 217, 272
wùhn 60, 130
wuht 183
wui 100, 182, 205, 208, 301, 319, 398
wuih 150
wùih 56, 102, 366
wun 25, 47, 130, 157, 183, 188, 205, 209, 230, 233, 306, 346, 367
wún 184, 244, 288
yáh 3
yahm 7
yàhm 38
yahn 5, 23, 77, 266, 404
yáhn 99, 232
yàhn 5
yahp 18
yaht 143, 191, 367
yaih 149
yam 97
yám 409
yàm 170, 405
yan 17, 286
yán 104, 399
yàn 56, 72, 107, 170, 173
yàp 130, 181, 371
yàt 1, 66
yau 9, 10, 56, 95, 96, 312, 319, 347, 404, 418

Cantonese (Pinyin)

yáu 154

yàu 1, 7, 17, 95, 114, 371

yauh 33, 34

yáuh 34, 150, 340

yàuh 84, 108, 155, 180, 189, 214, 224, 368, 373, 375

ye 218

yeh 67, 131

yéh 21, 111, 378

yèh 161, 209, 372

yeuhk 99, 149, 299, 315, 317, 391, 434

yeuhng 55, 66, 107, 165, 195, 345, 378

yéuhng 6, 176, 232, 410

yèuhng 129, 162, 182, 205, 278, 397

yeuih 330, 384

yeuk 266, 359

yeung 68, 106, 251

yèung 425

yi 111

yí 13

yì 7, 10, 328, 377

yih 4, 225, 278, 284, 349, 375

yíh 6, 91, 137, 240, 282

yìh 16, 18, 68, 72, 80, 226, 251, 281, 340

yihk 5, 101, 145, 156, 186, 227, 279, 280, 345, 365

yihm 204, 346, 416

yíhm 155

yìhm 55, 201, 429

yihn 101, 218, 342

yìhn 98, 99, 204, 207, 216, 242, 258, 335, 351

yihng 339

yìhng 6, 22, 23, 60, 101, 208, 234, 324, 326, 365

yihp 161, 307, 405

yiht 206

yìk 16, 116, 121, 234

yim 33, 89, 95, 187

Cantonese (Pinyin)

yím 62, 186
yin 55, 80, 207
yín 194, 328
yìn 41, 203
yíng 145
yìng 101, 115, 119, 300, 428
yip 377, 403
yiu 62, 333
yiú 70, 137, 274
yiù 68, 289, 370
yiuh 280
yiùh 254, 343, 369, 412
yò 47
yu 76, 81, 230, 306
yù 142
yuh 47, 79, 249, 331, 345, 368, 406
yúh 3, 178, 279, 293, 340, 400
yùh 16, 54, 69, 78, 111, 112, 194, 219, 234, 410, 420
yuhk 170, 184, 215, 216, 284, 285, 332, 364
yuhn 196, 273, 407
yúhn 360, 369
yùhn 17, 33, 43, 57, 79, 169, 181, 191, 215, 272, 382
yuhng 223
yúhng 27
yùhng 15, 81, 96, 117, 206, 269, 301, 309, 323
yuht 3, 109, 111, 150, 253, 264, 353, 393
yuk 87, 145
yùk 144, 178
yun 80, 105, 219
yún 2, 110, 396
yùn 81, 425
yung 64, 213
yúng 20, 135, 190, 356
yùng 279
zi 78, 100, 224

Mandarin (Yale)

a 45, 385
ai 41, 42, 60, 75
ái 43, 125, 231, 233
ài 112, 148, 221, 246, 296, 398
ăi 53, 241, 315, 402
an 79, 95, 96, 157, 176, 342, 426
án 404
àn 87, 124, 147, 157, 212, 287, 431
ăn 12, 61, 130, 383
ang 416
áng 144
àng 234
ao 22
áo 49, 97, 140, 206, 215, 280, 283, 324, 369, 389, 423
ào 15, 59, 69, 90, 116, 123, 197, 333, 415
ăo 74
ba 19, 35, 37, 86, 92, 126, 227, 256, 263, 298
bá 121, 300, 354, 419
bà 66, 201, 209, 277, 402, 420
bă 121, 380, 403
bai 129
bái 233
bài 123, 140, 251, 348
băi 9, 126, 137, 154, 233
ban 120, 132, 218, 230, 294
bán 141, 406
bàn 8, 31, 120, 123, 222, 268, 363
băn 153, 210, 294, 380, 395
bang 94, 158, 184, 371
bàng 159, 245, 308, 318, 343, 388
băng 163, 269, 290
bao 25, 28, 29, 78, 205, 286, 298, 332, 433
báo 313, 401
bào 62, 122, 148, 208, 347, 354, 381, 420
băo 11, 62, 83, 306, 332, 410, 425

Mandarin (Yale)

bei 31, 43, 109, 131, 153, 396, 426

béi 29, 243

bèi 12, 14, 77, 109, 115, 204, 213, 244, 285, 309, 329, 330, 348, 362, 372, 384, 391

běi 193

ben 68, 386

bèn 58, 256

běn 151, 225, 300

beng 50, 89, 274

béng 224

bèng 223, 241, 358, 365

bi 260, 368

bí 302, 432

bì 50, 65, 74, 76, 94, 95, 96, 98, 100, 103, 112, 140, 141, 174, 213, 221, 224, 225, 229, 244, 258, 260, 291, 305, 309, 310, 311, 313, 331, 333, 349, 357, 370, 382, 392, 396, 397, 417

bǐ 12, 29, 37, 70, 101, 174, 250, 257, 374

bian 205, 242, 272, 322, 371, 404

biàn 11, 31, 98, 104, 178, 262, 272, 345, 363, 364, 368

biǎn 30, 119, 253, 331, 348

biao 165, 230, 290, 389, 391, 408, 409, 415, 417

biáo 101, 151

biào 423

biǎo 74, 328, 385

bie 114, 424

bié 23, 358

biě 232

bin 17, 101, 141, 168, 199, 217, 275, 347, 350, 391

bìn 136, 173, 291, 417, 418

bing 19, 21

bìng 2, 12, 133, 228

bǐng 1, 154, 202, 250, 372, 410

bo 181, 232, 276, 304, 410

bó 5, 8, 27, 31, 92, 131, 134, 135, 180, 189, 217, 247, 259, 287, 290, 295, 296, 356, 381, 382, 413, 426

bò 136, 316

bǒ 262, 355

Mandarin (Yale)

bu 146, 367, 382
bú 378
bù 1, 8, 61, 92, 106, 171, 222, 262, 373, 381
bǔ 31, 43, 126, 331
ca 54, 137
cǎ 246
cai 213
cái 119, 151, 330, 348
cài 305, 311
cǎi 101, 128, 238, 356, 378
can 410, 415
cán 114, 172, 327
càn 78, 208, 221, 264
cǎn 114, 431
cang 12, 14, 192, 295, 309
cáng 314
cao 136, 265
cáo 50, 149, 165, 194, 295, 324
cǎo 296, 302
cè 14, 20, 96, 112, 189, 257
cén 86, 185
céng 85
cèng 358
cha 33, 47, 91, 120, 130, 152, 386
chá 82, 132, 155, 162, 164, 168, 244, 301
chà 24, 86, 177, 328, 338
chai 123, 379
chái 155, 347
chài 326
chan 138, 334
chán 74, 97, 196, 197, 249, 275, 325, 326, 345, 359, 412
chàn 117, 279, 408
chǎn 223, 311, 341, 389, 395
chang 12, 73, 144, 214, 305, 394, 422
cháng 17, 50, 63, 76, 93, 102, 289, 305, 392

Mandarin (Yale)

chàng 13, 44, 110, 148, 226, 419
chăng 97, 110, 140, 145, 175
chao 106, 121, 204, 353, 380
cháo 51, 91, 145, 196
chăo 38, 202
che 243, 360
chè 59, 86, 103, 129, 134, 197
chĕ 120
chen 48, 122, 218
chén 64, 81, 105, 146, 179, 292, 342, 364, 397
chèn 169, 333, 346, 353, 433
chĕn 245
cheng 51, 134, 167, 190, 239, 251, 326
chéng 3, 37, 60, 63, 116, 117, 121, 146, 160, 166, 195, 251, 330, 338, 339, 376, 385
chèng 250
chĕng 367, 414
chi 35, 49, 229, 237, 256, 286, 287, 318, 325, 420, 425
chí 29, 59, 64, 99, 124, 178, 260, 356, 370, 413
chì 45, 101, 140, 142, 207, 236, 279, 352, 409
chĭ 10, 84, 108, 282, 332, 346, 433
chong 104, 115, 178, 293, 295, 328
chóng 17, 82, 88, 317, 326
chòng 383
chou 122, 231
chóu 5, 17, 94, 110, 111, 226, 251, 262, 270, 345, 359, 376
chòu 292
chŏu 1, 238, 377
chu 22, 23, 165, 328, 433
chú 97, 169, 192, 297, 321, 358, 359, 384, 397, 400
chù 4, 107, 131, 240, 317, 335, 430
chŭ 17, 116, 153, 161, 162, 246
chuai 131
chùai 51, 356
chŭai 130
chuan 91, 175, 253

487

Mandarin (Yale)

chúan 15, 161, 295, 368
chùan 2, 380
chǔan 47, 294
chuang 230, 253
chúang 94, 95, 209, 226
chùang 25, 113
chǔang 394
chui 160, 201
chúi 38, 59, 127, 129, 131, 160, 164, 386, 387, 397
chun 162, 323
chún 43, 145, 187, 267, 310, 376, 427
chǔn 327
chuo 118, 356
chùo 45, 271, 362, 364, 433
ci 227
cí 111, 222, 244, 248, 301, 337, 363, 400, 427
cì 170, 350
cǐ 171
cong 29, 56, 165, 220, 283, 310, 311
cóng 34, 102, 187, 219
còu 189, 289, 362
cú 101, 172, 263
cù 11, 214, 261, 310, 357, 358, 377
cuan 138, 177, 359
cùan 208, 254, 260
cui 15, 45, 88, 133, 163, 220
cùi 110, 174, 187, 204, 229, 264, 280, 287, 304
cun 151, 234
cún 77
cùn 83
cǔn 104
cuo 131, 135, 245, 357
cúo 89, 228, 230, 241, 429
cùo 33, 125, 128, 384, 386
cǔo 287

488

Mandarin (Yale)

da 53, 132, 230, 282, 332
dá 106, 256, 258, 369, 404
dà 67
dǎ 120
dái 37, 172
dài 6, 61, 87, 93, 102, 105, 118, 217, 223, 268, 329, 349, 365, 367, 430
dǎi 172
dan 2, 31, 47, 173, 236, 261, 282, 360, 374
dán 136
dàn 8, 45, 115, 143, 176, 187, 198, 231, 306, 318, 339
dǎn 134, 227, 291
dang 54, 333, 390
dàng 79, 167, 177, 235, 244, 305, 312
dǎng 18, 136, 346, 431
dao 22, 34, 103, 175
dáo 83
dào 24, 110, 208, 235, 252, 276, 369
dǎo 13, 88, 131, 249, 357
dé 103
deng 52, 207, 232, 261, 358
dèng 22, 90, 168, 239, 245, 374, 390
děng 118, 257
di 8, 62, 73, 175, 193, 278
dí 50, 76, 140, 193, 212, 256, 265, 280, 302, 334, 365, 388
dì 58, 93, 99, 160, 233, 237, 244, 257, 272, 308, 342, 369
dǐ 95, 122, 155, 242, 337, 372, 416
diǎ 49
dian 91, 128, 192, 232, 408
diàn 9, 64, 69, 95, 110, 173, 186, 217, 224, 232, 261, 382, 395, 401, 403
diǎn 19, 244, 356
diao 21, 22, 35, 243, 347, 400, 422
diào 36, 99, 126, 321, 379
die 209, 354
dié 46, 60, 62, 130, 210, 222, 226, 244, 281, 323, 341, 356, 365, 422
dím 431

Mandarin (Yale)

dīng 1, 5, 35, 216, 226, 235, 282, 379
dìng 80, 243, 289, 335, 384, 386
dǐng 375, 405, 432
diu 2
dong 21, 40, 152, 176, 426
dòng 21, 27, 59, 87, 107, 160, 183, 225, 242
dǒng 116, 307
dou 311
dóu 18
dòu 228, 254, 346, 366, 418
dǒu 121, 141, 318, 396
du 51, 238, 373
dú 169, 174, 199, 210, 211, 215, 244, 345, 417, 431
dù 70, 95, 152, 189, 284, 297, 327, 387
dǔ 63, 238, 255, 260, 351
duan 255
dùan 142, 161, 173, 204, 261, 272, 387
dǔan 241
dui 62
dùi 18, 83, 114, 116, 243, 398
dun 53, 65, 140, 246, 358, 390
dùn 56, 179, 207, 236, 242, 368, 380, 406
dǔn 236, 358
duo 39, 41, 67, 127, 331
dúo 69, 357, 391
dùo 59, 65, 111, 180, 295, 355
dǔo 42, 151, 360
e 73, 85, 381, 396
é 12, 56, 73, 87, 303, 320, 336, 385, 407, 426
è 33, 38, 53, 62, 109, 112, 120, 306, 342, 360, 368, 373, 387, 407, 410, 424, 427
en 49, 107, 309
èn 132
ér 18, 421, 425
èr 4, 281, 349
ěr 183, 209, 218, 282, 371, 410

490

Mandarin (Yale)

fa 233

fá 2, 7, 257, 277, 393

fà 219, 417

fǎ 180, 242

fan 94, 225, 280, 315

fán 22, 34, 92, 165, 205, 207, 246, 273, 311, 330, 358, 379

fàn 159, 177, 181, 212, 224, 259, 348, 409

fǎn 364

fang 29, 58, 142, 153, 298

fáng 70, 119, 285, 395, 420

fàng 139

fǎng 7, 101, 266, 294, 336

fei 45, 69, 119, 270, 304, 401, 403, 409, 421

féi 285, 288

fèi 37, 97, 181, 212, 229, 285, 349

fěi 30, 109, 141, 163, 260, 279, 298, 321, 340

fen 38, 175, 298, 375

fén 65, 159, 179, 204, 266, 432

fèn 7, 23, 69, 105, 115, 200, 265

fěn 263

feng 88, 161, 200, 203, 229, 307, 320, 374, 384, 408

féng 21, 83, 272, 346, 367, 413

fèng 12, 68, 425

fěng 43, 342

fó 9

fǒu 37, 276

fu 68, 77, 141, 290, 354, 372, 429

fú 7, 11, 29, 78, 79, 93, 99, 106, 121, 123, 150, 158, 175, 184, 185, 247, 249, 257, 267, 268, 276, 297, 300, 303, 305, 318, 321, 322, 330, 362, 424, 431

fù 6, 15, 25, 40, 67, 74, 81, 103, 209, 273, 289, 323, 332, 333, 335, 348, 350, 351, 353, 395, 412, 413, 420, 422

fǔ 12, 52, 95, 123, 134, 142, 223, 288, 361, 379, 431

ga 40, 50, 144

gá 50, 53, 84

gà 84, 416

gǎ 83

Mandarin (Yale)

gai 59, 286, 339, 350, 396
gài 1, 118, 163, 191, 195, 309, 380
găi 139
gan 3, 59, 84, 94, 152, 154, 181, 223, 227, 241, 256, 284, 300, 375
gán 15
gàn 94, 144, 187, 268, 352
găn 111, 135, 140, 158, 166, 197, 251, 353
gang 86, 270, 276, 277, 284, 294, 385
gáng 25
gàng 164
găng 88, 189
gao 164, 233, 239, 264, 278, 290, 292
gào 37, 340, 385
găo 131, 152, 164, 252, 273, 314, 388
gau 260, 417
ge 25, 42, 117, 137, 171, 226, 286, 295, 426
gé 48, 64, 129, 156, 290, 307, 319, 388, 393, 398, 403, 416
gè 13, 36, 317, 382
gĕ 43
gen 156, 355
gèn 296, 301
geng 42, 95, 149, 279, 281, 350
gĕng 60, 158, 269, 282, 421
gong 10, 19, 27, 80, 98, 139, 285, 318, 335, 360, 434
góng 91, 99, 108
gòng 19, 348
gŏng 124, 178, 217, 404
gou 9, 29, 191, 260, 272, 381, 404
gòu 67, 75, 100, 164, 334, 338, 351, 369
gŏu 154, 212, 256, 299
gu 8, 40, 71, 78, 178, 180, 233, 259, 304, 305, 319, 335, 363, 376, 425
gù 15, 56, 139, 158, 211, 229, 385, 408, 422
gŭ 34, 50, 210, 240, 277, 284, 291, 327, 337, 346, 362, 381, 416, 427, 432
gua 24, 38, 409, 426
gúa 222

492

Mandarin (Yale)

gùa 32, 128, 331, 339
gŭa 25, 82
guai 3
gùai 106
gŭai 122, 155
guan 12, 80, 303, 334, 395, 423
gúan 20
gùan 113, 133, 185, 200, 235, 276, 349, 428
gŭan 259, 411
guang 18, 157
gùang 367
gŭang 97, 216
gui 57, 172, 220, 334, 393, 421, 434
gùi 26, 156, 167, 168, 349, 355, 424
gŭi 30, 79, 147, 232, 261, 338, 360, 419
gùn 159
gŭn 2, 193, 271, 329, 362, 421
guo 88, 282, 325, 373, 387
gúo 57, 94, 132, 412
gùo 60, 368
gŭo 152, 165, 213, 322, 331
gwan 160
gwang 286
gwo 62
ha 42
hai 4, 49
hái 78, 417
hài 80, 176, 414
hăi 184, 377
hàk 51
han 114, 276, 319, 375, 406, 432
hán 22, 38, 81, 146, 186, 203, 372, 405
hàn 109, 116, 126, 134, 135, 144, 177, 194, 199, 203, 280, 305, 379, 384, 407
hăn 32, 46
hang 406

Mandarin (Yale)

háng 153, 268, 294

hàng 179

hao 54, 309, 313

háo 49, 54, 65, 174, 198, 327, 347

hào 144, 184, 201, 233, 281, 317, 408

hǎo 70, 372

he 39, 47, 49, 337

hé 9, 27, 36, 39, 149, 156, 180, 186, 234, 249, 266, 280, 302, 304, 347, 393, 394, 406

hè 65, 332, 349, 352, 427

hei 430

hén 228

hèn 108

hěn 102, 212

heng 5, 42

héng 107, 156, 167, 316, 328

hó 35

hong 203, 314, 335, 363

hóng 79, 99, 181, 183, 266, 307, 313, 317, 392, 425, 430

hòng 336, 419

hou 260

hóu 10, 46, 214, 229, 416

hòu 36, 62, 102, 366, 424

hǒu 33, 38

hu 2, 39, 44, 105, 110, 119, 193, 202, 316

hú 66, 99, 141, 165, 190, 212, 214, 219, 264, 286, 307, 323, 335, 377, 418, 426, 427

hù 4, 21, 87, 106, 119, 193, 222, 247, 256, 297, 345

hǔ 43, 193, 218, 317

hua 297

húa 26, 31, 193, 214, 304, 390, 415

hùa 26, 29, 166, 225, 338

húai 102, 117, 164, 187, 356

hùai 66

huan 171, 216

húan 57, 82, 157, 183, 221, 275, 306, 370, 387

hùan 47, 80, 94, 108, 130, 136, 184, 188, 195, 205, 230, 347, 367, 421

Mandarin (Yale)

hǔan 272

huang 284, 302

húang 22, 103, 111, 113, 190, 195, 204, 221, 231, 233, 259, 261, 322, 325, 368, 398, 422, 430

hùang 246

hǔang 93, 107, 146, 343

hui 41, 130, 147, 201, 219, 339, 362, 399, 430

húi 56, 103, 108, 182, 301, 319, 366

hùi 31, 47, 100, 107, 109, 113, 146, 150, 208, 252, 274, 275, 312, 313, 326, 340, 343, 350

hǔi 108, 173, 207, 317

hun 74, 144, 308, 394

hún 189, 411, 419

hùn 188, 192, 342

huo 26, 137, 281

húo 183

hùo 54, 111, 118, 215, 248, 252, 315, 327, 346, 348, 391, 401

hǔo 67, 201

hwa 52

ji 25, 41, 43, 52, 58, 72, 85, 89, 197, 211, 221, 225, 226, 245, 252, 257, 259, 271, 274, 277, 284, 359, 400, 409, 411, 433

jí 4, 22, 32, 33, 36, 61, 75, 86, 89, 105, 118, 136, 159, 162, 167, 172, 178, 227, 230, 256, 262, 267, 309, 313, 344, 362, 399

jì 7, 20, 24, 26, 54, 70, 78, 81, 100, 104, 110, 120, 143, 148, 182, 198, 248, 252, 266, 275, 297, 313, 314, 334, 335, 336, 355, 398, 402, 416, 418, 421, 424

jǐ 91, 95, 118, 127, 136, 269, 287, 325, 429

jia 9, 14, 27, 50, 68, 81, 185, 217, 227, 257, 307, 329, 354, 365, 388

jiá 87, 107, 118, 303, 320, 330, 373, 384, 407

jià 16, 75, 155, 252, 414

jiǎ 13, 224, 230, 285, 350, 382

jian 19, 63, 72, 84, 173, 190, 205, 211, 235, 259, 271, 273, 285, 296, 304, 308, 404, 423, 427

jián 61, 393

jiàn 7, 14, 26, 98, 161, 168, 174, 195, 196, 199, 259, 289, 296, 313, 334, 342, 351, 356, 387, 390, 391, 410

jiǎn 16, 25, 56, 129, 135, 155, 158, 168, 188, 240, 258, 261, 275, 280, 343, 345, 354, 357, 429

jiang 16, 72, 83, 195, 226, 246, 346, 404

Mandarin (Yale)

jiáng 178, 312

jiàng 30, 182, 211, 265, 269, 377, 396

jiǎng 69, 164, 215, 282, 311, 343

jiao 4, 72, 76, 161, 196, 204, 246, 290, 296, 301, 311, 320, 355, 372, 415, 421, 428

jiáo 55

jiào 35, 51, 90, 103, 140, 253, 361, 363, 376, 378

jiǎo 16, 26, 28, 134, 138, 140, 213, 233, 241, 268, 275, 289, 335, 383, 410

jie 46, 48, 233, 397

jié 14, 24, 27, 32, 74, 77, 118, 123, 127, 128, 130, 156, 157, 195, 232, 238, 244, 255, 258, 268, 278, 328, 336, 338, 421

jiè 5, 13, 85, 117, 224, 227, 297, 314, 318, 340

jiě 71, 335

jin 6, 92, 142, 183, 240, 257, 329, 333, 379

jìn 27, 52, 146, 185, 208, 235, 248, 314, 352, 364, 367, 403

jǐn 16, 62, 97, 165, 220, 271, 344, 386, 411

jing 5, 18, 143, 147, 185, 237, 258, 264, 269, 288, 302, 303, 304, 415, 422

jìng 64, 74, 100, 102, 140, 187, 228, 255, 287, 367, 389, 403, 405

jǐng 4, 25, 115, 147, 285, 345, 395, 407

jiong 20, 119

jiǒng 201, 202, 254, 365

jiu 46, 265, 353, 418, 419, 424

jiú 130

jiù 40, 84, 139, 155, 156, 226, 253, 293, 428

jiǔ 2, 3, 201, 216, 375, 405

ju 85, 122, 128, 161, 212, 227, 300, 304, 331, 353, 399, 404, 413

jú 10, 84, 166, 305

jù 12, 19, 26, 35, 86, 91, 117, 122, 135, 202, 240, 254, 283, 299, 337, 355, 356, 370, 381, 385, 409

jǔ 39, 164, 169, 180, 241, 293, 303, 357, 433

juan 73, 125, 185, 327, 390, 426

jùan 13, 32, 157, 213, 237, 269, 373, 400

jǔan 127

jue 52, 133

júe 3, 13, 21, 26, 33, 53, 77, 88, 121, 128, 138, 158, 166, 179, 208, 209, 215, 217, 240, 268, 312, 334, 335, 336, 344, 358

jun 36, 58, 234, 360, 380, 429

Mandarin (Yale)

jún 304

jùn 11, 88, 125, 184, 255, 372, 414

ka 40

kà 46

kǎ 32, 40

kai 130, 392

kái 112

kài 113

kǎi 22, 26, 63, 113, 162, 308, 387, 388

kan 23, 28, 62, 118, 434

kàn 236, 239, 395

kǎn 9, 58, 241, 304

kang 96, 265, 392

káng 114, 120

kàng 4, 7, 121, 202, 380

kao 84

kào 211, 383, 403

kǎo 124, 156, 203, 280

ke 155, 160, 217, 227, 239, 245, 250, 251, 254, 299, 323, 360, 406, 407, 417

ké 41, 173

kè 18, 24, 48, 80, 108, 176, 191, 271, 319, 340, 385, 414

kě 59, 189

kèn 330

kěn 44, 65, 115, 285

keng 37, 58, 389

kong 88, 253

kòng 128

kǒng 77, 107

kou 132, 297

kòu 35, 81, 120, 258, 380

kǒu 34

ku 24, 43, 61, 154, 254, 416

kù 55, 96, 268, 332, 376

kǔ 299

kua 339

497

Mandarin (Yale)

kùa 124, 286, 355
kǔa 60
kùai 16, 53, 64, 104, 197, 215, 258, 291, 374
kǔai 308
kuan 417
kúan 82
kǔan 170
kuang 30, 257, 339
kúang 212, 339
kùang 21, 66, 149, 157, 181, 237, 246, 275, 349
kui 14, 90, 109, 234, 238, 317
kúi 67, 68, 129, 147, 254, 308, 323, 367, 412, 419
kùi 30, 47, 112, 115, 196, 261, 283, 312, 412
kǔi 355
kun 144, 218, 377, 385, 417, 422
kún 59
kùn 56
kǔn 108, 126, 393
kùo 97, 123, 137, 319, 394
la 45, 58, 123, 371
lá 144, 242
là 24, 229, 292, 327, 363
lǎ 46
lái 9, 102, 188, 306
lài 199, 232, 238, 262, 350, 351
lǎm 194
lán 44, 73, 89, 138, 141, 169, 200, 262, 314, 316, 333, 345, 391, 394
làn 198, 208
lǎn 116, 138, 170, 276, 334
lang 45
láng 96, 163, 213, 220, 251, 323, 372, 384, 393
làng 184, 303
lao 134
láo 28, 79, 90, 210, 231, 377
lào 197, 203, 376

Mandarin (Yale)

lǎo 10, 72, 156, 196, 280, 383

láu 52

le 3

lè 5, 35, 181, 423

lei 28, 50

léi 75, 136, 167, 273, 279, 390, 401

lèi 187, 284, 376, 408

lěi 66, 245, 267, 281, 313, 339

léng 63, 160, 162

lèng 112

lěng 21

li 44

lí 75, 158, 193, 211, 213, 220, 263, 277, 315, 316, 320, 327, 332, 379, 400, 416, 424, 428, 430, 431

lì 10, 17, 23, 27, 28, 33, 36, 54, 66, 119, 156, 169, 171, 200, 213, 228, 232, 246, 255, 256, 260, 263, 265, 302, 308, 327, 338, 359, 363, 374, 399, 402, 419, 429

lǐ 11, 42, 72, 152, 197, 218, 249, 331, 371, 378, 385, 421, 424

lián 97, 115, 194, 198, 262, 283, 310, 326, 332, 367, 390, 423

liàn 117, 162, 173, 200, 204, 272, 387, 389

liǎn 141, 221, 291, 316

liáng 64, 157, 160, 165, 186, 264, 265, 296, 379

liàng 5, 147, 341, 356, 361

liǎng 12, 19, 150, 420

liáo 16, 51, 82, 135, 207, 215, 231, 274, 282, 370, 428

liào 97, 133, 141, 390

liǎo 3, 310, 379

lie 40

liè 23, 27, 126, 182, 203, 216, 330, 353, 359, 418

lin 123

lín 90, 153, 186, 207, 219, 240, 246, 264, 292, 363, 370, 374, 402, 424, 429

lìn 36, 315, 350, 359

lǐn 21, 98, 116, 167

líng 8, 21, 56, 154, 169, 181, 217, 271, 278, 279, 282, 299, 305, 319, 374, 381, 397, 401, 402, 422, 433

lìng 6, 34, 38

lǐng 90, 406

Mandarin (Yale)

liu 191

liú 26, 143, 163, 184, 199, 218, 225, 230, 243, 388

liù 19, 369, 411, 427

liŭ 155, 270

long 399

lóng 54, 151, 169, 200, 222, 231, 246, 262, 283, 316, 398, 434

lŏng 66, 138

lou 89

lóu 51, 165, 282, 310, 325, 417

lòu 194, 231, 389, 396

lŏu 133, 261

lu 37, 54

lú 66, 98, 168, 169, 199, 208, 235, 292, 296, 315, 363, 393, 408, 416, 424, 428

lù 102, 114, 118, 176, 187, 188, 194, 199, 221, 243, 248, 261, 270, 349, 355, 361, 363, 367, 385, 397, 402, 428, 429

lŭ 10, 85, 86, 126, 135, 143, 168, 273, 290, 317, 332, 384, 420, 428

lúan 77, 79, 90, 138, 170, 201, 292, 392, 428

lùan 3

lŭan 32

lùe 128, 225, 384

lún 10, 13, 57, 88, 127, 187, 270, 362

lùn 341

lúo 169, 216, 263, 277, 316, 324, 371, 391, 415

lùo 41, 133, 183, 195, 199, 211, 217, 269, 306, 400, 414

lŭo 231, 326, 331

ma 49, 50, 75, 77

má 229, 325, 430

mà 163, 277, 414

mă 214, 220, 245, 324, 412

mái 60, 402

mài 31, 49, 51, 287, 351, 370, 429

măi 312, 349

man 389, 408

mán 239, 327, 411, 423

màn 64, 93, 113, 149, 194, 273, 310, 344

mǎn 193, 325

máng 104, 175, 235, 296, 301, 371

mǎng 195, 304, 325

mao 348

máo 142, 174, 240, 300, 323, 324, 386, 418

mào 20, 93, 115, 220, 238, 281, 300, 329, 347, 349

mǎo 32, 87, 145, 181, 382

mǎu 300

me 430

méi 74, 89, 153, 158, 162, 179, 189, 205, 217, 236, 303, 376, 431

mèi 71, 74, 81, 145, 180, 329, 419

měi 174, 185, 278, 387

men 11

mén 126, 392

mèn 109, 115, 206, 392

méng 151, 168, 223, 235, 239, 246, 295, 306, 308, 317

mèng 67, 78

měng 116, 214, 295, 321, 327, 386, 432

mi 20, 40, 239

mí 100, 216, 265, 273, 316, 343, 365, 377, 429

mì 20, 81, 178, 181, 247, 250, 265, 321, 334, 343

mǐ 99, 263, 287, 403

mián 79, 159, 236, 271

miàn 403, 430

miǎn 18, 20, 27, 73, 179, 190, 197, 236, 272

miáo 129, 238, 299

miào 70, 97

miǎo 152, 188, 189, 236, 250, 272, 315, 371

mie 40, 278

miè 192, 261, 310, 327

mín 87, 175, 216, 271, 299

mǐn 111, 115, 123, 139, 182, 234, 392, 393, 423

míng 20, 36, 144, 148, 191, 239, 300, 324, 382, 425

mìng 39

mǐng 376

Mandarin (Yale)

miù 344
mo 133
mó 76, 133, 165, 245, 290, 315, 344, 411, 420
mò 65, 82, 151, 172, 180, 191, 231, 250, 300, 304, 347, 348, 389, 396, 415, 430
mǒ 121
mou 42
móu 210, 237, 274, 319, 342, 387
mǒu 33, 155
mù 22, 28, 64, 93, 114, 148, 151, 179, 210, 235, 238, 252, 300, 381
mǔ 71, 122, 174, 225
ná 125
nà 38, 127, 266, 329, 371, 380
nái 68
nài 155, 281, 306, 432
nǎi 2, 42, 69, 175
nan 56
nán 31, 46, 162, 224
nàn 400
nǎn 289, 352
náng 55, 412
nǎng 139, 149
nao 78
náo 39, 134, 166, 214, 326, 390
nào 187, 393, 419
nǎo 112, 220, 289
nè 336
nèi 19, 20
něi 410
nèn 76
néng 287
ni 71
ní 84, 106, 182, 213, 401, 422
nì 30, 148, 192, 238, 291, 365
nǐ 8, 59, 137, 143, 248
nian 122, 311

502

nián 94, 421, 422

niàn 44, 60, 98, 105, 430

niǎn 127, 134, 137, 245, 362

niáng 73

niàng 378

niào 84, 288

niǎo 77, 311, 330, 424

nie 126, 130

niè 54, 55, 79, 185, 283, 292, 359, 388, 391, 398, 408

nín 108

níng 22, 54, 82, 168, 215, 283

nìng 198

nǐng 137

niu 70

niú 210

niǔ 105, 120, 212, 266, 381

nóng 16, 53, 198, 291, 364

nòng 98

nòu 282

nú 69, 78, 413

nù 106, 107, 328

nǔ 27, 69, 99, 380

nuǎn 147

nüè 230, 317

núo 17, 73, 125

nùo 46, 116, 132, 265, 342

o 39

ó 42

ou 171, 173, 222, 344, 427

òu 113, 194

ǒu 14, 50, 281, 315

pa 45, 307, 354

pá 119, 209, 219, 281

pà 92, 106

pǎ 153

Mandarin (Yale)

pai 122
pái 12, 102, 127, 210
pài 184, 189
pan 137, 196
pán 209, 235, 245, 325, 357
pàn 23, 34, 182, 225, 236, 333
pang 3, 192
páng 98, 103, 142, 323
pàng 286
pǎng 282
pao 123, 288
páo 23, 29, 39, 95, 212, 329
pào 181, 202, 234
pǎo 354
pei 39, 59, 286, 376
péi 61, 331, 351, 397
pèi 9, 92, 143, 178, 363, 375, 401
pen 52
pén 190, 234
peng 51, 106, 121, 197, 203, 242
péng 62, 101, 150, 160, 243, 260, 290, 310, 325, 426
pèng 244
pěng 126
pi 1, 26, 53, 120, 122, 241, 267, 372, 402
pí 45, 61, 153, 174, 219, 227, 234, 277, 288, 297, 318, 321, 348, 373, 381
pì 16, 75, 84, 188, 198, 223, 238, 345, 364, 395
pǐ 6, 30, 57, 95, 136, 226, 228, 231, 299
pian 211, 259, 280
pián 13, 287, 341, 357, 414
piàn 210, 414
piao 26, 194, 324, 409
piáo 75, 222
piào 50, 248
piǎo 172, 239, 273
pie 134, 175, 239

piě 2

pin 71, 124

pín 75, 348, 407, 408

pìn 210, 283

pǐn 40

ping 3, 72

píng 59, 85, 94, 114, 154, 222, 250, 304, 316, 337, 420

po 59, 195, 379, 406

pó 73, 233, 374

pò 151, 217, 242, 263, 365, 419

pǒ 35, 257

pou 25

póu 126, 330

pu 52, 135, 139, 385

pú 15, 29, 198, 221, 288, 303, 305, 307, 308

pù 149, 199

pǔ 56, 60, 147, 167, 184, 191, 344, 358

qi 1, 50, 58, 71, 118, 160, 164, 165, 170, 179, 186, 194, 306

qí 19, 68, 86, 88, 143, 146, 150, 159, 171, 218, 225, 247, 248, 270, 281, 291, 298, 316, 321, 326, 406, 414, 423, 429, 433

qì 24, 53, 68, 114, 161, 175, 176, 177, 179, 181, 241, 245, 308, 336, 364

qǐ 3, 7, 45, 86, 139, 152, 270, 296, 346, 353

qia 127

qià 108, 184, 417

qian 6, 30, 111, 114, 120, 132, 262, 297, 382, 385, 395, 414, 427

qián 24, 128, 196, 211, 317, 343, 370, 380, 381, 386, 430

qiàn 64, 89, 113, 164, 170, 297, 301

qiǎn 22, 188, 275, 345, 369

qiang 49, 118, 164, 278, 288, 388, 389

qiáng 76, 100, 167, 210, 313

qiàng 206, 357

qiǎng 129, 278, 332, 390

qiao 140, 166, 246, 358, 386

qiáo 15, 26, 47, 115, 166, 239, 280, 312, 344

qiào 11, 87, 135, 254, 340, 404

Mandarin (Yale)

qiǎo 91, 109, 112
qié 8, 299
qiè 23, 71, 106, 112, 124, 255, 260, 386
qiě 1
qin 10, 52, 170, 329, 334, 380
qín 28, 82, 136, 167, 192, 219, 249, 250, 297, 298, 324
qìn 135, 179
qing 15, 32, 57, 176, 188, 322, 403, 422
qíng 110, 136, 147, 168, 176, 361, 431
qìng 245, 276
qǐng 168, 341, 344, 405
qiong 383
qióng 204, 221, 253, 254, 257, 320, 355, 371
qiu 1, 162, 190, 318, 371, 422
qiú 55, 91, 177, 180, 212, 218, 250, 317, 322, 330, 350, 366, 369, 375, 432
qiǔ 264
qu 30, 90, 149, 247, 319, 337, 360, 415, 430, 431
qú 27, 73, 85, 161, 175, 188, 221, 312, 316, 328, 353, 425
qù 33, 334, 353, 394
qǔ 34, 434
quan 109
qúan 19, 124, 169, 228, 258, 302, 321, 338, 361, 377, 383, 408, 418
qùan 24, 28, 182
quǎn 56, 212, 224, 270
que 202, 276
qúe 231
qùe 32, 112, 163, 244, 394, 399, 426
qun 366
qún 278, 331
rán 204, 207, 319, 418
rǎn 20, 155, 299
ráng 138, 222, 249, 252
ràng 66, 345
rǎng 55
ráo 76, 311, 412

Mandarin (Yale)

rào 274
rǎo 137
rè 206
rě 111
rén 5, 17, 66
rèn 6, 7, 23, 70, 266, 329, 339, 360, 404, 409
rěn 104, 251, 302
reng 119
réng 6
rì 143
róng 81, 90, 117, 163, 164, 192, 206, 213, 269, 301, 309, 323, 327
rǒng 20
rou 129
róu 155, 249, 357, 404
ròu 284
rǒu 264
rú 16, 54, 69, 78, 198, 301, 314, 326, 333, 383
rù 18, 183, 192, 273, 309, 332, 364
rǔ 3, 178
ruǎn 150, 360, 395
rui 238
rúi 312
rùi 153, 220, 298, 318, 384
rǔi 312
rùn 196, 393
rùo 99, 259, 299
sá 134
sà 31, 314, 408
sǎ 200
sai 53, 63, 289, 423
sài 351
san 1, 33, 174
sàn 140
sǎn 14, 265, 411
sang 47, 157

Mandarin (Yale)

sāng 48, 132, 245, 408
sao 274, 415
sào 61, 230
sǎo 75, 127
sau 131, 291
sè 49, 198, 220, 252, 296, 383
sen 159
seng 16
sha 48, 173, 179, 205, 229, 241, 330, 389, 421
shá 266
shà 44, 45, 97, 170, 402
shǎ 15
shai 260
shài 149
shan 23, 71, 86, 100, 132, 151, 196, 206, 217, 279, 291, 294, 297, 328, 355
shàn 25, 46, 76, 119, 136, 177, 226, 274, 299, 326, 336, 352, 374, 415, 424
shǎn 133, 392, 396
shang 15, 44, 173, 206, 331, 335
sháng 64
shàng 1, 84, 271
shǎng 146, 351
shao 27, 125, 207, 251, 258, 295
sháo 28, 159, 296, 405
shào 42, 196, 268, 372
she 350
shé 69, 293, 319
shè 83, 117, 138, 171, 185, 200, 247, 293, 324, 336, 352, 429
shě 126
shéi 340
shen 8, 33, 39, 73, 187, 224, 242, 267, 285, 303, 339, 359
shén 5, 248
shèn 113, 193, 223, 289, 307, 321
shěn 41, 77, 82, 188, 199, 240
sheng 28, 30, 211, 223, 256, 283, 396
shéng 275

Mandarin (Yale)

shèng 25, 235, 282

shěng 236, 237

shi 68, 84, 93, 215, 309, 323, 338, 378, 382

shí 30, 63, 82, 123, 142, 146, 198, 202, 241, 322, 344, 409, 423

shì 1, 4, 6, 8, 10, 28, 48, 53, 66, 80, 92, 99, 107, 124, 145, 155, 175, 247, 248, 258, 294, 308, 334, 339, 343, 349, 361, 366, 369, 378, 381, 410

shǐ 9, 35, 71, 85, 240, 346, 413

shou 139

shòu 34, 44, 66, 127, 213, 216, 230, 270

shǒu 79, 119, 412

shu 34, 72, 121, 137, 149, 159, 172, 173, 174, 186, 226, 266, 294, 305, 312, 362

shú 65, 78, 166, 206, 250, 352

shù 65, 96, 107, 117, 140, 152, 166, 180, 195, 197, 328, 346, 365

shǔ 86, 147, 148, 277, 314, 320, 430, 432

shua 24, 44

shuǎ 281

shuai 133, 329

shuài 93, 216, 325

shuǎi 223

shuan 125, 156, 392

shùan 185

shuang 77, 400, 402

shuǎng 209

shùi 238, 251

shǔi 176

shun 37

shùn 239, 294, 406

shuo 340

shùo 69, 131, 150, 164, 208, 244, 309, 391

si 35, 51, 52, 97, 105, 134, 142, 197, 323, 387, 428

sí 250, 269

sì 9, 11, 18, 49, 55, 71, 83, 91, 177, 181, 247, 256, 281, 284, 410, 413

sǐ 172

song 89, 104, 153, 305, 418

sòng 21, 79, 336, 340, 365, 406

Mandarin (Yale)

sōng 109, 113, 114, 255, 283
sou 48, 131, 192, 295, 323, 409, 411
sòu 49
sǒu 34, 49, 137, 239, 315
su 252, 316, 376
sú 11
sù 48, 63, 67, 81, 112, 185, 192, 261, 263, 267, 284, 310, 337, 343, 366
suan 228, 376
sùan 258, 308
sui 40, 237, 238, 302, 400
súi 269, 398
sùi 171, 207, 243, 248, 252, 340, 368, 370, 398
sǔi 417
sun 78, 214, 309, 409
sǔn 131, 163, 258, 399
suo 42, 48, 73, 126, 159, 260, 273, 278, 303, 308
sǔo 43, 119, 220, 267, 388
ta 6, 63, 192, 354, 369, 382
tá 70, 79
tà 48, 135, 164, 178, 216, 356, 357, 395
tǎ 423
tai 286
tái 122, 168, 202, 292, 299, 314, 354, 372, 413, 420
tài 67, 112, 178, 182, 285, 375, 380
tǎi 38, 63
tan 58, 138, 232, 348
tán 65, 100, 148, 167, 196, 200, 229, 311, 333, 341, 344, 386, 390
tàn 50, 128, 171, 202, 244, 351
tǎn 58, 104, 174, 329
tang 190, 278, 389
táng 17, 43, 61, 63, 132, 161, 191, 220, 264, 290, 324
tàng 207, 353
tǎng 13, 92, 186, 360
tao 193, 198, 269, 405, 412
táo 45, 127, 157, 183, 187, 305, 366, 397, 403

tào 69
tăo 335
tè 104, 113, 211
téng 193, 227, 315, 343, 415
ti 25, 383
tí 46, 130, 159, 269, 271, 302, 356, 357, 377, 407, 426
tì 25, 54, 85, 109, 110, 150, 185, 331, 366
tĭ 417
tian 67, 188
tián 64, 108, 223, 224, 394
tiàn 128
tiăn 105, 172, 288, 294
tiao 9, 248
tiáo 13, 124, 157, 299, 322, 341, 365, 418, 423, 433
tiào 237, 265, 355
tiăo 253
tie 92, 306
tié 349
tiè 411
tiĕ 391
ting 98, 177, 203, 283
tíng 5, 14, 74, 96, 98, 303, 321, 401
tĭng 125, 158, 224, 295
tong 367
tóng 10, 36, 101, 157, 196, 240, 242, 255, 301, 376, 382
tòng 114, 228
tŏng 126, 158, 257, 267
tou 14
tóu 4, 120, 407, 416
tòu 366
tŏu 380
tu 253
tú 18, 22, 57, 63, 85, 102, 249, 302, 366, 376
tù 62, 305
tŭ 36, 57, 379

Mandarin (Yale)

tuan 190
túan 57, 133
tùan 100
tŭan 226
tui 127
túi 407
tùi 320, 366
tŭi 290
tun 148
tún 37, 86, 291, 347, 409
tùn 332
tŭn 177
tuo 120, 121, 288, 336
túo 59, 167, 180, 242, 354, 365, 375, 396, 413, 425, 432
tùo 44, 122, 154, 262
tŭo 70, 96, 167
wa 41, 124, 254, 320
wá 72
wà 290, 333
wă 222
wai 42, 67, 171
wăi 89
wan 25, 100, 201, 322, 346
wán 2, 79, 217, 266, 406
wàn 230, 307
wăn 74, 80, 110, 125, 146, 219, 233, 244, 270, 287, 288, 304
wang 178
wáng 4, 216
wàng 70, 104, 144, 150
wăng 101, 110, 153, 270, 276, 361, 420
wei 13, 72, 205, 307, 313, 368, 398
wéi 32, 44, 55, 57, 89, 93, 103, 110, 157, 191, 196, 198, 202, 209, 270, 369, 394, 404
wèi 8, 39, 46, 83, 113, 151, 189, 225, 285, 310, 323, 328, 342, 420
wĕi 13, 14, 71, 72, 84, 183, 205, 214, 219, 229, 272, 306, 307, 341, 398, 405, 421
wen 191, 230

Mandarin (Yale)

wén 141, 266, 283, 318, 393, 401

wèn 45, 179, 221, 392

wěn 23, 38, 252, 267

weng 48, 279

wèng 223, 312

wěng 309

wo 254, 306, 322

wò 46, 130, 141, 178, 189, 292, 434

wǒ 117

wu 49, 57, 76, 91, 177, 203, 340, 373, 388

wú 37, 85, 158, 174, 184, 203, 211, 311, 321, 432

wù 17, 28, 29, 63, 74, 82, 109, 117, 146, 152, 203, 210, 228, 298, 340, 384, 402, 414, 427

wǔ 4, 7, 10, 30, 97, 104, 115, 125, 171, 294, 364, 426

xi 16, 19, 38, 43, 51, 69, 76, 85, 92, 107, 110, 145, 147, 149, 153, 166, 170, 177, 186, 191, 206, 207, 211, 233, 243, 251, 253, 263, 279, 295, 322, 323, 325, 333, 357, 378, 386, 432

xí 67, 75, 93, 108, 167, 279, 290, 333, 334, 399

xì 11, 30, 118, 248, 265, 267, 274, 293, 398, 411, 419

xǐ 47, 102, 182, 221, 249, 307, 310

xia 39, 239, 322

xiá 11, 30, 88, 147, 154, 212, 213, 219, 243, 362, 368, 402, 431

xià 1, 54, 67, 276

xian 6, 18, 127, 148, 175, 247, 250, 276, 313, 359, 421

xián 41, 73, 75, 76, 99, 185, 231, 295, 351, 383, 393, 428

xiàn 88, 114, 216, 218, 271, 273, 278, 289, 303, 396, 397, 402, 411

xiǎn 208, 215, 257, 316, 320, 355, 383, 399, 408

xiang 190, 271, 313, 333, 391, 412, 416

xiáng 96, 236, 248, 259, 279, 339, 373

xiàng 15, 36, 54, 92, 167, 325, 347, 405

xiǎng 5, 111, 405, 410, 412, 422

xiao 52, 55, 81, 154, 158, 185, 200, 243, 262, 269, 314, 320, 366, 384, 401, 415, 419

xiáo 42, 89, 186

xiào 52, 139, 156, 256, 284

xiǎo 83, 148, 258

xie 4, 161, 170, 326

Mandarin (Yale)

xié 14, 31, 82, 125, 137, 138, 141, 275, 287, 341, 371, 404, 407
xiè 32, 85, 98, 116, 159, 163, 183, 189, 199, 200, 207, 215, 267, 314, 326, 332, 343, 359, 370
xin 103, 105, 142, 145, 170, 298, 314, 363, 384, 391, 412
xìn 11, 56, 378
xing 111, 145, 214, 289, 293, 328
xíng 23, 60, 101, 192, 243, 371, 396, 411
xìng 71, 94, 106, 110, 152, 302
xǐng 136, 377
xiong 18, 22, 29, 179, 183, 287, 297
xióng 17, 206, 399
xiu 7, 12, 96, 278, 347, 411, 418, 426
xiù 48, 87, 192, 249, 274, 330, 384
xiǔ 151
xu 52, 65, 117, 146, 235, 241, 285, 317, 401, 406, 418
xú 102
xù 28, 34, 74, 95, 108, 140, 144, 183, 205, 225, 268, 271, 275, 309, 375
xǔ 156, 264, 286, 337, 338
xuan 4, 47, 80, 129, 148, 204, 306, 342, 360
xúan 116, 143, 194, 216, 221, 227
xùan 162, 182, 190, 202, 236, 269, 382, 390
xǔan 232, 370
xue 24, 313, 403
xúe 78, 355
xùe 327, 343, 423
xǔe 401
xun 28, 64, 149, 206, 215, 314, 378
xún 83, 87, 103, 107, 143, 183, 196, 302, 338, 364, 424
xùn 92, 102, 172, 177, 311, 336, 364, 369, 413
ya 36, 38, 122, 161, 425
yá 7, 86, 88, 186, 210, 218, 237, 298, 318, 328
yà 4, 61, 130, 176, 241, 336, 360, 364
yǎ 45, 399
yan 41, 75, 89, 116, 186, 190, 203, 205, 286, 374, 394
yán 17, 55, 70, 87, 98, 181, 201, 242, 258, 262, 335, 377, 392, 394, 395, 407, 429

Mandarin (Yale)

yàn 33, 43, 55, 62, 80, 101, 146, 201, 204, 207, 243, 296, 342, 346, 352, 378, 399, 412, 416

yǎn 18, 33, 68, 128, 194, 219, 237, 277, 328, 373, 420, 432

yang 68, 172, 182, 251, 404, 425

yáng 9, 102, 129, 162, 182, 203, 205, 229, 278, 320, 397

yàng 106, 107, 165, 195

yǎng 6, 176, 232, 410

yao 36, 68, 70, 94, 289, 370

yáo 62, 72, 103, 131, 209, 218, 220, 254, 274, 343, 369, 383, 423

yào 149, 208, 280, 315, 333, 391, 427

yǎo 41, 152, 253, 293

ye 51, 128

yé 131, 161, 209, 282, 372

yè 67, 124, 148, 149, 161, 186, 206, 288, 307, 342, 374, 403, 405

yě 3, 21, 61, 378

yi 1, 7, 10, 41, 53, 66, 160, 194, 214, 328, 377, 383, 431

yí 16, 40, 58, 68, 72, 80, 90, 100, 106, 130, 178, 226, 228, 251, 286, 337, 349, 370, 375, 407, 410

yì 5, 16, 23, 26, 48, 55, 61, 68, 86, 90, 98, 99, 101, 109, 111, 116, 117, 121, 125, 145, 173, 191, 206, 225, 227, 230, 234, 272, 274, 278, 279, 280, 284, 291, 313, 315, 321, 330, 338, 340, 345, 361, 367, 371, 388, 416

yǐ 3, 6, 13, 91, 143, 240, 295, 299, 326, 379

yin 46, 56, 62, 72, 97, 173, 176, 301, 405

yín 38, 60, 67, 81, 187, 213, 374, 383, 402, 433

yìn 32, 254, 301

yǐn 37, 98, 99, 232, 318, 399, 409

ying 55, 76, 138, 169, 219, 222, 275, 276, 291, 427, 428

yíng 63, 76, 115, 162, 199, 200, 205, 208, 220, 234, 272, 300, 324, 326, 352, 365, 388

yìng 75, 145, 243

yǐng 101, 195, 232, 252, 373

yo 44, 47

yong 15, 64, 65, 96, 113, 224, 232, 291, 371, 389, 400, 412

yóng 46, 135

yòng 223

yǒng 11, 27, 108, 176, 182, 190, 320, 338, 356

you 17, 38, 95, 108, 114, 139

yóu 84, 180, 189, 214, 224, 226, 312, 319, 322, 368, 373, 382, 420

515

Mandarin (Yale)

yòu 8, 9, 10, 33, 34, 56, 80, 95, 154, 340, 378, 432

yǒu 32, 34, 150, 210, 303, 319, 375, 431

yu 187, 229, 266, 364

yú 12, 19, 70, 73, 89, 111, 112, 129, 142, 163, 171, 188, 194, 213, 219, 234, 249, 254, 255, 289, 293, 306, 317, 322, 334, 341, 362, 368, 397, 400, 410, 420

yù 35, 47, 60, 81, 87, 111, 145, 170, 174, 184, 204, 207, 215, 216, 249, 263, 283, 285, 297, 312, 321, 331, 342, 345, 347, 368, 382, 394, 406, 409, 413, 419, 426, 428

yǔ 3, 15, 52, 56, 76, 79, 90, 96, 230, 249, 254, 279, 293, 340, 400, 434

yuan 20, 81, 188, 237, 425

yúan 17, 33, 43, 57, 60, 64, 74, 130, 169, 179, 191, 209, 215, 272, 298, 324, 329, 362, 432

yùan 105, 129, 219, 298, 396, 407

yǔan 369

yue 53, 149, 266

yúe 253

yùe 23, 87, 109, 150, 165, 166, 200, 264, 353, 359, 381, 393, 434

yun 147, 176

yún 29, 144, 258, 267, 281, 298, 373, 401

yùn 77, 112, 113, 206, 315, 368, 373, 377, 405

yǔn 17, 172, 398

za 29, 39, 124

zá 242, 400

zai 41, 157, 201

zài 16, 20, 57, 361

zǎi 6, 39, 80, 89

zan 261

zán 41

zàn 148, 222, 346, 352, 389

zǎn 138, 145, 354

zang 292, 352, 417

zàng 69, 292, 307

zǎng 413

zao 265, 370

záo 392

zào 53, 201, 208, 233, 358, 367

zǎo 143, 159, 197, 275, 315, 318

Mandarin (Yale)

zé 24, 51, 136, 197, 257, 261, 294, 348, 351, 365
zè 5, 144
zéi 350
zèn 344
zěn 105
zeng 65, 115, 150, 277
zèng 223, 352
zha 119, 131, 190, 227
zhá 151, 267, 387, 393
zhà 3, 132, 154, 155, 163, 202, 318, 337
zhǎ 236, 242
zhai 433
zhái 79, 132
zhài 15, 36, 82, 231
zhǎi 253
zhan 31, 142, 175, 180, 240, 263, 338, 345
zhán 85
zhàn 118, 160, 190, 255, 270, 316, 415
zhǎn 90, 132, 142, 235, 362
zhang 101, 166, 195, 215, 221, 325, 374, 405
zháng 100, 255
zhàng 1, 6, 90, 93, 94, 152, 195, 231, 288, 351, 398
zhǎng 129
zhao 44, 122, 145, 379
zháo 150
zhào 18, 34, 160, 205, 256, 277, 284, 337, 353
zhǎo 121, 180
zhe 321, 369, 387
zhé 42, 120, 132, 324, 344, 361, 363
zhè 154, 184, 310, 367, 427
zhě 281, 332, 352
zhen 14, 141, 161, 162, 163, 217, 222, 236, 242, 249, 259, 286, 293, 309, 379
zhén 348
zhèn 58, 125, 150, 350, 388, 397, 401, 425
zhěn 152, 225, 227, 273, 337, 361

Mandarin (Yale)

zheng 88, 103, 106, 128, 203, 214, 237, 259, 308, 381, 386
zhéng 209
zhèng 93, 139, 171, 228, 341, 344, 374
zhěng 124, 141
zhi 32, 37, 139, 158, 177, 240, 247, 274, 284, 287, 296, 322, 361, 399
zhí 2, 13, 61, 133, 153, 160, 172, 235, 273, 283, 357, 359
zhì 24, 87, 92, 94, 100, 104, 133, 137, 147, 157, 168, 180, 193, 201, 228, 250, 251, 253, 277, 290, 292, 320, 331, 335, 339, 347, 351, 359, 372, 396, 400, 414, 427
zhǐ 35, 40, 58, 66, 124, 144, 171, 247, 267, 298, 354, 361, 431
zhong 2, 105, 234, 268, 324, 329, 387, 390
zhòng 7, 237, 378
zhǒng 20, 251, 289, 356
zhou 91, 183, 263, 294, 343, 368
zhóu 71, 360
zhòu 40, 80, 146, 234, 262, 266, 272, 375, 416
zhǒu 92, 284
zhu 10, 151, 156, 168, 169, 181, 182, 200, 218, 301, 320, 339, 342, 372, 382
zhú 208, 229, 255, 294, 347, 358, 366
zhù 7, 8, 27, 153, 154, 202, 248, 259, 260, 280, 300, 319, 337, 349, 391, 413
zhǔ 2, 55, 123, 188, 204, 205, 240, 429
zhua 121, 135
zhǔa 209
zhuan 83, 245, 407
zhùan 55, 135, 259, 351, 411
zhǔan 363
zhuang 70, 263, 303, 330
zhúang 165
zhùang 66, 117, 134, 212
zhui 366, 385, 399, 414
zhùi 65, 111, 270, 352
zhun 253, 285, 341
zhǔn 21, 191
zhuo 31, 123, 125, 156, 186
zhúo 44, 137, 142, 184, 197, 198, 201, 218, 268, 300, 306, 341, 375, 390
zi 19, 39, 40, 72, 78, 186, 191, 224, 241, 264, 271, 350, 353, 361, 386, 418, 421, 433

zí 301, 350

zì 77, 107, 194, 237, 292

zǐ 71, 77, 158, 193, 250, 256, 263, 268, 300, 338

ziào 77

ziu 41

zong 80, 159, 269, 288, 418

zóng 358

zòng 264, 273

zǒng 274

zou 341, 373, 397, 415, 422

zòu 68, 129

zǒu 353

zu 250

zú 31, 143, 354, 389

zǔ 11, 247, 268, 337, 395

zuan 392

zùan 138

zǔan 275, 276

zùi 150, 277, 312, 377

zǔi 51

zun 83, 166, 370, 424

zǔn 134

zúo 145

zùo 9, 14, 58, 96, 105, 247, 286, 375

zǔo 8, 91

www.ingramcontent.com/pod-product-compliance
Lightning Source LLC
Chambersburg PA
CBHW060417010526
44118CB00017B/2246